2004

Common Sense, Reasoning, & Rationality

Common Sense, Reasoning, & Rationality

Edited by Renée Elio

OXFORD
UNIVERSITY PRESS
2002

OXFORD
UNIVERSITY PRESS

Oxford   New York
Athens   Auckland   Bangkok   Bogotá   Buenos Aires   Cape Town
Chennai   Dar es Salaam   Delhi   Florence   Hong Kong   Istanbul   Karachi
Kolkata   Kuala Lumpur   Madrid   Melbourne   Mexico City   Mumbai   Nairobi
Paris   São Paulo   Shanghai   Singapore   Taipei   Tokyo   Toronto   Warsaw

and associated companies in
Berlin   Ibadan

Copyright © 2002 by Oxford University Press

Published by Oxford University Press, Inc.
198 Madison Avenue, New York, New York 10016

Oxford is a registered trademark of Oxford University Press

Library of Congress Cataloging-in-Publication Data
Common sense, reasoning, and rationality / edited by Renée Elio.
    p.   cm.   (New directions in cognitive science)
  ISBN 0-19-514766-9; ISBN 0-19-514767-7 (pbk.)
  1. Reasoning—Congresses.
  I. Elio, Renée.   II. Series.
  BC177 C657 2001
  128'.33—dc21   2001133043

9 8 7 6 5 4 3 2 1

Printed in the United States of America
on acid-free paper

Acknowledgments

In February 1998 an interdisciplinary symposium on common sense, reasoning, and rationality was held as the Eleventh Vancouver Studies in Cognitive Science conference in Vancouver, Canada. This event brought together researchers in computer science, artificial intelligence, philosophy, and psychology, whose work on issues central to rationality and reasoning has made contributions to both descriptive theories of human cognition and prescriptive theories of artificial cognition. The chapters in this volume are among those presented as invited talks at that event.

The conference would not have been possible without sponsorship from Simon Fraser University, through the Vice-President Academic (Bruce Clayman), the Center for Systems Science, the Faculty of Arts, the Department of Philosophy, and the School of Computing Science; from the University of Alberta, through the Department of Computing Science; and from the Natural Sciences and Engineering Research Council of Canada, through research funding to Renée Elio. I also thank other members of the Simon Fraser community, including Steven Davis and Phil Hanson, who assisted with aspects of the event's organization and financing. And finally, a special thanks goes to the invited speakers who contributed the outstanding essays that make up this volume.

Contents

Contributors, ix

1. Issues in Commonsense Reasoning and Rationality, 3
   Renée Elio
2. Rationality and Intelligence, 37
   Stuart Russell
3. The Logical Foundations of Means-End Reasoning, 60
   John L. Pollock
4. Induction and Consistency, 78
   Henry E. Kyburg, Jr.
5. The Logic of Ordinary Language, 93
   Gilbert Harman
6. Knowledge and Coherence, 104
   Paul Thagard, Chris Eliasmith, Paul Rusnock, and Cameron Shelley
7. The Evolutionary Roots of Intelligence and Rationality, 132
   Denise Dellarosa Cummins
8. How Good Are Fast and Frugal Heuristics?, 148
   Gerd Gigerenzer, Jean Czerlinski, and Laura Martignon
9. Commonsense Reasoning, Logic, and Human Rationality, 174
   Mike Oaksford and Nick Chater
10. Reasoning Imperialism, 215
    Lance J. Rips
11. Ending the Rationality Wars: How to Make Disputes about Human Rationality Disappear, 236
    Richard Samuels, Stephen Stich, and Michael Bishop

Name Index, 269
Subject Index, 274

Contributors

Michael Bishop
  Department of Philosophy, Iowa State University
Nick Chater
  Department of Psychology, University of Warwick
Denise Dellarosa Cummins
  Department of Philosophy, University of California, Davis
Jean Czerlinski
  Center for Adaptive Behavior and Cognition, Max Planck Institute for
  Human Development, Berlin
Chris Eliasmith
  Department of Philosophy, University of Waterloo
Renée Elio
  Department of Computing Science, University of Alberta
Gerd Gigerenzer
  Center for Adaptive Behavior and Cognition, Max Planck Institute for
  Human Development, Berlin
Gilbert Harman
  Department of Philosophy, Princeton University
Henry E. Kyburg, Jr.
  Departments of Philosophy and Computer Science, University of
  Rochester
Laura Martignon
  Center for Adaptive Behavior and Cognition, Max Planck Institute for
  Human Development, Berlin
Mike Oaksford
  Department of Psychology, Cardiff University
John L. Pollock
  Department of Philosophy, University of Arizona
Lance J. Rips
  Department of Psychology, Northwestern University
Paul Rusnock
  Department of Philosophy, University of Waterloo

Stuart Russell
Department of Computer Science, University of California, Berkeley
Richard Samuels
Department of Philosophy, University of Pennsylvania
Cameron Shelley
Department of Philosophy, University of Waterloo
Stephen Stich
Department of Philosophy, Rutgers University
Paul Thagard
Department of Philosophy, University of Waterloo

Common Sense, Reasoning, & Rationality

1

Issues in Commonsense Reasoning and Rationality

RENÉE ELIO

1. Introduction

The notions of common sense and rationality are integral parts of "folk psychology." We have no trouble saying, "That's a matter of common sense," "That person just doesn't have a lot of common sense," or "That seems completely irrational to me." If we turn to *Webster's New Collegiate Dictionary* (1981) as a source for folk psychology definitions, we find that *common sense* is "sound and prudent but often unsophisticated judgment" and "the un-reflective opinions of ordinary [persons]." Unsophisticated and unreflective notwithstanding, common sense seems to be a *good* thing that most ordinary people possess. Similarly, there would seem to be little argument that ratio-nality is also "a good thing," for *Webster's* informs us that *irrational* means "not endowed with reason or understanding" and "lacking usual or normal mental clarity or coherence." Although it is not explicitly stated in these definitions, it seems fair to say that "usual" and "normal" are relativized to people. Any notion that humans on the whole are irrational in significant, systematic ways would seem, well, irrational to most of us. However, even *Webster's* eventually intimates that there might be some sort of objective standard for rationality. *Rational* is defined as "having reason or under-standing." If we track down *reason* and *understanding*, we find that they both concern "the power of intellect by which man [*sic*] attains to truth or knowledge." Putting all these definitions together, we might conclude that it is through careful, reasoned rationality that we discover "the truth" and through unreflective common sense that we make judgments that are "sound enough" for dealing with matters that arise in the everyday world. How these might be fundamentally different aspects of a common cognitive architecture, either for machines or for people, is the question at hand.

The folk psychology definitions offered in *Webster's* underscore two issues that emerge when common sense and rationality are considered more formally. The first concerns what these aspects of intelligence *are*. That is, what phenomena, behavior, or abilities are thought to constitute or define common sense and rationality? The second issue concerns what these aspects *ought to be*. Are the standards for common sense and rationality defined by what (ordinary) people do or by some a priori independent-of-people considerations? By some accounts, people are very good at common-sense reasoning in a rather uncertain and complex everyday world and yet rather bad at rational decision making and inference on formal problems. Conversely, computer programs can be designed to get the "right [rational] answer" for certain types of questions in application domains (e.g., medical diagnosis) once we circumscribe and formalize the questions carefully enough for our current programs and methods. But there is no generally accepted formalism and computational method that enable us to build systems that accomplish the same broad scope of commonsense reasoning that we observe in people. Implicitly or explicitly, it seems that common sense and rationality are often viewed as two distinct features of a single cognitive architecture held to rather different normative standards.[1] In reviewing certain aspects of common sense and rationality, I consider how this perceived distinction is detrimental to understanding either of these notions.

I begin by reviewing the issue of normative standards and particularly what role human performance plays in specifying these standards for common sense and rationality. The issue of whether there are independent-of-people normative standards reflects a general tension that characterizes how common sense and rationality have been defined, investigated, and debated within various sectors of the cognitive science community. I then consider the scope and definitions for common sense and rationality in turn. In the case of common sense, a computational formalization that can embrace all its aspects has been elusive and yielded many competing views. But at least we seem to know common sense when we see it. For the matter of rationality, this does not seem to be the case and much of the debate turns on what should serve as normative standards for rationality. I conclude with brief summaries of the contributed chapters in this volume, as they address many of the issues raised by these considerations.

2. Normative Standards

A normative standard specifies how something *ought* to be, based on a priori considerations that, if followed, yield "success" on some dimension. Broadly speaking, we can take three approaches to defining normative standards for rationality and commonsense reasoning. First, we can define normative standards in these realms in terms of *what people actually do*. This would be a form of psychologism. Second, we might believe that there are some truths about these matters that are *independent of what people do*, in a "world apart" from humans. The normative standards are to be discovered. We can call this view Platonism because of its commitment to a realm of truths independent of humans. Third, we might or might not believe there are truths to be discovered in some realm but instead decide that normative standards for some particular purpose can just *be invented*. We might call this constructionism. For example, in a medical diagnosis system, all that pragmatically matters is whether adhering to certain designed normative standards manages to produce the desired outcome (a diagnosis that can be independently validated). It is not relevant whether the mechanisms involved correspond to any broad theory of reasoning or rationality.

Within philosophy, psychologism emerged in the early eighteenth century as a kind of methodological stance that advocated an empirical or naturalistic approach to questions in epistemology and metaphysics. As M. Kusch (1995) relates, this perspective reached its peak in the late 1800s with certain British empiricists and German logicians, who argued that the laws of logic and, in some cases, mathematics were suitably generalized accounts of patterns of human thought and reasoning. Today it is difficult to find anyone who adopts psychologism with regards to logic, geometry, or arithmetic, due mostly to E. Husserl's (1900) and G. Frege's (1894) arguments that logic is not a subjective matter but instead is an objective matter of the relations among propositions, predicates, and terms. Propositional logic, the syllogism, probability theory, and the like were designed to describe some *independent-of-people purpose*, according to the Frege-Husserl view. And what is a correct inference in these systems is given by those purposes. Although these specific systems are invented, they are regarded as describing some antecedently existing realm (i.e., they count as discovery) because they reflect and obey truth-preserving properties of the world.

When used to set standards for correct inference and decision making, these systems thereby create the possibility for people to go wrong in using these systems. It is only if we reject psychologism in logic that we can say that most people "make mistakes" in logic, for example, fail to apply correctly *modus tollens* as an inference rule (see Evans 1987 and Evans, Newstead, and Byrne 1993 for reviews of such results). In the field of probabilistic reasoning, experimenters discover that subjects typically make errors in assigning probabilities to conjunctions (Tversky and Kahneman 1973), at least under some circumstances. These human behaviors are considered as "errors" because we believe that psychologism is *false* with respect to these theories. If we believe that there is a single, objective theory for logic and probability, which is independent of how people reason about it, then this objective or normative theory sets the standard with which we can make these judgments about how people make mistakes.

What roles do normative standards of the independent-of-people sort play in the enterprise of describing and explaining human cognition? First, the acceptance of some normative system can have theoretical implications for how data on human reasoning is interpreted. For example, G. Gigerenzer and his colleagues have argued that the received (Bayesian) probability theory is flawed. Hence, the so-called errors that investigators have found people making in their probabilistic judgments (e.g., those reported in Tversky and Kahneman 1973, 1974) are only thought to be errors, in part because of a misplaced acceptance of the idea that probabilities can be associated with single events (Gigerenzer 1994). Second, deciding to adopt one normative standard instead of another can directly influence the theoretical characterizations offered for human performance. If we take a normative specification like deductive logic as a starting point, then our account of people's correct and incorrect responses takes on a particular flavor. The competence/performance distinction is an example of this. Using this distinction, errors in some circumstances become understood as the result of "interfering factors" (e.g., Cohen 1981; Macnamara 1986; Rips 1994, 1995) with respect to some underlying machinery that would have otherwise worked correctly (by some standard), *except for* these interfering factors. Third, there are pragmatic implications for adopting a particular normative standard for decision making and action, since this defines, by exclusion, a wrong pattern of behavior in some domain. What we characterize as a bias or factor that impedes a desired type of reasoning can motivate particular tutorial interventions, frameworks for decision support systems, or other strategies to counteract the bias. For example, some researchers advocate the design of human-computer collaboration systems specifically with an eye toward "de-biasing" human judgment and decision-making patterns (e.g., Raghavan 1991; Silverman 1992). In sum, without deeming some particular standard to be normative per se, its adoption as a reference point at the very least defines what counts as errors, which in turn requires theoretical constructs (e.g., competence/performance) to explain these errors and shapes applied research agendas to fix these errors.

By Kusch's reckoning (1995, pp. 9–12), psychologism is making a comeback with some philosophers of logic and epistemology who maintain that human psychology does—or must—inform the investigation of these matters (even if there is no direct agreement on exactly how). The field of artificial intelligence (AI) has also had a somewhat ambivalent stance on whether or not psychologism is a useful perspective for developing computational models of intelligence. F. J. Pelletier and I (1997) cite many historic and contemporary quotations in which AI researchers believe that human behavior defines the standard, if not the process specification, for intelligent activity, particularly in the realm of nonmonotonic reasoning (discussed in more detail in section 3). J. McCarthy, who has done much to both motivate and investigate commonsense reasoning, often used humans as the standard bearers in this realm. Yet he also argues that the activity of AI should be "studying the structure of information and the structure of problem solving processes independently of applications and *independently of their realization in animals and humans* . . . [because] intellectual activity takes place in a world that has certain physical and intellectual structure" (1974, p. 64, emphasis mine). This view of intelligence is both Platonic (especially the italicized portion) and situated, at least insofar as its character is to be understood as governed in part by the structure of the environment. And it is fair to say that the successes enjoyed by AI systems have come from an understanding of how to structure problems in a way that the current architectures—and programs that can be run on those architectures—can exploit. This is a theme we will return to later. At this point, we can observe that normative standards for reasoning and action are important for AI, if only as a means whereby current programs, architectures, and techniques can be evaluated relative to one another.

The usual independent-of-people contenders for normative standards of inference and decision making are deductive logic, probability theories, and economic theory. Deductive logic specifies rules of inference that manipulate facts about the world, so that some desirable properties (e.g., truth preservation) are maintained. Under the logical view of rationality, it is rational to accept-as-true those and only those consequences of independently known facts that are sanctioned by those inference rules. Basic axioms of probability define ways in which independently known probabilities that describe some situation can be manipulated so that a consistent view of the situation results. Under a probability-theory view of rationality, it is irrational to manipulate those independently known probabilities in such a way that these axioms, which ensure consistency, are violated. An economic model of rationality holds that a decision maker is in possession of independently specified preferences and utilities; rational choices are ones that maximize those utilities, given a set of preferences.

Many matters arise from the use of these standards for rationality, in a practical sense, either for understanding human cognition or for designing machine intelligence (see, for example, Doyle 1992 for a thoughtful consideration of the latter issue). First, none of these standards specifies what to believe in the first place. Instead, they are all of the form "If you *already* accept X as true, or assign this probability to X, or possess this preference about X, then you must also conclude this statement, or assign that probability, or make that selection." They are silent on how the reasoner is to *get* the first set of acceptances, probabilities, or preferences. And so it seems that there is some sort of mismatch between what these theories specify and what gets discussed as "here is what a reasoner *ought* to believe." Second, these standards specify the rational outcome when there is *exactly* such-and-so input and no other input. They are silent on what constitutes rational outcome when the input is *not* exactly such-and-so. Third, because they focus on outcomes and not processes, these frameworks of normative correctness are silent on *how* to build agents that would produce rational decisions. Nor can they contribute much in the way of developing explanatory process models for human reasoning—they do not specify how the relevant knowledge is to be normatively computed and brought to bear on rendering the correct decision or inference. As a result, it is difficult to use them to guide accounts of how and why humans might deviate from the normative standard. Fourth, while many research communities routinely tout logic or probability frameworks as the normative standards for rationality, many of these same communities are occupied with *extending* the representational and inferential adequacy of these rationality frameworks to handle commonsense reasoning! This is surprising if we view commonsense reasoning as somehow leveraged off the reasoner's underlying "core" rationality. So it is helpful at this juncture to consider next what it is about common sense that has made building it upon these commonly accepted ways of framing rationality such a challenge.

3. Commonsense Knowledge and Commonsense Reasoning

Our dictionary-based folk psychology view of common sense defines it as prudent, sound, albeit possibly unreflective, judgments by ordinary people. McCarthy (1984) distinguishes between commonsense knowledge ("what everyone knows") and commonsense reasoning ("the human ability to use commonsense knowledge") (pp. 191–193). So we can ask two questions: What are ordinary people making unreflective but sound judgments *about?* And what is the *means* by which they do so? Formalizing answers to these questions would take us rather close to considering all of human cognition.[2] Wishing to stop well short of that, I nonetheless want to consider a few matters that have typically been thought to characterize the *content* of commonsense knowledge and the *nature* of commonsense reasoning.

The Domains of Commonsense Knowledge

So what does "everyone" know? Some time ago, McCarthy and P. Hayes (1969) and McCarthy (1984) offered the AI community a list of topics relevant to commonsense knowledge that still defines many crucial research questions in the field of knowledge representation and reasoning. Those topics include time and space; causality; approximate or qualitative theories of motion, force, substances, and energy; continuous change; and quantities. In short, what "everyone" knows is mainly concerned with an understanding of changes, actions, cause, and effect in the physical world (sometimes called naive physics). Since our own actions and those we observe also involve other human beings, we might augment the domain of commonsense knowledge to include folk psychology concepts like goals, beliefs, and desires. Finally, we use this knowledge not only to reason about action and change we actually make or observe in the world but also to *talk about* actions and changes in the world (see chapter 5). Commonly shared commonsense knowledge thereby enables much of the discourse among people in describing, predicting, or explaining everyday events. Our knowledge in these matters appears to be established well before we undergo formal education and certainly some of it before we are very far out of infancy. Indeed, the acquisition of concepts like causality, the persistence of objects and properties over time, and even a theory of mind are core theoretical and empirical concerns of developmental psychology. The attribution of causality by adult reasoners has long been an active area of empirical research within cognitive psychology.[3] In sum, one way to define the domain of commonsense knowledge is by exclusion, contrasting it with highly structured domains such as mathematics and other subjects about which we receive formal, direct instruction. Commonsense knowledge seems to be that which people come to know in the course of growing up and living in the world.[4]

The Nature of Commonsense Reasoning

Once various realms of commonsense knowledge have been identified, one agenda might be as follows: (1) write down—axiomatize—what everyone knows about some domain (e.g., solid substances) and (2) apply a formal proof procedure for this axiomatization as the machinery of reasoning. When AI researchers adopted this agenda, two matters soon became apparent. First, it is unclear there is any coherent independent-of-use content base for knowledge—commonsense or otherwise—that could be itemized, axiomatized, and then used by any algorithm for any purpose. This is both a general epistemological issue as well as an issue that shows up in practical endeavors.

Second, even if we imagined we *could* write down independent-of-purpose axioms that represented a subdomain of commonsense knowledge, it was soon believed by many that we couldn't write it *all* down.[5] Consider a famous commonsense problem: what knowledge comes into play in formulating a simple plan to crack an egg on the side of a bowl, with the intention that the egg contents will be in the bowl? We could prove such a plan would succeed only if we knew at least the following: that the egg is brought into contact with the bowl's edge (and not elsewhere); that this action is done neither too fast nor not too slow; that the bowl is neither upside down, smaller than the egg, nor made of (say) paper; and that the egg itself is not hard-boiled. Furthermore, we must also know that an object cannot be two places at once—the contents of the egg cannot be both in the egg and in the bowl. Nor will an inanimate object move unless the force applied to it is sufficient to counteract any other force. Gravity will cause the egg contents to fall into the bowl only if the opening made by the crack is facing downward. We further assume that the act of cracking an egg does not change the structure of the bowl but does change the structure of the eggshell (and possibly the contents of the egg). Throughout this detailing of what is known and assumed, there is appeal both to domain specific knowledge and to a general understanding of materials, time, and forces. When do we stop writing down all specifications of all conditions that we know to be relevant to this problem? And writing it all down is necessary so that if we ever could have access to a complete deductive logic inference machine, it would derive all and only the consequences of making an inference or taking some action in a situation.

Formalizing Aspects of Commonsense Reasoning

The egg-cracking example requires not only knowledge about our physical world. Its analysis also depends on assumptions about the objects involved; for example, we assume for the particular plan under consideration that the egg is not hard-boiled. It is these assumptions that render any conclusion or inference we might make subject to reversal. Nonetheless, people draw conclusions and form beliefs even while admitting that there are likely many concurrently true facts or events about which they have no direct knowledge that could influence the validity of their beliefs, beliefs that in turn form the basis of plans and actions. For example, the success of the simple plan of using the family car to pick up a visitor at the airport depends, in part, on many such assumptions and beliefs. These include my assumption that the car will indeed start when I turn the key in the ignition. But this truly is an assumption: the alternator might be broken; other drivers may have left the gas tank empty; I may have left the car door ajar overnight, causing the inside passenger light to be on all night and eventually deplete the battery. Strictly speaking, I do not possess all the knowledge that allows me to conclude with certainty that my plan for using the car is going to succeed, nor could I ever prove it would succeed (see chapter 3). In short, much of the knowledge we have about even familiar objects, events, and people is ill-defined, approximate, and often inherently uncertain.

Because of this, much commonsense reasoning became equated with the problem of formalizing the (vaguely distressing) notion of "jumping to conclusions" based on default assumptions about what is usually or typically true and not on facts known to be true. But once researchers began to formalize, represent, and use these default assumptions in inference, three further aspects of commonsense reasoning emerged. The first is that a reasoner may have different default assumptions that in turn can lead to inconsistent beliefs or conclusions. For example, I might accept as true the following two heuristic rules: typically, colleagues with children in day care don't attend late-afternoon seminars, and typically, colleagues attend any seminar held in their research area. If both default assumptions apply to the same colleague, I would have contradictory beliefs about whether or not he will be at a particular seminar held late in the day, generated by apparently correct default inferences.

Merely computing these alternative belief sets is not enough, since presumably a reasoner must adopt one of them in order to proceed with the next inference or determine a particular action. If I accept as true the belief that this colleague will be there, I can give him some urgently needed material he requested; if I don't, I'll adopt some different plan. Thus, there is the second matter of formalizing how to decide which alternative belief set to adopt, given the different default assumptions from which they arose. And even after I make this decision, there is still a third matter that arises in commonsense reasoning, namely, how to *revise* the adopted belief set in light of new and possibly contradictory information about the world. This is likely to occur, because the belief set itself was, after all, based on various default assumptions. If I believe my colleague has a child in day care and adopt a belief set that does not predict my colleague's attendance at the 5:00 P.M. seminar, seeing him at the seminar presents an inconsistency between my beliefs about the world and how the world really is. Assuming that I accept as true what I see (I am not hallucinating; I see him clearly), I could resolve this inconsistency by abandoning my belief that he has a child in day care. This belief itself might have rested on other beliefs, which in turn might need to be revised. As an alternative, I might decide to reject as true the default assumption that colleagues with day-care children don't attend 5:00 P.M. seminars. While this assumption might have some general utility, perhaps the regularity it describes does not hold in this particular situation.[6] This kind of revision might also necessitate changing other beliefs that I had accepted as true. In short, new information may arrive that contradicts a reasoner's current model or belief set; resolving this contradiction may require the reasoner to abandon one or more previously accepted beliefs. Inferences that previously followed from the now-retracted beliefs may no longer be valid. In this regard, much of everyday, commonsense reasoning is recognized to have a strong *nonmonotonic* nature: the same conclusions once entailed by those beliefs accepted as true may no longer follow once new information is taken into account.[7]

Within AI, there are many proposals about how the nonmonotonic nature of commonsense reasoning might be formalized and achieved computationally. These approaches range from those more geared to implementations (e.g., mechanisms for reasoning with semantic networks, as reviewed in Sowa 1991, and J. Pearl's [1988] Bayesian networks) to those that are presented from a formal or logical stance (such as default logic, circumscription, autoepistemic logic, probabilistic logics, and fuzzy logics). Within the latter group it is common to distinguish those approaches that are quantitative (probabilistic and fuzzy logics) from the other qualitative ("symbolic") approaches. Quantitative approaches address the issue of uncertain or unavailable knowledge characteristic of commonsense reasoning by formalizing rules for associating a degree of certainty with statements and for computing degrees of certainty for inferences derived from those statements (see chapter 4). These approaches aim to ground the uncertainty aspect of reasoning with incomplete or imperfect information ("most of the time, X is true" or "Y can be concluded in this context with nearly complete certainty") in probability theories. Rather than assigning numerical values to individual sentences (as the quantitative approaches do), qualitative approaches attempt to build upon the machinery of first-order logic. This is accomplished in various ways, such as adding additional rules of inference, sometimes introducing new modal operators, and sometimes conjecturing the boundaries of what is known to be true within some model, in order that the machinery of first-order logic could then apply (e.g., McCarthy 1980; Reiter 1980). Finally, since both classical belief revision and defeasible reasoning are concerned with nonmonotonicity, it is possible to view belief revision as a kind of nonmonotonic reasoning, or vice versa (Gärdenfors 1988, 1990; Gärdenfors and Makinson 1994). These topics and detailed accounts of each of these frameworks are covered in Gabbay, Hogger, and Robinson 1993. L. Morgenstern (1996) discusses how many of these approaches purport to solve elements of AI's frame *problem*, a canonical matter of commonsense reasoning.[8]

Psychological Studies of Commonsense Reasoning

During the same decades that AI researchers worked on extending formal logic and probability theories to achieve elements of people's commonsense reasoning, cognitive psychologists were working to understand how and why people's formal reasoning fell short of the very same theories that AI-ers aimed to extend. There has been considerably less investigation within cognitive psychology of everyday reasoning per se than there has been of logical and probabilistic inference. Notable exceptions include A. Collins and R. Michalski's (1989) framework for plausible reasoning, as well as a long history of research on inductive inference (e.g., Osherson et al. 1990) and causal reasoning (e.g., Cheng 1997). More recently, increasing attention has been given to so-called assumption-based or belief-based inference—how people's everyday reasoning rests on premises that they do not fully accept (e.g., Evans and Over 1996; Evans, Over, and Manktelow 1993; Oaksford and Chater 1995, chapter 9 in this volume). And psychologists' proposals for extending models of human propositional inference to encompass subjective or probabilistic elements (e.g., George 1995; Johnson-Laird 1994; Stevenson and Over 1995) address issues similar to those found in probabilistic treatments of plausible inference offered in the AI literature (e.g., Bacchus et al. 1992; Kyburg 1994). The matter of belief revision—updating one's confidence in or acceptance of previously accepted beliefs in light of new information—has been studied extensively in management science and psychology literature (e.g., Ashton and Ashton 1990; Baron 1994; Einhorn and Hogarth 1981); in social cognition literature, where it is explored as a matter of stereotypes and attitude change (Petty, Priester, and Wegener 1994); as plausible inference problems (Elio 1997, 1998); and as theory revision (Thagard 1989, chapter 6 in this volume).

The preceding examples are only a fragment of what can be viewed as the empirical study of commonsense reasoning, since much of cognitive psychology is concerned in some way or other with understanding how the human cognitive architecture makes sense of the everyday world. So surely we must include extensive literatures on the cognitive skills and knowledge that people seem to have without formal training, such as spatial reasoning and navigation skills, world knowledge that supports language understanding and discourse, and the like. But regardless of how widely we cast the net, it is fair to say that in studies of commonsense reasoning—unlike studies of formal reasoning—there is relatively little appeal to independent-of-people standards in formulating theories or models. It is generally accepted that people excel in these realms, and the goal is to understand how.

Normative Standards for Commonsense Reasoning

What then can we say about normative standards for commonsense reasoning when these matters are so broadly defined in both AI and psychology? Is psychologism a correct perspective to apply in devising computational models of commonsense reasoning? Pelletier and I (1997) argued that for at least some sorts of default reasoning problems, empirical studies of what people give as correct answers to default reasoning problems ought to be taken as the correct "commonsense answer." At least, the patterns that arise from empirical studies should be the preferred standard over whatever commonsense answers are deemed intuitively correct by an individual researcher or even by the consensus of a research community (this reliance on introspection in itself is an extreme form of psychologism). However, one can argue that it is preferable to have artificial agents engage in uncertain reasoning according to some provably correct method (e.g., a qualitative probability theory). Such a perspective is committed to claiming that there *is* an independent-of-people's performance metric that can be used to evaluate a proposed plausible inference system. Some researchers within AI take this pragmatic view, according to which there may be different (invented) answer patterns that could be considered correct for nonmonotonic reasoning and different logics that are appropriate for different interpretations of default assumptions and different applications (Halpern 1993). For example, within a medical diagnosis domain, we can validate the different approaches and methods for dealing with uncertain information and incomplete theories quite easily: we assess which ones yield the desired diagnosis, whose correctness is open to independent validation. Generally speaking, for any particular application area, AI practitioners can apply (their) commonsense knowledge to structure the problem in ways that are amenable to the kinds of algorithms they currently develop for their systems. These systems can then produce answers in accordance with some formal standard that the designers have in mind.

What happens when the problems are not well structured, as most of the commonsense problems that have thus far eluded a common formalization seem to be? There are two perspectives to consider here that indirectly speak to the role of rationality norms as applied to commonsense reasoning. The first perspective holds that much of what passes as commonsense reasoning has a strong inductive component. N. Rescher (1980) argues that induction is the mechanism by which reasoning proceeds in the face of imperfect or incomplete information, the very realm we have associated with commonsense reasoning. In some frameworks (e.g., Holland et al. 1986), the term *induction* is used to encompass any and all mechanisms that expand knowledge in the face of uncertainty. In addition to learning from past cases in order to predict new cases, this more expansive view of induction would include other sorts of inference processes, such as reasoning to the best explanation, scientific hypothesis induction, abduction, and the like. R. J. Stevenson (1993, p. 69) presents a similar characterization of induction as the cognitive mechanism that is "sensitive to the constraints of reality" and, as such, enables thinking and reasoning successfully about the everyday world. From this perspective, everyday commonsense reasoning may (only) be possible via induction (but see chapter 10).

This brings us to the second, related perspective. Certain accounts of human error in formal reasoning problems appeal to the notion that people employ, quite automatically, certain heuristic methods that are computationally biased in some way or other (e.g., Tversky and Kahneman 1974).[9] While these heuristic methods may serve people well in commonsense reasoning, they can lead people astray in formal reasoning. However, many problems resist a "logical or formal" solution, for once they are stated with due formal diligence, it is unclear that anything *but* heuristic methods would be able to solve them. For example, a normative standard for rationality within a probabilistic framework is that a reasoner should assign probabilities to statements in a model so that no probability axioms are violated. That is, there should be some probabilistic coherence. Thus, if statement A is thought to be true only 50 percent of the time and statement B depends only on A, then statement B ought not to be assigned a probability of being true more than 50 percent of the time. However, D. N. Osherson (1995) presents a relatively restricted problem that requires assigning just two probability values ("greater than .5" and "not greater than .5") and reveals that maintaining probabilistic coherence would require a Boolean circuit with 10^{123} gates, a very large number indeed. From this perspective, the heuristic nature that we accord to human probabilistic reasoning might be the most effective response possible to complex problems, that is, problems afforded by the real-world environment. M. Ginsberg argues that commonsense reasoning is fundamentally a heuristic activity and the need for heuristic activities is no less for machine intelligence than it is for human intelligence. He promotes a definition of commonsense reasoning as "the technique whereby an inference problem is solved by reducing it (perhaps unsoundly) to a modified . . . problem on which exhaustive search is practical" (1996, p. 623), that is, suitable for the kinds of algorithms that are realizable and effective on the current machine architectures.

If commonsense reasoning is the necessarily heuristic, necessarily inductive means by which any architecture solves ill-defined, underspecified, or intractable problems, then what counts as the normatively correct commonsense answer may be relative to the problem being solved and the heuristic methods supported by the architecture for solving it. And this sounds very much like some current perspectives on rationality.

4. Rationality

Commonsense knowledge seems to be something that people *have* and commonsense reasoning seems to be something that people *do*. Rationality, however, seems to be an abstract pronouncement of reasoners, reasoning methods, or reasoning patterns as defined by some normative standard. Hence, the discussions of rationality have been primarily discussions of normative standards for rationality and what counts and does not count as rational behavior.[10]

Earlier I suggested that the folk definition of rationality was relativized to humans, since the dictionary states that irrationality is "lacking usual or normal mental clarity or coherence"—presumably what is usual and normal for people. So it would seem that *Webster's* (and Socrates) takes an optimistic view of humans: humans *are* rational *by virtue of* their ability to reason, and it is not conceptually possible for humans to be irrational in any systematic manner. But there is an opposing, pessimistic view that a correct standard of rationality exists and people fall short of this standard.

This pessimistic view of human rationality is fueled by empirical evidence about the ways in which human inference and decision making deviate from what would be sanctioned by various normative standards. Careful and considered experiments over the last few decades have chronicled the manner and circumstances in which people's responses to categorical and conditional syllogisms, to other logic problems, and to probability problems do and do not match the inferences sanctioned by deductive rules of inference or probability axioms. L. J. Cohen (1981) began a debate that continues today about what, if anything, these sorts of empirical studies mean for attributing rationality to humans. The body of empirical results on human formal reasoning continues to be reconsidered and expanded. Opposing views fuel the debate about the role of empirical investigations in the pronouncements about human rationality, from both methodological and theoretical viewpoints (e.g., Manktelow and Over 1993; Stanovich 1999; Stein 1996). There is even argument offered that the very opposing views that define these debates actually agree more than they disagree (chapter 11).

Rationality and Cognitive Architecture

Here I wish to focus on matters that arise from what might be called a situated view of rationality, in which what counts as part of the situation includes the reasoner's cognitive architecture. Cognitive architecture and rationality have been conjoined considerations, either implicitly or explicitly, since H. A. Simon (1982) introduced the notion of bounded or limited rationality. Simon recognized that the decision maker's available information and the available computational resources limit a decision's rationality, however measured. The role of computational resources must be understood in a wide sense to include the manner in which information and knowledge is acquired, assimilated, retrieved, and manipulated to make a decision or inference in support of an action. In brief, the decision maker's rationality is constrained in part by properties of the decision maker's cognitive architecture. Hence, the decision-maker must often make do with what Simon called satisficing—making inferences or taking actions that are good enough, rather than being optimal in some regard.

The notion that architecture is central to enabling, constraining, and possibly defining what counts as rational is pervasive, at least in some communities that are concerned with computational accounts of intelligence. A few representative quotations illustrate this position well:

> An architecture with twice the processing speed and memory size of another has the potential to be more rational. The underlying speed and size are only the crudest measures . . . and realistic assessments of relative rationality must look to details of the architecture. . . . The very architecture itself [is] a limitation on the agent's capabilities. (Doyle 1992, p. 14)

> The [human cognitive] architecture shows up through many ways, large and small. Indeed much of cognitive psychology is counting these ways— speed of processing, memory errors, linguistic slips, perceptual illusions, failures of rationality, decision making. These factors are grounded in part in the architecture. (Newell, Rosenbloom, and Laird 1993, p. 98)

This focus on the properties of the cognitive architecture surfaces explicitly or implicitly in many accounts of how and why human performance falls short on those formal reasoning problems that are taken to measure rationality. For example, A. Newell (1990) reports on a syllogistic reasoning system that was built within SOAR, a cognitive theory realized as a cognitive architecture with particular commitments to primitive operations, representations, and mechanisms. The syllogistic reasoning system modeled many of the answer patterns that people give on a variety of syllogistic problems. By Newell's reckoning, elements of this simulation map to the basic assumptions that inform one account for errors in formal reasoning, namely, the *mental models* theory expounded by P. N. Johnson-Laird and his colleagues (Johnson-Laird 1983; Johnson-Laird and Byrne 1991). Briefly, the mental model theory holds that reasoning procedures operate on internal models of world situations. Newell argues that model representations are useful for much of reasoning *because* they are presumably well suited for the quick matching and other essential primitive operations executed by the cognitive architecture (such as those proposed by the SOAR theory). But Newell contends that model representations are bad for reasoning with *propositions about* the world, particularly quantified propositions. Hence, one central reason that the simulation matched the observed errors in people's reasoning on syllogistic problems was thought to be its reliance on model-based representations.

Note that in this analysis the account for why the system gives the human answers on syllogistic inference problems is grounded in fairly specific assumptions about (1) the primitive processes that define a proposed cognitive architecture, (2) the nature of the architecture's default representation of information that those processes are effective in manipulating, and then (3) how that architecture thus defined is ill-suited for certain types of information and problems. The crucial argument here in explaining errors in human syllogistic reasoning is that representations that directly model the world and mechanisms that manipulate those representations may be ill-suited for modeling abstractions about the world and manipulating those abstractions in problem solving. Gigerenzer and his colleagues (Gigerenzer 1994, 1998, chapter 8 in this volume) make similar arguments, having shown that people's generally poor performance at manipulating probability information improves dramatically when the same information is presented in a frequency format. Their account of such results—that the world presents people with frequencies, not probabilities—appeals first to the structure of the everyday world and then to the kinds of representations that the human architecture might have evolved for effectively modeling such a world.

Similarly, other investigations show that people can give normative responses to formal reasoning problems if those problems are recast with certain types of contextualizations. On various formal logic problems it is well documented that people's response patterns can be made to obey different normative standards, merely by changing the sorts of semantic cover stories imposed on the problem's syntactic structure. For example, both adults and children give answers sanctioned by deductive logic on difficult inference problems if the logical structure of those problems is couched in a cover story about social behavior and compliance with social norms specified as obligations and permissions among different parties. Various theoretical constructs have been proposed to account for such findings, such as pragmatic reasoning schemas (Cheng and Holyoak 1985) and deontic reasoning rules (Manktelow and Over 1991). These in turn have been transformed into the stronger theoretical claim that cognitive facilities have evolved for reasoning with domain-specific content (e.g., permissions and obligations that define social hierarchies) that was particularly essential to evolutionary success (e.g., Cosmides 1989; Cosmides and Tooby 1996, chapter 7 in this volume). Without necessarily positing the evolution of specialized reasoning modules, several researchers have argued that broad aspects of human cognition are adaptive in an evolutionary sense (Anderson 1991; Oaksford and Chater 1994).

Many premises and assumptions are part and parcel of such a position, including whether human information processing has somehow been optimized (and what optimization might mean) by evolution or merely shaped in some way or other (see discussions by E. Stein [1996] and S. Stich [1990]). Perhaps less controversially, we might concede that the human cognitive architecture has mechanisms, default representations, and properties that are somehow attuned to the structure of the world in which it does its information processing. Crudely put, the fact that people can be swayed by particular reframings or semantic contextualizations of various logic or probability problems might be more properly viewed as a "feature," not a "bug," of their cognitive architecture. Indeed, the current jargon *AI complete* has emerged to denote problems for which the solution presupposes human-level intelligence, that is, problems that appear to be just "too hard" for artifacts because, in part, of the amount of contextual information their solution seems to require.

Normative Standards for a Situated Rationality

Given the evolutionary account, at least certain elements of rationality become framed in terms of ecological or adaptive validity within particular physical and social environments. In this perspective, rationality becomes a pragmatic and relativized property of creatures that are trying to perform a particular task within a particular environment. This is consistent with the goal-directed view of rationality implicitly adopted within much of the AI community and expressed in Newell's Principle of Rationality:

> A [rational agent] acts so as to attain his goals through rational action, given the structure of the task and his inputs of information and bounded by limitations on his knowledge and processing abilities. (1990, p. 33)

This principle governs what Newell calls the *knowledge-level* behavior of an agent, that is, an agent described only as having goals, receiving input from an environment, and taking actions within the environment to achieve those goals (see also Newell 1982). A perfect knowledge-level agent could achieve perfect rationality. Such an agent would have no constraints on its processing resources and no constraints imposed by the environment on the length of time it might use those unlimited resources to come up with a particular answer or action. Such perfect knowledge-level creatures are, of course, an abstraction and not real human or artificial agents. Both human and artificial agents have constraints on their processing resources. But it is not only the architecture that constrains reasoning and deliberation. Both types of agent do their problem solving within some kind of environment that defines the type and quality of information it makes available and the amount of time the agent has, pragmatically speaking, for any particular deliberation.

Are there ways of defining what "the best" or "most rational" answer or action might be, given this situated view? Yes, and not surprisingly the essential elements of this answer are shared in perspectives on both human rationality and machine rationality. In the realm of human cognition, Simon's position on bounded rationality brought attention to the notion of *prescriptive models* (Baron 1985; Simon 1956), a specification of how people ought to reason *given* their cognitive limitations. The relative match between the reasoning patterns specified by a prescriptive model and a normative model leads to fundamentally different theoretical positions on whether people behave rationally on that task (Stanovich 1999). When the prescriptive model for a task matches a descriptive model of how people actually perform on the task, then there is no sense in which the observed reasoning can be viewed as irrational. Any deviations there might be from the normative standard are accounted for by architectural limitations. But if there is a difference between observed performance and the performance specified by a prescriptive model, then it is possible to declare people irrational with respect to the standard set by the prescriptive model (and for some people to be more or less rational than others). Pragmatically, it follows that people could achieve the prescriptive model's standard via the proper instruction or training (Baron 1985). That is, the cognitive architecture does not preclude the acquisition of the "right programs" by which people might achieve the maximal reasoning performance as specified by a prescriptive model.

The essence of these ideas and analogous implications have been formalized within the AI community under the term *bounded optimality* (Horvitz 1989, chapter 2 in this volume). The bounded optimality perspective defines a reasoning agent as a particular program that is running on a particular machine. The program portion of the agent includes all the knowledge the agent might have about the task, as well as how that knowledge is brought to bear on the task under the invariant constraints imposed by the agent's software and hardware architecture. Thus defined, an agent is bounded optimal if it maximizes the utility of its behavior *given* the environmental and task demands. What counts as bounded optimal performance for any particular agent will thus depend in part on whether the environment is allowing five seconds or five minutes for a deliberation and whether it is providing complete or incomplete information for the task. A differently designed agent might behave better or worse on the same task with the environmental constraints. Like a prescriptive model for human reasoning performance, bounded optimality is offered as a way of formalizing rational reasoning and action for systems in a way that takes into account properties of the cognitive architecture that is operating with a particular task and with particular constraints imposed by the environment on computation time and information quality.[11]

We can now revisit the evolutionary perspective on human rationality and better appreciate its methodological implications for how empirical investigations of rationality and reasoning are designed and interpreted. Just as bounded optimality takes into account properties of both the environment and the agent (some program running on a particular architecture), so, too, is J. R. Anderson's (1991) adaptive rationality a joint function of the environment—or at least task structure—and the human cognitive architecture. Anderson contends that the human architecture has been "optimized somehow" (1991, p. 471) to perform cognitive functions in an environment that has a particular structure. Since the raison d'être of much of cognitive psychology is to reverse-engineer the human cognitive architecture from its observed behavior, Anderson uses these premises to formulate what he calls a rational analysis methodology for constructing an explanatory account of some cognitive behavior of interest. According to this methodology, one begins by specifying the goal of the behavior, the structure of the environment in which this behavior occurs, and (psychologically plausible) computational constraints. From these, one determines optimal behavior on the task, that is, a prescriptive model. Several researchers have applied this methodology to modeling human performance on certain formal reasoning tasks, finding that the response patterns historically viewed as non-normative by some standard (and hence indicative of irrationality) appear to be optimal under the rational analysis perspective (e.g., Oaksford and Chater 1994, chapter 9 in this volume).

If rational analysis is a sound methodology, then it may have some prescriptive advice about how to construct artificial agents as well. At the juncture of determining what the optimal behavior is for some task, we can consider what properties an architecture (and program running on that architecture) must have to support such behavior. In general, all these situated views of rationality bring us full circle to McCarthy's original characterization of intellectual activity as taking place in a world that has "a certain physical and intellectual structure." And the implication of any such view is that both the forward and reverse engineering of intelligent architectures must be guided by considering properties of that world structure.

The situated view of rationality, with its emphasis on cognitive architecture, is important from a philosophical sense as well. From this perspective, it seems that there can be no competence/performance distinction because the architecture simply operates as it operates. It can do no more and no less than what it actually does given a particular task in a particular environment. That it might perform in some realm according to one manner and be competent in the same realm in some other sense does not hold, once an integrated picture takes into account the environment and the task.

5. Uniting Common Sense and Rationality

A classical perspective about rationality in computational approaches to intelligence maintains that an agent (whether natural or artificial) has a "central system" that controls all the agent's decision-making activities, which would include commonsense reasoning. According to this perspective, good commonsense reasoning would arise when this central system possesses "rationality." Often this perspective has presumed that "rationality" is definable in terms other than what people in fact do. But adopting this perspective can be self-refuting, at least when we apply it to humans. When we discover that people do fall short of full rationality according to most normative standards and given the close tie that this perspective implicitly makes between rationality and common sense, we then call human commonsense reasoning into question. However, human commonsense reasoning is acknowledged by all sides to be excellent. In turn then, this leads us to question whether the normative standards were correct.

Such a paradoxical result is due in part to the assumption of a normative standard for rationality that is independent of the details of how people actually reason and rationally act in specific situations. A way out of this paradox is to abandon any definition of rational action and inference that is independent of how the reasoner is constituted (i.e., of the reasoner's cognitive architecture) and independent of the environment in which the reasoner is using this cognitive architecture to achieve its goals.

Clearly, people's ability to achieve certain epistemic and pragmatic goals is often limited by the nature of the human cognitive architecture. As Newell puts it, people must "overcome in each and every concrete case how knowledge is internally distributed and represented [by the human cognitive architecture]" (1990, p. 364). This fight between architecture limitations and information-processing goals is a difficult one, and not just for people. AI researchers do similar battles with architectures in constructing intelligent artifacts. The successes for AI have come when AI practitioners can structure problems in ways that exploit the strengths of current computational architectures and the programs supported by such architectures. A crucial theoretical position is whether a given architecture can in principle support the "right programs" for optimizing reasoning on a particular task within a particular environment. If an AI practitioner believes it cannot, then that belief defines a different research agenda, that is, the search for an alternative architecture that has a different set of invariants, for which the "right programs" can be formulated and implemented. One argument for paradigm shifts to connectionist architectures or behavior-based architectures (e.g., Brooks 1991) is based on exactly this belief: that the battle for achieving general intelligent behavior will be won with a different sort of architecture.

Still, we are left with wondering if there is an underlying rationality for the mechanisms that enable commonsense reasoning, for both people and machines. An evolutionary perspective holds that there is—commonsense reasoning is an adaptive accomplishment of the human cognitive architecture, through which we acquire and manipulate knowledge of the everyday world. As we saw earlier, commonsense reasoning has been characterized as heuristic rather than logical, perhaps fundamentally inductive (in the broad sense outlined earlier), and geared to integrating and assimilating incomplete and uncertain information to predict, to explain, and to achieve goals within the world. The pervasive success of this kind of reasoning in achieving a wide range of epistemic and pragmatic goals should be regarded as an indication of its rationality. If our artifacts are to exist in the same world as we do, with some constraints on their computational resources, they, too, will need some kind of adaptive rationality that is predicated on the structure of this world. This adaptive rationality might fall short of commonly adopted standards of normative rationality for them as well. In sum, these considerations point to the view that commonsense reasoning should be thought of as adaptive rationality.

Much of the theoretical and empirical effort that surrounds these issues turns on whether and how the rationality of commonsense reasoning is fundamentally at odds with the sense of rationality required by other sorts of epistemic and pragmatic goals. These other goals include ones involved in problem solving when using abstractions about the world and indirect representations of properties of the world, such as those provided by the languages of logic and probability. It is with these abstractions and indirect representations that the mechanisms that underlie commonsense reasoning appear to lead people astray, at least according to normative standards. For while people can in fact solve formal reasoning problems, it is also the case that their reasoning on such problems is influenced by semantic content, cued information, and information presentation modes (e.g., frequencies vs. probabilities).

To reconcile these matters, several theoretical accounts posit two different sorts of reasoning systems. K. E. Stanovich (1999) uses the term *dual-process theories* to denote these accounts, which include the positions put forward by J. St. B. T. Evans and D. E. Over (1996), J. L. Pollock (1993), and S. A. Sloman (1996). In these accounts, there is a group of processes that constitutes a reasoning system that "automatically" and "effortlessly" deals with certain types of information, but there is also another, more "reflective" reasoning system that can be called upon when needed. By Stanovich's (1999, p. 145) reckoning, there is a common depiction for each of these two types of reasoning systems across the many different proposals. Generally speaking, the first type of reasoning is holistic, automatic, and associative, making few demands on cognitive capacity and being relatively fast. It is generally thought that people are able to reason in this way "for free" as a consequence of their biology. The second type of reasoning, Stanovich notes, is variously characterized as deliberative, slower, analytic, rule-based, and acquired "by formal tuition."

Three themes emerge in this sort of account. First, we are invited to align the first type of reasoning with commonsense reasoning and then commonsense reasoning in turn with the cognitive architecture—its default representations for information, associated mechanisms for manipulating those representations, and some control system (a default operating system, if you will) that allocates memory and attention resources. By associating the commonsense reasoning with the cognitive architecture, we make commonsense reasoning cognitively impenetrable—beyond any direct influence of our knowledge or beliefs (Fodor 1983; Pylyshyn 1984). Under this view, it is not surprising that commonsense reasoning and the acquisition of commonsense knowledge has eluded any easy analysis and duplication by artificial systems, for its enabling mechanisms are not directly discernible by us.

A second theme in these dual-process accounts—motivated by the empirical data on human reasoning—is the idea that the mechanisms that enable commonsense reasoning are somehow at odds with the more deliberative, analytic reasoning required for normative success on formal problems, due to the former's automaticity and cognitive impenetrability. On the one hand, this holistic and associative commonsense reasoning system is credited with obtaining the normatively right answers when, say, logic problems are reframed as permission/obligation scenarios. On the other hand, it takes the blame for yielding those non-normative answers when semantic information leads reasoners astray from considering the underlying formal structure (e.g., to assigning higher probabilities to a conjunctive statement than to either of its parts, if the conjunctive statement fits some familiar real-world prototype). In such cases, the seat of rationality is seen as lying with the deliberative, analytic reasoning, whose job it is to recognize and "override" any nonoptimal decisions or actions recommended by the automatic reasoning mechanisms (e.g., Pollock 1993). More generally, the deliberative, analytic thinking is seen as primarily responsible for intentional-level goals, whose achievement might be jeopardized if the holistic, associative thinking were relied on exclusively.

A final theme in these dual-process analyses is that despite the manner in which this impenetrable commonsense reasoning may detract from normative performance in some realms, this reasoning is nonetheless seen as essential for achieving everyday epistemic and pragmatic goals. Such goals require belief revision, nonmonotonic reasoning, inference to the best explanation, and the like, all to be accomplished within an environment of imperfect and incomplete knowledge. Under this perspective, the emphasis on normative standards—abstracted from any particular cognitive agent within any particular environment—has obscured recognizing the potential value of whatever cognitive processes are responsible for certain systematic, nonnormative responses on formal reasoning problems. Whatever the ways in which our automatic and hard-wired reasoning mechanisms deviate from normative behavior in certain realms, we probably would not survive long in the everyday world without them.

If we align commonsense reasoning and its adaptive rationality with the human cognitive architecture—what we get for free from our biology—are we then led to conclude that deliberative, analytic thinking (and its promise of normative rationality) comes with a price, namely, formal education and tuition? This might invite us to see such deliberative thinking and reasoning as just so many different sorts of learned programs—running "on" the cognitive architecture but somehow not part of it. But this does not seem quite right, either: young children and even other primates appear to engage in complex problem-solving strategies that we would certainly categorize as deliberative, analytic, rule-based reasoning (e.g., see chapter 7). These capabilities, too, are demanded by the everyday world and presumably are enabled by the cognitive architecture. If this is right, both those mechanisms that enable commonsense reasoning and those mechanisms that enable some approximation to normative rationality must coexist within the same architecture. The theoretical issue that then remains is to describe the detailed interaction of these two components of the architecture, for both descriptive theories of human cognition and prescriptive theories of artificial cognition.

6. Overview of the Book

In the chapters that follow, readers will find considered treatments of common sense, reasoning, and rationality from computational, psychological, and philosophical perspectives. Some authors present position statements and analyses, while others offer detailed consideration of how to formalize particular elements thought to underlie cognitive or computational models of commonsense reasoning. In all cases, these essays speak to many of the issues and debates I have touched upon here and offer inroads into a diverse cognitive science literature on rationality and commonsense reasoning. While the reader might be drawn to some chapters before others, the order of their appearance in the volume has been set to allow certain themes and counterthemes to unfold.

Rationality and Intelligence

In his essay, Stuart Russell considers how to formalize intelligence or rationality in a way that has pragmatic and theoretical value for the development of agents built for some specific application and of general theories of intelligence. He presents and reviews three candidates that traditionally have stood as formalizations of intelligence: perfect rationality, calculative rationality, and meta-level rationality. Each characterization offered is problematic in some way or other. As in Newell's analysis of the perfect knowledge-level agent, perfect rationality is an abstraction that does not correspond to any physical reasoner. Calculative rationality—based on methods that we know would give the right answer in principle—fails to scale up to problems of sufficient and interesting complexity. Meta-level rationality—deliberating about how to maximize behavior and then deliberating about the extent to which such deliberation is optimal—pushes the problem into a never-ending regress. As an alternative, he considers the notion of bounded optimality as a workable proxy for theorizing about machine intelligence. This notion rests on two crucial elements: that behaviors and decisions happen in real time and that an agent is defined by a particular (software and hardware) architecture and a particular program that runs on that architecture. Under this view, an agent is bounded optimal if it maximizes the utility of its behavior for a task within the demands of the environment. Having laid this groundwork, Russell elaborates on the role of adaptive, inductive mechanisms as the means for making gains in calculative and meta-level rationality for real-world application systems and for bounded optimality more generally. He observes that the notion of bounded optimality shares much in spirit with computational models of human intelligence, which ultimately must account for the operation of the human cognitive architecture within the real-world environment.

The Logical Foundations of Means-Ends Reasoning

A good deal of commonsense reasoning is done in the service of determining how to get something done, that is, to achieve a goal. John L. Pollock presents this perspective as a matter of *epistemic cognition* being driven by the requirements of *practical cognition* or plan-construction. In particular, he argues that the epistemic cognition that supports planning in the real world must be a type of defeasible reasoning. He observes that much of AI's success in building successful planning systems rests on the prespecification of statements about the world known to be relevant and assumed to hold true across world states, unless otherwise specified. But he further observes that people plan quite easily in the absence of such guarantees and so, too, must a truly autonomous planning agent for which all necessary knowledge about the world cannot possibly be specified. Planning must proceed without the reasoner first being able to prove that the assumptions upon which the plan was formulated will still hold *while* the plan is being executed. In this chapter, Pollock is concerned with the defeasible aspects of means-ends reasoning, a common way through which people construct plans by identifying the circumstances in which they could achieve a desired goal and then making the achievement of these circumstances a subgoal. The expectation that a plan will succeed is grounded, Pollock argues, in defeasible expectations about features of the world that serve as preconditions for taking particular steps toward that goal. Pollock contends that these defeasible expectations about world features, in turn, are based on temporal projectability assumptions about which properties will be stable across time. This notion of temporal projectability is a crucial matter that underlies much of commonsense knowledge, induction, and plausible inference, according to Pollock. He goes on to offer not only a logical specification of defeasible means-ends planning by employing these temporal projectability principles but also a fully implemented version of the planner using his general defeasible reasoning system, OSCAR.

Induction and Consistency

How can a reasoning agent come to accept conclusions that are based on inductive or uncertain inference? This is an important matter for plausible inference, particularly given the groundwork laid earlier that puts induction at center stage for both common sense and rationality. The very evidence on which we base some inference may itself have some error associated with it, and yet it still forms the basis for subsequent inferences and reasoning. If everything is open for revision, then it is difficult to stipulate what counts as evidence in the first place. Henry E. Kyburg, Jr., considers two approaches to uncertainty in dealing with such matters. One is the Bayesian approach, which holds that observations or evidence is incorrigible, while all other statements have an associated number that indicates their degree of uncertainty. Under the Bayesian approach, there is no notion of nonmonotonicity: the inference generated is a classical deductive inference. There is a rule by which one can calculate a particular conditional probability given other conditional probabilities. There is no sense in which this sort of conclusion might have to be retracted upon learning new information: it is absolutely certain, and so whether or not to accept the resulting conclusion is not an issue. Kyburg notes that "updating" a conditional probability is really a matter of drawing an altogether different conclusion—one based on different knowledge—and not modifying one already drawn. The other is a nonmonotonic approach, which supposes that people come to accept statements tentatively and that we might reject them when more evidence is collected. Under this latter approach, it is the inferential step that has some associated uncertainty; the evidence itself may only be accepted with some degree of "practical certainty." The conclusion, therefore, has some associated practical certainty as well. Kyburg focuses on inductive inference and argues that the Bayesian reconstruction of induction is misguided both in its assumption that evidential statements are certain and in its attempt to avoid nonobservational acceptance. He also argues that there is a way of casting the nonmonotonic approach in terms of probability intervals. This method allows for the association of a level of error or uncertainty with individual statements and the recognition that the conjunction of all such statements is false, while still supporting the acceptance of each individual statement. Although the cost of this acceptance approach is that sometimes mistakes will be made, Kyburg contends that this approach is more realistic psychologically and more efficient computationally as a representation of rational inference.

The Logic of Ordinary Language

Gilbert Harman considers whether there is a naive or folk logic of ordinary language, a set of principles that plays the same role in our understanding and use of language as, say, the principles of naive physics play in our understanding of the everyday world. To introduce this matter, Harman makes a crucial distinction between true logical and nonlogical principles: the truth of the former is a matter of their form, while the truth of the latter is a matter of their content. Thus, he argues that logical principles can inform a reasoner about the acceptability of an argument's structure but not how the argument is to be assembled or even whether the argument's conclusion should warrant a change in belief state. In brief, Harman contends that logic is silent on which of several possible belief states a reasoner should adopt or on how a model ought to be revised, should new information prove inconsistent with already-accepted beliefs. Harman notes that logical form is a generalization about propositions of a language and, since logical inference operates on these forms, they might be taken to define the logic of ordinary language. He then considers a candidate logic rule of ordinary language, which he calls the knowledge rule: If someone knows something, then it is true. Harman identifies ways in which such a rule seems both like a logic rule, for there is a need to talk about truth in any way we might paraphrase this principle, but also unlike a logic rule, for its truth appears to depend on its content in addition to its structure. He offers by way of resolution a distinction between strict and loose logics, where the former appeals only to formal aspects of structure, while the latter appeals to the truth of propositions in order to state the relevant generalizations. And it is in this sense, Harman speculates, that a (loose) logic of ordinary language embodies our commonsense knowledge about language and how we use it to reason and speak fluidly about what is known in the world and what is said about the world.

Knowledge and Coherence

Consistent with Harman's epistemological position on models of belief and belief change, Paul Thagard, Chris Eliasmith, Paul Rusnock, and Cameron Shelley have developed and refined a computational notion of coherence as a property of belief states, models, and theories about the world. Simply put, coherence is meant to capture the degree to which the constituent elements of a belief state, model, or theory are mutually consistent or inconsistent with one another. Under this view, how we explain the world and integrate new information with already-accepted beliefs can be viewed as a matter of maximizing the coherence of our current belief sets. In their chapter, Thagard, Eliasmith, Rusnock, and Shelley extend this coherence theory for explanation to include analogical, deductive, perceptual, and conceptual coherence. For each type of coherence, they define the two facets required by the coherence account: the constituent elements (e.g., hypotheses, propositions, concepts, and interpretations) and the set of constraints that can connect these elements in mutually supportive or nonsupportive relationships. Maximizing the overall coherence of the element set is achieved by accepting and rejecting particular elements. The authors contend that this extended definition of epistemic coherence addresses many objections against coherence theories, which have traditionally concerned matters of computability, the preservation of truth, coherence versus justification, and circularity of inference. Furthermore, the parallel algorithms for computing coherence constitute an inference mechanism that is quite different from inference methods associated with deductive logic or even probability theories. In offering this broad framework, Thagard and his colleagues contribute a psychologically and computationally plausible account of the diverse ways in which people make sense of the everyday world around them.

The Evolutionary Roots of Intelligence and Rationality

While the influence of domain content on formal reasoning has traditionally been viewed as interfering with human rationality, it might also reflect an adaptive feature of the human reasoning architecture, one that is the product of natural selection. Denise Dellarosa Cummins argues in support of this latter view, weaving together data on animal behavior in dominance hierarchies, the development of theory of mind concepts in young children, and the ease with which people reason about problems that concern social norms. In the realm of animal behavior, dominance hierarchies dictate which individuals get access to potential mates and thereby influence reproductive opportunities. Seeing dominance hierarchies as defining a set of social norms, Cummins asks two questions: What cognitive abilities would ensure maintenance of the hierarchy and hence the reproductive success of individuals high in the hierarchy? And what cognitive abilities would enable a low-ranking individual to thwart the hierarchy and gain access to resources? The former, she argues, rests on the ability to recognize when low-ranking individuals are violating what the hierarchy forbids. The latter requires that such low-ranking individuals have certain deceptive skills and the ability to reason about the knowledge and beliefs of others. Could humans have evolved specialized cognitive facilities particularly tuned to reasoning about obligations and violations in social relationships and to manipulating complex representations about belief states and intentions of others? Cummins argues so, citing data that both young children and adults quite easily make deductively valid inferences on problems presented in the guise of enforcing social norms. She notes that children seem naturally to develop a theory of mind, particularly concerning belief states, knowledge states, and intentionality; furthermore, these concepts emerge developmentally in a pattern similar to that observed in other mammals. In presenting this evolutionary perspective, Cummins reframes elements of intelligence and rationality as matters of adaptation and survival in a social world.

How Good Are Fast and Frugal Heuristics?

Gerd Gigerenzer, Jean Czerlinski, and Laura Martignon argue that models of reasonable and rational judgment should look outside the mind to the structure of the environment in which the mind must operate. The authors note that the everyday world presents reasoners—who have finite computational resources—with limited time to solve problems for which there is often scarce and uncertain information. Although this observation has long supported the notion that the rationality of any physical creature is limited or bounded in some sense, Gigerenzer, Czerlinski, and Martignon point out that there are competing approaches to accomplishing even this bounded rationality. One approach is to maximize the computational deliberation as much as possible under the given constraints, possibly doing some metareasoning about the cost of further deliberation within the available time. As an alternative, a reasoner could opt to satisfice, coming up with a decision that is good enough by using what the authors call "fast and frugal" computational methods. Problem-solving heuristics that are fast (by requiring simple computations) and frugal (by using relatively little information to render a decision) would seem particularly effective in environments that offer limited time and uncertain information for making decisions. But is there an accuracy price associated with using such heuristics, particularly relative to more comprehensive (and hence arguably more rational) approaches, such as decision models that employ linear and multiple regression techniques? Using several real-world data sets, the authors demonstrate that certain fast and frugal heuristics performed nearly as accurately as and sometimes better than these optimality methods, with significantly fewer computations during learning and testing. The authors propose that such heuristics are ecologically valid satisficing strategies, that is, information-processing strategies that are effective for the real-world environment in which people must render most of their decisions. And it is plausible, they suggest, that the human mind could have evolved such strategies for rendering highly accurate decisions despite the uncertainty and scarcity of information that the environment provides.

Commonsense Reasoning, Logic, and Human Rationality

Mike Oaksford and Nick Chater advance a strong position: deductive inference plays *no* significant role in everyday commonsense reasoning, in formalizing scientific predictive and explanatory reasoning, or in considerations of human (and possibly machine) rationality. The crucial starting question, they contend, is whether deduction provides a satisfactory computational-level description of commonsense reasoning. They review and ultimately reject various arguments in support of this. For example, they contend that it is circular to discuss how well people perform some deductive tasks or how frequently deductive inferences appear in language statements. Such methodologies, they argue, presume that reasoning tasks and language statements are interpreted deductively in the first place by the individuals who are performing the task and making the statements. Oaksford and Chater also argue that while commitment to cognition as computation theoretically implies a logical interpretation for all behaviors, this level of analysis admits no useful distinctions about the function of particular computations. As such, it does not inform us about cognitive theory. Oaksford and Chater further note that some current epistemology and philosophy of science theories accord deduction at best a marginal role in the origin of knowledge. They also observe that formal and computational models of defeasible reasoning lie outside the realm of standard deductive logic. In the realm of human reasoning, the authors contend that many of the canonical tasks used in empirical studies are not necessarily deductive *in nature*. Their own empirical and theoretical work supports alternative analyses of such tasks and what would constitute rational patterns of responses and inferences. Oaksford and Chater ultimately conclude that psychological accounts of human reasoning are left with the three frameworks for defeasible inference that have long occupied AI's knowledge representation and reasoning community: nonmonotonic logics, specialized procedural accounts, and probabilistic approaches. It is the last framework that the authors themselves currently regard as most promising. In placing such a bet, they are betting against the notion that specialized reasoning modules—of the sort discussed by Cummins—will have a central role in accounting for commonsense reasoning.

Reasoning Imperialism

Although people can recognize and make deductively valid arguments on occasion, one perspective is that there might be no psychologically valid distinction between the deductive correctness of a conclusion and its inductive strength. This perspective, evidenced by Oaksford and Chater's position, is a case of what Lance J. Rips calls reasoning imperialism: the attempts of one theoretical camp to assimilate the data explained by another. An example of reasoning imperialism would be the argument that deductive inference is just a form of probabilistic inference where the (conditional) probability of the conclusion given the premises is 1.0. Equally imperialistic is the alternative position that probabilistic (or default) reasoning is simply deductive reasoning where degrees of invalidity and the possibility of counterexamples are allowed. Rips considers whether such strategic strikes are likely to be successful. Assuming first that people can reliably distinguish deductive correctness from inductive strength, Rips demonstrates that an element crucial to extending a mental models theory of deduction to handle inductive-strength judgments is unavailable, namely, the specification of constraints on what counts as relevant counterexamples to the inductive inference under consideration. Such relevance constraints play no role in deductive correctness but are required for the inductive case. Thus, Rips argues, the evaluation of inductive strength must be more than a "slightly different computation" on the mental models that also determine deductive correctness. Rips then considers abandoning the premise that people can in fact distinguish between deductive correctness and inductive strength only to note two problems with this position as well. First, people quite readily recognize the validity of certain elementary deductive inference rules, such as and-elimination, even when the content is arbitrary. Second, Rips cites intriguing, albeit preliminary, neuro-imaging studies that suggest that inductive and deductive tasks activate different areas of the brain. In sum, Rips concludes that reasoning imperialism may not work for deduction and induction, for people may hold different sorts of arguments to different sorts of standards and evaluate them in qualitatively different sorts of ways.

Ending the Rationality Wars: How to Make Disputes about Human Rationality Disappear

Richard Samuels, Stephen Stich, and Michael Bishop characterize the two opposing sides of the current rationality wars as the "heuristics and biases" researchers on the one hand and the evolutionary psychologists on the other. The former group cites decades of evidence that people have systematic devia-tions from rationality, as evidenced by their performance on certain types of formal reasoning tasks. The latter group asserts the implausibility of the human architecture evolving with an inaccurate sense of probability and offers evidence that a representation of various formal problems in more ecologically valid forms makes the so-called irrational response patterns disappear. Samuels, Stich, and Bishop contend, however, that there is less disagreement by the proponents of these two views than it might initially appear once they eliminate the so-called rhetorical flourishes and focus on the core claims that each side makes about cognitive judgments and cogni-tive mechanisms. The authors evaluate these core claims in the context of alternative normative perspectives on rationality: rationality derived from formal logic, probability, and decision theories; rationality based on accuracy of reasoning, in either the actual or proper domains for cognitive mecha-nisms; and rationality based on a mechanism's optimality with respect to the constraints under which it must operate. The authors contend that both sides of the rationality wars are in agreement about the rationality of mech-anisms or judgments given any one of these normative frameworks. While acknowledging that there are still areas of disagreement, Samuels, Stich, and Bishop make an even stronger claim, namely, that the evolutionary psychologists and the heuristics-and-biases proponents not only agree on human rationality but also must be committed to supporting the core claims of their opponents.

NOTES

This work was supported by NSERC research grant A0089. I thank Jeff Pelletier for comments on earlier versions of this material.

1. Of course, in both philosophy (e.g., Plato) and psychology (e.g., Freud) rationality and emotion have long been seen as opposing elements of the human psyche, where the role of the former is to tame the latter.

2. In thinking about how "what everyone knows" might be formalized, McCarthy (1979, p. 115) suggested that philosophy might be defined as an attempted "science of common sense" or, alternatively, that the science of common sense was a particular part of philosophy.

3. P. W. Cheng (1997) presents a new theory of causality and its relation to previous psychological and philosophical accounts.

4. See the Web site www-formal.stanford.edu/leora/cs for problems that some researchers in the formal reasoning community view as illustrative of these commonsense content areas and issues. The egg-cracking example that follows in the text is included there.

5. It should be noted here that D. Lenat's CYC project (Guha and Lenat 1990; Lenat and Guha 1990), by its very conception, takes issue with these claims.

6. Not only does belief revision have an explanatory role in terms of accounting for the unexpected, but the adoption of one belief set over another to remove an inconsistency has implications for future actions and planning as well. Suppose you have the beliefs "If I brought the new lecture slides with me, then they would be right next to the old lecture slides in my briefcase" and "I'm sure I brought the new slides with me." Jointly, these beliefs lead to a plan of looking only where the new slides are supposed to be and nowhere else in the briefcase. When the new slides are not found where expected, the reasoner is forced to accept that one of the initial beliefs is wrong and must adopt a belief set that excludes one or the other of them. Depending on which initial belief is abandoned, the reasoner will take different actions.

7. A monotonic reasoning procedure will continue to derive the same conclusions (as well as possibly some more) from a set of facts even after new information is added to the set of facts. More formally, a first-order logic system with a knowledge base KB will still derive conclusion P even after the KB is augmented with some new information Q. Other conclusions may also follow, but P itself is still entailed after Q is added to KB. A nonmonotonic reasoning procedure may retract P once Q is taken into account. In the example in the text, learning that my colleague's only child is a teenager causes me to retract the belief that my colleague has a child in day care. Thus, the set of conclusions derived from my knowledge base is not strictly increasing as new information arrives. This is also called *defeasible reasoning*: newly accepted beliefs defeat or undermine previously accepted beliefs.

8. Although the term *frame problem* originally designated a technical matter in the specification of axioms for reasoning about change, it is often used more generally to refer to the issue of knowing what does and does not change in the world after an action has been executed. See chapter 3 for a discussion of the frame problem in the context of planning.

9. The term *heuristic* has many definitions associated with it and is sometimes, incorrectly, regarded as somehow "nonalgorithmic." The crucial distinction concerning heuristics is a functional one, namely, that a heuristic method

is one that is successful most but not necessarily all of the time. See also Romany-cia and Pelletier 1985.

10. I note at this juncture that many scholars do not consider the decision-making and inference patterns discussed here as central to their own considerations of rationality, which focus instead on cases of weakness of will, self-deception, and the like. See Harman 1995 and Mele 1997 for discussion of some of these matters. For other philosophers and anthropologists, the crucial debate about rationality is whether it is culturally defined. See Hollis and Lukes 1982.

11. Note that this does not lead to a tautological definition of rationality as "the best that can be done with the available resources and constraints," for it presumes a function that can evaluate the utility of the resultant action with respect to the task. See chapter 2.

REFERENCES

Anderson, J. R. (1991). Is human cognition adaptive? *Behavioral and Brain Sciences* 14:471–517.

Ashton, R., and A. Ashton (1990). Evidence-responsiveness in professional judgment: Effects of positive vs. negative evidence and presentation mode. *Organizational Behavior and Human Decision Processes* 46:1–19.

Bacchus, F., A. Grove, J. Y. Halpern, and D. Koller (1992). From statistics to belief. In *Proceedings of the Tenth National Conference on Artificial Intelligence,* pp. 602–608. Cambridge: MIT Press.

Baron, J. (1985). *Rationality and Intelligence.* Cambridge: Cambridge University Press.

Baron, J. (1994). *Thinking and Deciding.* New York: Cambridge University Press.

Brooks, R. A. (1991). Intelligence without representation. *Artificial Intelligence* 47:139–159.

Cheng, P. W. (1997). From covariation to causation: A causal power theory. *Psychological Review* 104:367–405.

Cheng, P. W., and K. J. Holyoak (1985). Pragmatic reasoning schemas. *Cognitive Psychology* 17:391–416.

Cohen, L. J. (1981). Can human irrationality be experimentally demonstrated? *Behavioral and Brain Sciences* 4:317–370.

Collins, A., and R. Michalski (1989). The logic of plausible reasoning: A core theory. *Cognitive Science* 13:1–49.

Cosmides, L. (1989). The logic of social exchange: Has natural selection shaped how humans reason? Studies with the Wason selection task. *Cognition* 31:187–276.

Cosmides, L., and J. Tooby (1996). Are humans good intuitive statisticians after all? Rethinking some conclusions from the literature on judgement under uncertainty. *Cognition* 58:1–73.

Doyle, J. (1992). The roles of rationality in reasoning. *Computational Intelligence* 8:376–409.

Einhorn, H. J., and R. M. Hogarth (1981). Behavioral decision theory: Processes of judgement and choice. *Annual Review of Psychology* 32:53–88.

Elio, R. (1997). What to believe when inferences are contradicted: The impact of knowledge type and inference rule. In *Proceedings of the Nineteenth*

Annual Conference of the Cognitive Science Society, pp. 211–216. Hillsdale, NJ: Erlbaum.

Elio, R. (1998). How to disbelieve p → q: Resolving contradictions. In *Proceedings of the Twentieth Annual Conference of the Cognitive Science Society*, pp. 315–320. Hillsdale, NJ: Erlbaum.

Evans, J. (1987). *Bias in Human reasoning: Causes and Consequences*. Hillsdale, NJ: Erlbaum.

Evans, J. St. B. T., S. E. Newstead, and R. M. J. Byrne (1993). *Human Reasoning: The Psychology of Deduction*. Hillsdale, NJ: Erlbaum.

Evans, J. St. B. T., and D. E. Over (1996). *Rationality and Reasoning*. Hove, England: Psychology Press.

Evans, J. St. B. T., D. E. Over, and K. I. Manktelow (1993). Reasoning, decision making, and rationality. *Cognition* 49:165–187.

Fodor, J. A. (1983). *Modularity of Mind: An Essay on Faculty Psychology*. Cambridge: MIT Press.

Frege, G. (1894). Review of Husserl, *Philosophie der Arithmetic: Zeitschrift für Philosophie und philosophische Kritik* 103:313–332. Extracts translated and reprinted in P. Geach and M. Black (1952), *Translations from the Philosophical Writings of Gottlob Frege*, pp. 79–85. Oxford: Blackwell.

Gabbay, D., C. Hogger, and J. A. Robinson (1993). *Handbook of Logic in Artificial Intelligence and Logic Programming*, vol. 3: *Non-monotonic Reasoning and Uncertain Reasoning*. Hillsdale, NJ: Erlbaum.

Gärdenfors, P. (1988). *Knowledge in Flux: Modeling the Dynamics of Epistemic States*. Cambridge: MIT Press.

Gärdenfors, P. (1990). Belief revision and non-monotonic logic: Two sides of the same coin? In *Proceedings of the Ninth European Conference on Artificial Intelligence*, pp. 768–773. London: Pittman.

Gärdenfors, P., and D. Makinson (1994). Non-monotonic inference based on expectation. *Artificial Intelligence* 65:197–245.

George, C. (1995). The endorsement of the premises: Assumption-based or belief-based reasoning. *British Journal of Psychology* 86:93–111.

Gigerenzer, G. (1994). Why the distinction between single-event probabilities and frequencies is important for psychology (and vice versa). In G. Write and P. Ayton (eds.), *Subjective Probability*, pp. 129–161. New York: Wiley.

Gigerenzer, G. (1998). Ecological intelligence: An adaptation for frequencies. In D. Cummins and C. Allen (eds.), *The Evolution of Mind*, pp. 9–29. New York: Oxford University Press.

Ginsberg, M. (1996). Do computers need common sense? In *Proceedings of the Fifth Knowledge Representation and Reasoning Conference*, pp. 620–626. San Francisco: Morgan Kaufmann.

Guha, R. V., and D. Lenat (1990). CYC: A midterm report. *AI Magazine* 11:32–59.

Halpern, J. (1993). A critical re-examination of default logic, autoepistemic logic, and only knowing: Computational logic and proof theory. In *Proceedings of the Kurt Gödel Conference, Springer-Verlag Lecture Notes in Computer Science*, vol. 713, pp. 43–60. Berlin: Springer-Verlag.

Harman, G. (1995). Rationality. In E. E. Smith and D. N. Osherson (eds.), *Thinking: An Invitation to Cognitive Science*, vol. 3, pp. 175–212. Cambridge: MIT Press.

Holland, J. H., K. J. Holyoak, R. E. Nisbett, and P. R. Thagard (1986). *Induction: Processes of Inference, Learning, and Discovery*. Cambridge: MIT Press.

Hollis, M., and S. Lukes (1982). *Rationality and Relativism*. Oxford: Blackwell.

Horvitz, E. J. (1989). Reasoning about beliefs and actions under computational resource constraints. In L. N. Kanal, T. S. Levitt, and J. F. Lemmer (eds.), *Uncertainty in Artificial Intelligence*, vol. 3, pp. 301–324. Amsterdam: Elsevier Science.

Husserl, E. (1900). *Logical Investigations* (translated by J. Findley). London: Routledge and Kegan Paul.

Johnson-Laird, P. N. (1983). *Mental Models: Towards a Cognitive Science of Language, Inference, and Consciousness*. Cambridge: Harvard University Press.

Johnson-Laird, P. N. (1994). Mental models and probabilistic thinking. *Cognition* 50:189–209.

Johnson-Laird, P. N., and R. M. J. Byrne (1991). *Deduction*. Hillsdale, NJ: Erlbaum.

Kusch, M. (1995). *Psychologism*. London: Routledge.

Kyburg, H. E., Jr. (1994). Believing on the basis of evidence. *Computational Intelligence* 10:3–20.

Lenat, D., and R. V. Guha (1990). *Building Large Knowledge-based Systems*. Reading, MA: Addison-Wesley.

Macnamara, J. (1986). *A Border Dispute: The Place of Logic in Psychology*. Cambridge: MIT Press.

Manktelow, K. I., and D. E. Over (1991). Social rules and utilities in reasoning with deontic conditionals. *Cognition* 39:85–105.

Manktelow, K. I., and D. E. Over (eds.) (1993). *Rationality: Psychological and Philosophical Perspectives*. London: Routledge.

McCarthy, J. (1974). Review of Artificial Intelligence: A general survey. *Artificial Intelligence* 5:317–322. Reprinted in V. Lifschitz (ed.) (1990), *Formalizing Common Sense: Papers by John McCarthy*, pp. 64–69. Norwood, NJ: Ablex. Page cites refer to reprint.

McCarthy, J. (1979). Ascribing mental qualities to machines. In M. Ringle (ed.), *Philosophical Perspectives in Artificial Intelligence*, pp. 161–195. Atlantic Highlands, NJ: Humanities Press. Reprinted in V. Lifschitz (ed.) (1990), *Formalizing Common Sense: Papers by John McCarthy*, pp. 93–118. Norwood, NJ: Ablex. Page cites refer to reprint.

McCarthy, J. (1980). Circumscription—a form of non-monotonic reasoning. *Artificial Intelligence* 13:27–39.

McCarthy, J. (1984). Some expert systems need common sense. In H. Pagels (ed.), *Computer Culture: The Scientific, Intellectual, and Social Impact of the Computer*, vol. 426, pp. 129–137. New York: New York Academy of Sciences. Reprinted in V. Lifschitz (ed.) (1990), *Formalizing Common Sense: Papers by John McCarthy*, pp. 189–197. Norwood, NJ: Ablex. Page cites refer to reprint.

McCarthy, J., and P. Hayes (1969). Some philosophical problems from the standpoint of artificial intelligence. *Machine Intelligence* 4:463–502.

Mele, A. R. (1997). Real self-deception. *Behaviorial and Brain Sciences* 20:91–136.

Morgenstern, L. (1996). The problems with solutions to the frame problem. In K. Ford and Z. Pylyshyn (eds.), *The Robot's Dilemma Revisited*, pp. 99–133. Norwood, NJ: Ablex.

Newell, A. (1982). The knowledge level. *Artificial Intelligence* 18:87–127.

Newell, A. (1990). *Unified Theories of Cognition*. Cambridge: Harvard University Press.

Newell, A., P. S. Rosenbloom, and J. E. Laird (1993). Symbolic architectures for cognition. In M. I. Posner (ed.), *Foundations of Cognitive Science*, pp. 93–131. Cambridge: MIT Press.

Oaksford, N., and M. Chater (1994). A rational analysis of the selection task as optimal data selection. *Psychological Review* 101:608–631.

Oaksford, N., and M. Chater (1995). Theories of reasoning and the computational explanation of everyday inference. *Thinking and Reasoning* 1:121–152.

Osherson, D. N. (1995). Probability judgment. In E. E. Smith and D. N. Osherson (eds.), *Thinking: An Invitation to Cognitive Science*, vol. 3, pp. 35–76. Cambridge: MIT Press.

Osherson, D. N., E. E. Smith, O. Wilkie, A. Lopez, and E. Shafir (1990). Category-based induction. *Psychological Review* 97:185–200.

Pearl, J. (1988). *Probabilistic Reasoning in Intelligent Systems: Networks of Plausible Inference*. Reading, MA: Addison-Wesley.

Pelletier, F. J., and R. Elio (1997). What should default reasoning be, by default? *Computational Intelligence* 13:165–188.

Petty, R. E., J. R. Priester, and D. T. Wegener (1994). Cognitive processes in attitude change. In R. S. Wyer and T. K. Srull (eds.), *Handbook of Social Cognition*, vol. 2: *Applications*, pp. 69–142. Hillsdale, NJ: Erlbaum.

Pollock, J. L. (1993). The phlogeny of rationality. *Cognitive Science* 17:563–588.

Pylyshyn, Z. W. (1984). *Computation and Cognition: Toward a Foundation for Cognitive Science*. Cambridge: MIT Press.

Raghavan, S. A. (1991). JANUS: A paradigm for active decision support. *Decision Support Systems* 7:379–395.

Reiter, R. (1980). A logic for default reasoning. *Artificial Intelligence* 32:57–92.

Rescher, N. (1980). *Induction*. Oxford: Blackwell.

Rips, L. J. (1994). *The Psychology of Proof: Deductive Reasoning in Human Thinking*. Cambridge: MIT Press.

Rips, L. J. (1995). Deduction and cognition. In E. E. Smith and D. N. Osherson (eds.), *An Invitation to cognitive science*, vol. 3, pp. 297–344. Cambridge: MIT Press.

Romanycia, M., and F. J. Pelletier (1985). What is a heuristic? *Computational Intelligence* 1:47–58.

Silverman, B. G. (1992). *Critiquing Human Error: A Knowledge-Based Human–Computer Collaborative Approach*. London: Academic Press.

Simon, H. (1956). Rational choice and the structure of the environment. *Psychological Review* 63:129–138.

Simon, H. A. (1982). *Models of Bounded Rationality*. 2 vols. Cambridge: MIT Press.

Sloman, S. A. (1996). The empirical case for two systems of reasoning. *Psychological Bulletin* 119:3–22.

Sowa, J. (1991). *Principles of Semantic Networks*. San Francisco: Morgan Kaufmann.

Stanovich, K. E. (1999). *Who Is Rational? Studies of Individual Differences in Reasoning*. Mahwah, NJ: Erlbaum.

Stein, E. (1996). *Without Good Reason: The Rationality Debate in Philosophy and Cognitive Science*. Oxford: Clarendon Press.

Stevenson. R. J. (1993). Rationality and reality. In K. I. Manktelow and D. E. Over (eds.), *Rationality: Psychological and Philosophical Perspectives*, pp. 61–82. London: Routledge.

Stevenson, R. J., and D. E. Over (1995). Deduction from uncertain premises. *Quarterly Journal of Experimental Psychology* 48:613–643.

Stich, S. (1990). *The Fragmentation of Reason*. Cambridge: MIT Press.

Thagard, P. (1989). Explanatory coherence. *Behavioral and Brain Sciences* 12: 435–467.

Tversky, A., and D. Kahneman (1973). Availability: A heuristic for judging frequency and probability. *Cognitive Psychology* 5:207–232.

Tversky, A., and D. Kahneman (1974). Judgement under uncertainty: Heuristics and biases. *Science* 185:1124–1131.

Webster's New Collegiate Dictionary, 150th Anniversary Edition (1981). Springfield, MA: G. and C. Merriam.

2

Rationality and Intelligence

STUART RUSSELL

1. Artificial Intelligence

AI is a field whose ultimate goal has often been somewhat ill-defined and subject to dispute. Some researchers aim to emulate human cognition, others aim at the creation of intelligence without concern for human characteristics, and still others aim to create useful artifacts without concern for abstract notions of intelligence.

This variety is not *necessarily* a bad thing, since each approach uncovers new ideas and provides fertilization to the others. But one can argue that, since philosophers abhor a definition vacuum, many of the damaging and ill-informed debates about the feasibility of AI have been about definitions of AI to which we as AI researchers do not subscribe.

My own motivation for studying AI is to create and understand intelligence as a general property of systems, rather than as a specific attribute of humans. I believe this to be an appropriate goal for the field as a whole, and it certainly includes the creation of useful artifacts—both as spin-offs and as foci and driving forces for technological development. The difficulty with this "creation of intelligence" view, however, is that it presupposes that we have

This article previously appeared in *Artificial Intelligence Journal* 94 (1–2) (1997):57–77 and is reprinted by permission of Elsevier Science.

some productive notion of what intelligence is. Cognitive scientists can say, "Look, my model correctly predicted this experimental observation of human cognition," and artifact developers can say, "Look, my system is saving lives/megabucks," but few of us are happy with papers that say: "Look, my system is intelligent." This difficulty is compounded further by the need for theoretical scaffolding to allow us to design complex systems with confidence and to build on the results of others. "Intelligent" must be given a definition that can be related directly to the system's input, structure, and output. Such a definition must also be *general*. Otherwise, AI subsides into a smorgasbord of fields—intelligence as chess playing, intelligence as vehicle control, intelligence as medical diagnosis.

In this chapter, I shall outline the development of such definitions over the history of AI and related disciplines. I shall examine each definition as a predicate P that can be applied, supposedly, to characterize systems that are intelligence. For each P, I shall discuss whether the statement "Look, my system is P" is interesting and at least sometimes true and the sort of research and technological development to which the study of P-systems leads.

I shall begin with the idea that intelligence is strongly related to the capacity for successful behavior—the so-called agent-based view of AI. The candidates for formal definitions of intelligence are as follows:

- P_1: *Perfect rationality*, or the capacity to generate maximally successful behavior given the available information.
- P_2: *Calculative rationality*, or the in-principle capacity to compute the perfectly rational decision given the initially available information.
- P_3: *Meta-level rationality*, or the capacity to select the optimal combination of computation-sequence-plus-action under the constraint that the action must be selected by the computation.
- P_4: *Bounded optimality*, or the capacity to generate maximally successful behavior given the available information and computational resources.

All four definitions will be fleshed out in detail, and I will describe some results that have been obtained so far along these lines. Then I will describe ongoing and future work under the headings "Calculative Rationality" and "Bounded optimality."

I shall be arguing that of these candidates, bounded optimality comes closest to meeting the needs of AI research. There is always a danger, in this sort of claim, that its acceptance can lead to "premature mathematization," a condition characterized by increasingly technical results that have increasingly little to do with the original problem—in the case of AI, the problem of creating intelligence. Is research on bounded optimality a suitable stand-in for research on intelligence? I hope to show that P_4, bounded optimality, is more suitable than P_1 through P_3 because it is a real problem with real and desirable solutions and also because it satisfies some essential intuitions about the nature of intelligence. Some important questions about intelligence can only be formulated and answered within the framework of bounded optimality or some relative thereof. Only time will tell, however, whether bounded optimality research, perhaps with additional refinements, can generate enough theoretical scaffolding to support significant practical progress in AI.

2. Agents

Until fairly recently, it was common to define AI as the computational study of "mental faculties" or "intelligent systems," catalog various kinds, and leave it at that. This doesn't provide much guidance. Instead, one can define AI as the problem of designing systems that *do the right thing.* Now we just need a definition for "right."

This approach involves considering the intelligent entity as an *agent*, that is to say, a system that senses its environment and acts upon it. Formally speaking, an agent is defined by the mapping from percept sequences to actions that the agent instantiates. Let **O** be the set of percepts that the agent can observe at any instant and **A** be the set of possible actions the agent can carry out in the external world (including the action of doing nothing). Thus, the *agent function f*: $\mathbf{O}^* \rightarrow \mathbf{A}$ defines how an agent behaves under all circumstances. What counts in the first instance is what the agent does, not necessarily what it thinks or even whether it thinks at all. This initial refusal to consider further constraints on the internal workings of the agent (such as that it should reason logically, for example) helps in three ways: first, it allows us to view such "cognitive faculties" as planning and reasoning as occurring *in the service of* finding the right thing to do; second, it encompasses rather than excludes the position that systems can do the right thing without such cognitive faculties (Agre and Chapman 1987; Brooks 1989); third, it allows more freedom to consider various specifications, boundaries, and interconnections of subsystems.

The agent-based view of AI has moved quickly from workshops on "situatedness" and "embeddedness" to mainstream textbooks (Dean, Aloimonos, and Allen 1995; Russell and Norvig 1995) and buzzwords in *Newsweek*. Loosely speaking, *rational* agents are agents whose actions make sense from the point of view of the information possessed by the agent and its goals (or the task for which it was designed). Rationality is a property of actions and does not specify—although it does constrain—the process by which the actions are selected. This was a point emphasized by Simon (1958), who coined the terms *substantive rationality* and *procedural rationality* to describe the difference between the question of *what* decision to make and the question of *how* to make it. That R. A. Brooks's 1991 Computers and Thought lecture was titled "Intelligence without Reason" (see also Brooks 1991) emphasizes the fact that reasoning is (perhaps) a *derived* property of agents that might, or might not, be a good implementation scheme to achieve rational behavior. Justifying the cognitive structures that many AI researchers take for granted is not an easy problem.

One other consequence of the agent-based view of intelligence is that it opens AI up to competition from other fields that have traditionally looked

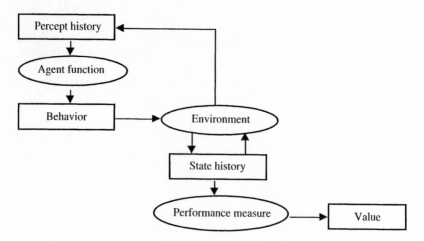

FIGURE 2.1. The agent receives percepts from the environments and generates a behavior that in turn causes the environment to generate a state history. The performance measure evaluates the state history to arrive at the value of the agent.

on the embedded agent as a natural topic of study. Control theory is foremost among these, but evolutionary programming and indeed evolutionary biology itself also have ideas to contribute.[1] The prevalence of the agent view has also helped the field move toward solving real problems, avoiding what Brooks calls the hallucination problem, which arises when the fragility of a subsystem is masked by having an intelligent human providing input to it and interpreting its outputs.

3. Perfect Rationality

Perfect rationality constrains an agent's actions to provide the maximum expectation of success given the information available. We can expand this notion as follows (see Figure 2.1). The fundamental inputs to the definition are the environment class E, in which the agent is to operate, and the performance measure U, which evaluates the sequence of states through which the agent drives the actual environment. Let $V(f, E, U)$ denote the expected value according to U obtained by an agent function f in environment class E, where (for now) we will assume a probability distribution over elements of E. Then a perfectly rational agent is defined by an agent function f_{opt} such that

$$f_{opt} = argmax_f \, V(f, E, U)$$

This is just a fancy way of saying that the best agent does the best it can. The point is that perfectly rational behavior is a well-defined function of E and U, which I will call the *task environment*. The problem of computing this function is addressed here.

The theoretical role of perfect rationality within AI is well described by Newell's paper on the knowledge level (1982). Knowledge-level analysis of AI systems relies on an assumption of perfect rationality. It can be used to establish an upper bound on the performance of any possible system, by establishing what a perfectly rational agent would do given the same knowledge.

Although the knowledge that a perfectly rational agent has determines the actions that will take given its goals, the question of where the knowledge comes from is not well understood. That is, we need to understand rational learning as well as rational action. In the logical view of rationality, learning has received almost no attention—indeed, Newell's analysis precludes learning at the knowledge level. In the decision-theoretic view, Bayesian updating provides a model for rational learning, but this pushes the question back to the prior (Carnap 1950). The question of rational priors, particularly for expressive representation languages, remains unanswered.

Another aspect of perfect rationality that is lacking is the development of a suitable body of techniques for the specification of utility functions. In economics, many results have been derived on the decomposition of overall utility into attributes that can be combined in various ways (Keeney and Raiffa 1976), yet such methods have made few inroads into AI (but see Bacchus and Grove 1995 and Wellman 1985). We also have little idea how to specify utility over time, and although the question has been raised often, we do not have a satisfactory understanding of the relationship between goals and utility.

The good thing about perfectly rational agents is that if you have one handy, you prefer it to any other agent. Furthermore, if you are an economist you can prove nice results about economies populated by them; and if you want to design distributed intelligent systems, assuming perfect rationality on the part of each agent makes the design of the interaction mechanisms much easier. The bad thing is that the theory of perfect rationality does not provide for the analysis of the internal design of the agent: one perfectly rational agent is as good as another. The *really* bad thing, as pointed out by Simon, is that perfectly rational agents do not exist. Physical mechanisms take time to process information and select actions; hence the behavior of real agents cannot immediately reflect changes in the environment and will generally be suboptimal.

4. Calculative Rationality

Before I discuss calculative rationality, it is necessary to introduce a distinction between the agent function and the *agent program*. In AI, an agent is implemented as a program, which I shall call l, running on a machine, which I shall call M. An agent program receives as input the current percept but also has an internal state that reflects, in some form, the previous percepts. It outputs actions when they have been selected. From the outside, the behavior of the agent consists of the selected actions *interspersed with inaction* (or whatever default actions the machine generates).

Calculative rationality is displayed by programs that, *if executed infinitely fast*, would result in perfectly rational behavior. Unlike perfect rationality, calculative rationality is a requirement that can be fulfilled by many real programs. Also unlike perfect rationality, calculative rationality is not necessarily a desirable property. For example, a calculatively rational chess program will choose the "right" move but may take 10^{50} time too long to do so.

The pursuit of calculative rationality has nonetheless been the main activity of theoretically well founded research in AI. In the early stages of the field, it was important to concentrate on "epistemological adequacy" before "heuristic adequacy"—that is, capability in principle rather than in practice.[2] Calculative rationality has been the mainstay of both the logical and the decision-theoretic traditions. In the logical tradition, the performance measure accepts behaviors that achieve the specified goal in all cases and rejects any others. Thus, Newell (1982) defines rational actions as those that are guaranteed to achieve one of the agent's goals. Logical planning systems, such as theorem provers that use situation calculus, satisfy the conditions of calculative rationality under this definition. In the decision-theoretic tradition, the design of calculatively rational agents has largely gone on outside AI—for example, in stochastic optimal control theory (Kumar and Varaiya 1986). Representations have usually been very impoverished (state-based rather than sentential), and solvable problems have been either very small or very specialized. Within AI, the development of probabilistic networks or belief networks has opened up many new possibilities for agent design, providing in many cases an exponential reduction in representational complexity. Systems based on influence diagrams (probabilistic networks with action and value nodes added) satisfy the decision-theoretic version of calculative rationality.

In practice, neither the logical nor the decision-theoretic traditions can avoid the intractability of the decision problems posed by the requirement of calculative rationality. One response is to rule out sources of exponential complexity in the representations and reasoning tasks addressed, so that calculative and perfect rationality coincide—at least, if we ignore the little matter of polynomial time computation. This position was expounded in two fascinating Computers and Thought lectures given by H. J. Levesque in 1985 (Levesque 1986; Levesque and Brachman 1987) and by Henry Kautz in 1989. The accompanying research results on tractable sublanguages are perhaps best seen as indications of where complexity may be an issue rather than a solution to the problem of complexity. The idea of restricting expressiveness was strongly opposed by J. Doyle and R. S. Patil (1991), who pointed out that it also restricts the applicability of the representation and inference services designed under such constraints.[3]

In the area of distributed AI, the system designer has control over that part of each agent's environment that involves negotiations with other agents. Thus, one possible way to control complexity is to constrain the negotiation problem so that optimal decisions can be made easily. For example, the Clarke Tax mechanism can be used to ensure that the best policy for each agent is simply to state its preferences truthfully (Ephrati and Rosenschein 1991). Of course, this approach does not necessarily result in optimal behavior by the *ensemble* of agents; nor does it solve the problem of complexity in interacting with the rest of the environment.

The most common response to complexity has been to use various speedup techniques and approximations in the hope of getting reasonable behavior. AI has developed a very powerful armory of methods for reducing complexity, including the decomposition of state representations into sentential form; sparse representations of environment models (as in STRIPS operators); solution decomposition methods such as partial-order planning and abstraction; approximate, parameterized representations of value functions for reinforcement learning; compilation (chunking, macro-operators, EBL, etc.); and the application of meta-level control. Although some of these methods can retain guarantees of optimality and are effective for moderately large problems that are well structured, it is inevitable that intelligent agents will be unable to act rationally in all circumstances. This observation has been a commonplace since the very beginning of AI. Yet systems that select suboptimal actions fall outside calculative rationality per se, and we need a better theory to understand them.

5. Meta-level Rationality

Meta-level rationality, also called Type II rationality by I. J. Good (1971), is based on the idea of finding an optimal trade-off between computational costs and decision quality. Although Good never made his concept of Type II rationality very precise—he defines it as "the maximization of expected utility *taking into account deliberation costs*"—it is clear that the aim was to take advantage of some sort of *meta-level architecture* to implement this trade-off. Meta-level architecture is a design philosophy for intelligent agents that divides the agent into two (or more) notional parts. The *object level* carries out computations concerned with the application domain—for example, projecting the results of physical actions, computing the utility of certain states, and so on. The *meta-level* is a second decision-making process whose application domain consists of the object-level computations themselves and the computational objects and states that they affect. Metareasoning has a long history in AI, going back at least to the early 1970s (see Russell and Wefald 1991a for historical details). One can also view selective search methods and producing strategies as embodying meta-level expertise that concerned the desirability of pursuing particular object-level search operations.

The theory of *rational metareasoning* formalizes the intuition that the meta-level can "do the right thinking." The basic idea is that object-level computations are actions with costs (the passage of time) and benefits (improvements in decision quality). A rational meta-level selects computations according to their expected utility. Rational metareasoning has a precursor, the theory of *information value* (Howard 1966)—the notion that one can calculate the decision-theoretic value of acquiring an additional piece of information by simulating the decision process that would be followed given each possible outcome of the information request, thereby estimating the expected improvement in decision quality averaged over those outcomes. The application to computational processes, by analogy to information gathering, seems to have originated with J. E. Matheson (1968). In AI, E. J. Horvitz (1987, 1989), J. S. Breese and M. R. Fehling (1990), and S. J. Russell and E. H. Wefald (1989, 1991a, 1991b) all showed how the idea of value of computation could solve the basic problems of real-time decision making.

The work done with Wefald looked in particular at search algorithms, in which the object-level computations extend projections of the results of various courses of actions further into the future. For example, in chess programs each object-level computation expands a leaf node of the game tree. The meta-level problem is then to select nodes for expansion and to terminate the search at the appropriate point. The principal problem with metareasoning in such systems is that the local effects of the computations do not *directly* translate into improved decisions, because there is also a complex process of propagating the local effects at the leaf back to the root and the move choice. It turns out that a general formula for the value of computation can be found in terms of the "local effects" and the "propagation function" such that the formula can be instantiated for any particular object-level system (such as minimax propagation), compiled, and executed efficiently at runtime. This method was implemented for two-player games, two-player games with chance nodes, and single-agent search. In each case, the same general metareasoning scheme resulted in efficiency improvements of roughly an order of magnitude over traditional, highly engineered algorithms.

Another general class of metareasoning problems arises with *anytime* (Dean and Boddy 1988) or *flexible* (Horvitz 1987) algorithms, which are algorithms designed to return results whose quality varies with the amount of time allocated to computation. The simplest type of metareasoning trades off the expected increase in decision quality for a single algorithm, as measured by a *performance profile*, against the cost of time (Simon 1955). A greedy termination condition is optimal if the second derivative of the performance profile is negative. More complex problems arise if one wishes to build complex real-time systems from anytime components. First, one has to ensure the *interruptibility* of the composed system—that is, to ensure that the system as a whole can respond robustly to immediate demands for output. The solution is to interleave the execution of all the components, allocating time to each component so that the total time for each complete iterative improvement cycle of the system doubles at each iteration. In this way, we can construct a complex system that can handle arbitrary and unexpected real-time demands exactly as if it knew the exact time available in advance, with just a small (≤ 4) constant factor penalty in speed (Russell and Zilberstein 1991). Second, one has to allocate the available computation optimally among the components to maximize the total output quality. Although this is NP-hard for the general case, it can be solved in time linear in program size when the call graph of the components is tree-structured

(Zilberstein and Russell 1996). Although these results are derived in the relatively clean context of anytime algorithms with well-defined performance profiles, there is reason to expect that the general problem of robust real-time decision making in complex systems can be handled in practice.

Over the last few years, an interesting debate has emerged concerning the nature of metaknowledge and metareasoning. Teiresias (Davis 1980) established the idea that explicit, domain-specific metaknowledge was an important aspect of expert system creation. Thus, metaknowledge is a sort of "extra" domain knowledge, over and above the object-level domain knowledge, that one has to add to an AI system to get it to work well. However, in the work on rational metareasoning described earlier it is clear that *the metatheory that describes the effects of computations is domain-independent* (Ginsberg and Geddis 1991; Russell and Wefald 1991a). In principle, no additional domain knowledge is needed to assess the benefits of a computation. In practice, metareasoning from first principles can be very expensive. To avoid this, the results of meta-level analysis for particular domains can be compiled into domain-specific metaknowledge, or such knowledge can be learned directly from experience (Minton 1996; Russell and Wefald 1991a, chapter 6). This view of emerging "computational expertise" leads to a fundamental insight into intelligence—namely, that there is an interesting sense in which *algorithms are not a necessary part of AI systems*. Instead, one can imagine a general process of rationally guided computation interacting with properties of the environment to produce more and more efficient decision making. To my mind, this way of thinking finesses one major puzzle of AI: If what is required for AI is incredibly devious and superbly efficient algorithms far surpassing the current best efforts of computer scientists, how did evolution (and how will machine learning) ever get there?

Significant open problems remain in the area of rational metareasoning. One obvious difficulty is that almost all systems to date have adopted a *myopic* strategy—a greedy, depth-one search at the meta-level. Obviously, the problem of optimal selection of computation *sequences* is at least as intractable as the underlying object-level problem. Nonetheless, sequences must be considered because in some cases the value of a computation may not be apparent as an improvement in decision quality until further computations have been done. This suggests that techniques from reinforcement learning could be effective, especially as the "reward function" for computation—that is, the improvement in decision quality—is easily available to the meta-level post hoc. Other possible areas for research include the creation of effective meta-level controllers for more complex systems such as abstraction hierarchy planners, hybrid architectures, and so on.

Although rational metareasoning seems to be a useful tool in coping with complexity, the concept of meta-level rationality as a formal framework for resource-bounded agents does not seem to hold water. The reason is that since metareasoning is expensive, it cannot be carried out optimally. The history of object-level rationality has repeated itself at the meta-level: perfect rationality at the meta-level is unattainable, and calculative rationality at the meta-level is useless. Therefore, a time/optimality trade-off has to be made for meta-level computations, as for example with the myopic approximation mentioned earlier. Within the framework of meta-level rationality, however, there is no way to identify the appropriate trade-off of time for meta-level decision quality. Any attempt to do so via a meta-meta-level simply results in a conceptual regress. Furthermore, it is entirely possible that in some environments the most effective agent design will do no metareasoning at all but will simply respond to circumstances. These considerations suggest that the right approach is to step outside the agent, as it were, to refrain from micromanaging the individual decisions made by the agent. This is the approach taken in bounded optimality.

6. Bounded Optimality

The difficulties with perfect rationality and meta-level rationality arise from the imposition of constraints on things (actions, computations) that the agent designer does not directly control. Specifying that *actions* or *computations* be rational is of no use if no real agents can fulfill the specification. The designer controls the *program*. In Russell and Subramanian 1993, the notion of *feasibility* for a given machine is introduced to describe the set of all agent functions that can be implemented by some agent program running on that machine. This is somewhat analogous to the idea of computability but is much stricter because it relates the operation of a program on a formal machine model with finite speed to the actual temporal behavior generated by the agent.

Given this view, one is led immediately to the idea that optimal feasible behavior is an interesting notion and to the idea of finding the program that generates it. Suppose we define $Agent(l, M)$ to be the agent function implemented by the program l running on machine M. Then the bounded optimal program l_{opt} is defined by

$$l_{opt} = arg\,max_{l \in \mathcal{L}_M}\, V(Agent(l,M),\mathbf{E},U)$$

where $\mathcal{L}_M$ is the finite set of all programs that can be run on M. This is P_4, bounded optimality.

In AI, the idea of bounded optimality floated around among several discussion groups interested in the general topic of resource-bounded rationality in the late 1980s, particularly those at Rockwell (organized by Michael Fehling) and Stanford (organized by Michael Bratman). The term *bounded optimality* seems to have been originated by E. J. Horvitz (1989), who defined it informally as "the optimization of computational utility given a set of assumptions about expected problems and constraints on resources."

Similar ideas have also surfaced recently in game theory, where there has been a shift from consideration of optimal decisions in games to a consideration of optimal decision-making programs. This leads to different results because it limits the ability of each agent to do unlimited simulation of the other, who is also doing unlimited simulation of the first, and so on. Even the requirement of computability makes a significant difference (Megiddo and Wigderson 1986). Bounds on the complexity of players have also become a topic of intense interest. C. H. Papadimitriou and M. Yannakakis (1994) have shown that a collaborative equilibrium exists for the iterated Prisoner's Dilemma game if each agent is a finite automaton with a number of states that is less than exponential in the number of rounds. This is essentially a bounded optimality result, where the bound is on space rather than speed of computation.

Philosophy has also seen a gradual evolution in the definition of rationality. There has been a shift from consideration of *act utilitarianism*—the rationality of individual acts—to *rule utilitarianism*, or the rationality of general policies for acting. The requirement that policies be feasible for limited agents was discussed extensively by C. Cherniak (1986) and Harman (1983). A philosophical proposal generally consistent with the notion of bounded optimality can be found in "The Moral First Aid Manual" (Dennett 1986). In this lecture, D. C. Dennett explicitly discusses the idea of reaching an optimum within the space of feasible decision procedures, using as an example the Ph.D. admissions procedure of a philosophy department. He points out that the bounded optimal admissions procedure may be somewhat messy and may have no obvious hallmark of "optimality"—in fact, the admissions committee may continue to tinker with it since bounded optimal systems may have no way to recognize their own bounded optimality.

In work with D. Subramanian, the general idea of bounded optimality has been placed in a formal setting so that one can begin to derive rigorous results on bounded optimal programs. This involves setting up completely specified relationships among agents, programs, machines, environments, and time. We found this to be a very valuable exercise in itself. For example, the "folk AI" notions of "real-time environments" and "deadlines" ended up with definitions rather different from those we had initially imagined. From this foundation, a very simple machine architecture was investigated in which the program consists of decision procedures of fixed execution time and decision quality. In a "stochastic deadline" environment, it turns out that the utility attained by running several procedures in sequence until interrupted is often higher than that attainable by any single decision procedure. That is, it is often better first to prepare a "quick and dirty" answer before embarking on more involved calculations in case the latter do not finish in time.

The interesting aspect of these results, beyond their value as a demonstration of nontrivial proofs of bounded optimality, is that they exhibit in a simple way what I believe to be a major feature of bounded optimal agents: the fact that the pressure toward optimality within a finite machine results in more complex program structures. Intuitively, efficient decision making in a complex environment requires a software architecture that offers a wide variety of possible computational options, so that in most situations the agent has at least some computations available that provide a significant increase in decision quality.

One possible objection to the basic model of bounded optimality outlined earlier is that solutions are not *robust* with respect to small variations in the environment or the machine. This in turn would lead to difficulties in analyzing complex system designs. Theoretical computer science faced the same problem in describing the running time of algorithms, because counting steps and describing instruction sets exactly gives the same kind of fragile results on optimal algorithms. The $O()$ notation was developed to deal with this and provides a much more robust way to describe complexity that is independent of machine speeds and implementation details. This robustness is also essential in allowing complexity results to develop cumulatively. In Russell and Subramanian 1993, the corresponding notation is asymptotic bounded optimality (ABO). As with classical complexity, we can define both average-case and worst-case ABO, where *case* here means the environment. For example, worst-case ABO is defined as follows:

> An agent program l is timewise (or spacewise) worst-case ABO in **E** on **M** iff $\exists k, n_o \ \forall l', n \ n > n_o \Rightarrow V^*(\text{Agent}(l, kM), \textbf{E}, U, n) \geq V^*(\text{Agent}(l', M),$ **E**, $U, n)$ where kM denotes a version of **M** speeded up by a factor k (or with k times more memory) and $V^*(f, \textbf{E}, U, n)$ is the minimum value of $V(f, E, U)$ for all E in **E** of complexity n.

In English, this means that the program is basically along the right lines if it just needs a faster (larger) machine to have worst-case behavior as good as that of any other program in all environments.

Another possible objection to the idea of bounded optimality is that it simply shifts the intractable computational burden of meta-level rationality from the agent's meta-level to the designer's object level. Surely, one might argue, the designer now has to solve off-line all the meta-level optimization problems that were intractable when on-line. This argument is not without merit—indeed, it would be surprising if the agent design problem turns out to be easy. There is, however, a significant difference between the two problems, in that the agent designer is presumably creating an agent for an entire class of environments, whereas the putative meta-level agent is working in a specific environment. That this can make the problem *easier* for the designer can be seen by considering the example of sorting algorithms. It may be very difficult indeed to sort a list of a trillion elements, but it is relatively easy to design an asymptotically optimal algorithm for sorting. In fact, the difficulties of the two tasks are unrelated. The unrelatedness would still hold for BO as well as ABO design, but the ABO definitions make it a good deal clearer.

It can be shown easily that worst-case ABO is a generalization of asymptotically optimal algorithms, simply by constructing a "classical environment" in which classical algorithms operate and in which the utility of the algorithm's behavior is a decreasing positive function of runtime if the output is correct and zero otherwise. Agents in more general environments may need to trade off output quality for time, generate multiple outputs over time, and so on. As an illustration of how ABO is a useful abstraction, one can show that under certain restrictions one can construct *universal* ABO programs that are ABO for any time variation in the utility function, using the doubling construction from Russell and Zilberstein 1991. Further directions for bounded optimality research are discussed later.

7. What Is to Be Done?

This section describes some of the research activities that will, I hope, help to turn bounded optimality into a creative took for AI system design. First, however, I shall describe work on calculatively rational systems that needs to be done in order to enrich the space of agent programs.

Components for Calculative Rationality

As mentioned earlier, the correct design for a rational agent depends on the task environment—the "physical" environment and the performance measure on environment histories. It is possible to define some basic properties of task environments that, together with the complexity of the problem, lead to identifiable requirements on the corresponding rational agent designs (Russell and Norvig 1995, chapter 2). The principal properties are whether the environment is *fully observable* or *partially observable*, whether it is *deterministic* or *stochastic*, whether it is *static* (i.e., does not change except when the agent acts) or *dynamic*, and whether it is *discrete* or *continuous*. Although crude, these distinctions serve to lay out an agenda for basic research in AI. By analyzing and solving each subcase and producing calculatively rational mechanisms with the required properties, theoreticians can produce the AI equivalent of bricks, beams, and mortar, with which AI architects can build the equivalent of cathedrals. Unfortunately, many of the basic components are currently missing. Others are so fragile and nonscalable as to be barely able to support their own weight. This presents many opportunities for research of far-reaching impact.

The logicist tradition of goal-based agent design, based on the creation and execution of guaranteed plans, is firmly anchored in fully observable, deterministic, static, and discrete task environments. (Furthermore, tasks are usually specified as logically defined goals rather than general utility functions.) This means that agents need keep no internal state and can even execute plans without the use of perception.

The theory of optimal action in stochastic, partially observable environments goes under the heading of POMDPs (Partially Observable Markov Decision Problems), a class of problems first addressed in the work of E. J. Sondik (1971) but almost completely unknown in AI until recently (Cassandra, Kaelbling, and Littman 1994). Similarly, very little work of a fundamental nature has been done in AI on dynamic environments, which require real-time decision making, or on continuous environments, which have been largely the province of geometry-based robotics. Since most real-world applications are partially observable, nondeterministic, dynamic, and continuous, the lack of emphasis is somewhat surprising.

There are, however, several new bricks under construction. For example, dynamic probabilistic networks (DPNs) (Dean and Kanazawa 1989) provide a mechanism to maintain beliefs about the current state of a dynamic, partially observable, nondeterministic environment and to project forward the effects of actions. Also, the rapid improvement in the speed and accuracy of computer vision systems has made interfacing with continuous physical environments more practical. In particular, the application of Kalman filtering (Kalman 1960), a widely used technique in control theory, allows robust and efficient tracking of moving objects; DPNs extend Kalman filtering to allow more general representations of world state. Reinforcement learning, together with inductive learning methods for continuous function representations such as neural networks, allows learning from delayed rewards in continuous, nondeterministic environments. Recently R. Parr and S. Russell (1995), among others, have had some success in applying reinforcement learning to partially observable environments. Finally, learning methods for static and dynamic probabilistic networks with hidden variables (i.e., for partially observable environments) may make it possible to acquire the necessary environment models (Lauritzen 1995; Russell et al. 1995).

The Bayesian Automated Taxi (aka BATmobile) project (Forbes et al. 1995) is an attempt to combine all these new bricks to solve an interesting application problem, namely, driving a car on a freeway. Technically, this can be viewed as a POMDP because the environment contains relevant variables (such as whether or not the Volvo on your left is intending to change lanes to the right) that are not observable and because the behavior of other vehicles and the effects of one's own actions are not exactly predictable. In a POMDP, the optimal decision depends on the joint probability distribution over the entire set of state variables. It turns out that a combination of real-time vision algorithms, Kalman filtering, and DPNs can maintain the required distribution when observing a stream of traffic on a freeway. The BATmobile currently uses a hand-coded decision tree to make decisions on this basis and is a fairly safe driver (although probably far from optimal) on our simulator. We are currently experimenting with lookahead methods to make approximately rational decisions, as well as supervised learning and reinforcement learning methods.

As well as extending the scope of AI applications, new bricks for planning under uncertainty significantly increase the opportunity for metareasoning to make a difference. With logical planners, a plan either does or does not work; it has proved very difficult to find heuristics to measure the "goodness" of a logical plan that does not guarantee success or to estimate the likelihood that an abstract logical plan will have a successful concrete instance. This means that it is very hard to identify plan elaboration steps that are likely to have high value. In contrast, planners designed to handle uncertainty and utility have built-in information about the likelihood of success and there is a continuum from hopeless to perfect plans. Getting metareasoning to work for such systems is a high priority. It is also important to apply those methods, such as partial-order planning and abstraction, that have been so effective in extending the reach of classical planners.

Directions for Bounded Optimality

Ongoing research on bounded optimality aims to extend the initial results of Russell and Subramanian (1993) to more interesting agent designs. In this section, I will sketch some design dimensions and the issues involved in establishing bounded optimality results.

The general scheme to be followed involves defining a virtual machine M that runs programs from a class $\mathcal{L}_M$. Typically, programs will have a "fixed part" that is shared across some subclass and a "variable part" that is specific to the individual program. Then comparisons are made between the best programs in different subclasses for the same machine. For example, suppose M is a machine capable of running any feedforward neural network. $\mathcal{L}_M$ consists of all such networks, and we might be interested in comparing the subclasses defined by different network topologies, while within each subclass individual programs differ in the weights on the links of the network. Thus, the boundary between machine and program depends to some extent on the range of comparisons that the designer wishes to consider.

At the most general level of analysis, the methodology is now quite straightforward: choose a machine, choose a program that runs on the machine, then dump the resulting agent into a class of environments **E**. The program with the best performance is bounded optimal for M in **E**. For example, M is an IBM PC with a C compiler; $\mathcal{L}_M$ consists of C programs up to a certain size; the environment consists of a population of human chess opponents; the performance measure is the chess rating achieved; the bounded optimal program is the one with the highest rating.

This rather blunt and unenlightening approach has no doubt occurred to many engaged in the construction of chess programs. As stated, the problem is ridiculously hard to solve and the solution, once found, would be very domain-specific. The problem is to define a research agenda for bounded optimality that provides a little more guidance and generality. This can be done by exploiting structure in the definition of the problem, in particular the orthogonality of time and content, and by using more sophisticated agent designs, particularly those that incorporate mechanisms for adaptation and optimization. In this way, we can prove bounded optimality results for more general classes of task environments.

MECHANISMS FOR OPTIMIZATION   Modular design that uses a hierarchy of components is commonly seen as the only way to build reliable complex systems. The components fulfill certain behavioral specifications and interact in well-defined ways. To produce a composite bounded optimal design, the optimization problem involves allocating execution time to components (Zilberstein and Russell 1996) or arranging the order of execution of the components (Russell and Subramanian 1993) to maximize overall performance. As illustrated earlier in the discussion of universal ABO algorithms, the techniques for optimizing temporal behavior are largely orthogonal to the *content* of the system components, which can therefore be optimized separately. Consider, for example, a composite system that uses an anytime inference algorithm over a belief network as one of its components. If a learning algorithm improves the accuracy of the belief network, the performance profile of the inference component will improve, which will result in a reallocation of execution time that is guaranteed to improve overall system performance. Thus, techniques such as the doubling construction and the time allocation algorithm in Zilberstein and Russell 1996 can be seen as domain-independent tools for agent design. They enable bounded optimality results that do not depend on the specific temporal aspects of the environment class. As a simple example, we might prove that a certain chess program design is ABO for all time controls ranging from blitz to full tournament play.

The results obtained so far for optimal time allocation have assumed a static, off-line optimization process with predictable component performance profiles and fixed connections among components. One can imagine far more subtle designs in which individual components must deal with unexpectedly slow or fast progress in processing and changing needs for information from other components. This might involve exchanging computational resources among components, establishing new interfaces, and so on. This is more reminiscent of a computational market, as envisaged by M. P. Wellman (1994), than of the classical subroutine hierarchies and would offer a useful additional level of abstraction in system design.

MECHANISMS FOR ADAPTATION   In addition to combinatorial optimization of the structure and temporal behavior of an agent, we can also use learning methods to improve the design:

- The *content* of an agent's knowledge base can of course be improved by inductive learning. In Russell and Subramanian 1993, it is shown that approximately bounded optimal designs can be guaranteed with high probability if each component is learned in such a way that its output quality is close to optimal among all components of a given execution time. Results from computational learning theory, particularly in the *agnostic learning* model (Kearns, Schapire, and Sellie 1992), can provide learning methods with the required properties. The key additional step is to analyze the way in which slight imperfection in each component carries through to slight imperfection in the whole agent.
- *Reinforcement learning* can be used to learn value information such as utility functions. Recent results (Tsitsiklis and Van Roy 1996) provide convergence guarantees for reinforcement learning with a fairly broad class of function approximators. One can use such learning methods for meta-level information, for example, the value of computation. In Russell and Wefald 1991a, chapter 6, this is shown to be an effective technique. Formal results on convergence to optimal control of search would be of great interest. Further work is needed, however, since current theorems assume a stationary distribution that generates the agent's experiences, whereas an agent that is improving its search control will presumably be exploring different populations of experiences over time.
- *Compilation* methods such as explanation-based learning can be used to transform an agent's representations to allow faster decision

making. Several agent architectures, including SOAR (Laird, Rosenbloom, and Newell 1986), use compilation to speed up all forms of problem solving. Some nontrivial results on convergence have been obtained by P. Tadepalli (1991), based on the observation that after a given amount of experience, novel problems for which no solution has been stored should be encountered only infrequently.

Presumably, an agent architecture can incorporate all these learning mechanisms. One of the issues to be faced by bounded optimality research is how to prove convergence results when several adaptation and optimization mechanisms are operating simultaneously. A "quasistatic" approach, in which one mechanism reaches convergence before the other method is allowed to take its next step, seems theoretically adequate but not very practical.

OFF-LINE AND ON-LINE MECHANISMS   One can distinguish between *off-line* and *on-line* mechanisms for constructing bounded-optimal agents. An off-line construction mechanism is not itself part of the agent and is not the subject of bounded optimality constraints. Let C be an off-line mechanism designed for a class of environments $\mathbf{E}$. Then a typical theorem will say that C operates in a specific environment $E \in \mathbf{E}$ and returns an agent design that is ABO (say for E—that is, an environment-specific agent).

In the on-line case, the mechanism C is considered part of the agent. Then a typical theorem will say that the agent is ABO for all $E \in \mathbf{E}$. If the performance measure used is indifferent to the transient cost of the adaptation or optimization mechanism, the two types of theorems are essentially the same. However, if the cost cannot be ignored—for example, if an agent that learns quickly is to be preferred to an agent that reaches the same level of performance but learns more slowly—then the analysis becomes more difficult. It may become necessary to define asymptotic equivalence for "experience efficiency" in order to obtain robust results, as is done in computational learning theory.

It is worth noting that one can easily prove the value of "lifelong learning" in the ABO framework. An agent that devotes a constant fraction of its computational resources to learning-while-doing cannot do worse, in the ABO sense, than an agent that ceases learning after some point. If some improvement is still possible, the lifelong learning agent will always be preferred.

FIXED AND VARIABLE COMPUTATION COSTS   Another dimension of design space emerges when one considers the computational cost of the "variable part" of the agent design. The design problem is simplified considerably when the cost is fixed. Consider again the task of meta-level reinforcement learning, and to make things concrete let the metalevel decision be made by a Q function mapping from computational state and action to value. Suppose further that the Q function is to be represented by a neural net. If the topology of the neural net is fixed, then all Q functions in the space have the same execution time. Consequently, the optimality criterion used by the standard Q-learning process coincides with bounded optimality, and the equilibrium reached will be a bounded-optimal configuration.[4] However, if the topology of the network is subject to alteration as the design space is explored, then the execution time of the different Q functions varies. In this case, the standard Q-learning process will not necessarily converge to a bounded-optimal configuration. A difference adaptation mechanism must be found that takes into account the passage of time and its effect on utility.

Whatever the solution to this problem turns out to be, the important point is that the notion of bounded optimality helps to distinguish adaptation mechanisms that will result in good performance from those that will not. Adaptation mechanisms derived from calculative rationality will fail in the more realistic setting where an agent cannot afford to aim for perfection.

FULLY VARIABLE ARCHITECTURES   The discussion so far has been limited to fairly sedate forms of agent architecture in which the scope for adaptation is circumscribed to particular functional aspects such as meta-level Q functions. However, an agent must in general deal with an environment that is far more complex than itself and that exhibits variation over time at all levels of granularity. Limits on the size of the agent's memory may imply that almost complete revision of the agent's mental structure is needed to achieve high performance. For example, one can imagine that a simple rule-based agent that lives through cycles of winter and summer may have to discard all of its summer rules as winter approaches and then relearn them from scratch the following year. Such situations may engender a rethinking of some of our notions of agent architecture and optimality and suggest a view of agent programs as dynamic systems with various amounts of compiled and uncompiled knowledge and internal processes of inductive learning, forgetting, and compilation.

TOWARD A GRAMMAR OF AI SYSTEMS   The approach that seems to be emerging for bounded optimality research is to divide up the space of agent designs into "architectural classes" such that in each class the structural variation is sufficiently limited. Then ABO results can be obtained either by analytical optimization within the class or by showing that an empirical adaptation process results in an approximately ABO design. Once this is done, it should be possible to compare architecture classes directly, perhaps to establish asymptotic dominance of one class over another. For example, it might be the case that the inclusion of an appropriate "macro-operator formation" or "greedy metareasoning" capability in a given architecture will result in an improvement in behavior in the limit of very complex environments—that is, one cannot compensate for the exclusion of the capability by increasing the machine speed by a constant factor. A central tool in such work will be the use of "no-cost" results where, for example, the allocation of a constant fraction of computational resources to learning or metareasoning can do no harm to an agent's ABO prospects.

Getting all these architectural devices to work together smoothly is an important unsolved problem in AI and must be addressed before we can make progress on understanding bounded optimality within these more complex architectural classes. If the notion of "architectural device" can be made sufficiently concrete, then AI may eventually develop a *grammar* for agent designs, describing the devices and their interrelations. As the grammar develops, so should the accompanying ABO dominance results.

8. Summary

I have outlined some directions for formally grounded AI research based on bounded optimality as the desired property of AI systems. This perspective on AI seems to be a logical consequence of the inevitable philosophical "move" from optimization over actions or computations to optimization over programs. I have suggested that such an approach should allow synergy between theoretical and practical AI research of a kind not afforded by other formal frameworks. In the same vein, I believe it is a satisfactory formal counterpart of the informal goal of creating intelligence. In particular, it is entirely consistent with our intuitions about the need for complex structure in real intelligent agents, the importance of the resource limitations faced by relatively tiny minds in large worlds, and the operation of evolution as a design optimization process. One can also argue that bounded optimality research is likely to satisfy better the needs of those who wish to emulate human intelligence, because it takes into account the limitations on computational resources that are presumably responsible for most of the regrettable deviation from perfect rationality exhibited by humans.

Bounded optimality and its asymptotic cousin are, of course, nothing but formally defined properties that one may want systems to satisfy. It is too early to tell whether ABO will do the same kind of work for AI that asymptotic complexity has done for theoretical computer science. Creativity in design is still the prerogative of AI researchers. It may, however, be possible to systematize the design process somewhat and to automate the process of adapting a system to its computational resources and the demands of the environment. The concept of bounded optimality provides a way to make sure the adaptation process is "correct."

My hope is that with these kinds of investigations it will eventually be possible to develop the conceptual and mathematical tools to answer some basic questions about intelligence. For example, *why* do complex intelligent systems (appear to) have declarative knowledge structures over which they reason explicitly? This has been a fundamental assumption that distinguishes AI from other disciplines for agent design, yet the answer is still unknown. Indeed, Rod Brooks, Hubert Dreyfus, and others flatly deny the assumption. What is clear is that it will need *something like* a theory of bounded optimal agent design to answer this question.

Most of the agent design features that I have discussed here, including the use of declarative knowledge, have been conceived within the standard methodology of "first build calculatively rational agents and then speed them up." Yet one can legitimately doubt that this methodology will enable the AI community to discover all the design features needed for general intelligence. The reason is that no conceivable computer will ever be remotely close to approximating perfect rationality for even moderately complex environments. Perfect rationality is, if you like, a "Newtonian" definition for intelligent agents, whereas the real world is a particle accelerator. It may well be the case that agents based on improvements to calculatively rational designs are *not even close* to achieving the level of performance that is potentially achievable given the underlying computational resources. For this reason, I believe it is imperative not to dismiss ideas for agent designs that do not seem at first glance to fit into the "classical" calculatively rational framework. Instead, one must attempt to understand the potential of the bounded optimal configurations within the corresponding architectural class and to see if one can design the appropriate adaptation mechanisms that might help in realizing these configurations.

As mentioned in the previous section, there is also plenty of work to do in the area of making more general and more robust "bricks" from which to construct AI systems for more realistic environments, and such work will provide added scope for the achievement of bounded optimality. In a sense, under this conception AI research is the same now as it always should have been.

NOTES

An earlier version of this essay appeared in the *Proceedings of the Fourteenth International Joint Conference on Artificial Intelligence*, published by IJCAII. That paper drew on previous work with Eric Wefald (Russell and Wefald 1991a) and Devika Subramanian (Russell and Subramanian 1993). The latter work contains a more rigorous analysis of many of the concepts presented here. Thanks to Michael Wellman, Michael Fehling, Michael Genesereth, Russ Greiner, Eric Horvitz, Henry Kautz, Daphne Koller, and Bart Selman for many stimulating discussions and useful suggestions on the topic of bounded rationality. The research was supported by NSF grants IRI-8903146, IRI-9211512, and IRI-9058427 and by a UK SERC Visiting Fellowship.

1. I view this as a very positive development. AI is a field defined by its problems, not its methods. Its principal insights—among them the learning, use, and compilation of explicit knowledge in the service of decision making—can certainly withstand the influx of new methods from other fields. This is especially true when other fields are simultaneously embracing the insights derived within AI.

2. Perhaps not coincidentally, this decision was taken before the question of computational intractability was properly understood in computer science.

3. Doyle and Patil propose instead the idea of "rational management of inference." Representation systems "should be designed to offer a broad mix of services varying in cost and quality" and should take into account "the costs and benefits (of computations) as perceived by the systems' user." That is, they suggest a solution based on rational metareasoning, as discussed in section 5.

4. A similar observation was made by Horvitz and Breese (1990) for cases where the object level is so restricted that the meta-level decision problem can be solved in constant time.

REFERENCES

Agre, P. E., and D. Chapman (1987). Pengi: An implementation of a theory of activity. In *Proceedings of the Tenth International Joint Conference on Artificial Intelligence (IJCAI-87)*, pp. 268–272. Palo Alto, CA: Morgan Kaufmann.

Bacchus, F., and A. Grove (1995). Graphical models for preference and utility. In *Proceedings of the Eleventh Conference on Uncertainty in Artificial Intelligence (UAI-95)*, pp. 3–10. Palo Alto, CA: Morgan Kaufmann.

Breese, J. S., and M. R. Fehling (1990). Control of problem-solving: Principles and architecture. In R. D. Shachter, T. Levitt, L. Kanal, and J. Lemmer (eds.), *Uncertainty in Artificial Intelligence*, vol. 4, pp. 59–68. Amsterdam: Elsevier Science.

Brooks, R. A. (1989). Engineering approach to building complete, intelligent beings. *Proceedings of the SPIE—the International Society for Optical Engineering* 1002:618–625.

Brooks, R. A. (1991). Intelligence without representation. *Artificial Intelligence* 47:139–159.

Carnap, R. (1950). *Logical Foundations of Probability*. Chicago: University of Chicago Press.

Cassandra, A. R., L. P. Kaelbling, and M. L. Littman (1994). Acting optimally in partially observable stochastic domains. In *Proceedings of the Twelfth National Conference on Artificial Intelligence (AAAI-94)*, pp. 1023–1028. Menlo Park, CA: AAAI Press.

Cherniak, C. (1986). *Minimal Rationality*. Cambridge: MIT Press.

Davis, R. (1980). Meta-rules: Reasoning about control. *Artificial Intelligence* 15:179–222.

Dean, T., and M. Boddy (1988). An analysis of time-dependent planning. In *Proceedings of the Seventh National Conference on Artificial Intelligence (AAAI-88)*, pp. 49–54. San Francisco: Morgan Kaufmann.

Dean, T., and K. Kanazawa (1989). A model for reasoning about persistence and causation. *Computational Intelligence* 5:142–150.

Dean, T. L., J. Aloimonos, and J. F. Allen (1995). *Artificial Intelligence: Theory and Practice*. Redwood City, CA: Benjamin/Cummings.

Dennett, D. C. (1986). The moral first aid manual. In S. M. McMurrin (ed.), *The Tanner Lectures on Human Values*, pp. 119–147. Salt Lake City: University of Utah Press.

Doyle, J., and R. S. Patil (1991). Two theses of knowledge representation: Language restrictions, taxonomic classification, and the utility of representation services. *Artificial Intelligence* 48:261–297.

Ephrati, E., and J. S. Rosenschein (1991). The Clarke Tax as a consensus mechanism among automated agents. In *Proceedings of the Ninth National Conference on Artificial Intelligence (AAAI-91)*, vol. 1, pp. 173–178. Menlo Park, CA: AAAI Press.

Forbes, J., T. Huang, K. Kanazawa, and S. J. Russell (1995). The BATmobile: Towards a Bayesian automated taxi. In *Proceedings of the Fourteenth International Joint Conference on Artificial Intelligence (IJCAI-95)*, pp. 1878–1885. San Francisco: Morgan Kaufmann.

Ginsberg, M. L., and D. F. Geddis (1991). Is there any need for domain-dependent control information? In *Proceedings of the Ninth National Conference on Artificial Intelligence (AAAI-91)*, vol. 1, pp. 452–457. Menlo Park, CA: AAAI Press/MIT Press.

Good, I. J. (1971). Twenty-seven principles of rationality. In V. P. Godambe and D. A. Sprott (eds.), *Foundations of Statistical Inference*, pp. 108–141. Toronto: Holt, Rinehart, Winston.

Harman, G. H. (1986). *Change in View: Principles of Reasoning*. Cambridge: MIT Press/Bradford.

Horvitz, E. J. (1987). Problem-solving design: Reasoning about computational value, trade-offs, and resources. In *Proceedings of the Second Annual NASA Research Forum*, pp. 26–43. Moffett Field, California, NASA Ames Research Center.

Horvitz, E. J. (1989). Reasoning about beliefs and actions under computational resource constraints. In L. N. Kanal, T. S. Levitt, and J. F. Lemmer (eds.), *Uncertainty in Artificial Intelligence*, vol. 3, pp. 301–324. Amsterdam: Elsevier Science.

Horvitz, E. J., and J. S. Breese (1990). *Ideal Partition of Resources for Metareasoning*. Technical Report KSL-90-26. Knowledge Systems Laboratory, Stanford University, Stanford, California.

Howard, R. A. (1966). Information value theory. *IEEE Transactions on Systems Science and Cybernetics* SSC-2:22–26.

Kalman, R. E. (1960). A new approach to linear filtering and prediction problems. *Journal of Basic Engineering* MAR:35–46.

Kearns, M., R. Schapire, and L. Sellie (1992). Toward efficient agnostic learning. In *Proceedings of the Fifth Annual ACM Workshop on Computational Learning Theory (COLT-92)*, pp. 341–352. New York: ACM Press.

Keeney, R. L., and H. Raiffa (1976). *Decisions with Multiple Objectives: Preferences and Value Tradeoffs*. New York: Wiley.

Kumar, P. R., and P. Varaiya (1986). *Stochastic Systems: Estimation, Identification, and Adaptive Control*. Englewood Cliffs, NJ: Prentice-Hall.

Laird, J. E., P. S. Rosenbloom, and A. Newell (1986). Chunking in SOAR: The anatomy of a general learning mechanism. *Machine Learning* 1:11–46.

Lauritzen, S. L. (1995). The EM algorithm for graphical association models with missing data. *Computational Statistics and Data Analysis* 19:191–201.

Levesque, H. J. (1986). Making believers out of computers. *Artificial Intelligence* 30:81–108.

Levesque, H. J., and R. J. Brachman (1987). Expressiveness and tractability in knowledge representation and reasoning. *Computational Intelligence* 3:78–93.

Matheson, J. E. (1968). The economic value of analysis and computation. *IEEE Transactions on Systems Science and Cybernetics* SSC-4:325–332.

Megiddo, N., and A. Wigderson (1986). On play by means of computing machines. In J. Y. Halpern (ed.), *Theoretical Aspects of Reasoning about Knowledge: Proceedings of the 1986 Conference (TARK-86)*, pp. 259–274. San Francisco: Morgan Kaufmann.

Minton, S. (1996). Is there any need for domain-dependent control information? A reply. In *Proceedings of the Thirteenth National Conference on Artificial Intelligence (AAAI-96)*, pp. 855–862. Menlo Park, CA: AAAI Press.

Newell, A. (1982). The knowledge level. *Artificial Intelligence* 18:82–127.

Papadimitriou, C. H., and M. Yannakakis (1994). On complexity as bounded rationality. In *Proceedings of the Twenty-Sixth Annual ACM Symposium on the Theory of Computing*, pp. 726–733. New York: ACM Press.

Parr, R., and S. Russell (1995). Approximating optimal policies for partially observable stochastic domains. In *Proceedings of the Fourteenth International*

Joint Conference on Artificial Intelligence (IJCAI-95). San Francisco: Morgan Kaufmann.

Russell, S. J., and P. Norvig (1995). *Artificial Intelligence: A Modern Approach.* Englewood Cliffs, NJ: Prentice-Hall.

Russell, S. J., and D. Subramanian (1993). Provably bounded-optimal agents. In *Proceedings of the Thirteenth International Joint Conference on Artificial Intelligence (IJCAI-93)*, pp. 338–344. San Francisco: Morgan Kaufmann.

Russell, S. J., and E. H. Wefald (1989). On optimal game-tree search using rational meta-reasoning. In *Proceedings of the Eleventh International Joint Conference on Artificial Intelligence (IJCAI-89)*, pp. 334–340. San Francisco: Morgan Kaufmann.

Russell, S. J., and E. H. Wefald (1991a). *Do the Right Thing: Studies in Limited Rationality.* Cambridge: MIT Press.

Russell, S. J., and E. H. Wefald (1991b). Principles of metareasoning. *Artificial Intelligence* 49:361–395.

Russell, S. J., and S. Zilberstein (1991). Composing real-time systems. In *Proceedings of the Twelfth International Joint Conference on Artificial Intelligence (IJCAI-91)*, pp. 212–217. San Francisco: Morgan Kaufmann.

Russell, S. J., J. Binder, D. Koller, and K. Kanazawa (1995). Local learning in probabilistic networks with hidden variables. In *Proceedings of the Fourteenth International Joint Conference on Artificial Intelligence (IJCAI-95)*, pp. 1146–1152. San Francisco: Morgan Kaufmann.

Simon, H. A. (1955). A behavioral model of rational choice. *Quarterly Journal of Economics* 69:99–118.

Simon, H. A. (1958). Rational choice and the structure of the environment. In *Models of Bounded Rationality*, vol. 2, pp. 259–268. Cambridge: MIT Press.

Sondik, E. J. (1971). The optimal control of partially observable Markov decision processes. Ph.D. diss., Stanford University, Stanford, California.

Tadepalli, P. (1991). A formalization of explanation-based macro-operator learning. In *Proceedings of the Twelfth International Joint Conference on Artificial Intelligence (IJCAI-91)*, pp. 616–622. San Francisco: Morgan Kaufmann.

Tsitsiklis, J. N., and B. Van Roy (1996). *An Analysis of Temporal-Difference Learning with function Approximation.* Technical Report LIDS-P-2322. Laboratory for Information and Decision Systems, MIT, Cambridge.

Wellman, M. P. (1985). *Reasoning about Preference Models.* Technical Report MIT/LCS/TR-340. Laboratory for Computer Science, MIT, Cambridge.

Wellman, M. P. (1994). A market-oriented programming environment and its application to distributed multi-commodity flow problems. *Journal of Artificial Intelligence Research* 9:1–23.

Zilberstein, S., and S. Russell (1996). Optimal composition of real-time systems. *Artificial Intelligence* 83:181–213.

3

The Logical Foundations of
Means-End Reasoning

JOHN L. POLLOCK

1. Introduction

Philosophers distinguish between epistemic cognition and practical cognition. Epistemic cognition is concerned with what to believe, and practical cognition is concerned with what to do. The logical structure of epistemic cognition has been studied extensively by epistemology, but less attention has been paid to the logical structure of some of the important parts of practical cognition. In this chapter I will focus on one aspect of practical cognition—plan-construction. Human plan-construction is generally based on *means-end reasoning*. Means-end reasoning is concerned with finding the means for achieving goals. The basic idea is a simple one, which goes back at least to Aristotle. To achieve a goal, we consider an action that would achieve it under some specified circumstances and then try to find a way of putting ourselves in those circumstances in order to achieve the goal by performing the action. Putting ourselves in those circumstances becomes a *subgoal*. The idea is to work backward from the goal through subgoals until we arrive at subgoals that are already achieved. The resulting sequence of actions constitutes a *plan* for achieving the goal. My ultimate objective is the formulation of a precise logical theory of plan-construction that completely characterizes means-end reasoning (Pollock 1998).

2. Goal-Regression Planning

Much work in artificial intelligence has been directed at the task of formalizing and automating means-end reasoning. This forms the basis of AI planning theory, and the result is what is called *goal-regression planning*. In this section I will formulate a somewhat more precise description of means-end reasoning, drawing upon the insights of AI planning theory. Because of its heavy reliance on familiar parts of AI planning theory, I will refer to this as the "conventional" theory of means-end reasoning. In section 3 I will argue that, assuming the basic correctness of the conventional theory, rational agents situated in a complex environment cannot in general perform means-end reasoning in quite the way AI planning theory proposes to implement it. In a sense to be explained, planning must be done defeasibly rather than algorithmically. In section 4 I will argue that even given the modifications of section 3, the conventional theory turns upon an indefensible assumption. In effect, the conventional theory runs afoul of the frame problem and must be modified to accommodate a solution to the frame problem. In section 5 I will show how the conventional theory of means-end reasoning must be modified to accomplish this.

Means-end reasoning is based upon *planning-conditionals* to the effect that if an action A is performed under circumstances C, the goal G will be achieved. I will write such a conditional as "$(A \ \& \ C) \blacktriangleright G$." I will refer to C as the *precondition* of the conditional, A as the *action*, and G as the *goal*. For the time being, I will not attempt to be more precise about the logical form of these conditionals.

Means-end reasoning aims to construct a plan for achieving a goal. But what exactly is a plan? Plans are constructed out of *plan-steps*, which prescribe actions. Plan-steps cannot be identified with the actions they prescribe, because the same action may be prescribed by more than one step in a single plan. The plan-steps must be executed in a proper order, so I will identify a plan with the ordered triple that consists of the set of its plan-steps, the ordering of the plan-steps, and the goal of the plan.

Goal-regression planning is performed by performing several different kinds of operations. Describing these operations constitutes a description of the logical structure of means-end reasoning.

Null-Plans

The simplest case of means-end reasoning is the degenerate case in which the goal to be achieved is already true and hence nothing needs to be done to achieve it. A *null-plan* for the goal *goal* is a plan with no plan-steps. The degenerate case of means-end reasoning can then be regarded as proceeding in accordance with the following operation:

PROPOSE NULL-PLAN
Given an interest in finding a plan for achieving *goal*, if *goal* is already true, propose a null-plan for *goal*.

Goal-Regression

The core of means-end reasoning consists of goal-regression. This can be formulated as follows:

GOAL-REGRESSION
Given an interest in finding a plan for achieving G and given a planning-conditional $(A \& C) \succ G$, adopt an interest in finding a plan for achieving C. If a plan *subplan* is proposed for achieving C, construct a plan by (1) adding a new step to the end of *subplan* where the new step prescribes the action A, and (2) ordering the new step after all steps of *subplan*. Propose the new plan as a plan for achieving G.

Splitting Conjunctive Goals

The operations PROPOSE-NULL-PLAN and GOAL-REGRESSION formalize what people normally think of as means-end reasoning but do not by themselves constitute a complete description of means-end reasoning. The subgoals generated by GOAL-REGRESSION will usually be conjunctions. For example, if my goal is to light a fire, I may observe that I could do so by lighting a match, provided I have a match and I have tinder. GOAL-REGRESSION will thus generate the conjunctive subgoal *I have a match and I have tinder*. We will generally be unable to make further progress in our plan construction by applying GOAL-REGRESSION once more to such a conjunctive subgoal $(C_1 \& C_2)$. To do so would require our having a planning-conditional of the form $(A \& C) \succ (C_1 \& C_2)$. But it is rare that we will have a single planning-conditional like this that will achieve both conjuncts of a conjunctive subgoal. The most we can generally hope for is to have two separate planning-conditionals $(A \& C) \succ C_1$ and $(A^* \& C^*) \succ C_2$, which will allow us to construct separate subplans for the individual conjuncts. Given subplans for achieving each conjunct, we can then attempt to construct a plan for achieving the conjunction by merging the plans for the conjuncts. Given two plans $plan_1$ and $plan_2$, let $plan_1 + plan_2$ be the plan that results from combining the plan-steps and ordering-constraints of each. Then it appears that we can plan for conjunctive goals by using the following operation:

SPLIT-CONJUNCTIVE-GOAL
Given an interest in finding a plan for achieving a conjunctive goal $(G_1 \& G_2)$, adopt interest in finding plans $plan_1$ for G_1 and $plan_2$ for G_2. If such plans are proposed, propose $plan_1 + plan_2$ as a plan for $(G_1 \& G_2)$.

Note that when SPLIT-CONJUNCTIVE-GOAL is used to merge independent plans, the resulting plan $plan_1 + plan_2$ simply combines the ordering-constraints of $plan_1$ and $plan_2$. This can leave plan-steps from one of the subplans unordered with respect to plan-steps from the other. Such a plan is called a *partial-order plan*.

There is a logical problem for planning for conjunctive goals using SPLIT-CONJUNCTIVE-GOAL. The difficulty is that planning separately for the individual conjuncts can produce plans that destructively interfere with each other, in the sense that although the separate subplans can each be expected to achieve their goals in isolation, the merged plan cannot be expected to achieve both goals. One of the plans may achieve a subgoal for the purpose of achieving a later goal, but then before the subgoal can be used for that purpose some step of the other plan may may make the subgoal false again.

The fact that $plan_1 + plan_2$ cannot automatically be expected to achieve $(G_1 \& G_2)$ suggests that the operation that should actually be employed in planning for conjunctive goals is not SPLIT-CONJUNCTIVE-GOAL but rather:

SPLIT-CONJUNCTIVE-GOAL-SAFELY
Given an interest in finding a plan for achieving a conjunctive goal $(G_1 \& G_2)$, adopt interest in finding plans $plan_1$ for G_1 and $plan_2$ for G_2. If such plans are proposed *and do not destructively interfere with each other*, propose $plan_1 + plan_2$ as a plan for $(G_1 \& G_2)$.

The difference between SPLIT-CONJUNCTIVE-GOAL and SPLIT-CONJUNCTIVE-GOAL-SAFELY is that the former must be viewed as a *defeasible* rule of practical reasoning. That is, if a plan is proposed on the basis of SPLIT-CONJUNCTIVE-GOAL, the planning-agent must be prepared to withdraw the proposal if destructive interference is subsequently discovered. SPLIT-CONJUNCTIVE-GOAL must then be supplemented with additional principles aimed at proposing new plans constructed on the basis of $plan_1 + plan_2$ but avoiding the interference. This is vague about how to repair plans that exhibit destructive interference, but I do not have time to describe how to make it precise. In fact, what is required is promotion, demotion, and confrontation, as described in the AI planning literature.[1]

Conventional AI planning algorithms are based upon SPLIT-CONJUNCTIVE-GOAL-SAFELY, ruling out the possibility of internal defects before proposing plans. I will argue later that the conventional AI approach cannot work for general-purpose means-end reasoning, but before doing that I must lay some additional groundwork.

Achieving Goals

Thus far I have relied on little more than common sense and introspection in describing the structure of means-end reasoning. To make further progress, we must consider what the objective of means-end reasoning is supposed to be. If we can make that precise, we can use it to evaluate proposals for how to perform means-end reasoning.

Presumably, the objective of means-end reasoning is to produce plans that will achieve their goals. Under what circumstances will a plan achieve its goal? Contemporary AI planning theory is based upon a particular answer to this question. First consider partial-order plans. A *linearization* of a partial-order plan is a linear plan that results from adding additional ordering constraints sufficient to linearly order the plan-steps. To adopt a partial-order plan is to be indifferent between its various linearizations. Accordingly, we should define:

A partial-order plan will achieve its goal iff every linearization of it will achieve its goal.

Under what circumstances will a linear plan achieve its goal? The standard answer to this question proceeds in terms of the technical notion of a "result of an action-sequence." To make the standard answer work, we must also make some assumptions. The assumptions are (1) that goals are always literals[2] or conjunctions of literals, and (2) that in a planning-conditional $(A \mathrel{\&} C) \blacktriangleright P$, C and P are either literals or finite conjunctions of literals. Where P is atomic, it will be convenient to identify $\sim\sim P$ with P, so that the negation of a literal is a literal.

Let us take an *action-sequence* to be a linear sequence of actions. Given an action-sequence $\langle A_1, \ldots, A_n \rangle$, define:

(R1) Where *start-state* is a state of affairs and *conditionals* is a set of planning-conditionals, P is a *result* of $\langle A_1, \ldots, A_n \rangle$ relative to *start-state* and *conditionals* iff either:

1. $n = 0$ and P is true in *start-state*; or
2. $n > 0$ and *conditionals* contains a conditional $(A_n \mathrel{\&} C) \blacktriangleright P$ such that C is a result of $\langle A_1, \ldots, A_{n-1} \rangle$; or
3. $n > 0$, P is a result of $\langle A_1, \ldots, A_{n-1} \rangle$, and *conditionals* does not contain a conditional of the form $(A_n \mathrel{\&} C) \blacktriangleright \sim Q$ such that Q is either P or a conjunct of P and C is a result of $\langle A_1, \ldots, A_{n-1} \rangle$; or
4. $n > 0$ and P is a conjunction whose conjuncts are results of $\langle A_1, \ldots, A_n \rangle$.

In other words, P is a result of an action-sequence iff either P is made true by the final step of the action-sequence in accordance with a planning-conditional whose precondition is a result of the preceding subsequence of the action-sequence or an initial segment of the action-sequence makes P true and subsequent actions in the sequence do not reverse that. Conventional AI planning theory makes the following assumption:

Soundness Assumption
A linear plan will achieve its goal relative to a state *start-state* iff its goal is a result of the sequence of actions prescribed by its plan-steps relative to *start-state* and the set of all true planning-conditionals.

For the moment, let us follow AI planning theory in assuming this. I will return to the evaluation of the Soundness Assumption in section 4.

The Soundness Assumption provides the mathematical basis for a complete theory of means-end reasoning. It enables us to prove the correctness of a recursive characterization of plans that will achieve their goals. The steps of the recursion are formulated to correspond to procedures of plan-construction used in means-end reasoning. The rules in question are those formulated earlier, together with five more that I will not discuss due to lack of time. The end result is a proof that when means-end reasoning is performed in accordance with these rules, the plans it produces will achieve their goals, and if there is a plan that will achieve a particular goal, some such plan will be found by following these rules of means-end reasoning. So this is a kind of soundness and completeness proof for means-end reasoning.

3. Algorithmic Planning and Defeasible Planning

Contemporary AI planning theory is based upon *algorithmic planners*. Given a planning problem, an algorithmic planner runs a program that systematically searches the space of possible plans until it returns one that purports to solve the problem. The sense in which the planner is algorithmic is that it executes an effective computation; that is, the set of pairs ⟨problem, solution⟩ that characterize the planner is recursively enumerable. In effect, such planners are based upon the three operations PROPOSE-NULL-PLAN, GOAL-REGRESSION, and SPLIT-CONJUNCTIVE-GOAL-SAFELY. There is, however, an insuperable logical problem for attempting to perform general-purpose means-end reasoning by running such an algorithm.

Assuming that a planner is a goal-regression planner that works as described earlier by splitting conjunctive goals into their conjuncts and merging the plans for the conjuncts, an algorithmic planner will only be possible if the set of destructive interferences is effectively computable, that is, recursive. If the set of destructive interferences is not effectively computable, the planner will not be able to use SPLIT-CONJUNCTIVE-GOAL-SAFELY to determine whether two plans can be merged or, when there is destructive interference, whether it can be repaired.

In order for destructive interference to be computable, it must be computable whether a particular condition (the negation of a precondition of one of the plan steps) is a consequence of an action under specifiable circumstances. Standard AI planning systems accomplish this by assuming that all relevant planning-conditionals are contained in a database at the time planning begins, and hence the consequences of actions can be determined by simply looking them up in a table (using unification). Such planners do no reasoning or very little reasoning about the consequences of actions, relying instead on precompiled knowledge.[3]

It is useful to make a distinction between applied planning systems and planning systems that are intended to formalize and automate the planning of an autonomous rational agent (e.g., a human being). AI planning theory has had a number of practical applications and is one of the success stories of AI. However, practical applications of AI planning theory have been confined largely to well-behaved domains in which the goals are fixed and all the relevant information can be precompiled and supplied to the planner. The planner then runs a program that searches the space of possible plans (relative to the given information) until it finds a plan whose execution is guaranteed to achieve the goals. In such "applied planning," a planner is a tool used by a human being, and in order to use the tool effectively the human must prepare the ground very carefully, being sure to give the planner all the knowledge needed to solve the planning problem.

One of the ideals to which AI aspires is the construction of autonomous rational agents capable of maneuvering through a complex, variable, and often uncooperative environment. A special case of this is the attempt to build a system that models human rationality. Planning will be an essential ingredient in any such agent. However, the planning problem faced by such an agent contrasts in important ways with the kind of applied planning problem that is solved by current AI planning technology. The most obvious difference is that, in sharp contrast to applied planning, it cannot be assumed that a planning agent has exactly the knowledge it needs to solve a planning problem. An autonomous agent must build its own knowledge base. The system designer can get things started by providing background knowledge, but the agent must be provided with cognitive machinery that enables its knowledge base to grow and evolve as it gains experience of its environment, senses its immediate surroundings, and reasons about the consequences of beliefs it already holds. The more complex the environment, the more the autonomous agent will have to be self-sufficient for knowledge acquisition. I have distinguished between practical cognition and epistemic cognition. The principal function of epistemic cognition in an autonomous agent is to provide the information needed for practical cognition. As such, the course of epistemic cognition is driven by practical interests. Rather than coming to the planning problem equipped with all the knowledge required for its solution, the planning problem itself directs epistemic cognition, focusing epistemic endeavors on the pursuit of information that will be helpful in solving current planning problems.

Paramount among this information is knowledge about what will happen if certain actions are taken under certain circumstances. Sometimes the agent already knows what will happen, but often it has to figure it out. At the very least this will require reasoning from current knowledge. In many cases it will require the empirical acquisition of new knowledge that cannot be obtained just by reasoning from what is already known. For example, in order to construct a plan the planning agent may have to find out what time it is and may be able to do that only by examining the world in some way (e.g., it may have to go into the next room and look at the clock). In general, such empirical investigations are carried out by performing actions (not just by reasoning). Figuring out what actions to perform is a matter of engaging in further planning. The agent acquires the epistemic goal of acquiring certain information and then plans for how to accomplish that. So planning drives epistemic investigation, which may in turn drive further planning. It follows that an essential characteristic of planning agents is that planning and epistemic cognition are interleaved. Unlike applied planning, it is impossible to require of a planning agent capable of functioning in realistically complex environments that it acquire all the requisite knowledge before beginning the plan search.

Now let us apply this to the question of whether human beings (and other rational agents) can perform their planning by implementing planning algorithms. As I have argued, that is only possible if destructive interference is computable, which in turn requires that the consequences of actions be computable. As we have seen, autonomous planning agents cannot rely on precompiled knowledge. They must engage in genuine reasoning about the consequences of actions, and we should not expect that reasoning to be any simpler than general epistemic reasoning. Realistically, epistemic reasoning must be defeasible, which makes the set of conclusions at best Δ_2.[4] But even if we could construct an agent that did only first-order deductive reasoning, the set of conclusions is not effectively computable—it is recursively enumerable. Even for such an unrealistically oversimplified planner, destructive interference will not be computable—the set of destructive interferences will be only r.e. This means that when the planning algorithm computes plans for the conjuncts of a conjunctive goal and then considers whether they can be merged without destructive interference, the reasoning required to find any particular destructive interference may take indefinitely long, and if there is no destructive interference, there will be no point at which the planner can draw the conclusion that there is none simply on the grounds that none has been found. Thus, the planning algorithm will bog down at this point and will never be able to produce the merged plan for the conjunctive goal.[5]

If destructive interference is not computable, how can a planner get away with dividing conjunctive goals into separate conjuncts and planning for each conjunct separately? The key to this problem emerges from considering how human beings solve it. Humans assume defeasibly that the separate plans do not destructively interfere with one another and so infer defeasibly that the merged plan is a good plan for the conjunctive goal. In other words, human means-end reasoning is based on SPLIT-CONJUNCTIVE-GOAL rather than SPLIT-CONJUNCTIVE-GOAL-SAFELY. Having made this defeasible inference, human planners then look for destructive interference that would defeat it, but they do not regard it as essential to establish that there is no destructive interference before they make the inference. And if, at the time plan execution is to begin, no destructive interference has been discovered, then we humans go ahead and execute the plan despite the fact that we have not *proven conclusively* that there is no destructive interference.

One may be tempted to suppose that human beings are making an unreasonable leap of faith here and that a more rational agent would postpone plan execution until it has been established that there is no destructive interference. However, the logic of the epistemic search for destructive interference makes that impossible. Given a logically complex knowledge base, there will not, in general, be a point at which an agent can conclude with certainty that there is no destructive interference within a plan, so an agent that required such certainty would be unable to execute any of its plans.

The upshot of this is that a rational agent that is operating in a realistically complex environment must make defeasible assumptions in the course of its planning and then be prepared to change its planning decisions later if subsequent epistemic reasoning defeats those defeasible assumptions. In other words, the reasoning involved in planning must be a species of defeasible reasoning. *Planning in autonomous agents cannot be done algorithmically.*

The general way means-end reasoning must work is by performing goal regression, splitting conjunctive goals into their conjuncts and planning for them separately and then merging the plans for the individual conjuncts into a combined plan for the conjunctive goal. The practical reasoner will infer defeasibly that the merged plan is a solution to the planning problem. A defeater for this defeasible inference consists of discovering that the plan contains destructive interference. Whenever a defeasible reasoner makes a defeasible inference, it must adopt interest in finding defeaters, so in this case the agent will adopt interest in finding destructive interference. Finding such interference should lead the agent to try various ways of repairing the plan to eliminate the interference and then lead to a defeasible inference that the repaired plan is a solution to the planning problem. The tentative conclusion being adopted is that the plan will achieve its goal. Means-end reasoning becomes a form of epistemic reasoning to the effect that if a plan is executed (in any way consistent with the ordering) then it is defeasibly reasonable to expect the goal to be achieved.

4. Planning and the Frame Problem

I have presented a tentative account of the logical structure of means-end reasoning. This account differs in some important ways from conventional AI planning theory, but it also makes heavy reliance on certain aspects of the conventional theory. In particular, it turns on the Soundness Assumption, according to which a linear plan achieves a goal relative to a start-state iff the goal is a result of the sequence of actions prescribed by the plan-steps relative to the start-state and the set of all true planning-conditionals, where "result" is a technical concept that was defined as follows:

(R1)   Where *start-state* is a state of affairs and *conditionals* is a set of planning-conditionals, P is a *result* of $\langle A_1, \ldots, A_n \rangle$ relative to *start-state* and *conditionals* iff either:

1. $n = 0$ and P is true in *start-state*; or
2. $n > 0$ and *conditionals* contains a conditional $(A_n \& C) \blacktriangleright P$ such that C is a result of $\langle A_1, \ldots, A_{n-1} \rangle$; or
3. $n > 0$, P is a result of $\langle A_1, \ldots, A_{n-1} \rangle$ and *conditionals* does not contain a conditional of the form $(A_n \& C) \blacktriangleright \sim Q$ such that Q is either P or a conjunct of P and C is a result of $\langle A_1, \ldots, A_{n-1} \rangle$; or
4. $n > 0$ and P is a conjunction whose conjuncts are results of $\langle A_1, \ldots, A_n \rangle$.

To evaluate the Soundness Assumption we must consider more carefully what it means. It seems to say the following:

Necessarily, a linear plan will achieve a goal G when executed from a start-state iff G is a result of the sequence of actions prescribed by its plan-steps relative to the start-state and the set of all true planning-conditionals.

But so interpreted, the Soundness Assumption is obviously false. The difficulty concerns clause (3) of the definition of "result." Clause (3) asserts that once a subgoal has been established, it will remain true unless some later step of the plan makes it false. There is no logical guarantee of this. To take a simple example, suppose my goal is to start a fire. I have a match, and it is dry, and I am given the conditionals "If a dry match is struck it will light" and "If a lit match is placed under kindling then a fire will start." By GOAL-REGRESSION I adopt interest in finding a plan for having a lit match. By a second application of GOAL-REGRESSION I adopt interest in finding a plan for having a dry match. Observing that I already have a dry match, I conclude that the latter subgoal is achieved by a null-plan. To the end of the null-plan I add the two steps *strike the match* and *place the match under the kindling*, thus obtaining a plan for starting the fire. But this plan will only work if the match, which is initially dry, is still dry when it is struck and if the match, which is lit by striking it, is still lit when it is placed under the kindling. All sorts of things can go wrong. The match might be be drenched by a rainstorm before I get a chance to strike it. Another agent might blow it out after it is lit, or I might take too long in lighting the kindling and the match will burn out. The world is a dynamic, continually changing place. It is certainly not a necessary truth that subgoals established by earlier steps of a plan will not be made false by events extraneous to the plan before the subgoals can be used in establishing further goals.

In AI it is often claimed that goal-regression planning relies upon the so-called STRIPS assumption, according to which nothing changes in the world unless it does so as a result of executing a step of the plan.[6] But such an assumption is obviously silly. We engage in goal-regression planning all the time without believing the STRIPS assumption, so the STRIPS assumption cannot provide the logical basis for our planning.

The STRIPS assumption is much too strong. We do not expect that nothing will change in the world unless we change it, but we do expect our plan to work. This means that we have a *limited* expectation, not that nothing will change but that the particular subgoals established by initial steps of the plan will not change unless executing later steps of the plan causes them to change. We certainly do not believe that plans will *never* be disrupted by extraneous events, but we do expect that not to happen in any particular case. We are, however, always prepared to be proven wrong. In other words, our expectation is defeasible. We know that things change, but there is a presumption against it in any particular case.

Providing the logical foundations for such a defeasible expectation is just the *frame problem*. Early attempts in AI to give a logical reconstruction of reasoning about the consequences of actions tried doing so by axiomatizing the domain and then reasoning about it deductively. However, AI researchers quickly gave up the attempt to solve the frame problem deductively and proposed instead that there is a defeasible presumption that things don't change. The thinking was that given such a defeasible presumption, the only substantive principles we need for reasoning about change are causal principles that override the defeasible presumption in specific cases (McCarthy and Hayes 1969). I have recently explored ways of making this reasoning precise

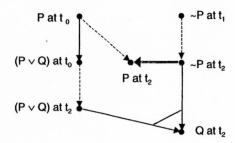

FIGURE 3.1. The need for a temporal projectibility constraint

within the OSCAR system of defeasible reasoning, and I will summarize my results here (Pollock 1997, 1998).

Temporal-Projection

As a first approximation, we can formulate a defeasible presumption against change as follows:

(1)   If $t_0 < t_1$, believing P-at-t_0 is a defeasible reason for the agent to believe P-at-t_1, the strength of the reason being a monotonic decreasing function of $t_1 - t_0$.

Principle 1 is a principle of *temporal-projection*. It amounts to a presumption that P's being true is a stable property of a time. A stable property is one such that if it holds at one time, the probability is high that it will continue to hold at a later time. Some such principle seems to be presupposed by much of our reasoning about the world.[7] However, as formulated, principle 1 is too strong. A constraint must be imposed on P. This is best demonstrated with an example, diagrammed in Figure 3.1. Let P and Q be unrelated propositions. Suppose we know that P is true at t_0 and false at the later time t_1. Consider a third time t_2 later than t_1. P-at-t_0 gives us a defeasible reason for expecting P-at-t_2, but $\sim P$-at-t_1 gives us a stronger reason for expecting $\sim P$-at-t_2, because $(t_2 - t_1) < (t_2 - t_0)$. Thus, an inference to P-at-t_2 is defeated, but an inference to $\sim P$-at-t_2 is undefeated. This is as it should be. However, from P-at-t_0 we can deductively infer $(P \vee Q)$-at-t_0. Without any restrictions on the proposition-variable in temporal-projection, $(P \vee Q)$-at-t_0 gives us a defeasible reason for expecting $(P \vee Q)$-at-t_2. Given the inference to $\sim P$-at-t_2, we can then infer Q-at-t_2. In diagramming these inferences in Figure 3.1, the solid arrows symbolize deductive inferences and bars that connect arrows indicate that the inference is from multiple premises. The "bold" arrow symbolizes a defeat relation. In this inference-graph, the conclusion Q-at-t_2 is undefeated. But this is unreasonable. Q-at-t_2 is inferred from $(P \vee Q)$-at-t_2. $(P \vee Q)$ is expected to be true at t_2 only because it was true at t_0, and it was only true at t_0 because P was true at t_0. This makes it reasonable to believe $(P \vee Q)$-at-t_2 only insofar as it is reasonable to believe P-at-t_2, but the latter is defeated. This example illustrates clearly that temporal-projection does not work equally well for all propositions. In particular, the set of propositions for which temporal-projection works is not closed under disjunction. Let us label those propositions for which it does work *temporally projectible*. A principle of temporal-projection must be restricted to temporally projectible propositions:

TEMPORAL-PROJECTION
If P is temporally projectible and $t_0 < t_1$, believing P-at-t_0 is a defeasible reason for the agent to believe P-at-t_1, the strength of the reason being a monotonic decreasing function of $t_1 - t_0$.

What are called projectibility problems arise in a number of places in philosophical epistemology. N. Goodman (1955) first showed that inductive reasoning does not work equally well for all properties—that principles of induction require a projectibility constraint. In Pollock 1972 I showed that many projectibility problems result from attempting to employ induction with respect to disjunctions. In Pollock 1990 I showed that similar projectibility problems arise in other contexts—the statistical syllogism, direct inference, and statistical induction. In all of these contexts, disjunctions create major difficulties. Apparently, the same conclusion must be drawn for temporal-projection.[8]

The need for a projectibility constraint is clear, but the exact content of the constraint is not. Disjunctions create projectibility problems but are not the only culprits. It is easy to see that conjunctions of temporally projectible propositions are temporally projectible. If we have an undefeated reason for believing P-at-t_1 and an undefeated reason for believing Q-at-t_1, then we can infer $(P \& Q)$-at-t_1 deductively, so the latter inference cannot be problematic. However, the negation of a conjunction is equivalent to a disjunction, so the negations of temporally projectible propositions are not automatically temporally projectible. We can make many such observations about temporal-projectibility, but I do not have a general criterion of temporal-projectibility to propose. The literature contains no good theories of projectibility in any of its guises.[9] Constructing such a theory is at this time an unsolved philosophical problem.

The Frame Problem Resurrected

TEMPORAL-PROJECTION was originally proposed as a solution to the frame problem. However, TEMPORAL-PROJECTION turns out to be only part of the solution, as was first shown by S. Hanks and D. McDermott (1986). To illustrate (with a different example from theirs), suppose there is a causal law to the effect that if a match is dry and it is struck then it will burn. Suppose we have a match that is initially known to be dry, at time t_0. Shortly thereafter, at time t_1, it is struck. We want to be able to conclude that it will light at some time t_2 ($> t_1$). It may seem that TEMPORAL-PROJECTION allows us to make this inference. The match was known to be dry at t_0, so TEMPORAL-PROJECTION gives us a reason for expecting it to still be dry at t_1. Then on the basis of the law we can infer that the match will burn at some time $t_2 > t_1$. However, as Hanks and McDermott observed, we also know that the match is not burning

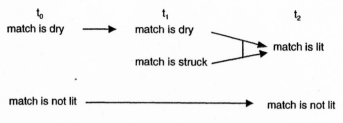

FIGURE 3.2. The Yale Match Lighting Problem

at time t_0, and so (assuming temporal-projectibility) TEMPORAL-PROJECTION gives us a reason for thinking it will not be burning at time t_2. This conflicts with the conclusion that it will burn at time t_2. Thus, TEMPORAL-PROJECTION does not favor either the conclusion that the match will burn or the conclusion that the match will not burn. This is diagrammed in Figure 3.2. But, intuitively, we want to conclude defeasibly that the match will still be dry at t_1 and hence will burn at t_2. Thus, TEMPORAL-PROJECTION does not solve the frame problem.[10]

There is a kind of consensus that the solution to this problem lies in performing the temporal-projections in temporal order.[11] We first use TEMPORAL-PROJECTION to infer that the match is still dry at time t_1. At that point, nothing has yet happened to block the application of TEMPORAL-PROJECTION, so we make this inference. From this we can infer that the match will burn at t_2. At time t_2, we can also try to use TEMPORAL-PROJECTION to infer that the match will not burn, but this time something has already happened (the match was struck while dry) to block the projection, and so we do not infer that the match will not burn. This general idea was first suggested by Y. Shoham (1986) and subsequently endorsed by Hanks and McDermott (1987), V. Lifschitz (1987a), and others. I will follow the literature in calling this *chronological minimalization* (changes are minimized in chronological order).

In Pollock 1996, 1997, and 1998 I suggested a way of making this precise and implementing the reasoning. For present purposes, most of the details of that account are irrelevant. It does have implications for planning-conditionals, however. A planning-conditional $(A \ \& \ C) \blacktriangleright G$ must be an instantiation of a general causal law where C refers to times that precede the performance of the action A and G refers to times that succeed the performance of the action. This is required if we are to use such conditionals to reason causally about the results of executing plan-steps. I turn to the details of this reasoning in the next section.

5. Planning and Temporal-Projectibility

The conventional theory of means-end reasoning as developed in section 2 was based upon the Soundness Assumption, which was formulated as follows:

Soundness Assumption

A linear plan will achieve a goal G relative to a state *start-state* iff G is a result of the sequence of actions prescribed by its plan-steps relative to *start-state* and the set of all true planning-conditionals.

This employs the concept of a result of a sequence of actions, which was defined as follows:

(R1)   Where *start-state* is a state of affairs and *conditionals* is a set of planning-conditionals, P is a *result* of $\langle A_1, \ldots, A_n \rangle$ relative to *start-state* and *conditionals* iff either:

1. $n = 0$ and P is true in *start-state*; or
2. $n > 0$ and *conditionals* contains a conditional $(A_n \mathbin{\&} C) \blacktriangleright P$ such that C is a result of $\langle A_1, \ldots, A_{n-1} \rangle$; or
3. $n > 0$, P is a result of $\langle A_1, \ldots, A_{n-1} \rangle$, and *conditionals* does not contain a conditional of the form $(A_n \mathbin{\&} C) \blacktriangleright \sim Q$ such that Q is either P or a conjunct of P and C is a result of $\langle A_1, \ldots, A_{n-1} \rangle$; or
4. $n > 0$ and P is a conjunction whose conjuncts are results of $\langle A_1, \ldots, A_n \rangle$.

The observations of section 4 require modifications to both the Soundness Assumption itself and the definition of result, and these in turn require modifications to the rules of means-end reasoning that are based upon the Soundness Assumption. First, the inferences that underlie the definition of "result" are only defeasible inferences, based upon TEMPORAL-PROJECTION. As such, the term *result* is a misnomer. We are not characterizing what *will definitely* happen if the action-sequence is performed. We are just characterizing what can be reasonably expected to happen. So it would be better to use the term *expectable-result*. Second, because the inferences are based upon TEMPORAL-PROJECTION, they are subject to temporal-projectibility constraints. We must make some changes to the definition to accommodate these constraints. Clause (1) is unproblematic. It follows that PROPOSE-NULL-PLAN is correct as it was originally formulated. Clause (4) also requires no modification to accommodate temporal-projectibility, because it only concerns relations between expectable-results that have already been projected forward to the appropriate times. However, clauses (2) and (3) require temporal-projectibility constraints.

Clause (2) describes causal inferences of the sort to which the frame problem is relevant. If we can expect C to be achieved by executing the sequence of actions $\langle A_1, \ldots, A_{n-1} \rangle$, and C is temporally projectible, then we can infer defeasibly that C will remain true until action A_n is performed, and given the conditional $(A_n \mathbin{\&} C) \blacktriangleright P$ we can infer that P will be made true. For this reasoning to work, a projectibility constraint must be added to clause (2):

2. $n > 0$ and *conditionals* contains a conditional $(A_n \mathbin{\&} C) \blacktriangleright P$ such that C is a temporally projectible expectable-result of $\langle A_1, \ldots, A_{n-1} \rangle$

GOAL-REGRESSION is based directly on clause 2, so it must contain a corresponding constraint:

GOAL-REGRESSION
Given an interest in finding a plan for achieving G, adopt interest in finding planning-conditionals $(A \& C) \blacktriangleright G$ having G as their consequent. Given such a conditional, adopt an interest in finding a plan for achieving C. If a plan *subplan* is proposed for achieving C, construct a plan by (1) adding a new step to the end of *subplan* where the new step prescribes the action A, (2) ordering the new step after all steps of *subplan*, and (3) adjusting the causal-links appropriately. Infer nondefeasibly that the new plan will achieve G.

Although clause (4) required no modification, SPLIT-CONJUNCTIVE-GOAL, which is based on clause 4, does require a temporal-projectibility constraint. The difficulty is that the conjuncts G_1 and G_2 will not normally be achieved at the same time. Whichever one is achieved first must be temporally projectible if we are to be able to infer that it will still be true when the second is achieved. Furthermore, the achievement of G_1 and G_2 will be unordered with respect to each other by $plan_1 + plan_2$, so we cannot predict which will be achieved first. Thus SPLIT-CONJUNCTIVE-GOAL must include the constraint that they are both temporally projectible:

SPLIT-CONJUNCTIVE-GOAL
Given an interest in finding a plan for achieving a conjunctive goal $(G_1 \& G_2)$, *if G_1 and G_2 are temporally projectible*, adopt interest in finding plans $plan_1$ for G_1 and $plan_2$ for G_2. If such plans are proposed, infer defeasibly that $plan_1 + plan_2$ will achieve $(G_1 \& G_2)$.

Clause (3) is, in effect, a statement of TEMPORAL-PROJECTION applied to the expectable-results of an action-sequence, together with the statement of a defeater for the application of TEMPORAL-PROJECTION. For TEMPORAL-PROJECTION to be applicable, we must require that P be temporally projectible. Given that constraint, if it is defeasibly reasonable to expect P to be true after executing $A_1, \ldots, A_{n-1}$, then it is defeasibly reasonable to expect P to remain true after executing A_n as well. A defeater for this defeasible expectation consists of having a reason for thinking that P will not be true. Given that C is temporally projectible and it is defeasibly reasonable to expect C to be true after executing $A_1, \ldots, A_{n-1}$, it follows in accordance with the preceding discussion of the frame problem that, given the conditional $(A_n \& C) \blacktriangleright \sim Q$, it is defeasibly reasonable to expect Q to become false after executing A_n. So (3) should be reformulated as follows:

3. $n > 0$, P is a temporally projectible expectable-result of $\langle A_1, \ldots, A_{n-1} \rangle$ and *conditionals* does not contain a conditional of the form $(A_n \& C) \blacktriangleright \sim Q$ such that Q is either P or a conjunct of P and C is a temporally projectible expectable-result of $\langle A_1, \ldots, A_{n-1} \rangle$

Combining these observations, we are led to the following definition of expectable-result:

(R2)   Where *start-state* is a state of affairs and *conditionals* is a set of planning-conditionals, P is an expectable-result of $\langle A_1, \ldots, A_n \rangle$ relative to *start-state* and *conditionals* iff either:

1. $n = 0$ and P is true in *start-state*; or
2. $n > 0$ and *conditionals* contains a conditional $(A_n \ \& \ C) \blacktriangleright P$ such that C is a temporally projectible expectable-result of $\langle A_1, \ldots, A_{n-1} \rangle$; or
3. $n > 0$, P is a temporally projectible expectable-result of $\langle A_1, \ldots, A_{n-1} \rangle$ and *conditionals* does not contain a conditional of the form $(A_n \ \& \ C) \blacktriangleright \sim Q$ such that Q is either P or a conjunct of P and C is a temporally projectible expectable-result of $\langle A_1, \ldots, A_{n-1} \rangle$; or
4. $n > 0$ and P is a conjunction whose conjuncts are expectable-results of $\langle A_1, \ldots, A_n \rangle$.

The Soundness Assumption must now be reinterpreted as giving us merely a defeasible expectation that a plan will achieve its goal:

Soundness Assumption
Executing a linear plan can be defeasibly expected to achieve a goal G relative to a state *start-state* iff G is an expectable-result of the sequence of actions prescribed by the plan-steps of the plan relative to *start-state* and the set of all true planning-conditionals.

The definition (R2) of expectable-result constitutes a semantics, relative to which we can prove the soundness and completeness of a set of rules for means-end reasoning. These rules consist of PROPOSE-NULL-PLAN, SPLIT-CONJUNCTIVE-GOAL, the revision of GOAL-REGRESSION that incorporates temporal-projectibility constraints, and some further rules that deal with finding and repairing desctructive interference.

6. Conclusions

Although (R2) is an improvement on (R1), there are still some problems with (R2) that require further revision. Fortunately, that can be done, and a set of rules for means-end reasoning can be produced that is provably sound and complete for the corrected version of (R2).

The theory of means-end reasoning developed in this chapter draws heavily on conventional AI planning theory, but there are also important differences. One important difference is that on the theory proposed here, planning is not algorithmic. It has been argued that a planning agent embedded in a complex environment must interleave planning with epistemic cognition aimed at providing information needed for planning, and this makes algorithmic planning logically impossible. Instead, planning must be done defeasibly. To accomplish this I have proposed taking means-end reasoning to be a species of epistemic cognition whose purpose is to generate defeasibly reasonable conclusions of the form "Plan p would achieve its goal if the prescribed plan-steps were executed in any order consistent with its ordering-constraints."

Viewing planning as an epistemic endeavor generates a different kind of semantic foundation for planning. The conventional approach adopts the definition (R1) of result and then attempts to prove the soundness and completeness of a planning algorithm. This concept of result is intended to be an objective concept that describes the way the world will be as a result of executing the plan. But once it is recognized that planning is based upon defeasible expectations rather than objectively determinate results of actions, it becomes apparent that no such definition of result is possible. The semantics of planning must instead be based upon the epistemic concept of an expectable-result.

It has been argued here that means-end reasoning presupposes a certain kind of solution to the frame problem, and this generates the second important difference from conventional AI planning theory. The solution to the frame problem uses TEMPORAL-PROJECTION at crucial points in the process of inferring that a plan can be expected to achieve its goal, and that requires the imposition of temporal-projectibility constraints in the definition of expectable-result and on the subgoals generated by GOAL-REGRESSION.

The system of defeasible means-end reasoning described in section 5 and based upon (R2) has been implemented in the OSCAR planner, which is based upon the OSCAR system of defeasible reasoning.[12]

NOTES

This work was supported by NSF grant IRI-9634106.

1. Promotion and demotation were first described in McAllester and Rosenblitt 1991, and confrontation is due to Penberthy and Weld 1992.
2. A literal is either an atomic formula or the negation of an atomic formula.
3. This originated with STRIPS (Fikes and Nilsson 1971), which built the requisite planning-conditionals into the plan operators themselves. Subsequent AI planners have followed suit.
4. For a discussion of this, see Pollock 1995, chapter 3.
5. Notice that a similar problem arises in applying PROPOSE-NULL-PLAN, which may require an indeterminate amount of reasoning to determine that the subgoal is already true. If the requisite reasoning is not at least r.e., then the planning cannot be algorithmic.
6. See Allen 1987 and Lifschitz 1987b.
7. For arguments to the effect that such reasoning is pervasive, see Pollock 1997.
8. I first showed this in Pollock 1997.
9. See Stalker 1994 for a compendium of work on projectibility.
10. This is formulated more precisely in Pollock 1998.
11. See Hanks and McDermott 1987. A number of more recent papers explore this same idea.
12. An experimental version of the OSCAR planner can be downloaded from http://www.u.arizona.edu/~pollock/.

REFERENCES

Allen, J. (1987). Formal models of planning. In J. Allen, J. Hendler, and A. Tate (eds.), *Readings in Planning*. Los Altos, CA: Morgan Kaufmann.

Fikes, R. E., and N. J. Nilsson (1971). STRIPS: A new approach to the application of theorem proving to problem solving. *Artificial Intelligence* 2:189–208.

Goodman, N. (1955). *Fact, Fiction, and Forecast*. Cambridge: Harvard University Press.

Hanks, S., and D. McDermott (1986). Default reasoning, nonmonotonic logics, and the frame problem. In *Proceedings of the Fifth National Conference on Artificial Intelligence (AAAI-86)*, pp. 328–333. Los Altos, CA: Morgan Kaufmann.

Hanks, S., and D. McDermott (1987). Nonmonotonic logic and temporal projection. *Artificial Intelligence* 33:379–412.

Kautz, H. A. (1986). The logic of persistence. *Proceedings of the Fifth National Conference on Artificial Intelligence (AAAI-86)*, pp. 401–405.

Lifschitz, V. (1987a). Formal theories of action. In F. Brown (ed.), *The Frame Problem in Artificial Intelligence: Proceedings of the 1987 Workshop*, pp. 35–57. Los Altos, CA: Morgan Kaufmann.

Lifschitz, V. (1987b). On the semantics of STRIPS. In M. Georgeff and A. Lansky (eds.), *Reasoning about Actions and Plans*, pp. 1–9. Los Altos, CA: Morgan Kaufmann.

McAllester, D., and D. Rosenblitt (1991). Systematic nonlinear planning. In *Proceedings of the Ninth National Conference on Artificial Intelligence (AAAI-91)*, pp. 634–639. Menlo Park, CA: AAAI Press/MIT Press.

McCarthy, J., and P. Hayes (1969). Some philosophical problems from the standpoint of artificial intelligence. In B. Meltzer and D. Michie (eds.), *Machine Intelligence*, vol. 4. pp. 463–502. Edinburgh: Edinburgh University Press.

Penberthy, J. S., and D. Weld (1992). UCPOP: A sound, complete, partial order planner for ADL. In *Proceedings of the Third International Conference on Principles of Knowledge Representation and Reasoning*, pp. 103–114. San Francisco: Morgan Kaufmann.

Pollock, J. (1972). The logic of projectibility. *Philosophy of Science* 39:302–314.

Pollock, J. (1990). *Nomic Probability and the Foundations of Induction*. New York: Oxford University Press.

Pollock, J. (1995). *Cognitive Carpentry*. Cambridge: MIT Press.

Pollock, J. (1996). Reason in a changing world. In D. M. Gabbay and H. J. Ohlbach (eds.), *Practical Reasoning*, pp. 495–509. Berlin: Springer-Verlag. This can be downloaded from http://www.u.arizona.edu/~pollock/.

Pollock, J. (1997). Reasoning about change and persistence: A solution to the frame problem. *Nous* 31:143–169.

Pollock, J. (1998). Perceiving and reasoning about a changing world. *Computational Intelligence* 14:498–562.

Pollock, J. (1998). The logical foundations of goal-regression planning in autonomous agents. *Artificial Intelligence* 106:267–335.

Shoham, Y. (1986). *Time and Causation from the Standpoint of Artificial Intelligence*. Computer Science Research Report No. 507. Yale University, New Haven, Connecticut.

Shoham, Y. (1987). *Reasoning about Change*. Cambridge: MIT Press.

Stalker, D. (ed.) (1994). *Grue! The New Riddle of Induction*. Chicago: Open Court.

4

Induction and Consistency

HENRY E. KYBURG, JR.

1. Introduction: The Problem

Let us begin by sketching one view of what we are about. We know that people make uncertain inferences, in some sense. Part of our project is to understand in what sense or senses that is so. Another part of our project is to develop standards for arguments that involve uncertainty. Again, there is plenty of ambiguity in this characterization of what we are about. The fundamental issue I want us to focus on is that of whether or not inductive or uncertain inference leads to the *acceptance* of conclusions. Of course this depends on what the conclusions are taken to be.

A clear-cut characterization of the issue is given by C. Hempel in Hempel (1965, p. 383). Let "$p(T, R) \approx 1.0$" stand for the sentence that asserts that the long-run frequency or propensity of Rs to be Ts is approximately 1, that is, is close to 1.0. If we know *only*[1] the two facts "$p(T, R) \approx 1.0$" and "Ra" we are surely entitled to be pretty sure of Ta. The issue is how, exactly, to express this.

Hempel distinguishes two ways of expressing what goes on epistemically. One way is the Bayesian way: we infer from the two premises cited the *conclusion*: "Ta" is highly probable.

$$\frac{\text{``}p(T, R) \approx 1.0\text{''}}{\text{``}Ra\text{''}}$$
"Ta" *is highly probable*

The other way to describe what is going on is to take the qualification "is highly probable" to characterize not the conclusion but the *inference*. Thus, under this description the conclusion is the categorical "*Ta*" and the double line *itself* is characterized by the qualification.

$$\text{"}p(T,R)\approx 1.0\text{"}$$

$$\frac{\text{"}Ra\text{"}}{\text{"}Ta\text{"}} \quad \textit{is highly probable}$$

R. Carnap (Kyburg 1968, "Discussion," pp. 146–150) has argued that "acceptance" merely reflects a sloppy but convenient way of talking. W. Salmon, however (Kyburg 1968b, "Discussion," pp. 139–144), sees acceptance as fundamental to the process of science, as does I. Levi (1980).

2. A Bayesian View

I would not presume to characterize all Bayesian views, but a general picture that will serve our purpose has a first-order formal language and a probability measure associated with it.

This probability measure is a function $\mathcal{P}$ defined on the language $\mathcal{L}$ that assigns a real number in [0, 1] to each sentence in the language. The basic Bayesian claim is that this function ought to be a probability function. Various arguments have been offered supporting this claim, from the Dutch Book argument to appeals to our intuitions of fairness (Howson and Urbach 1993). None of these arguments strike me as in the least compelling, but let us leave that issue to one side for our present purposes. The approach of E. Bolker (1967) and R. C. Jeffrey (1965) is pretty persuasive, but it is focused on decision theory, rather than on epistemology or inference.

One feature of the function is that it assigns the values 1 and 0 to certain sentences. For example, it assigns the value 1 to logical truths and the value 0 to their negations. This bothers some Bayesians, but it doesn't bother me. Most Bayesian views also allow the assignment of probability 1 to other statements as well: evidence statements and perhaps statements that belong to "background knowledge." In virtue of the theorem

$$A \vdash B \rightarrow P(A) \leq P(B)$$

the set of sentences assigned probability 1 is a *theory*: it is deductively closed.

In what follows, we shall suppose there is such a theory, constituting the evidence relative to which we perform our inferences. We will represent the theory in two parts: *BK*, which will embody our empirical background knowledge, and *E*, which will represent the empirical evidence we are taking account of at a given time. We will suppose that both parts are finitely axiomatizable, so that we may think of both *BK* and *E* as statements.[2]

Note that the probability function $\mathcal{P}$ is regarded as *given*; it does not change. When we talk about probabilities changing in response to evidence or being "updated," we are indulging in a bit of poetic license. The probability $P(S \mid BK)$ does not change when E becomes a new item of evidence. It retains its value as the (relatively) prior probability of *S*. What changes is that a probability with a different *argument* becomes of interest: $P(S \mid E \wedge BK)$. In making decisions, computing expectations, and assessing degrees of belief, this, rather than $P(S \mid BK)$, is the relevant number.

The *inference* that takes us from $P(S \mid BK)$ to $P(S \mid E \wedge BK)$ is an absolutely classical deductive inference. It is a trivial bit of probability theory:

$$P(S \mid E \wedge BK) = P(S \wedge E \mid BK)/P(E \mid BK)$$

There is nothing inductive or nonmonotonic going on at all—no leaping to new conclusions, no withdrawing of anything once added to *BK*. The only inferences we make are *valid* inferences: the conclusions *must* be true whenever the premises are true. This is a comfy and secure world. If it is less than totally familiar to some of us, that may only be because we have not adequately internalized the rules of the probability calculus.

Three things are required in order to implement this view.

1. we must specify the *kinds* of statement that can occupy the positions of *E* and *BK*,
2. we must specify the conditions under which a statement of this kind can be added to *BK*, and
3. we must specify the prior distribution.

We will have more to say about these requirements in the sequel.

3. An Acceptance View

Let us now sketch an alternative view. This view is based on probability, too, but in a different way. Let the language be the same as before, but this time we require rather than merely allow that the language have enough expressive power to include statements about long-run frequencies or propensities or chances or distributions of them. Thus, we should be able to say that the distribution of heads on tosses of a coin is binomially distributed with a parameter between 0.4 and 0.6 or that the distribution of errors characteristic of a measurement method $\mathcal{M}$ has some distribution bounded by N(−0.1, 0.3) and N(0.1, 0.4).

We pick out a set of statements to serve as background knowledge *BK*. For reasons that will become apparent, we will construe *BK* strictly as a set of statements, rather than as a finitely axiomatiable theory. We *define* probability relative to sets of statements. The probability function $\mathcal{P}$ is defined for every sentence *S* of $\mathcal{L}$; its value is an *interval*. In every case the probability is based on some statement in *BK* that expresses a fact about long-run frequencies, or chances or distributions. This is the reason that probabilities are interval-valued: they are based on known statistics—statistics known in *BK*—and our statistical knowledge is generally approximate.

There is, of course, the problem of determining *which* bit of statistical knowledge in *BK* should determine the probability of *S*. This is the very neglected problem of the reference class, whose solution is a major part of finding the best definition of probability. It is also a major part of finding the best realistic approach to decision theory.

We now define a *new* set of statements $(BK)_\varepsilon$: this is to be the set of statements S in $\mathcal{L}$ such that $P(S \mid BK) \subseteq [1 - \varepsilon, 1]$.

The small positive number ε corresponds to the ordinary-language, commonsense "incredible," "unbelievable"; $1 - \varepsilon$ thus corresponds to the commonsense "practically certain." We do *not* construe it as the commonsense "probable," in the sense of having a probability greater than $1/2$.

Note that $(BK)_\varepsilon$ is *not* deductively closed: it is easy to see that $P(S \mid BK) \subseteq [1 - \varepsilon, 1]$ and $P(T \mid BK) \subseteq [1 - \varepsilon, 1]$ may hold when $P(S \wedge T \mid BK) \subseteq [1 - \varepsilon, 1]$ does not. Of course this raises the possibility of inconsistency. As Pollock has observed (1990), the lottery problem is rather special and artificial. Instead, think of *the* most common and universal scientific use of probability: the use of probability to characterize the accuracy of measurements.

4. Errors of Measurement

Learning how errors of measurement are distributed in the results of a certain method of measurement is a matter (a complex matter, to be sure) of statistical inference. Typically it is alleged that errors of measurement are distributed normally with a variance d characteristic of the method or instrument of measurement and a mean that can (typically) be taken to be 0 in a calibrated instrument.

This is a casual statement, generally made without justification. Gauss offered a theoretical argument for the normal (or Gaussian) distribution of error. He assumed (1) that the total error in a measurement was the sum of a very large number of contributing factors, (2) that an error is as likely to be positive as to be negative, and (3) that large errors are less likely than small errors. The upshot of the last requirement is just that among the errors that make up the sum, no one kind of error will dominate, in the long run.

If these conditions are made precise in a plausible way and the "large number" is allowed to approach infinity, the resulting distribution approaches the normal or Gaussian distribution. (Indeed, this distribution is sometimes called the error distribution or the Gaussian distribution of error.)

Of course we know that these conditions do not hold in the real world, since the distribution of errors of measurement cannot literally be taken to be normal. In measuring a distance, for example, the normal distribution would require that for any $m > 0$ and any true value μ, there is a finite probability that the result of measurement will be less than $\mu - m$. This will be so even if $\mu < m$; that is, we must sometimes get negative readings from our meterstick. Since this is false, the Gaussian conditions don't hold literally.

So what is going on? Am I just being too literal-minded about a harmless approximation that no sensible person would take literally? No. What I am concerned with is a plausible way in which to *understand* this approximation, since I take it to be typical of many other useful approximations in statistics, many (if not most) of which cannot be taken literally.

I suppose there is a literal truth about the distribution of errors of measurement characteristic of measurement method $\mathcal{M}$. This may be construed as hypothetical (as the distribution of errors of a hypothetical countable number of applications of $\mathcal{M}$) or as real (the distribution of errors in the actual large finite number of applications of $\mathcal{M}$ or $\mathcal{M}$-like methods —the reference class problem again!). In either case, the distribution is *bounded* (we do not make errors of measurement of arbitrarily large size or negative errors of measurement of distances). Under the latter construal (toward which I lean), the distribution of error must be a *discrete* distribution.

In either case, we can ask how the normal distribution (unbounded, continuous) can be an "approximation" to the real distribution. The obvious answer is that "the" normal distribution of error must itself be construed as an approximation to a *set* of normal distributions. When we say that the distribution of error characteristic of $\mathcal{M}$ is approximately $N(o, d)$, what we really mean—the commonsense interpretation of what we are saying—is that the distribution is captured by $N(\varepsilon, d + \delta)$, where $|\varepsilon| < \varepsilon^*$ and $|\delta| < \delta^*$ for some fixed, implicitly specified, positive ε^* and δ^*.[3]

Now that we have a *set* of normal distributions, we can interpret the claim about the distribution of error characteristic of measurement method $\mathcal{M}$ as follows: The actual (bounded, possibly discrete) distribution of error characteristic of $\mathcal{M}$ is some distribution F_E *bounded* by this set of distributions. This means that for every $y > x > o$ that is not too close together and is in the plausible range,

$$F_E(y) - F_E(x) \in$$
$$\left[\min\left\{ \int_x^y dN(\varepsilon, d+\delta) : |\varepsilon| < \varepsilon^* \wedge |\delta| < \delta^* \right\}, \right.$$
$$\left. \max\left\{ \int_x^y dN(\varepsilon, d+\delta) : |\varepsilon| < \varepsilon^* \wedge |\delta| < \delta^* \right\} \right]$$

"Not too close together" merely spells out a natural granularity determined by our commonsense concerns. Similarly, "in the plausible range" spells out the commonsense condition that in measuring a length we cannot make an error so large that our measurement is negative or that, in using a micrometer, we cannot make an error of a hundred yards.

5. Contrasting Views of Measurement

The point of this long digression on the applied theory of errors of measurement is that this theory is a fragment of probability theory that throws into stark relief the practical contrast between Bayesian and acceptance views of the growth of knowledge.

According to the Bayesian view, what we obtain as a result of measurement is a *probability distribution* that characterizes the quantity being measured. This is similar to R. A. Fisher's *fiducial distribution* when the original distribution of error is taken to be continuous. If D_E is the Normal distribution of error E (note that it must be a single distribution on the standard

Bayesian view) and m_Q is the measured value of the quantity Q, then we obtain the distribution of the quantity Q by way of the pivotal quantity $Q - E = m_Q$. Note that our posterior beliefs about Q are distributed normally with mean m_Q and variance equal to the variance of D_E.

The Bayesian view can be rendered a bit more plausible by means of a couple of ploys. First we can construe the normative dimension in the fashion of *robust Bayesianism*: this would allow the same kind of approximation we considered before. Second, while under any Bayesian view, measurement errors are *not* independent—knowing something about one error would tell you something about the next error—we could, in line with the robust treatment of error distributions, simply suppose that the effect of a few observations on the distribution is negligible.

In contrast, the acceptance view would hold that for some small ε we just tolerate a probability of less than ε of making a mistake and *accept* the proposition that Q lies in the interval $[m_Q - k\delta^*, m_Q + k\delta^*]$, where δ^* represents the variance of bounding set of normal distributions and k is chosen to ensure that the probability of the interval claim is greater than $1 - \varepsilon$.

One might adopt an "ordinary-language" or "commonsense" argument and say that common sense argues for an acceptance view measurement, since that is the way we treat measurement in the real world of science and engineering. We do want to be guided, as much as we can be, by commonsense practice. I do not think that such an argument should be dismissed lightly. But a little more attention to detail will show that there are a number of issues that should not be disregarded.

There are certainly awkwardnesses entailed by even the robust Bayesian view. The typical scientific or engineering pronouncement that the quantity Q is $6.38 \pm .05$ meters becomes simply unjustified and irrational. According to Carnap, that most tolerant of men, this way of talking is just a casual and harmless way of saying what should *strictly* be expressed as "the probability of Q being $6.38 \pm .05$ meters is high, given the (measurement) evidence we have" (Kyburg 1968b, "Discussion," pp. 146–150).

There are further difficulties associated with the requirements briefly alluded to before: the requirement that we stipulate what kinds of statements may be accepted as evidence; the circumstances under which they may be so accepted; the difficulty that once accepted, evidence statements are with us forever; and the existence, and particularly the justification, of the required prior distribution.

The difficulties attendant on the acceptance view, as I have simplemindedly articulated it here, may seem at first sight to be even more serious. The acceptance view does seem to reflect the way scientists and engineers and even ordinary people tend to talk: "What is the melting point of compound X?" "About 49 degrees." Or "49.42 ± .05 degrees."

What happens that is so bad? There is the threat of regress: If everything we accept is based on high probability (practical certainty), how do we get the show on the road? If nothing is immune from revision, how do we handle evidence, which may need to be withdrawn? How do we decide on a plausible value of "incredibility" ε? All these are serious issues, and most of them have been touched upon elsewhere (Kyburg 1990, 1994). The problem I want to focus on here is the problem of potential inconsistency.

6. Inconsistency

Let us denote our *acceptance level* by $1 - \alpha$. We suppose that we are *just* willing to be in error a fraction α of the time. If, as a result of measurement, we are just allowed to accept "$Q_1 \in [p_1, q_1]$" and "$Q_2 \in [p_2, q_2]$," then their conjunction, "$Q_1 \in [p_1, q_1] \wedge Q_2 \in [p_2, q_2]$," will *not* be probable enough for acceptance, because in general $P(S) \geq 1 - \alpha$ and $P(T) \geq 1 - \alpha$ do not imply $P(S \wedge T) \geq 1 - \alpha$.

One answer to the failure of conjunction seems simple enough: it is the answer typically provided by the creators of nonmonotonic logics. Typically, in such cases one characterizes *extensions* of a set of evidence statements or "facts" as the deductive closures of the application of a maximal sequence of nonmonotonic rules. Thus, if we treated probabilistic acceptance as a kind of nonmonotonic rule, we would be assured that if there is an extension that contains both S and T, that extension would also contain $(S \wedge T)$.

So why not stipulate that probabilistic acceptance be treated as a non-monotonic rule? A construction along these lines, called sequential thresholding, has been suggested by C. M. Teng (1997). Consider a sequence of applications of probabilistic acceptance at the $1 - \alpha$ level: accept S_1 as a result of the first application just in case the probability of S_1 relative to the background knowledge BK and evidence E is greater than or equal to $1 - \alpha$; accept S_i as a result of the i'th application just in case the probability of S_i relative to the union of BK, E, and the set of sentences accepted as a result of the first $i - 1$ applications of the acceptance rule, is greater than $1 - \alpha$.

Formally, $EX_{1-\alpha}(BK, E)$ is a probabilistic extension of level $1 - \alpha$ generated from evidence E and background knowledge BK just in case there is a sequence of statements S_i, $i \leq n$ such that

1. $P(S_1 \mid BK \cup E) \subseteq [1 - \alpha, 1]$,
2. $P(S_i \mid BK \cup E \cup \bigcup_{j<i}\{S_j\}) \subseteq [1 - a, 1]\{S_j\})$,
3. $\forall S(P(S \mid BK \cup E \cup \bigcup_{j \leq n}\{S_j\}) \subseteq [1 - a, 1] \rightarrow BK \cup E \cup \bigcup_{j \leq n} \{S_j\} \vdash S)$, and
4. $EX_{1-\alpha}(BK, E) = \{S: BK \cup E \cup \bigcup_{j \leq n}\{S_j\} \vdash S\}$.

As Teng points out, this would give what many people would regard as a satisfactory treatment of the lottery. Suppose there are n tickets and that m is the largest integer such that $1 - 1/(n - m) \geq 1 - \alpha$. Then we have $\binom{n}{m}$ extensions, each of which specifies m losers. Since these are distinct extensions, each is perfectly consistent and even deductively closed.

How does the paradox of the preface fare? Just the way Pollock would like it to: we can believe everything in the book (as long as the demurrer in the preface is not regarded as part of the book). Measurement turns out equally well: sequential thresholding helps precisely because errors of measurement are, for good empirical reasons, known to be independent; the error made on the second measurement is independent of the error made on the first measurement.

Let us examine the way Teng's idea applies to measurement. Let the statements $S_1, \ldots, S_n$, be the high-probability results of measurement: $S_i = \ulcorner Q_i \in I_i \urcorner$. In each case we have $P(S_i \mid BK \cup E) = [p_i, q_i]$ where $p_i \geq 1 - \alpha$. Since the probability of error made in one measurement is probabilistically independent of the error made in another measurement,[4] $P(Q_i \in I_i \mid BK \cup E \cup \bigcup_{j<i}\{Q \in I_j\}) = P(Q_i \in I_i \mid BK \cup E)$. Thus, any number of measurement statements can appear in a deductively closed extension. We need not worry, on this construction, about the fact that the probability of $(S \wedge T)$ is generally less than the probability of T.

This is a very nice result. But before we celebrate too much, let us see what happens when $q^m < \alpha$, that is, when $1 - q^m > 1 - \alpha$. Let C_m be the conjunction of m measurement statements $S_i = \ulcorner Q_i \in I_i \urcorner$, where m is the least natural number such that $q^m < \alpha$. Each of these measurements is to be made by a method M that yields a result $\ulcorner Q_i \in I_i \urcorner$ whose probability is $[p, q]$, where $p \geq 1 - \alpha$. The probability that the ith result is false, that is, the probability of $\ulcorner \neg Q_i \in I_i \urcorner$, is $[1 - q, 1 - p]$. Since all the errors are independent, the probability that all the measurement statements are true is the product of the probabilities that each is true. We are talking of intervals, but the intervals are derived from distributions, and from the underlying distribution we may derive, with the independence of the errors, that $P(C_m \mid E \cup BK) \subseteq [p^m, q^m]$ and thus that $P(\neg C_m \mid E \cup BK) \subseteq [1 - q^m, 1 - p^m]$. But note that we have $q^m \leq \alpha$ and thus $1 - q^m \geq 1 - \alpha$.

This is not a total disaster, because of course when we have added $\neg C_m$ to our extension, that will eventually have a bearing on the probabilities of the statements, S_i for $i < m$. Specifically, consider accepting $\neg C_m$. Compute the probability of S_i given $\neg C_m$, $P(S_1 \mid BK \cup E \cup \{\neg C_m\})$. This may well exceed $1 - \alpha$. But there will come a k such that $P(S_k \mid BK \cup E \cup \bigcup_{i<k}\{S_i\} \cup \{\neg C_m\}) < 1 - \alpha$. At that point our extension runneth over. Of course there will also be a lot of other extensions; but that just means that we are back in the difficult multiextension situation that characterized the lottery problem.

Although many nonmonotonic logicians seem to see nothing wrong with multiple extensions, from a normative point of view it is hard to know how to interpret them. If my group needs six measurements to complete the design of a widget, we may be out of luck unless we each *happen* to adopt an extension in which that conjunction occurs. If I have preferred some other set of measurements, so that the sixth measurement is not acceptable in *my* extension, the project may be doomed!

7. A Commonsense Solution?

We seem to be caught between a rock (the implausibility and unreality of Bayesianism) and a hard place (multiplicity of extensions). Note that if we take α to be something reasonable, like .01 or .001, m is only 458 or 6,904. These are numbers that will quickly be exceeded by any busy laboratory.

Thus, this is a real problem if we are trying to represent realistic, common sense, inference from a normative philosophical point of view or from the point of view of computer science, where we seek to find rules that machines can follow uniformly.

One idea worth exploring is that of adopting a slightly different logic—one that allows us to be more tolerant of inconsistency. A useful side effect of this approach would be that it is independently desirable when we need to use large databases. Any realistic database is going to embody implicit, if not explicit, contradictions. It will embody an explicit contradiction if one operator enters "$F(a) = 6.0$" and another enters "$F(a) = 7.0$," where "F" is a function symbol, like "age of." The database will embody an implicit contradiction if one operator enters "$green(a)$" and another (color-blind) operator enters "$red(a)$." Even more to the point (and this is an actual instance), the database may contradict common sense by containing such a pair of entries as "vehicle n; first oil change: Koblenz, May 10, 17,500 Km" and "vehicle n; second oil change: Geneva, May 1, 20,000 Km." Common sense says that something is wrong.

There are a number of "paraconsistent" logics to which we may turn for help. Recall the definition of a probabilistic extension: the final clause said that closed under deduction. But perhaps classical deduction should be replaced by some species of paraconsistent deduction. In particular, the paraconsistent logic that seems to do the least violence to our classical intuitions is that of P. Schotch and R. Jennings (1989, p. 311).

Schotch and Jennings introduce a derivability relation they call forcing that is very close in spirit to the classical one. It is characterized in terms of structural rules in a Gentzen style system. We write "$\Gamma \mathrel{\Box\!\!-} \Delta$" to mean that the set of formulas Γ forces one of the formulas in Δ to be true. The rules of the system differ only slightly from the rules of the classical system. To state them, we must introduce the notion of level (Schotch and Jennings 1989, p. 311).

DEFINITION 7.1
$Con(\Gamma, \xi)$ iff there is a family of sets $\{a_i\}_{i \in \xi \leq w}$ such that $\bigcup_{i \in \xi} a_i = \Gamma$ and each set a_i is classically consistent.

Con spells out a kind of consistency: how much can you swallow before you get logical indigestion? The minimum number of ways of splitting Γ into subsets, each of which is consistent, is the level of Γ (Schotch and Jennings 1989, p. 311):

DEFINITION 7.2
$\ell(\Gamma) = \text{Min}_\xi(Con[\Gamma, \xi])$ if this limit exists; infinite otherwise.

We have similar definitions that are to be thought of as applying to conclusion sets:

DEFINITION 7.3
$Con'(\Delta, \xi)$ iff there is a family of sets $\{a_i\}_{i \in \xi \leq w}$ such that $\bigcup_{i \in \xi} a_i = \Delta$ and none of the sets a_i is provable.

DEFINITION 7.4

$\ell'(\Delta) = \text{Min}_\xi(Con'[\Delta, \xi])$ if this limit exists; infinite otherwise.

In the classical framework, the rule of monotonicity holds:

$$\frac{\Gamma\vdash\Delta\ \&\ \Gamma\subseteq\Gamma'\ \&\ \Delta\subseteq\Delta'}{\Gamma'\vdash\Delta'}$$

In the new system, this only holds when the inclusion is between sets of the same level. Let $\Gamma\subseteq^*\Gamma'$ stand for $\Gamma\subseteq\Gamma'$ and $\ell(\Gamma)=\ell(\Gamma')$ and $\Delta\subseteq^*\Delta'$ stand for $\Delta\subseteq\Delta'$ and $\ell(\Delta)=\ell(\Delta')$. Monotonicity becomes:

$$\frac{\Gamma\square\vdash\Delta\ \&\ \Gamma\subseteq^*\Gamma'\ \&\ \Delta\subseteq^*\Delta'}{\Gamma'\square\vdash\Delta'}$$

In order to preserve as much as we can of classical logic, we incorporate the rule:

$$\frac{\Gamma\vdash\Delta}{\Gamma\square\vdash\Delta},$$

where Γ and Δ are singular, that is, $\{\alpha\}$ for some α, or $\emptyset$.

Two of the usual rules must be constrained by considerations of level:

$$\frac{\Gamma\square\vdash\alpha_1,\Delta\ \&\ \dots\&\ \Gamma\square\vdash\alpha_k,\Delta}{\Gamma\square\vdash\{\alpha_i\wedge\alpha_j\},\Delta},\quad 1\leq i\neq j\leq k=\ell(\Gamma)+1$$

$$\frac{\Gamma,\alpha_1\square\vdash\Delta\ \&\ \dots\&\ \Gamma,\alpha_k\square\vdash\Delta}{\Gamma,\{\alpha_i\wedge\alpha_j\}\square\vdash\Delta},\quad 1\leq i\neq j\leq k=\ell(\Delta)+1$$

In addition, some rules that concern the conditional and negation are restricted:

$$\frac{\beta\square\vdash\Delta\ \&\ \Gamma\square\vdash\alpha,\Delta}{\Gamma,\alpha\to\beta\square\vdash\Delta}$$

$$\frac{\square\vdash\alpha,\Delta}{\neg\alpha\square\vdash\Delta}$$

$$\frac{\Gamma,\alpha\square\vdash\bot}{\Gamma\square\vdash\neg\alpha}$$

But the rule for introducing the conditional remains the same:

$$\frac{\Gamma,\alpha\square\vdash\beta,\Delta}{\Gamma\square\vdash\alpha\to\beta,\Delta}$$

Suppose now that we replace the symbol $\vdash$ in the definition of an extension by the symbol $\square\vdash$. The last clause becomes: $EX_{1\text{-}d}(BK, E) = \{S : BK \cup E \cup \bigcup_{j\leq n}\{S_j\}\square\vdash S\}$.

We can accept the results of all our measurements, as well as the result that any conjunction of (say) 458 of them is false without losing our ability to distinguish good inferences from bad ones. We also then have a *single* extension, however many measurements we have: no howling discontinuity occurs at the magic numbers 458 or 6,904. The *levels* of the sets of sentences that comprise the extensions, in these two cases, are not easy to compute even in the simple cases we've been looking at. Suppose we have made 458 measurements and that that is all that is involved in our bodies of knowledge. Then the level of our corpus is two: drop any of those sentences or the sentence $\neg C_{458}$, and we have achieved consistency.

But if α is 0.01 and we have N measurements, then the number of candidates for $\neg C_{458}$ is $\binom{N}{458}$. Consider a conjunction of k distinct statements of the form $\neg C_{458}$. We can find a k such that it would be incredible that the conjunction of k of them would be true; so here is a new sort of inconsistency. When one is calculating the levels of consistency of a corpus that contains the results of N measurements, each accepted at the .01 level should be possible, but I find it a bit mind-boggling.

Nevertheless, in this scheme, if we have made a lot of measurements, we can know that some of them are wrong and yet treat them all as if they were correct, so long as we are not considering a conjunction of too many of them. So long as we are dealing with a limited number of measurements, it is rational to assume that they are all correct (within their stipulated bounds).

8. Other Applications

This idea applies more broadly than to measurement, of course. For example, classical statistical testing involves the *nonmonotonic* rejection of a statistical hypothesis H_0, the null hypothesis, at a certain level α, based on the fact that the chance of making an *erroneous* rejection is less than α. To "reject" H_0 is to accept its complement in the set of hypotheses under consideration; it is to add $\overline{H_0}$ to the extension that represents the results of uncertain inference.

But typically a research program will eventuate in the rejection of many null hypotheses. It is, of course, almost certain that, given a lot of rejections, some of them will be erroneous. The situation is parallel to that in measurement.

On Teng's sequential acceptance model we can accept the denials of a finite sequence of (unrelated) null hypotheses, H_0, H_0', H_0'', . . . without getting into conflict with the fact that we know we are going to be wrong some of the time.

A similar treatment may be provided for other sorts of statistical inference: confidence interval inference, ANOVA, and so on. This is important for our general approach, since it is exactly the results of such inference that provide the statistical data that, together with a principled way of determining reference classes, yield our interval-valued probabilities.

Ordinary errors of observation can be treated in this way, too. We may know, on the basis of experience, that in general about one color judgment in a hundred is in error or that about one record in a hundred is entered incorrectly. A given judgment or a given record may, relative to what we know about it, be a random judgement or record with respect to the property of being in error. If so, the probability that it is correct is about .99, and it may be accepted into the corpus or extension of level .99, together with its equally justified pals. At the same time, we should be practically certain that the conjunction of enough of these judgments is false or that in a large number of records there is an error. If we adopt the logic of Schotch and Jennings, all this can be represented safely in a single extension.

There is one drawback to the sequential approach. It strikes me as a bit inflationary. Consider a pair of measurement statements. We can calculate, quite straightforwardly on the assumption of independent error, what the probability is that they are both correct. If $P(Q_1 \in I_1 \mid BK \cup E) = [\mathrm{I} - \alpha, q_1]$ and $P(Q_2 \in I_2 \mid BK \cup E \cup \{Q_1 \in I_1\}) = [\mathrm{I} - \alpha, q_2]$, then $P(Q_1 \in I_1 \land Q_2 \in I_2 \mid BK \cup E) \not\subseteq [\mathrm{I} - \alpha, \mathrm{I}]$. Nevertheless, we are allowing ourselves, according to this treatment, to take as acceptable the conjunction that is not probable enough to get into our extension. There is something odd about this. It makes me feel uncomfortable.

All is not lost if we forgo the sequential approach. We can still get the six measurements we need for the design of our widget, just by requiring that the probability of the conjunctive measurement be high enough. For the conjunction of six measurement statements to be acceptable at the .99 level, assuming the errors are independent, each individual statement should have a lower probability a bit higher than 0.998.

We simply require that the extensions be closed only under the consequences of single accepted statements: no form of adjunction would be allowed. The probability calculus will ensure that all the consequences of any statement that is accepted will also be accepted: $P(S \mid E \cup BK) \subseteq [\mathrm{I} - \alpha, \mathrm{I}]$ and $S \vdash T$ entail that $P(T \mid E \cup BK) \subseteq [\mathrm{I} - \alpha, \mathrm{I}]$.

9. Conclusion

There are some puzzles here, but there are also some observations that are worth making. The route of acceptance certainly seems to conform, as even Carnap recognized, to the way people talk and act. This observation carries only a limited weight. For example, I would not want to reject the classical probability calculus to take account of the fact that human probability judgments that concern very common or very rare events tend to be (as we ordinarily put it) mistaken. No more would I want to modify the laws of arithmetic to take account of common arithmetical mistakes.

A rather stronger argument rests on the proposal that we should be seeking normative standards for uncertain inference. As in the case of arithmetic or the probability calculus, while one may make mistakes, while one may not be able to live up to the normative ideal, one can, by being careful, by seeking the help of machines and other experts, *approach* that ideal. One can't be 100 percent accurate in adding up large columns of figures, but there are various aids one can employ.

An argument against acceptance and in favor of assigning probabilities can be based on the fact that it is probabilities we need as a guide to decision.

Clearly a set of probabilities on the alternatives contemplated in any decision problem is exactly what we want for making decisions: if we can calculate the mathematical expectation of each alternative action, then we're home free.

If we accept that $\ulcorner Q_1 \in I_1 \urcorner$ there is no way in which we can get guidance as to the odds to give on this claim being in error. To be sure, $1 - \alpha$ tells us something: it tells us that the probability of error *relative to BK and E* is at most α. But this is relative to our initial evidence, not relative to our nonmonotonic extension. Relative to that extension, the probability of error is 0.

All this supposes we have the choice between the Bayesian theory and a nonmonotonic acceptance theory. Do we really have such a choice?

A rational human may, as Bayesian enthusiasts claim, have an implicit probability distribution over the statements of his language. (Personally, I doubt it.) Discovering that distribution would be a nontrivial matter. Note that the points of the sample space on which this distribution must be defined are essentially maximally specific stories in the language of the person. But representing that distribution may be simply infeasible. This has been noted by Gil Harman (1986).

In the case of any language powerful enough to be of interest, a probability distribution can only be "given" in some systematic manner. But no such systematic probability distribution has been agreed upon by any significant number of scholars. Furthermore, computing with these probability distributions must be very expensive: the distribution must be updated with every increment in evidence; almost everything must be regarded as relevant to everything else (errors of measurement are not independent); the distributions must be based on something analogous to Carnap's state descriptions (1950) in level of detail.

The nonmonotonic views I have been describing also refer to probabilities, of course. The difference is that these can be construed as objective, frequency-based probabilities. Although there is as yet no agreed-upon solution to the problem of the reference class (*which* frequency do we base a probability on?), the prospects for a computationally feasible solution to the problem are encouraging (Loui 1988). The upshot, as I foresee it, would be a set of interval-valued probabilities for the statements of a regimented language, relative to a set of background statements *BK*; but many of these probabilities could be represented by the uninformative interval [0, 1].

Although interval-valued probabilities may be feasible in a way that a priori probabilities are not, they also fail to provide the nice solution to the problem of decision that a priori probabilities provide. From interval-valued probabilities what we get are interval-valued expectations and thus perhaps no unique maximal expectation. This makes decision theory more difficult; however, since the interval values are related to empirical frequencies or chances, there is at least some kind of connection between expectation and what happens in the world. While the occasion of our decision is unique and thus not a fit subject for either frequencies or chances, intuitively there is something reassuring about such a connection.

None of this can be construed as a knockdown argument against the Bayesian view of the world. The strongest part of the argument, to my mind, is that which involves the feasibility of the computations required. But neither sort of epistemology has really been implemented in a fully satisfactory manner, and both deserve further exploration and development. Nevertheless, I'm betting on some form of the acceptance view.

As for the difference between sequential and nonsequential nonmonotonic acceptance, I am simply unsure what to say. On the one hand, demanding of each statement in the extension that it have a probability relative to BK and E that is over $1 - \alpha$ may be thought to cramp too severely our ability to use information that is "practically certain." On the other hand, to accept the forceful closure of an extension, while it does not lead to the kind of explosive disaster that full classical deductive closure would entail, does lead to anomalies. For example, if we have $\neg C_n$ in our extension, we may treat as perfectly acceptable premises the conjunction of the first $n - 1$ measurement statements and $\neg C_n$. But this conjunction, while perfectly consistent, entails that the $n + 1$'st measurement statement is false. But surely, given what we have taken ourselves to know about the measurement process, we should not be certain that the $n + 1$'st measurement statement is false!

NOTES

1. Of course we can't know "only" these two facts; any realistic use of this idea must come to terms with the fact that we not only know a lot of other stuff but know stuff about a beyond "Ra."
2. We may include mathematics as part of our language by taking the language to be two-sorted as suggested in Kyburg 1997.
3. This is plausible, since there are classical confidence interval tests for the mean and variance of a normal (or approximately normal!) distribution.
4. This is so on the view under discussion; it is not true from a Bayesian point of view.

REFERENCES

Bolker, E. (1967). A simultaneous axiomatization of utility and subjective probability. *Philosophy of Science* 34:333–340.

Carnap, R. (1950). *Logical Foundations of Probability*. Chicago: University of Chicago Press.

Harman, G. H. (1986). *Change in View: Principles of Reasoning*. Cambridge: MIT Press-Bradford.

Hempel, C. (1965). *Aspects of Scientific Explanation*, pp. 331–496. New York: Free Press.

Howson, C., and P. Urbach (1993). *Scientific Reasoning: The Bayesian Approach*. LaSalle, IL: Open Court.

Jeffrey, R. C. (1965). *The Logic of Decision*. New York: McGraw-Hill.

Kyburg, H. E. Jr. (1968a). Full belief. *Theory and Decision* 25:137–162.

Kyburg, H. E. Jr. (1968b). The rule of detachment in inductive logic. In I. Lakatos (ed.), *The Problem of Inductive Logic*, pp. 98–165. Amsterdam: North-Holland.

Kyburg, H. E. Jr. (1990). Theories as mere conventions. In W. Savage (ed.), *Scientific Theories*, pp. 158–174. Minneapolis: University of Minnesota Press.

Kyburg, H. E. Jr. (1994). Believing on the basis of evidence. *Computational Intelligence* 10:3–20.

Kyburg, H. E. Jr. (1997). Combinatorial semantics. *Computational Intelligence* 13:215–257.

Levi, I. (1980). *The Enterprise of Knowledge*. Cambridge: MIT Press.

Loui, R. P. (1988). Computing reference classes. In *Proceedings of the Second Conference on Uncertainty in Artificial Intelligence (UAI-1988)*, pp. 273–290. Amsterdam: North-Holland.

Pollock, J. L. (1990). *Nomic Probability and the Foundations of Induction*. New York: Oxford University Press.

Schotch, P., and R. Jennings (1989). On detonating. In *Paraconsistent Logic: Essays on the Inconsistent*, pp. 306–327. Hamden, CT: Philosophia Verlag.

Teng, C. M. (1997). Sequential thresholds: Context-sensitive default extensions. In *Proceedings of the Thirteenth Conference on Uncertainty in Artificial Intelligence (UAI-1997)*, pp. 437–444. San Francisco: Morgan Kaufmann.

5

The Logic of Ordinary Language

GILBERT HARMAN

1. Introduction

Is there a logic of ordinary language? Not obviously. Formal or mathematical logic is, like algebra or calculus, a useful tool that requires its own symbol system, improving on ordinary language rather than analyzing it (Quine 1972). As with algebra and calculus, people need to study this sort of logic in order to acquire any significant facility with it. (Introductory logic teachers can testify to the troubles that ordinary people have with basic principles of formal logic.) Psychologists have demonstrated that almost everyone has difficulty applying abstract principles of formal logic, for example, in the Selection Task (Wason 1983). And, despite claims that logic courses help people reason better, training in formal logic does not appreciably affect how people reason in situations to which abstract logical principles are relevant (Nisbett 1993, 1995).

However, even if modern logic is an *improvement* on ordinary thought and practice, some sort of logic may be built into ordinary language or reflected in ordinary practice. Physics, too, is concerned with improving ordinary thinking, not analyzing it, and ordinary students often have trouble applying principles of physics in solving "word problems." But we can also study naive or folk physics as reflected in ordinary language and in expectations about the behavior of objects in the world (Gentner and Stevens 1983; Hayes

1979, 1985; Ranney 1987). Perhaps we can study naive or folk logic in the same way that we can study naive physics.

But what might distinguish principles of ordinary logic from other ordinary principles? Traditionally, at least three points have been thought to be relevant in distinguishing logic from other subjects. First, logical principles are principles of logical implication or inference; second, logical principles are concerned with *form* rather than content; third, logical principles of implication or inference cannot in general be replaced by corresponding premises.

2. Logical Rules as Normative Rules of Inference

It is sometimes said that some logical principles are normative rules of inference (Blackburn 1994). This isn't quite right, but let us pursue the idea for a while.

The idea is that the principle of disjunctive syllogism, for example, is the principle that it is normatively correct to infer from a disjunction, *P or Q*, together with its denial of one disjunct, *not P*, to its other disjunct, *Q*. This inference would be direct or elementary, warranted by a single principle of inference. More complex inferences or arguments would involve several steps, each step following from premises or previous steps by some acceptable principle of inference.

What is meant here by "inference" and "argument"? If an inference is simply defined as doing whatever accords with the acceptable principles of inference, then we do not learn anything about logic from the remark that logical principles are normative principles of inference or argument. The remark reduces to the empty claim that logical principles are normative principles for doing what satisfies logical principles.

It is natural to suppose that inference and argument are connected with something that ordinary people regularly do—they reason; they infer; they argue. More precisely, people reach conclusions and arrive at new beliefs; as a result of reasoning, they reason to new conclusions or to the abandonment of prior beliefs. Reasoning in this sense is reasoned change in view.

So one version of the idea we are considering takes the logical principle of disjunctive syllogism to be a rule for arriving at new beliefs on the basis of prior beliefs:

Disjunctive Syllogism as a Rule of Inference
If you believe a disjunction *P or Q* and you believe the denial of one of its disjuncts, *not P*, then it is normatively permitted for you to infer and so believe its other disjunct, *Q*.

Using this idea to try to help specify what logic is, we now have that principles of logic are or are among the normative principles of reasoned change in view.

Accepting this idea as a first approximation, we might next ask whether we can distinguish *logical* rules, like disjunctive syllogism, from what G. Ryle (1950) calls "inference tickets" and what contemporary cognitive scientists (e.g., J. R. Anderson [1983] and S. K. Card, T. P. Moran, and A. Newell [1983]) call "productions," as in

Today is Thursday. So tomorrow is Friday.

or

This burns with a yellow flame. So it is sodium.

W. Sellars (1982) argues that a sense of nomic or causal necessity arises from the acceptance of nonlogical inference tickets. Accepting an inference ticket that allows one to infer directly from the premise that something is copper to the conclusion that it conducts electricity is a way of treating the relation between copper and conducting electricity as a necessary or lawlike relation.

One issue, then, for this approach is whether logical principles can be distinguished from nonlogical productions or inference tickets.

3. Logical Rules as Formal and as Irreplaceable by Premises

Here we might turn to the second and third ideas about logic mentioned earlier. The second idea was that logic has to do with *form* rather than content. Perhaps the logical principles are the formal inference tickets. But to explore that thought we need to know how to distinguish "formal" principles from others.

It may help to consider also the third idea, that the acceptance of logical principles is not in general replaceable by the acceptance of premises. Accepting nonlogical productions or inference tickets is in some sense equivalent to accepting certain general conditional statements as premises, statements like "If something is copper, it conducts electricity." But not all productions or inference tickets can be replaced with such premises.

In particular, there is no straightforward generalization that corresponds to disjunctive syllogism (Quine 1970). We can't simply say, "If something or something else and not the first, then the second." To capture the relevant generalization, we might talk of the truth of certain propositions: "If a disjunction is true and the denial of one disjunct is true, then the other disjunct is true." Or we can appeal to a schema "If *P or Q* and *not P*, then *Q*," where this is understood to mean that all instances of this schema are true.

Not only does this provide an interesting interpretation of the notion that logical principles do not derive from corresponding generalizations that concern the relevant subject matter, but it also suggests a way to distinguish form from content for the purposes of saying that logical generalizations are formal. Logical generalizations are formal in that they refer most directly to statements or propositions as having a certain form rather than to nonlinguistic aspects of the world. The logical generalization that corresponds to disjunctive syllogism refers to *disjunctions*, that is, to propositions that have disjunctive form, whereas the nonlogical generalization refers to copper and electricity.

The fact that logical generalizations are generalizations about propositions of a certain linguistic form makes it plausible to suppose that there might be such a thing as the logic *of* a given language—a logic whose generalizations refer to linguistic forms of that language. So it might make sense to speak of the logic of ordinary language or at least of a logic of a particular ordinary language.

Of course, it might turn out that a given ordinary language (or even all ordinary languages) lacked sufficient regularity of form or grammar to permit the statement of logical generalizations. In the early 1950s, many researchers agreed with P. F. Strawson (1950) when he said: "Ordinary language has no exact logic." This is the only claim of Strawson that B. Russell (1957) was willing to endorse. But after Chomsky (1957) and other linguists began to develop generative grammar, many researchers came to think it might be possible after all to develop a logic of ordinary language.

4. Implication and Inference

Before considering further the connection between grammar and logical form, I need to clear up a point left hanging earlier: the relation between implication and inference or, more generally, the relation between arguments as structures of implications and reasoning as reasoned change in view.

The generalization that corresponds to disjunctive syllogism says that whenever a certain two propositions are true, a certain other proposition is true; in other words, the first two propositions *imply* the third. The rule of disjunctive syllogism is a rule of implication or perhaps a rule for recognizing certain implications. All so-called logical rules of inference are really rules of implication in this way.

Logical rules are universally valid; they have no exceptions. But they are not exceptionless universally valid *rules of inference*. So it is not always true that when you believe a disjunction and also believe the denial of one disjunct you may infer and thus believe the other disjunct. For one thing, you may already believe (or have reason to believe) the denial of that other disjunct, so that recognition of the implication indicates that you need to abandon one of the things you started out believing and not just add some new belief. Even if you have no reason to believe the denial of the other disjunct, you may also have no reason to care whether the consequent is true. You may have other things to worry about, such as where you have left your car keys. When you are faced with such a practical problem it is not at all reasonable to make random inferences of conclusions implied by your current beliefs.

Even if logical rules have *something* to do with reasoning, they are in the first instance rules of implication. Rules of implication are distinct from rules of inference even if inference involves the recognition of implication and the construction of arguments (structures of implications). To understand how logic can be relevant to reasoning, we therefore need to understand how the recognition of implication can be relevant to reasoning.

Reasoning may involve the construction of an argument, with premises, intermediate steps, and a final conclusion. Notice, however, that an argument is sometimes constructed backward, starting with the conclusion and working back to the premises, and sometimes in a more complex way, starting in the middle and working in both directions. It is of the utmost importance to distinguish the rules that have to be satisfied for such a structure to be an acceptable argument from procedures to be followed by the reasoner who constructs the argument. The rules of logic may be (among the) rules that have to be satisfied by an argument structure. They are not procedures to be followed for constructing that argument.

A further point is that even when an inference involves the construction of an argument, the conclusion of the inference is not always the same as the conclusion of the argument. The argument may provide an inferred explanation of some data. In that case, the conclusion of the argument is something originally believed and one or more premises of the argument are inferred in an inference to the best explanation.

Of course, there are cases in which the conclusion of an accepted argument is also a new conclusion of one's reasoning; one sometimes does accept something because it is implied by things one previously believes. But it is important that there are other cases of reasoning to which implications and arguments are similarly relevant. In all cases of argument construction, one's most immediate conclusion is probably best taken to be the argument as a whole: one accepts the parts as parts of that whole. There are also cases in which one accepts an argument as valid without accepting all of its parts, although that is no doubt a relatively sophisticated achievement.

Sometimes one accepts an explanatory argument as a whole or chunk, as it were, instantiating a template for the whole argument. In coming to believe what another person says, one typically accepts a complex explanation of the following general form:

P

S is in a position to know whether P.

So S comes to know that P.

S wants me to know whether P.

So S says something to me that means that P.

Presumably, this sort of explanation does not have to be discovered from scratch each time someone tells one something.

5. Principles of Reasoned Change in View

A full account of the relation between rules of logic and principles of reasoning would have to specify the principles of reasoned change in view

(Harman 1986, 1995). Here I can only vaguely sketch the relevant principles with respect to three factors: conservatism, goals, and coherence.

Reasoned change in view is *conservative* in at least two related respects. First, the default position is *no change*. Change in view is what requires justification, not continuing to believe as one already believes. Second, when a change is called for, one seeks, as it were, to minimize the needed change so that one will make the least change that will eliminate inconsistency or answer one's questions.

Reasoned change in view is *goal-directed* in that new views typically arise only because one is interested in answering certain questions (Harman 1997). One's interests control one's reasoning. (This is *not* to say that it is reasonable to accept a conclusion simply because one wants it to be true!)

We can use the term *coherence* to stand in for all the other factors relevant to change in view. Following Pollock (1979), let us distinguish *negative coherence* (lack of incoherence) from *positive coherence* (positive features of a view that justify its acceptance over other views that are at least equally good with respect to answering questions in which one is interested and minimizing changes in one's initial view). Explanation is a coherence-giving factor, as is a certain sort of simplicity (Harman 1994). This is why much inference is inference to the best explanation.

I cannot present here a detailed account of inference. For my purposes here, my main point is that logical rules like disjunctive syllogism are not directly rules of inference but are rules of implication. To "possess" such a rule might mean to have a recognitional capacity—an ability to directly recognize instances of, say, disjunctive syllogism as implications. So-called non-logical inference tickets might also be conceived in this way. They would not really be inference tickets but would be capacities to recognize implications— implication tickets!

The psychology of deduction seeks to discover what procedures people use to decide what follows from what, especially where the implication is not immediate. (It's like studying what procedures people use to add columns of numbers or solve problems in physics.) One theory, defended, for example, by Rips (1994), is that people try to construct arguments in accordance with rules of natural deduction. Another theory, defended by Johnson-Laird (1993), says that people use something like truth tables. That is, they try to consider various possible cases in which the premises could be true in order to see whether the conclusion holds in all those cases. Both of these theories allow that certain implications are recognized directly and immediately while others are recognized indirectly and more slowly, if at all.

6. Knowledge, Truth, and Form

I now want to return to the distinction between form and content, where the logical rules are those that hold by virtue of form and where the nonlogical rules are those that hold by virtue of content. I noted a connection between this idea and the idea that the logical rules are those for which the corresponding generalizations require talk of relations of truth among propositions of certain related forms. However, there are cases in which, although the generalizations that correspond to certain rules appear to require such talk of truth, the rules in question seem less "formal" than other more strictly logical rules.

Consider the rule that *S knows that P* implies P. As with logical principles, there is no appropriate generalization at the same level as the instances of this rule. For example, it does not make sense to say, "If someone knows something, then it." Instead, we have to refer to the truth of the relevant sentences or propositions, as in "All instances of the following implication schema are true: if S knows that P, then P." Or perhaps we can say, "If S knows something, then it is true."

We might try to avoid mention of truth via a principle like the following (suggested to me but not endorsed by David Lewis):

(K*)   If someone knows that something is a certain way, then it is that way.

(K*) does not by itself cover all the instances we want, for example:

(I)   Jack knows that either grass is green or snow is white.

In order to apply (K*) to (I), we might suppose that (I) is equivalent to "Jack knows that the world is such that either grass is green or snow is white." But the principle that lies behind that equivalence is formally similar to the knowledge principle but stronger:

(W*)   The world is such that P implies (and is implied by) P.

Using this principle together with (K*) does not get rid of the need for talk of truth. (Indeed, "the world is such that P" looks like a terminological variant of "it is true that P.")

I mentioned two possible generalizations about truth that correspond to the knowledge principle:

(K1)   All instances are true of "If someone knows that P, then P."
(K2)   If someone knows something, it is true.

Scott Soames observes (private communication) that there is an apparent problem with (K2). Although (K2) seems correct at least at first, puzzles arise concerning what it is that is known and what it is that is true. Ordinary language distinguishes propositions from facts. Propositions can be true or false, can be stated, believed, and disbelieved, and can have certain sorts of structure. Facts can obtain and be known. To know that either grass is green or snow is white is to know the fact that either grass is green or snow is white, not just to know the proposition that grass is green or snow is white. (To know that proposition is to be familiar with it, not necessarily to know that it is true.) But then it is unclear what we would be quantifying over in saying, "If someone knows something, it is true." The thing known is a fact, which is not the sort of thing that is true in the relevant sense. The thing that is true is a proposition, which is not what is known in the relevant sense.

Despite this, (K2) seems a perfectly acceptable remark in ordinary English. And there seem to be many other cases in which ordinary language mixes ontological categories in this way: "The book on the table with the red cover, which weighs three pounds, took four years to write, has been translated into several languages, and has been read by millions of people" (Chomsky forthcoming). The book on the table is a particular physical object. That physical object didn't take four years to write, and it hasn't been read by millions of people. What to say about this very common type of apparent ontological confusion in ordinary language is unclear.

In any event, the immediate point is that we cannot state a generalization that corresponds to the knowledge schema without invoking truth or something equivalent to truth. So, in that respect, the knowledge schema resembles the rule of disjunctive syllogism. So should we say that this principle of knowledge is a logical principle? Is there a logic of knowledge in ordinary language?

The trouble is that the knowledge rule seems less formal and so less like a rule of logic than disjunctive syllogism. So we may be pulled in two different directions. In one respect the rule is like standard logical rules; in another respect it is not.

7. Using (Real) Grammar and Logic to Specify Form

Why does the rule about knowledge seem less formal than disjunctive syllogism? Perhaps because of the difference between *or* and *know*, namely, that *or* is a member of a very small closed lexical class of atomic sentential connectives, whereas *know* is a member of a large and open-ended lexical class of atomic relations (Harman 1976, 1979). To describe a proposition as of the form *P or Q* is therefore to describe it in contrast with a very small closed class of similar structures, perhaps only *P and Q* and *P but Q*. To describe a proposition as of the form *S knows that P* is to describe it in contrast with a large and open-ended class of similar structures in which *knows* is replaced with *believes, hopes, expects, fears, intends, says, denies,* and so forth. A pattern seems relatively formal to the extent that it contrasts with a small closed class of structures and a pattern seems less formal to the extent that it contrasts with a large open class of similar structures.

By an "open lexical class" I mean a class of vocabulary items of the language to which new members are easily added. A "closed lexical class" is a class of vocabulary items to which it is difficult to add new members.

It seems plausible that the logic of ordinary language should be relatively fixed, whereas the nonlogical principles and vocabulary should be relatively easy to change, the form relatively fixed and the content more variable. The vocabulary items that stand for sentential connectives, in other words, the atomic sentential connectives, are relatively fixed; the atomic predicates are not; so particular atomic sentential connectives count as part of form and particular atomic predicates count as part of content. By this criterion, then, to identify a proposition as having the form *S knows that P* is to make a less purely formal identification than to identify a proposition as having the form *P or Q*.

Almost any two vocabulary items differ syntactically in some respect or other, so grammar will not always be preserved when one term replaces the other in an expression in the same class. For example, *and* and *or* do not have exactly the same syntactic distribution; nor do *know* and *believe*. The relevant classes of lexical entries (atomic vocabulary items) are logical classes—the class of atomic predicates, the class of atomic sentential connectives, and so forth.

8. Looser and Stricter Conceptions of Logic

Much more needs to be said here, but suppose that some sort of distinction along these lines between form and content can be made out. Does that mean that the logic of ordinary language does not include the knowledge rule? By one criterion—formality—the answer seems to be that the knowledge rule is not part of the logic of ordinary language. By another criterion, in terms of lack of a straightforward generalization and the resulting need for talk of truth, the answer seems to be that the knowledge rule is part of the logic of ordinary language.

It is not obvious that ordinary reasoning is sensitive to any distinction between logical rules and nonlogical implication tickets. We recognize immediate implications of both sorts. So when we make such a distinction on the basis of ordinary practice and the grammar of ordinary language, we may not be making a distinction that matters to ordinary reasoners.

If it makes no psychological difference, we could simply allow for two senses, looser and stricter, in which a rule is a logical rule. So let us say that a rule is at least *loosely logical* if there is no straightforward corresponding generalization so that we need instead to talk of the truth of certain propositions in order to state the relevant generalization. Let us say that a rule is also *strictly logical* if it is at least a loosely logical rule that appeals only to (relatively) formal aspects of structure. Then, disjunctive syllogism is not only loosely but also strictly logical, whereas the knowledge rule is only loosely logical. Disjunctive syllogism is part of the strict logic of ordinary language, whereas the knowledge rule is only part of the loose logic of ordinary language.

9. Further Issues

A fuller discussion must say something about quantification in ordinary language, as well as identity theory and set theory. In each of these cases there are at least some loosely logical principles, because the corresponding generalization talks of the truth of certain propositions—quantificational principles of generalization and instantiation, a principle of the substitutivity of identity, and a principle of set abstraction. Are there also strictly logical principles of quantification, identity, or set theory built into ordinary language?

What words represent quantifiers? It might seem that there are indefinitely many such words, *all, some, few, many, most, several lots, one, two, three, four* . . . This would mean that quantifier words formed a large open set and thus were not logical constants. So the relevant principles of quantification would only be loosely logical principles, not strictly logical principles by the criterion given here.

But perhaps a better syntactic-semantic analysis distinguishes some of these words from others, treating most of them as predicates or relations of sets of groups of things. The quantifiers as atomic variable-binding operators would be the smaller group *a, the, some, all, each,* and *every.* Notice we can say "the many apples," "every few years," or "all nine ministers," but not "the all apples," "every some years," "nine few years," or "all many apples." We say the apples were most, all, or some of the fruit, treating *most, all,* and *some* as indicating relations between sets.

This approach needs to be developed further in order to determine what, if any, strict quantificational logic it would find in ordinary language. Clearly, this logic would not be the logic of the syllogism, which treats *all* and *some* as logical constants.

As far as the logic of identity and the logic of sets are concerned, if these logics are expressed using atomic relational predicates (perhaps the copula *be* used in one or another sense), then they must be loose logics only, because the class of atomic predicates is large and open-ended. However, we have just seen that some sort of reference to sets is tied into the ordinary system of quantification. Furthermore, a notion of nonidentity or distinctness is also involved in the system of quantification in ordinary language (Wittgenstein 1922). Two different quantifiers with the same scope cannot be treated as referring to the same things, so, for example, the remark "everyone is loved by someone" is not made true simply because (if it happens) everyone loves him- or herself. Similarly, assumptions about distinctness are built into certain grammatical constructions, so that the subject and object of a verb cannot be interpreted to refer to the same thing unless a reflexive construction is used. Compare *Mark saw the chairman in the mirror* and *Mark saw himself in the mirror.*

Therefore, it is quite likely that if there is a strict logic of quantification built into ordinary language, that logic will also incorporate some aspects of the logic of identity and the logic of sets. However, it is unclear to me just what the relevant principles would be.

REFERENCES

Anderson, J. R. (1983). *The Architecture of Cognition.* Hillsdale, NJ: Erlbaum.
Blackburn, S. (1994). Rule of inference. *The Oxford Dictionary of Philosophy,* pp. 334–335. New York: Oxford University Press.
Card, S. K., T. P. Moran, and A. Newell (1983). *The Psychology of Human–Computer Interaction.* Hillsdale, NJ: Erlbaum.
Chomsky, N. (1957). *Syntactic Structures.* The Hague: Mouton.
Chomsky, N. (forthcoming). Internalist explorations. Unpublished manuscript.

Gentner, D., and A. L. Stevens (eds.) (1983). *Mental Models*. Hillsdale, NJ: Erlbaum.

Harman, G. (1976). Logic and grammar. In C. Rameh (ed.), *Semantics: Theory and Application. Georgetown University Round Table on Languages and Linguistics*, pp. 173–180. Washington, DC: Georgetown University Press.

Harman, G. (1979). If and modus ponens: A study of the relations between grammar and logical form. *Theory and Decision* 11:41–53.

Harman, G. (1986). *Change in View: Principles of Reasoning*. Cambridge: MIT Press/Bradford.

Harman, G. (1994). Simplicity as a pragmatic criterion for deciding what hypotheses to take seriously. In D. Stalker (ed.), *Grue: The New Riddle of Induction*, pp. 153–171. Peru, IL: Open Court.

Harman, G. (1995). Rationality. In E. E. Smith and D. N. Osherson (eds.), *Thinking: An Invitation to Cognitive Science*, vol. 3, pp. 175–212. Cambridge: MIT Press.

Harman, G. (1997). Pragmatism and reasons for belief. In C. B. Kulp (ed.), *Realism/Antirealism and Epistemology*, pp. 123–147. Lanham, MD: Rowman and Littlefield.

Hayes, P. J. (1979). The naive physics manifesto. In D. Michie (ed.), *Expert Systems in the Microelectronic Age*, pp. 242–270. Edinburgh: Edinburgh University Press.

Hayes, P. J. (1985). The second naive physics manifesto. In J. R. Hobbs and R. C. Moore (eds.), *Formal Theories of the Commonsense World*, pp. 1–36. Norwood, NJ: Ablex.

Johnson-Laird, P. N. (1993). *Human and Machine Thinking*. Hillsdale, NJ: Erlbaum.

Nisbett, R. (1993). *Rules for Reasoning*. Hillsdale, NJ: Erlbaum.

Nisbett, R. (1995). Which inferential rules are easy to change, and which hard? Lecture at the Rutgers Conference on Epistemology and Evolutionary Psychology, New Brunswick, NJ, April 22.

Pollock, J. (1979). A plethora of epistemological theories. In G. Pappas (ed.), *Justification and Knowledge*, pp. 93–114. Dordrecht, Holland: D. Reidel.

Quine, W. V. (1970). *Philosophy of Logic*. Englewood Cliffs, NJ: Prentice-Hall.

Quine, W. V. (1972). Methodological reflections on current linguistic theory. In D. Davidson and G. Harman (eds.), *Semantics of Natural Language*, pp. 442–454. Dordrecht, Holland: D. Reidel.

Ranney, M. (1987). Changing naive conceptions of motion. Ph.D. diss., University of Pittsburgh, Learning Research and Development Center.

Rips, L. J. (1994). *The Psychology of Proof: Deductive Reasoning in Human Thinking*. Cambridge: MIT Press.

Russell, B. (1957). Mr. Strawson on referring. *Mind* 66:385–389.

Ryle, G. (1950). "If," "so," and "because." In M. Black (ed.), *Philosophical Analysis: A Collection of Essays*, pp. 323–340. Ithaca, NY: Cornell University Press.

Sellars, W. (1982). *Science and Metaphysics: Variations on Kantian Themes*. New York: Humanities Press.

Strawson, P. F. (1950). On referring. *Mind* 59:320–344.

Wason, P. C. (1983). Realism and rationality in the selection task. In J. St. B. T. Evans (ed.), *Thinking and Reasoning: Psychological Approaches*, pp. 44–75. London: Routledge and Kegan Paul.

Wittgenstein, L. (1922). *Tractatus Logico-Philosophicus*. London: Routledge & Kegan Paul.

6

Knowledge and Coherence

PAUL THAGARD, CHRIS ELIASMITH,
PAUL RUSNOCK, &
CAMERON SHELLEY

1. Introduction

Many contemporary philosophers favor coherence theories of knowledge
(Bender 1989; BonJour 1985; Davidson 1986; Harman 1986; Lehrer 1990).
But the nature of coherence is usually left vague, with no method provided
for determining whether a belief should be accepted or rejected on the
basis of its coherence or incoherence with other beliefs. S. Haack's (1993)
explication of coherence relies largely on an analogy between epistemic
justification and crossword puzzles. We show in this chapter how epistemic
coherence can be understood in terms of maximization of constraint satisfaction, in keeping with computational models that have had a substantial
impact in cognitive science. A coherence problem can be defined in terms of
a set of elements and sets of positive and negative constraints between pairs
of those elements. Algorithms are available for computing coherence by
determining how to accept and reject elements in a way that satisfies
the most constraints. Knowledge involves at least five different kinds of
coherence—explanatory, analogical, deductive, perceptual, and conceptual
—each requiring different sorts of elements and constraints.

Portions of this chapter previously appeared in Paul Thagard, *Coherence in
Thought and Language* (Cambridge: MIT Press, 2000), chapter 3, and are reprinted
by permission.

After specifying the notion of coherence as constraint satisfaction in more detail, we show how explanatory coherence subsumes Haack's recent "foundherentist" theory of knowledge. We show how her crossword puzzle analogy for epistemic justification can be interpreted in terms of explanatory coherence and describe how her use of the analogy can be understood in terms of analogical coherence. We then give an account of deductive coherence, showing how the selection of mathematical axioms can be understood as a constraint satisfaction problem. Moreover, visual interpretation can also be understood in terms of satisfaction of multiple constraints. After a brief account of how conceptual coherence can also be understood in terms of constraint satisfaction, we conclude with a discussion of how our "multi-coherence" theory of knowledge avoids many criticisms traditionally made of coherentism.

2. Coherence as Constraint Satisfaction

Although coherence theories have been very popular in contemporary epistemology and ethics, coherence has been very poorly specified compared to deductive logic and probability theory. Coherence can be understood in terms of maximal satisfaction of multiple constraints, in a manner informally summarized as follows (Thagard and Verbeurgt 1998):

1. Elements are representations such as concepts, propositions, parts of images, goals, actions, and so on.
2. Elements can cohere (fit together) or incohere (resist fitting together). Coherence relations include explanation, deduction, similarity, association, and so on. Incoherence relations include inconsistency, incompatibility, and negative association.
3. If two elements cohere, there is a positive constraint between them. If two elements incohere, there is a negative constraint between them.
4. Elements are to be divided into ones that are accepted and ones that are rejected.
5. A positive constraint between two elements can be satisfied either by accepting both of the elements or by rejecting both of the elements.
6. A negative constraint between two elements can be satisfied only by accepting one element and rejecting the other.
7. A coherence problem consists of dividing a set of elements into accepted and rejected sets in a way that satisfies the most constraints.

More precisely, consider a set E of elements that may be propositions or other representations. Two members of E, e_1 and e_2, may cohere with each other because of some relation between them, or they may resist cohering with each other because of some other relation. We need to understand how to make E into as coherent a whole as possible by taking into account the coherence and incoherence relations that hold between pairs of members of E. To do this, we can partition E into two disjoint subsets, A and R, where A contains the accepted elements of E and R contains the rejected elements of E. We want to perform this partition in a way that takes into account the local coherence and incoherence relations. For example, if E is a set of propositions and e_1 explains e_2, we want to ensure that if e_1 is accepted into A, then so is e_2. However, if e_1 is inconsistent with e_3, we want to ensure that if e_1 is accepted into A, then e_3 is rejected into R. The relations of explanation and inconsistency provide constraints on how we decide what can be accepted and rejected. Different constraints can be of different strengths, represented by a number w, the weight of a constraint.

This informal characterization of coherence as maximization of constraint satisfaction can be made mathematically precise, and algorithms are available for computing coherence (see appendix A). Connectionist (neural network) models that are commonly used in cognitive science provide a powerful way of approximately maximizing constraint satisfaction. In such models, each element is represented by a neuronlike unit, positive constraints are represented by excitatory links between units, and negative constraints are represented by inhibitory links between units. Appendix A outlines in more detail how connectionist networks can be used to compute solutions to coherence problems.

Characterizing coherence in terms of constraint satisfaction does not in itself provide a theory of epistemic coherence, for which we need a description of the elements and the constraints relevant to establishing knowledge. Epistemic coherence is a composite of five kinds of coherence, each with its own kinds of elements and constraints. We will first review explanatory coherence, showing how it subsumes Haack's recent foundherentist epistemology.

3. Haack's Foundherentism and Explanatory Coherence

Haack's 1993 book, *Evidence and Inquiry: Towards Reconstruction in Epistemology,* presents a compelling synthesis of coherentist and foundationalist epistemologies. From coherentism she incorporates the insights that there are no indubitable truths and that beliefs are justified by the extent to which they fit with other beliefs. From empiricist foundationalism she incorporates the insights that not all beliefs make an equal contribution to the justification of beliefs and that sense experience deserves a special, if not completely privileged, role. She summarizes her foundherentist view with the following two principles (1993, p. 19):

(FH1)   A subject's experience is relevant to the justification of his empirical beliefs, but there need be no privileged class of empirical beliefs justified exclusively by the support of experience, independently of the support of other beliefs.

(FH2)   Justification is not exclusively one-directional but involves pervasive relations of mutual support.

Haack's explication of "pervasive relations of mutual support" relies largely on an analogy with how crossword puzzles are solved by fitting together clues and possible interlocking solutions.

To show that Haack's epistemology can be subsumed within our account of coherence as constraint satisfaction, we will reinterpret her principles in terms of Thagard's theory of explanatory coherence (TEC) and describe how crossword puzzles can be solved as a constraint satisfaction problem by the computational model (ECHO) that instantiates TEC. TEC is informally stated in the following principles (Thagard 1989, 1992a, 1992b):

> *Principle E1: Symmetry.* Explanatory coherence is a symmetrical relation, unlike, say, conditional probability.

> *Principle E2: Explanation.* (1) A hypothesis coheres with what it explains, which can be either evidence or another hypothesis; (2) hypotheses that together explain some other proposition cohere with each other; and (3) the more hypotheses it takes to explain something, the lower the degree of coherence.

> *Principle E3: Analogy.* Similar hypotheses that explain similar pieces of evidence cohere.

> *Principle E4: Data Priority.* Propositions that describe the results of observations have a degree of acceptability on their own.

> *Principle E5: Contradiction.* Contradictory propositions are incoherent with each other.

> *Principle E6: Competition.* If *P* and *Q* both explain a proposition and if *P* and *Q* are not explanatorily connected, then *P* and *Q* are incoherent with each other. (*P* and *Q* are explanatorily connected if one explains the other or if together they explain something.)

> *Principle E7: Acceptance.* The acceptability of a proposition in a system of propositions depends on its coherence with them.

The last principle, "Acceptance," states the fundamental assumption of coherence theories that propositions are accepted on the basis of how well they cohere with other propositions. It corresponds to Haack's principle FH2 that acceptance does not depend on any deductionlike derivation but on relations of mutual support. Principle E4, "Data Priority," makes it clear that TEC is not a pure coherence theory that treats all propositions equally in the assessment of coherence but, like Haack's principle FH1, gives a certain priority to experience. Like Haack, however, TEC does not treat sense experience as the source of given, indubitable beliefs but allows the results of observation and experiment to be overridden based on coherence considerations. For this reason, it is preferable to treat TEC as affirming a kind of discriminating coherentism rather than as a hybrid of coherentism and foundationalism (see the discussion of indiscriminateness in section 8).

TEC goes beyond Haack's foundherentism in specifying more fully the nature of the coherence relations. Principle E2, "Explanation," describes how coherence arises from explanatory relations: when hypotheses explain

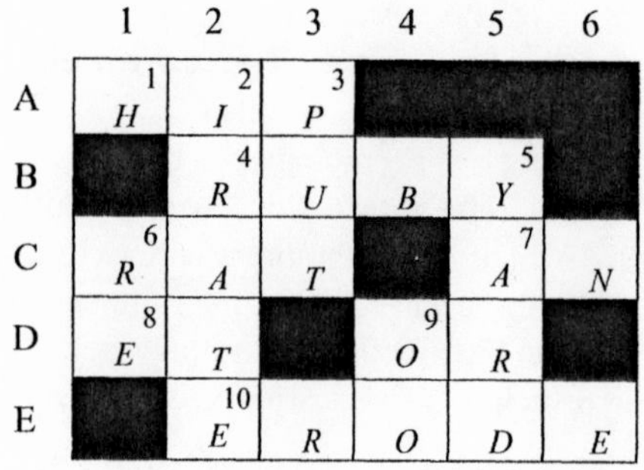

	1	2	3	4	5	6
A	¹H	²I	³P	■	■	■
B	■	⁴R	U	B	⁵Y	■
C	⁶R	A	T	■	⁷A	N
D	⁸E	T	■	⁹O	R	■
E	■	¹⁰E	R	O	D	E

ACROSS	DOWN
1 A cheerful start (3)	2 Angry Irish rebels (5)
4 She's a jewel (4)	3 Have a shot at an Olympic event (3)
6 No, it's Polonius (3)	5 A measure of one's back garden (4)
7 An article (2)	6 What's this all about? (2)
8 A visitor from outside fills this space (2)	9 The printer hasn't got my number (2)
9 What's the alternative? (2)	
10 Dick Turpin did this to York; it wore 'im out (5)	

Consider 4 across — Ruby

How reasonable it is to think this is correct depends on:
(1) the clue
(2) how likely it is that IRATE is correct
(3) how likely it is that PUT is correct
(4) how likely it is that YARD is correct

How reasonable it is to think that IRATE is correct depends on:
(i)   the clue
(ii)   how likely it is that HIP is correct (which also depends on IRATE and PUT)
(iii) how likely it is that RAT is correct (which also depends on IRATE and RE)
(iv)   how likely it is that ET is correct (which also depends on IRATE and RE)
(v)   how likely it is that ERODE is correct (which also depends on IRATE, OO, and YARD)
(vi)   how likely it is that RUBY is correct

How reasonable it is to think that PUT is correct depends on:
(a)   the clue
(b)   how likely it is that HIP is correct (which also depends on IRATE and PUT)
(c)   how likely it is that RAT is correct (which also depends on IRATE and RE)
(d)   how likely it is that RUBY is correct

How reasonable it is to think that YARD is correct depends on:
(a)   the clue
(b)   how likely it is that AN is correct (which also depends on YARD)
(c)   how likely it is that OR is correct (which also depends on YARD and OO)
(d)   how likely it is that ERODE is correct (which also depends on YARD, IRATE, and OO)
(e)   how likely it is that RUBY is correct.

FIGURE 6.1. Crossword used to illustrate coherence relations, adapted from Haack 1993, p. 85.

a piece of evidence, the hypotheses cohere with the evidence and with each other. These coherence relations establish the positive constraints required for the global assessment of coherence in line with the characterization of coherence in section 2. When a hypothesis explains evidence, this establishes a positive constraint that tends to make them either accepted together or rejected together. Principle E3, "Analogy," also establishes positive constraints between similar hypotheses. The negative constraints required for a global assessment of coherence are established by principles E5 and E6, "Contradiction" and "Competition," respectively. When two propositions are incoherent with each other because they are contradictory or in explanatory competition, there is a negative constraint between them that will tend to make one of them accepted and the other rejected. Principle E4, "Data Priority," can also be interpreted in terms of constraints, by positing a special element, EVIDENCE, that is always accepted and has positive constraints with all evidence derived from sense experience. The requirement to satisfy as many constraints as possible will tend to lead to the acceptance of all elements that have positive constraints with EVIDENCE, but their acceptance is not guaranteed. Constraints are *soft*, in that coherence maximizing will tend to satisfy them, but not all constraints will be satisfied simultaneously.

As appendix A shows, the idea of maximizing constraint satisfaction is sufficiently precise that it can be computed using a variety of algorithms. The theory of explanatory coherence TEC is instantiated by a computer program, ECHO, that uses input about explanatory relations and contradiction to create a constraint network that performs the acceptance and rejection of propositions on the basis of their coherence relations. We have used ECHO to simulate the solution of Haack's crossword puzzle analogy for foundherentism. Figure 6.1 is the example that Haack uses to illustrate how foundherentism envisages mutual support. In the crossword puzzle, the clues are analogous to sense experience and provide a basis for filling in the letters. But the clues are vague and do not themselves establish the entries, which must fit with the other entries. Filling in each entry depends not only on the clue for it but also on how the entries fit with one another. In terms of coherence as constraint satisfaction, we can say that there are positive constraints that connect particular letters with one another and with the clues. For example, in 1 across the hypothesis that the first letter is H coheres with the hypotheses that the second letter is I and the third letter is P. Together, these hypotheses provide an explanation of the clue, since "hip" is the start of the cheerful expression "hip hip hooray." Moreover, the hypothesis that I is the second letter of 1 across must cohere with the hypothesis that I is the first letter of 2 down, which, along with other hypotheses about the word for 2 down, provides an answer for the clue for 2 down. These coherence relations are positive constraints that a computation of the maximally coherent interpretation of the crossword puzzle should satisfy. Contradictions can establish incoherence relations: only one letter can fill each square, so if the first letter of 1 across is H, it cannot be another letter.

Appendix B shows in detail how a solution to the crossword can be simulated by the program ECHO, which takes input of the form:

(explain (hypothesis1 hypothesis2 ...) evidence).

For the crossword puzzle, we can identify each square using a system of letters *A–E* down the left side and numbers 1–6 along the top, so that location of the first letter of 1 across is A1. Then we can write A1 = H to represent the hypothesis that the letter *H* fills this square. Writing "C1A" for the clue for 1 across, ECHO can be given the input:

(explain (A1 = H A2 = I A3 = P) C1A)

This input establishes positive constraints among all pairs of the four elements listed, so that the hypothesis that the letters are *H*, *I*, and *P* tends to be accepted or rejected together in company with the clue C1A. Since the clue is given, it is treated as data, and therefore the element C1A has a positive constraint with the special EVIDENCE element that is accepted. For real crossword puzzles, explanation is not quite the appropriate relation to describe the connection between entries and clues, but it is appropriate here because Haack is using the crossword puzzle example to illuminate explanatory reasoning.

The crossword puzzle analogy is useful in showing how beliefs can be accepted or rejected on the basis of how well they fit together. But TEC and ECHO go well beyond the analogy, since they demonstrate how coherence can be computed. ECHO not only has been used to simulate the crossword puzzle example; it also has been applied to many of the most important cases of theory choice in the history of science, as well as to examples from legal reasoning and everyday life (Eliasmith and Thagard 1997; Nowak and Thagard 1992a, 1992b; Thagard 1989, 1992b, 1998). Moreover, ECHO has provided simulations of the results of a variety of experiments in social and educational psychology, so it meshes with a naturalistic approach to epistemology tied with human cognitive processes (Byrne 1995; Read and Marcus-Newhall 1993; Schank and Ranney 1992). Thus, the construal of coherence as constraint satisfaction, through its manifestation in the theory of explanatory coherence and the computational model ECHO, subsumes Haack's foundherentism.

4. Analogical Coherence

Although explanatory coherence is the most important contributor to epistemic justification, it is not the only kind of coherence. In contrast to the central role that the crossword puzzle analogy plays in her presentation of foundherentism, Haack nowhere acknowledges the important contributions of analogies to epistemic justification. TEC's principle E3 allows such a contribution, since it establishes coherence (and hence positive constraints) among analogous hypotheses. This principle was based on the frequent use of analogies by scientists, for example, Darwin's use of the analogy between artificial and natural selection in support of his theory of evolution.

Using analogies, as Haack does when she compares epistemic justification to crossword puzzles, requires the ability to map between two analogs, the

TABLE 6.1. Mapping between epistemic justification and crossword puzzle completion

Epistemic justification	Crossword puzzles
Observations	Clues
Explanatory hypotheses	Words
Explanatory coherence	Words that fit with clues and one another

target problem to be solved and the source that is intended to provide a solution. Mapping between source and target is a difficult computational task, but in recent years a number of computational models have been developed that perform it effectively. Haack's analogy between epistemic justification and crossword puzzles uses the mapping shown in Table 6.1.

Analogical mapping can be understood in terms of coherence and multiple constraint satisfaction, where the elements are hypotheses that concern what maps to what and the main constraints are similarity, structure, and purpose (Holyoak and Thagard 1989). To highlight the similarities and differences with explanatory coherence, we now present principles of analogical coherence:

Principle A1: Symmetry. Analogical coherence is a symmetrical relation among mapping hypotheses.

Principle A2: Structure. A mapping hypothesis that connects two propositions, R(a, b) and S(c, d), coheres with mapping hypotheses that connect R with S, a with c, and b with d; and all those mapping hypotheses cohere with one another.

Principle A3: Similarity. Mapping hypotheses that connect elements that are semantically or visually similar have a degree of acceptability on their own.

Principle A4: Purpose. Mapping hypotheses that provide possible contributions to the purpose of the analogy have a degree of acceptability on their own.

Principle A5: Competition. Mapping hypotheses that offer different mappings for the same object or concept are incoherent with one another.

Principle A6: Acceptance. The acceptability of a mapping hypothesis in a system of mapping hypotheses depends on its coherence with them.

In analogical mapping, the coherence elements are hypotheses that concern which objects and concepts correspond to one another. Initially, mapping favors hypotheses that relate similar objects and concepts (A3). Depending on whether analogs are represented verbally or visually, the relevant kind of similarity is either semantic or visual. For example, when Darwin drew an analogy between natural and artificial selection, both analogs had the verbal representations of selection that had similar meaning. In visual analogies, perceptual similarity can suggest possible correspondences—for example, when the atom with its electrons circling the nucleus is pictorially compared to the solar system with its planets revolving around the sun. We then get the positive constraint: if two objects or concepts in an analogy are visually or semantically similar to each other, then an analogical mapping that puts them in correspondence with each other should tend to be accepted. This kind of similarity is much more local and direct than the more general overall similarity that is found between two analogs. Another positive constraint is pragmatic, in that we want to encourage mappings that can accomplish the purposes of the analogy such as problem solving or explanation (A4).

Additional positive constraints arise because of the need for structural consistency (A2). In the verbal representations (CIRCLE [ELECTRON NUCLEUS]) and (REVOLVE [PLANET SUN]), maintaining structure (i.e., keeping the mapping as isomorphic as possible) requires that if we map CIRCLE to REVOLVE, then we must map ELECTRON to PLANET and NUCLEUS to SUN. The need to maintain structure establishes positive constraints, so that, for example, the hypothesis that CIRCLE corresponds to REVOLVE will tend to be accepted with or rejected with the hypothesis that ELECTRON corresponds to PLANET. Negative constraints occur between hypotheses that represent incompatible mappings—for example, between the hypothesis that the atom corresponds to the sun and the hypothesis that the atom corresponds to a planet (A5). Principles A2 and A5 together incline but do not require analogical mappings to be isomorphisms. Analogical coherence is a matter of accepting the mapping hypotheses that satisfy the most constraints.

The multiconstraint theory of analogy just sketched has been applied computationally to a great many examples and has provided explanations for numerous psychological phenomena. Additional epistemological importance lies in the fact that the constraint-satisfaction construal of coherence provides a way of unifying explanatory and analogical epistemic issues. Take, for example, the traditional philosophical problem of other minds: You know from your conscious experience that you have a mind, but how are you justified in believing that other people, whose consciousness you have no access to, have minds? One common solution to this problem is analogical inference: other people's actions are similar to yours, so perhaps these people are also similar to you in having minds. Another common solution to the problem of other minds is inference to the best explanation: the hypothesis that other people have minds is a better explanation of their behavior than any other available hypothesis, for example, that they are radiocontrolled robots. From the perspective of coherence as constraint satisfaction, analogical inference and best-explanation inference are complementary, not alternative, justifications, because analogical and explanatory coherence considerations can simultaneously work to justify as acceptable the conclusion that other people have minds. Figure 6.2 shows how analogy-based positive constraints mesh with explanation-based positive constraints to establish the acceptability of the hypothesis that other people have minds.

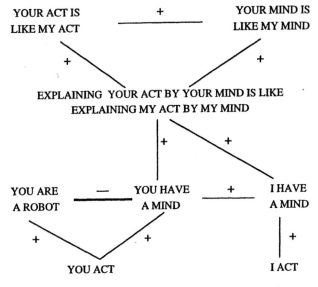

FIGURE 6.2. The problem of other minds incorporating both explanatory and analogical coherence. Plus signs indicate positive constraints and minus signs indicate negative constraints. The hypothesis that you have a mind is evaluated both by comparison of its explanatory power with other hypotheses that explain your behavior and by analogy with my explanations of my own behavior.

Thus, metaphysics, like science, can employ a combination of explanatory and analogical coherence to defend important conclusions. Mathematical knowledge, however, is more dependent on deductive coherence.

5. Deductive Coherence

For millennia, epistemology has been enthralled by mathematics, taking mathematical knowledge as the purest and soundest type. The Euclidean model of starting with indubitable axioms and deriving equally indubitable theorems has influenced many generations of philosophers. Surprisingly, however, Bertrand Russell, one of the giants of the axiomatic method in the foundations of mathematics, had a different view of the structure of mathematical knowledge. In an essay he presented in 1907, Russell remarked on the apparent absurdity of proceeding from recondite propositions in symbolic logic to the proof of such truisms as $2 + 2 = 4$. He concluded:

> The usual mathematical method of laying down certain premises and proceeding to deduce their consequences, though it is the right method of exposition, does not, except in the more advanced portions, give the order of knowledge. This has been concealed by the fact that the propositions traditionally taken as premises are for the most part very obvious, with the fortunate exception of the axiom of parallels. But when we push analysis farther, and get to more ultimate premises, the obviousness becomes less,

and the analogy with the procedure of other sciences becomes more visible. (1973, p. 282)

Just as science discovers hypotheses from which facts of the senses can be deduced, so mathematics discovers premises (axioms) from which elementary propositions (theorems) such as $2 + 2 = 4$ can be derived. Unlike the logical axioms that Russell, following Frege, used to derive arithmetic, these theorems are often intuitively obvious. Russell contrasts the a priori obviousness of such mathematical propositions with the lesser obviousness of the senses but notes that obviousness is a matter of degree and even where there is the highest degree of obviousness we cannot assume that the propositions are infallible, since they may be abandoned because of conflict with other propositions. Thus, for Russell, adoption of a system of mathematical axioms and theorems is much like the scientific process of acceptance of explanatory hypotheses. Let us try to exploit this analogy to develop a theory of deductive coherence.

The elements are mathematical propositions—potential axioms and theorems. The positive and negative constraints can be established by coherence and incoherence relations specified by a set of principles that are adapted from the seven principles of explanatory coherence in section 3.

Principle D1: Symmetry. Deductive coherence is a symmetrical relation among propositions, unlike, say, deducibility.

Principle D2: Deduction. (1) An axiom or other proposition coheres with propositions that are deducible from it; (2) propositions that together are used to deduce some other proposition cohere with each other; and (3) the more hypotheses it takes to deduce something, the less the degree of coherence.

Principle D3: Intuitive Priority. Propositions that are intuitively obvious have a degree of acceptability on their own. Propositions that are obviously false have a degree of rejectability on their own.

Principle D4: Contradiction. Contradictory propositions are incoherent with each other.

Principle D5: Acceptance. The acceptability of a proposition in a system of propositions depends on its coherence with them.

When a theorem is deduced from an axiom, the axiom and theorem cohere symmetrically with each other, which allows the theorem to confer support on the axiom as well as vice versa, just as an explanatory hypothesis and the evidence it explains confer support on each other (D1, D2). Principle D2, "Deduction," is just like the second principle of explanatory coherence, but with the replacement of the coherence-producing relation of explanation by the similarly coherence-producing relation of deduction. These coherence relations are the source of positive constraints: when an axiom and theorem cohere because of the deductive relation between them, there is a positive constraint between them so that they will tend to be accepted together or rejected together. Clause (3) of the principle has the consequence that the weight of the constraint will be reduced if the deduction requires other propositions. Just as scientists prefer simpler theories, other things being equal, Russell looked for simplicity in axiom systems: "Assuming then, that elementary arithmetic is true, we may ask for the fewest and simplest logical principles from which it can be deduced" (1973, pp. 275–276).

Although some explanations are deductive, not all are, and not all deductions are explanatory (Kitcher and Salmon 1989). So explanatory coherence and deductive coherence cannot be assimilated to each other. The explanatory coherence principle E4, "Data Priority," discriminated in favor of the results of sensory observations and experiments, but deductive coherence in mathematics requires a different kind of intuitive obviousness. Russell remarks that the obviousness of propositions such as $2 + 2 = 4$ derives remotely from the empirical obviousness of such observations as "2 sheep + 2 sheep = 4 sheep." Principle D3, "Intuitive Priority," does not address the source of the intuitiveness of mathematical propositions but simply takes into account that it exists. Different axioms and theorems will have different degrees of intuitive priority. D3 provides discriminating constraints that encourage the acceptance of intuitively obvious propositions such as $2 + 2 = 4$. Russell stressed the need to avoid having falsehoods as consequences of axioms, so we have included in D3 a specific mention of intuitively obvious falsehoods being rejected, even though it is redundant: a falsehood can be indirectly rejected because it contradicts an obvious truth. Principle D4, "Contradiction," establishes negative constraints that prevent two contradictory propositions from being accepted simultaneously. For mathematics, these should be constraints with very high weights. The contradiction principle is obvious, but it is much less obvious whether there is competition between mathematical axioms in the same way that there is between explanatory hypotheses.

Whereas there are ample scientific examples of the role of analogy in enhancing explanatory coherence, cases of an analogical contribution to deductive coherence in mathematics are rarer, so our principles of deductive coherence do not include an analogy principle, although analogy is important in mathematical discovery (Polya 1957). Moreover, analogical considerations can enter indirectly into the choice of mathematical principles, by virtue of isomorphisms between areas of mathematics that allow all the theorems in one area to be translated into theorems in the other, as when geometry is translated into Cartesian algebra.

Russell does not explicitly defend a coherentist justification of axiom systems, but he does remark that "we tend to believe the premises because we can see that their consequences are true, instead of believing the consequences because we know the premises to be true" (1973, pp. 273–274; there are additional noncoherence considerations such as independence and convenience that contribute to selection of an axiom set). P. Kitcher (1983, p. 220) sees the contribution of important axiomatizations by Euclid, Cayley, Zermelo, and Kolmogorov as analogous to the uncontroversial cases in which scientific theories are adopted because of their power to unify. Principle D5, "Acceptance," summarizes how axioms can be accepted on the basis

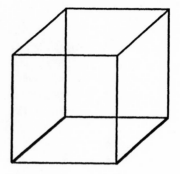

FIGURE 6.3. The Necker cube. The top edge can be seen as being either at the front or at the back of the cube. Try to make it flip back and forth by concentrating on different edges.

of the theorems they yield, while at the same time theorems are accepted on the basis of their derivation from axioms. The propositions to be accepted are just the ones that are most coherent with one another, as shown by finding a partition of propositions into accepted and rejected sets in a way that satisfies the most constraints.

We have discussed deductive coherence in the context of mathematics, but it is also relevant to other domains, such as ethics. According to J. Rawls's notion of reflective equilibrium, ethical principles such as "Killing is wrong" are to be accepted or rejected on the basis of how well they fit with particular ethical judgments such as "Killing Salman Rushdie is wrong" (1971). Ethical coherence is not just deductive coherence, however, since *wide* reflective equilibrium requires finding the most coherent set of principles and particular judgments in the light of background information, which can introduce considerations of explanatory, analogical, and deliberative coherence (Thagard 2000).

6. Perceptual Coherence

Explanatory and deductive coherence both involve propositional elements, but not all knowledge is verbal. Perceptual knowledge can also be thought of as a coherence problem, in accord with modern views of perception as involving inference and constraint satisfaction (Kosslyn 1994; Rock 1983). Vision is not simply a matter of taking sensory inputs and transforming them directly into interpretations that form part of conscious experience, because the sensory inputs are often incomplete or ambiguous. For example, the Necker cube in Figure 6.3 can be seen in two different ways with different front faces. We shall not attempt here anything like a full theory of different kinds of perception but want to sketch how vision can be understood as a coherence problem similar to but different from the kinds of coherence discussed so far.

Visual perception begins with two-dimensional image arrays on the retina, but the visual interpretations that constitute sensory experience are much more complex than these arrays. How does the brain construct a coherent understanding of sensory inputs? In visual coherence, the elements are nonverbal representations of input images and full-blown visual interpretations, which fit together in accord with the following principles:

Principle V1: Symmetry. Visual coherence is a symmetrical relation between a visual interpretation and a sensory input.

Principle V2: Interpretation. A visual interpretation coheres with a sensory input if they are connected by perceptual principles such as proximity, similarity, and continuity.

Principle V3: Sensory Priority. Sensory inputs are acceptable on their own.

Principle V4: Incompatibility. Incompatible visual interpretations are incoherent with each other.

Principle V5: Acceptance. The acceptability of a visual interpretation depends on its coherence with sensory inputs, other visual interpretations, and background knowledge.

Principle V2, "Interpretation," asserts that how an interpretation fits with sensory input is governed by innate perceptual principles such as the ones described in the 1930s by Gestalt psychologists (Koffka 1935). According to the principle of proximity, visual parts that are near each other join together to form patterns or groupings. Thus, an interpretation that joins two visual parts together in a pattern will cohere with sensory input that has the two parts close to each other. According to the Gestalt principle of similarity, visual parts that resemble one another in respect to form size, color, or direction unite to form a homogeneous group. Hence an interpretation that combines parts in a pattern will cohere with sensory input that has parts that are similar to one another. Other Gestalt principles encourage interpretations that find continuities and closure (lack of gaps) in sensory inputs. The visual system also has built into it assumptions that enable it to use cues such as size constancy, texture gradients, motion parallax, and retinal disparity to provide connections between visual interpretations and sensory inputs (Medin and Ross 1999, chapter 5). These assumptions establish coherence relations between visual interpretations and sensory inputs, and thereby provide positive constraints that tend to make visual interpretations accepted along with the sensory inputs with which they cohere.

Image arrays on the retina are caused by physical processes not subject to cognitive control, so we can take them as given (V3). But even at the retinal level considerable processing begins and many layers of visual processing occur before a person has a perceptual experience. The sensory inputs may be given, but sensory experience certainly is not. Sensory inputs may fit with multiple possible visual interpretations that are incompatible with one another and are therefore incoherent and the source of negative constraints (V4).

Thus, the Gestalt principles and other assumptions built into the human visual system establish coherence relations that provide positive constraints that link visual interpretations with sensory input. Negative constraints arise between incompatible visual interpretations, such as the two ways of seeing the Necker cube. Our overall visual experience arises from accepting the visual interpretation that satisfies the most positive and negative constraints. Coherence thus produces our visual knowledge, just as it establishes our explanatory and deductive knowledge.

We cannot attempt here to sketch coherence theories of other kinds of perception—smell, sound, taste, touch. Each would have a different version of Principle V2, "Interpretation," which would involve its own kinds of coherence relations based on the innate perceptual system for that modality.

7. Conceptual Coherence

Given the preceding discussions of explanatory analogical, deductive, and perceptual coherence, the reader might now be worried about the proliferation of kinds of coherence: just how many are there? We see the need to discuss only one additional kind of coherence—conceptual—that seems important for understanding human knowledge.

Different kinds of coherence are distinguished from one another by the different kinds of elements and constraints they involve. In *explanatory* coherence, the elements are propositions and the constraints are explanation-related, but in *conceptual* coherence the elements are concepts and the constraints are derived from positive and negative associations among concepts. Much work has been done in social psychology to examine how people apply stereotypes when forming impressions of other people. For example, you might be told that someone is a woman pilot who likes monster truck rallies. Your concepts of *woman, pilot,* and *monster truck fan* may involve a variety of concordant and discordant associations that need to be reconciled as part of the overall impression you form of this person.

> *Principle C1: Symmetry.* Conceptual coherence is a symmetrical relation between pairs of concepts.
>
> *Principle C2: Positive Association.* A concept coheres with another concept if they are positively associated, that is, if there are objects to which they both apply.
>
> *Principle C3: Given Concepts.* The applicability of a concept to an object may be given perceptually or by some other reliable source.
>
> *Principle C4: Negative Association.* A concept incoheres with another concept if they are negatively associated, that is, if an object that falls under one concept tends not to fall under the other concept.
>
> *Principle C5: Acceptance.* The applicability of a concept to an object depends on the applicability of other concepts.

The stereotypes that some Americans have of Canadians include associations with other concepts such as *polite, law-abiding, beer-drinking,* and

TABLE 6.2. Kinds of coherence and their constraints

	Elements	Positive constraints	Discriminating constraints	Negative constraints
Explanatory	hypotheses, evidence	E2: Explanation E3: Analogy	E4: Data Priority	E5: Contradiction E6: Competition
Analogical	mapping hypotheses	A2: Structure	A3: Similarity A4: Purpose	A5: Competition
Deductive	axioms, theorems	D2: Deduction	D3: Intuitive Priority	D4: Contradiction
Visual	visual interpretations	V2: Interpretation	V3: Sensory Priority	V4: Incompatibility
Conceptual	concepts	C2: Positive Association	C3: Given Concepts	C4: Negative Association

Note: Names such as E2 refer to principles stated in the text.

hockey-playing, where these concepts have different kinds of associations with one another. The stereotype that Canadians are polite (a Canadian is someone who says "thank you" to bank machines) conflicts with the stereotype that hockey players are somewhat crude. If you are told that someone is a Canadian hockey player, what impression do you form of him? Applying stereotypes in complex situations is a matter of conceptual coherence, where the elements are concepts and the positive and negative constraints are positive and negative associations among concepts (C2, C4). Some concepts cohere with each other (e.g., *Canadian* and *polite*), while other concepts resist cohering with each other (e.g., *polite* and *crude*). The applicability of some concepts is given, as when you can see that someone is a hockey player or told by a reliable source that he or she is a Canadian (C3). Many psychological phenomena that concern how people apply stereotypes can be explained in terms of conceptual constraint satisfaction (Kunda and Thagard 1994).

There are thus five primary kinds of coherence relevant to assessing knowledge: explanatory, analogical, deductive, perceptual, and conceptual. (A sixth kind, deliberative coherence, is relevant to decision making; see Millgram and Thagard [1996] and Thagard and Millgram [1995]). Each kind of coherence involves a set of elements and positive negative constraints, including constraints that discriminate to favor the acceptance or rejection of some of the elements, as summarized in Table 6.2. A major problem for the kind of multifaceted coherence theory of knowledge we have been presenting concerns how these different kinds of coherence relate to one another. To solve this problem, we would need to describe in detail the interactions involved in each of the fifteen different pairs of kinds of coherence. Some of these pairs are straightforward. For example, explanatory and deductive coherence involve both propositional elements and very similar kinds of constraints. In addition, section 4 showed earlier how explanatory and analogical coherence can interact in the problem of other minds.

The relation, however, between propositional elements (explanatory and deductive) on the one hand and visual and conceptual elements on the other is obscure, so that it is not obvious how, for example, a system of explanatory coherence can interface with a system of visual coherence. One possibility is that a deeper representational level, such as the systems of vectors used in neural networks, may provide a common substratum for propositional, perceptual, and conceptual coherence (see Eliasmith and Thagard 2001 for a discussion of vector representations of propositions and their use in analogical mapping).

Note that simplicity plays a role in most kinds of coherence. It is explicit in explanatory and deductive coherence, where an increase in the number of propositions required for an explanation or deduction decreases simplicity; and deliberative coherence is similar. Simplicity is implicit in analogical coherence, which encourages 1–1 mappings. Perhaps simplicity plays a role in perceptual coherence as well.

Explanatory, analogical, deductive, perceptual, and conceptual coherence add up to a comprehensive, computable, naturalistic theory of epistemic coherence. Let us now see how this theory can handle some of the standard objections that have been made to coherentist epistemologies.

8. Objections to Coherence Theories

Vagueness

One common objection to coherence theories is *vagueness*: in contrast to fully specified theories of deductive and inductive inference, coherence theories have generally been vague about what coherence is and how coherent elements can be selected. Our general characterization of coherence shows how vagueness can be overcome. First, for a particular kind of coherence, it is necessary to specify the nature of the elements and define the positive and negative constraints that hold between them. This task has been accomplished for the kinds of coherence discussed earlier. Second, once the elements and constraints have been specified, it is possible to use connectionist algorithms to compute coherence, accepting and rejecting elements in a way that approximately maximizes compliance with the coherence conditions (appendix A). Computing coherence then can be as exact as deduction or probabilistic reasoning and can avoid the problems of computational intractability that arise with them. Being able to do this computation does not, of course, help with the problem of generating elements and constraints, but it does show how to make a judgment of coherence with the elements and constraints on hand. Arriving at a rich, coherent set of elements—scientific theories, ethical principles, or whatever—involves a very complex process that intermingles both (1) assessment of coherence and (2) generation of new elements; the parallel constraint satisfaction algorithm shows only how to do the first of these. Whether a cognitive task can be construed as a coherence problem depends on the extent to which it involves evaluation of how existing elements fit together rather than generation of new elements.

Indiscriminateness

The second objection to coherence theories is *indiscriminateness*: coherence theories fail to allow that some kinds of information deserve to be treated more seriously than others. For example, in epistemic justification it has been argued that perceptual beliefs should be taken more seriously in determining general coherence than mere speculation. The abstract characterization of coherence given in section 2 is indiscriminating, in that all elements are treated equally in determinations of coherence.

But all the kinds of coherence discussed earlier are discriminating in the sense of allowing favored elements of E to be given priority in being chosen for the set of accepted elements A. We can define a discriminating coherence problem as one where members of a subset D of E are favored to be members of A. Favoring them does not guarantee that they will be accepted: if there were such a guarantee, the problem would be foundationalist rather than coherentist, and D would constitute the foundation for all other elements. As Audi (1993) points out, even foundationalists face a coherence problem in trying to decide what beliefs to accept in addition to the foundational ones. Explanatory coherence treats hypothesis evaluation as a discriminating coherence problem, since it gives priority to propositions that describe observational and experimental results. That theory is not foundationalist, since evidential propositions can be rejected if they fail to cohere with the entire set of propositions. Similarly, Table 6.2 makes it clear that the other five kinds of coherence are also discriminating.

Computing a solution to a discriminating coherence problem involves only a small addition to the characterization of coherence given in section 2:

> For each element d in the discriminated set D, construct a positive constraint between d and a special element e_s, which is assigned to the set A of accepted elements.

The effect of having a special element that constrains members of the set D is that the favored elements will tend to be accepted, without any guarantee that they will be accepted. For the connectionist algorithm (appendix A), this new discriminating condition is implemented by having an excitatory link between the unit that represents d and a special unit that has a fixed, unchanging maximum activation (i.e., 1). The effect of constructing such links to a special unit is that when activation is updated it flows directly from the activated special unit to the units that represent the discriminated elements. Hence those units will more strongly tend to end up activated than nondiscriminated ones and will have a greater effect on which other units get activated. The algorithm does not, however, enforce the activation of units that represent discriminated elements, which can be deactivated if they have strong inhibitory links with other activated elements. Thus, a coherence computation can be discriminating while remaining coherentist.

We can thus distinguish between three kinds of coherence problems: A *pure* coherence problem is one that does not favor any elements as potentially worthy of acceptance. A *foundational* coherence problem selects a set of favored elements for acceptance as self-justified. A *discriminating* coherence problem favors a set of elements, but their acceptance still depends on their coherence with all the other elements. We have shown how coherence algorithms can naturally treat problems as discriminating without being foundational.

Isolation

The *isolation* objection has been characterized as follows:

> This objection states that the coherence of a theory is an inadequate justification of the theory, because by itself it doesn't supply the necessary criteria to distinguish it from illusory but consistent theories. Fairy tales may sometimes be coherent as may dreams and hallucinations. Astrology may be as coherent as astronomy, Newtonian physics as coherent as Einsteinian physics. (Pojman 1993, p. 191)

Thus, an isolated set of beliefs may be internally coherent but should not be judged to be justified.

Our characterization of coherence provides two ways of overcoming the isolation objection. First, as we just saw, a coherence problem may be discriminating, giving nonabsolute priority to empirical evidence or other elements that are known to make a relatively reliable contribution to solution of the kind of problem at hand. The comparative coherence of astronomy and astrology is thus in part a matter of coherence with empirical evidence, of which there is obviously far more for astronomy than astrology. Second, the existence of negative constraints such as inconsistency shows that we cannot treat astronomy and astrology as isolated bodies of beliefs. The explanations of human behavior offered by astrology often conflict with those offered by psychological science. Astrology might be taken to be coherent on its own, but once it offers explanations that compete with psychology and astronomy, it becomes a strong candidate for rejection. The isolation objection may be a problem for underspecified coherence theories that lack discrimination and negative constraints, but it is easily overcome by the constraint satisfaction approach.

Having negative constraints, however, does not guarantee consistency in the accepted set A. The second coherence condition, which encourages dividing negatively constrained elements between A and R, is not rigid, so there may be cases where two negatively constrained elements both end up being accepted. For a correspondence theory of truth, this is a disaster, since two contradictory propositions cannot both be true. It would probably also be unappealing to most advocates of a coherence theory of truth. To overcome the consistency problem, we could revise the second coherence condition by making it rigid: a partition of elements (propositions) into accepted and rejected sets must be such that if e_i and e_j are inconsistent, then if e_i is in A then e_j *must* be in R. We do not want, however, to defend a coherence theory of truth, since there are good reasons for preferring a correspondence theory based on scientific realism (Thagard 1988, chapter 8).

For a coherence theory of epistemic justification, inconsistency in the set A of accepted propositions is also problematic, but we can leave open the possibility that coherence is temporarily maximized by adopting an inconsistent set of beliefs. One way of dealing with the lottery and proofreading paradoxes is simply by being inconsistent, believing that a lottery is fair while believing of each ticket that it will not win or believing that a paper must have a typographical error in it somewhere while believing of each sentence that it is flawless. A more interesting case is the relation between quantum theory and general relativity, two theories that individually possess enormous explanatory coherence. According to the eminent mathematical physicist Edward Witten,

> The basic problem in modern physics is that these two pillars are incompatible. If you try to combine gravity with quantum mechanics, you find that you get nonsense from a mathematical point of view. You write down formulae which ought to be quantum gravitational formulae and you get all kinds of infinities. (Davies and Brown 1988, p. 90)

Quantum theory and general relativity may be incompatible, but it would be folly given their independent evidential support to suppose that one must be rejected. Another inconsistency in current astrophysics derives from measurements that suggest that the stars are older than the universe. But astrophysics carries on, just as mathematics did when Russell discovered that Frege's axioms for arithmetic lead to contradictions.

From the perspective of formal logic, contradictions are disastrous, since from any proposition and its negation any formula can be derived: from *p* to *p or q* by addition, then from *not-p* to *q* by disjunctive syllogism. Logicians who have wanted to deal with inconsistencies have been forced to resort to relevance or paraconsistent logics. But from the perspective of a coherence theory of inference, there is no need for any special logic. It may turn out that at a particular time that coherence is maximized by accepting a set A that is inconsistent, but other coherence-based inferences need not be unduly influenced by the inconsistency, whose effects may be relatively isolated in the network of elements.

Related to the isolation objection is concern with the epistemic goal of achieving truth. A set of beliefs may be maximally coherent, but what guarantee is there that the maximally coherent system will be true? Assuming a correspondence theory of truth and the consistency of the world, a contradictory set of propositions cannot all be true. But no one ever suggested that coherentist methods guarantee the avoidance of falsehood. All that we can expect of epistemic coherence is that it is generally reliable in accepting the true and rejecting the false. Scientific thinking based on explanatory and analogical coherence has produced theories with substantial technological application, intersubjective agreement, and cumulativity. Our visual systems are subject to occasional illusions, but these are rare compared with the great preponderance of visual interpretations that enable us successfully to interact with the world. Not surprisingly, there is no foundational justification of coherentism, only the coherentist justification that coherentist principles fit well with what we believe and what we do. Temporary tolerance of contradictions may be a useful strategy in accomplishing the long-term aim of accepting many true propositions and few false ones. Hence there is no incompatibility between our account of epistemic coherence and a correspondence theory of truth.

Conservatism

Coherence theories of justification may seem unduly conservative in that they require new elements to fit into an existing coherent structure. This charge is legitimate against serial coherence algorithms that determine for each new element whether accepting it increases coherence or not. The connectionist algorithm in appendix A, however, allows a new element to enter into the full-blown computation of coherence maximization. If units have already settled into a stable activation, it will be difficult for a new element with no activation to dislodge the accepted ones, so the network will exhibit a modest conservatism. But if new elements are sufficiently coherent with other elements, they can dislodge previously accepted ones. Connectionist networks can be used to model dramatic shifts in explanatory coherence that take place in scientific revolutions (Thagard 1992b).

Circularity

Another standard objection to coherence theories is that they are circular, licensing the inference of p from q and then of q from p. The theories of coherence and the coherence algorithms presented here make it clear that coherence-based inferences are very different from those familiar from deductive logic, where propositions are derived from other propositions in linear fashion. The characterization of coherence and the algorithms for computing it (appendix A) involve a global, parallel, but effective means of assessing a whole set of elements simultaneously on the basis of their mutual dependencies. Inference can be seen to be holistic in a way that is nonmystical, computationally effective, and psychologically and neurologically plausible (pairs of real neurons do not excite each other symmetrically, but neuronal groups can). Deductive circular reasoning is inherently defective, but the foundational view that conceives of knowledge as building deductively on indubitable axioms is not even supportable in mathematics, as we saw in section 5. Inference based on coherence judgments is not circular in the way in the way feared by logicians, since it effectively calculates how a whole set of elements fit together, without linear inference of p from q and then of q from p.

9. Conclusion

This chapter has described epistemic coherence in terms of five contributory kinds of coherence: explanatory, analogical, deductive, perceptual, and conceptual. By analogy to previously presented principles of explanatory coherence, it has generated new principles to capture existing theories of analogical and conceptual coherence, and it has developed new theories of deductive and visual coherence. All of these kinds of coherence can be construed in terms of constraint satisfaction and computed using connectionist and other algorithms. We showed that Haack's foundherentist epistemology can be subsumed within the more precise framework offered here and that many of the standard philosophical objections to coherentism can be answered within this framework.

Further work remains to be done on the "multicoherence" theory of knowledge offered here. The most pressing is the "intercoherence" problem that requires finding additional connections among the elements and constraints involved in the different kinds of coherence. In the tradition of naturalistic epistemology, the intercoherence problem is also a problem in cognitive science, to explain how people make sense of their world using a variety of kinds of representations and computations. We have made only a small contribution to that problem here but have shown how satisfaction of various constraints that involve multiple different elements provides a novel and comprehensive account of epistemic coherence.

APPENDIX A: FORMAL DETAILS

Thagard and K. Verbeurgt (1998) define a *coherence problem* as follows: Let E be a finite set of elements $\{e_i\}$ and C be a set of constraints on E understood as a set $\{(e_i, e_j)\}$ of pairs of elements of E. C divides into $C+$, the positive constraints on E, and $C-$, the negative constraints on E. With each constraint is associated a number w, which is the weight (strength) of the constraint. The problem is to partition E into two sets, A and R, in a way that maximizes compliance with the following two *coherence conditions*:

1. If (e_i, e_j) is in $C+$, then e_i is in A if and only if e_j is in A.
2. If (e_i, e_j) is in $C-$, then e_i is in A if and only if e_j is in R.

Let W be the weight of the partition, that is, the sum of the weights of the satisfied constraints. The coherence problem is then to partition E into A and R in a way that maximizes W. Maximizing coherence is a difficult computational problem: Verbeurgt has proved that it belongs to a class of problems generally considered to be computationally intractable, so that no algorithms are available that are both efficient and guaranteed correct. Nevertheless, good approximation algorithms are available, in particular connectionist algorithms from which the preceding characterization of coherence was originally abstracted.

Here is how to translate a coherence problem into a problem that can be solved in a connectionist network:

1. For every element e_i of E, construct a unit u_i that is a node in a network of units U. These units are very roughly analogous to neurons in the brain.

2. For every positive constraint in C+ on elements e_i and e_j, construct an excitatory link between the corresponding units u_i and u_j.
3. For every negative constraint in C– on elements e_i and e_j, construct an inhibitory link between the corresponding units u_i and u_j.
4. Assign each unit u_i an equal initial activation (say .01), then update the activation of all the units in parallel. The updated activation of a unit is calculated on the basis of its current activation, the weights on links to other units, and the activation of the units to which it is linked. A number of equations are available for specifying how this updating is done (McClelland and Rumelhart 1989). Typically, activation is constrained to remain between a minimum (e.g., –1) and a maximum (e.g., 1).
5. Continue the updating of activation until all units have settled—achieved unchanging activation values. If a unit u_i has final activation above a specified threshold (e.g., 0), then the element e_i represented by u_i is deemed to be accepted. Otherwise, e_i is rejected.

We then get a partition of elements of E into accepted and rejected by virtue of the network U settling in such a way that some units are activated and others rejected. Intuitively, this solution is a natural one for coherence problems. Just as we want two coherent elements to be accepted or rejected together, so two units connected by an excitatory link will be activated or deactivated together. Just as we want two incoherent elements to be such that one is accepted and the other is rejected, so two units connected by an inhibitory link will tend to suppress each other's activation with one activated and the other deactivated. A solution that enforces the two conditions on maximizing coherence is provided by the parallel update algorithm that adjusts the activation of all units at once based on their links and previous activation values. Certain units (e.g., ones that represent evidence in an explanatory coherence calculation) can be given priority by linking them positively with a special unit whose activation is kept at 1. Such units will strongly tend to be accepted but may be rejected if other coherence considerations overwhelm their priority.

APPENDIX B: ECHO SIMULATION OF HAACK'S CROSSWORD PUZZLE

Here is a formulation of Haack's crossword puzzle example as presented in Figure 6.1 earlier. The propositions that represent clues and possible solutions are taken from Haack's sample crossword puzzle, and we have added alternate solutions to produce a problem that is solved by the computer program ECHO. In the possible solutions following, A1 = H means that the entry for square in the top right is H. 2A1 = J is a second possible entry for that square.

Hypotheses—Possible Solutions

(proposition 'A1 = H)   (proposition 'B3 = U)
(proposition 'A2 = I)   (proposition 'B4 = B)
(proposition 'A3 = P)   (proposition 'B5 = Y)
(proposition '2A1 = J)   (proposition '2B2 = S)
(proposition '2A2 = O)   (proposition '2B3 = T)
(proposition '2A3 = Y)   (proposition '2B4 = A)
(proposition 'B2 = R)   (proposition '2B5 = R)

(proposition 'C1 = R)
(proposition 'C2 = A)
(proposition 'C3 = T)
(proposition '2C1 = C)
(proposition 'C5 = A)
(proposition 'C6 = N)
(proposition '2C6 = X)
(proposition 'D1 = E)
(proposition 'D2 = T)
(proposition '2D1 = I)
(proposition 'D4 = O)
(proposition 'D5 = R)
(proposition '2D4 = N)
(proposition '2D5 = O)
(proposition 'E2 = E)
(proposition 'E3 = R)
(proposition 'E4 = O)
(proposition 'E5 = D)
(proposition 'E6 = E)
(proposition '2E4 = A)
(proposition '2E5 = S)
(proposition 'A2 = I)
(proposition 'B2 = R)
(proposition 'C2 = A)
(proposition 'D2 = T)
(proposition 'E2 = E)

(proposition '2A2 = F)
(proposition '2B2 = E)
(proposition '2C2 = I)
(proposition '2D2 = N)
(proposition '2E2 = S)
(proposition 'A3 = P)
(proposition 'B3 = U)
(proposition 'C3 = T)
(proposition '2A3 = T)
(proposition '2B3 = R)
(proposition '2C3 = Y)
(proposition 'B5 = Y)
(proposition 'C5 = A)
(proposition 'D5 = R)
(proposition 'E5 = D)
(proposition '2B5 = F)
(proposition '2C5 = O)
(proposition '2D5 = O)
(proposition '2E5 = T)
(proposition 'C1 = R)
(proposition 'D1 = E)
(proposition '2C1 = O)
(proposition '2D1 = F)
(proposition 'D4 = O)
(proposition 'E4 = O)
(proposition '2E4 = A)

Clues That Provide Discriminating Positive Constraints

(proposition 'C1A "A cheerful start [3].")
(proposition 'C4A "She's a jewel [4].")
(proposition 'C6A "No, it's Polonius [3].")
(proposition 'C7A "An article [2].")
(proposition 'C8A "A visitor from outside fills this space [2].")
(proposition 'C9A "What's the alternative? [2].")
(proposition 'C10A "Dick Turpin did this to York; it wore 'im out [5].")
(proposition 'C2D "Angry Irish rebels [5].")
(proposition 'C3D "Have a shot at an Olympic event [3].")
(proposition 'C5D "A measure of one's back garden [4].")
(proposition 'C6D "What's this all about? [2].")
(proposition 'C9D "The printer hasn't got my number [2].")

Explanations That Provide Solutions to Clues and Produce Positive Constraints

(explain '[A1 = H A2 = I A3 = P] 'C1A)
(explain '[B2 = R B3 = U B4 = B B5 = Y] 'C4A)
(explain '[C1 = R C2 = A C3 = T] 'C6A)
(explain '[C5 = A C6 = N] 'C7A)
(explain '[D1 = E D2 = T] 'C8A)
(explain '[D4 = O D5 = R] 'C9A)
(explain '[E2 = E E3 = R E4 = O E5 = D E6 = E] 'C10A)
(explain '[A2 = I B2 = R C2 = A D2 = T E2 = E] 'C2D)

(explain '[A3 = P B3 = U C3 = T] 'C3D)
(explain '[B5 = Y C5 = A D5 = R E5 = D] 'C5D)
(explain '[C1 = R D1 = E] 'C6D)
(explain '[D4 = O E4 = O] 'C9D)

Other Explanations That Provide Alternative Solutions and Additional Positive Constraints

(explain '[2A1 = J 2A2 = O 2A3 = Y] 'C1A)
(explain '[2B2 = S 2B3 = T 2B4 = A 2B5 = R] 'C4A)
(explain '[2C1 = C C2 = A C3 = T] 'C6A)
(explain '[C5 = A 2C6 = X] 'C7A)
(explain '[2D1 = I D2 = T] 'C8A)
(explain '[2D4 = N 2D5 = O] 'C9A)
(explain '[E2 = E E3 = R 2E4 = A 2E5 = S E6 = E] 'C10A)
(explain '[2A2 = F 2B2 = E 2C2 = I 2D2 = N 2E2 = S] 'C2D)
(explain '[2A3 = T 2B3 = R 2C3 = Y] 'C3D)
(explain '[2B5 = F 2C5 = O 2D5 = O 2E5 = T] 'C5D)
(explain '[2C1 = O 2D1 = F] 'C6D)
(explain '[D4 = O 2E4 = A] 'C9D)

Contradictory Solutions for a Letter's Square That Provide Negative Constraints

(contradict '2A2 = O '2A2 = F)
(contradict '2A3 = Y '2A3 = T)
(contradict '2B2 = S '2B2 = E)
(contradict '2B3 = T '2B3 = R)
(contradict '2B5 = R '2B5 = F)
(contradict '2C1 = C '2C1 = O)
(contradict 'C2 = A '2C2 = I)
(contradict 'C3 = T '2C3 = Y)
(contradict 'C5 = A '2C5 = O)
(contradict '2D1 = I '2D1 = F)
(contradict 'D2 = T '2D2 = N)
(contradict '2D5 = F '2D5 = O)
(contradict 'E2 = E '2E2 = S)
(contradict '2E5 = D '2E5 = T)

Additional Contradictions That Say That Two Different Letters Can't Be in the Same Space and Provide Additional Negative Constraints

(contradict '2A2 = O 'A2 = I)
(contradict '2C1 = C 'C1 = R)
(contradict '2C6 = X 'C6 = N)
(contradict '2D1 = I 'D1 = E)

More of the Same, but Not Necessary for Correct Answer

(contradict '2A1 = J 'A1 = H)
(contradict '2A3 = Y 'A3 = P)
(contradict '2B2 = S 'B2 = R)
(contradict '2B3 = T 'B3 = U)
(contradict '2B4 = A 'B4 = B)

(contradict '2B5 = R 'B5 = Y)
(contradict '2D4 = N 'D4 = O)
(contradict '2D5 = O 'D5 = R)
(contradict '2E4 = A 'E4 = O)
(contradict '2E5 = S 'E5 = D)
(contradict '2A2 = F 'A2 = I)
(contradict '2B2 = E 'B2 = R)
(contradict '2C2 = I 'C2 = A)
(contradict '2D2 = N 'D2 = T)
(contradict '2E2 = S 'E2 = E)
(contradict '2A3 = T 'A3 = P)
(contradict '2B3 = R 'B3 = U)
(contradict '2C3 = Y 'C3 = T)
(contradict '2B5 = F 'B5 = Y)
(contradict '2C5 = O 'C5 = A)
(contradict '2D5 = O 'D5 = R)
(contradict '2E5 = T 'E5 = D)
(contradict '2C1 = O 'C1 = R)
(contradict '2D1 = F 'D1 = E)
(contradict '2E4 = A 'E4 = O)

When this input is given to ECHO, it creates a constraint network and uses a connectionist algorithm to select the entries shown in Figure 6.1.

NOTE

We are grateful to Elijah Millgram for comments on an earlier draft and to the Natural Science and Engineering Research Council of Canada for funding.

REFERENCES

Audi, R. (1993). Fallibilist foundationalism and holistic coherentism. In L. P. Pojman (ed.), *The Theory of Knowledge: Classic and Contemporary Readings* (pp. 263–279). Belmont, CA: Wadsworth.

Bender, J. W. (ed.). (1989). *The Current State of the Coherence Theory*. Dordrecht: Kluwer.

BonJour, L. (1985). *The Structure of Empirical Knowledge*. Cambridge: Harvard University Press.

Byrne, M. D. (1995). The convergence of explanatory coherence and the story model: A case study in juror decision. In *Proceedings of the Seventeenth Annual Conference of the Cognitive Science Society*, pp. 539–543. Mahwah, NJ: Erlbaum.

Davidson, D. (1986). A coherence theory of truth and knowledge. In E. Lepore (ed.), *Truth and Interpretation*, pp. 307–319. Oxford: Basil Blackwell.

Davies, P., and J. Brown (1988). *Superstrings*. Cambridge: Cambridge University Press.

Eliasmith, C., and P. Thagard (1997). Waves, particles, and explanatory coherence. *British Journal for the Philosophy of Science* 48:1–19.

Eliasmith, C., and P. Thagard (2001). Integrating structure and meaning: A distributed model of analogical mapping. *Cognitive Science* 25:245–286.

Haack, S. (1993). *Evidence and Inquiry: Towards Reconstruction in Epistemology.* Oxford: Blackwell.

Harman, G. H. (1986). *Change in View: Principles of Reasoning.* Cambridge: MIT Press/Bradford.

Holyoak, K., and P. Thagard (1989). Analogical mapping by constraint satisfaction. *Cognitive Science* 13:295–355.

Kitcher, P. (1983). *The Nature of Mathematical Knowledge.* New York: Oxford University Press.

Kitcher, P., and W. Salmon (1989). *Scientific Explanation.* Minneapolis: University of Minnesota Press.

Koffka, K. (1935). *Principles of Gestalt Psychology.* New York: Harcourt Brace.

Kosslyn, S. M. (1994). *Image and Brain: The Resolution of the Imagery Debate.* Cambridge: MIT Press.

Kunda, Z., and P. Thagard (1996). Forming impressions from stereotypes, traits, and behaviors: A-parallel constraint-satisfaction theory. *Psychological Review* 103:284–308.

Lehrer, K. (1990). *Theory of Knowledge.* Boulder: Westview.

McClelland, J. L., and D. E. Rumelhart (1989). *Explorations in Parallel Distributed Processing.* Cambridge: MIT Press.

Medin, D. L., and B. Ross (1999). *Cognitive Psychology.* 2d ed. Fort Worth, TX: Harcourt College Publishers.

Millgram, E., and P. Thagard (1996). Deliberative coherence. *Synthese* 108:63–88.

Nowak, G., and P. Thagard (1992a). Copernicus, Ptolemy, and explanatory coherence. In R. Giere (ed.), *Cognitive Models of Science,* vol. 15, pp. 274–309. Minneapolis: University of Minnesota Press.

Nowak, G., and P. Thagard (1992b). Newton, Descartes, and explanatory coherence. In R. Duschl and R. Hamilton (eds.), *Philosophy of Science, Cognitive Psychology and Educational Theory and Practice,* pp. 69–115. Albany: SUNY Press.

Pojman, L. P. (ed.). (1993). *The Theory of Knowledge: Classic and Contemporary Readings.* Belmont, CA: Wadsworth.

Polya, G. (1957). *How to Solve It.* Princeton: Princeton University Press.

Rawls, J. (1971). *A Theory of Justice.* Cambridge: Harvard University Press.

Read, S., and A. Marcus-Newhall (1993). The role of explanatory coherence in the construction of social explanations. *Journal of Personality and Social Psychology* 65:429–447.

Rock, I. (1983). *The Logic of Perception.* Cambridge: MIT Press/Bradford.

Russell, B. (1973). *Essays in Analysis.* London: Allen and Unwin.

Schank, P., and M. Ranney (1992). Assessing explanatory coherence: A new method for integrating verbal data with models of on-line belief revision. In *Proceedings of the Fourteenth Annual Conference of the Cognitive Science Society,* pp. 599–604. Hillsdale, NJ: Erlbaum.

Thagard, P. (1988). *Computational Philosophy of Science.* Cambridge: MIT Press/Bradford.

Thagard, P. (1989). Explanatory coherence. *Behavioral and Brain Sciences* 12:435–467.

Thagard, P. (1992a). Adversarial problem solving: Modelling an opponent using explanatory coherence. *Cognitive Science* 16:123–149.

Thagard, P. (1992b). *Conceptual Revolutions.* Princeton: Princeton University Press.

Thagard, P. (1998). Ulcers and bacteria I: Discovery and acceptance. *Studies in History and Philosophy of Science. Part C. Studies in History and Philosophy of Biology and Biomedical Sciences* 29:107–136.

Thagard, P., and E. Millgram (1995). Inference to the best plan: A coherence theory of decision. In A. Ram and D. B. Leake (eds.), *Goal-Driven Learning*, pp. 439–454. Cambridge: MIT Press.

Thagard, P., and K. Verbeurgt (1998). Coherence as constraint satisfaction. *Cognitive Science* 22:1–24.

Thagard, P. (2000). *Coherence in Thought and Action*. Cambridge: MIT Press.

7

The Evolutionary Roots of Intelligence and Rationality

DENISE DELLAROSA CUMMINS

1. Introduction

Consider the fundamental question: *What is reasoning for?* Decades of research in disciplines as diverse as psychology, AI, robotics, and philosophy seem to converge on the following answer:

> The function of reasoning is to ensure that there is a nonarbitrary relation between the inputs a system receives on the one hand and its thoughts (inferences) and actions on the other.

This nonarbitrary relation requires reasoning be *constrained* in some way. Without constraints, the reasoning process can take on the unproductive characteristics of a runaway freight train, yielding an explosion of inferences, most of which are irrelevant to the problem at hand. A common solution to this problem is to *allow the reasoner's goals or interests to constrain the inference process by focusing attention on some inputs and some inference paths at the expense of others.* Binding action-sequences too tightly to goals, however, can produce a brittleness in the reasoning process that once again leads to unproductive action, as this example of the *Sphex* wasp's nest-building shows:

> For example, the wasp's routine is to bring the paralyzed cricket to the burrow, leave it on the threshold, go inside to see that all is well, emerge,

and then drag the cricket in. If the cricket is moved a few inches away while the wasp is inside making her preliminary inspection, the wasp, on emerging from the burrow, will bring the cricket back to the threshold, but not inside, and will then repeat the preparatory procedure of entering the burrow to see that everything is right . . . The wasp never thinks of pulling the cricket straight in. On one occasion, this procedure was repeated forty times, always with the same result. (Wooldridge 1963, p. 82, as cited in Dennett 1984, p. 11)

Intelligent reasoning must be *flexible*, that is, *capable of opportunistically exploiting variable environmental constraints*, as in this example of orangutan behavior from Byrne and Russon 1998:

Supinah's goal appeared to be using the soap and laundry possessed by camp staff . . . While she could directly take the goods from the staff by intimidating them (they were afraid of her), they were protected by a guard stationed on the dock to block her access. Her overall strategy to get the soap and laundry required foiling the humans and this entailed two different tactics—bypassing the guard, then taking the goods from the staff. Bypassing the guard meant detouring around him, which meant travelling through water because the end part of the dock where Supinah lurked stood knee-deep in water. Below this part of the dock was a dugout canoe. These orangutans are well-known for cruising down the river in pilfered canoes, but this one was moored and half full of water. Supinah dealt with this situation with two more subroutines—preparing the canoe for use, then riding it past the guard to the raft. Preparing the canoe had two subroutines—freeing it and baling it out . . . Riding the canoe required reorienting it relative to the dock and raft, then propelling it alongside the dock towards the raft. Taking soap and laundry from the staff was then easy; Supinah merely hopped onto the raft, staff obligingly shrieked and jumped into the water, abandoning soap and laundry. Supinah immediately set to work washing the clothes.

As this example dramatically illustrates, walking the tightrope between goal-constrained action and opportunistic planning requires the capacity to do deep embedding, that is, *the capacity to form hierarchically embedded goal structures*.

To be intelligent, then, an agent must be capable of opportunistic planning, which typically necessitates the capacity to construct and negotiate hierarchically embedded goals. Further, if one is interested in reasoning as instantiated in biological organisms (as opposed to artificial or normative systems), then one must seriously confront the fact that the mind is a product of evolution.

2. Cognition and Evolution

If you are a materialist, then you are committed (at least implicitly) to the view that

the mind (collection of cognitive functions) is what the brain does.

That is, our cognitive processes are instantiated as neurological processes. And unless you are a creationist, you are also committed to the view that

the brain was shaped by natural selection.

If you accept these two premises, you are also committed to accepting their logical conclusion, namely, that

the mind (collection of cognitive functions) was shaped by natural selection.

If you accept this conclusion (which is clearly entailed by the premises), then reasoning is readily seen as a cognitive adaptation, that is, as a function that was shaped by pressures exerted by the environment. In this chapter, I argue that several important cognitive functions were shaped (through natural selection) by the exigencies of the *social* environment. These functions include (1) a *biological predisposition* to rapidly and effectively acquire implicit rules that specify what we are *permitted, obligated,* or *forbidden* to do within our social groups and (2) a domain-specific embedding function that enables us to effortlessly form hierarchically structured representations of what is socially crucial but essentially hidden from view, namely, *the minds of others.* The implication is that our capacity to form deeply embedded mental representations (and hence deeply embedded goal structures) emerged as an adaptation to the social environment. The pressure to compete and cooperate successfully with conspecifics constituted a crucible that necessitated and forged this crucial cognitive function.

How Natural Selection Works

Let me begin by providing a brief summary of how natural selection works: Variation exists in the traits of the members of most species, and some of this variation is heritable. Because of their particular heritable attributes, some individuals will be better able to cope with survival pressures than others within the same environmental niche. These individuals will survive better or longer and hence leave more living offspring than others in their species. The differential reproductive success of individuals based on their genetic differences is called *natural selection.* The outcome of this process is that organisms will evolve behavioral or other traits that promote individual reproductive success within a particular environmental niche, which is referred to as *reproductive success* (or fitness) and is defined in terms of *the number of one's offspring that live to reproduce themselves.*

From an evolutionary standpoint, therefore, the fundamental problem that an organism must solve is *maximizing reproductive success.* This problem reduces in turn to solving the problems of acquiring mates, accessing sufficient food to feed oneself and one's progeny, and avoiding or reducing the risk of death due to predation. Many of these problems can be greatly reduced by living in social groups. Social living yields a reduction in predator pressure by improved detection or repulsion of enemies, improved foraging and hunting efficiency, improved defense of limited resources against conspecific intruders, and improved care of offspring through communal feeding and protection.

But there are also costs associated with sociality, including increased competition within the group for food, mates, nest sites, and other limited resources. In most mammalian and avian species, competition and cooperation among conspecifics produces a complex social structure called the *dominance hierarchy*. In functional terms, this means that

certain individuals have priority of access to resources in competitive situations. (Clutton-Brock and Harvey 1976)

These individuals are referred to as dominant or higher ranking, while those who have lower priority of access are called subordinate or lower ranking. In its most developed form, the dominance hierarchy is transitive, meaning that if A has priority over B and B has priority over C, then A has priority over C, and so on. The role of dominance is most pronounced in situations characterized by high levels of competition for resources, such as high population density or the onset of breeding season (Clutton-Brock and Harvey 1976).

In most species, there is a direct relationship between rank and reproductive success, with higher ranking members being less likely to die of predation or starvation (Cheney and Seyfarth 1990, pp. 33–34) and more likely to leave living offspring (e.g., Bertram 1976; Bygott, Bertram, and Hanby 1979; Clutton-Brock 1988; de Waal 1982; Dewsbury 1982; Ellis 1995; Fedigan 1983; Hausfater 1975; McCann 1981; Nishida 1983; Robinson 1982; Silk 1987; Tutin 1979; Watts and Stokes 1971). Among primates, the relationship is even more striking because dominance status is unstable; for this reason, the level of reproductive success achieved by any individual is directly related to the length of time during which the individual is high-ranking (Altmann et al. 1996).

From a cognitive standpoint, a dominance hierarchy is a set of *implicit social norms*. These social norms are reflected in virtually every activity, including who is allowed to sit next to, play with, share food with, groom, or mate with whom (Aruguete 1994; Hall 1964). Dominant individuals not only have priority of access to resources; they also typically take on the role of protecting "the social contract," aggressing against those who violate social norms and breaking up disputes between lower ranking individuals (see, e.g., Boehm 1992). Indeed, K. R. L. Hall (1964) designated perceived violations of the social code as the single most common cause of aggression in primate groups.

To summarize, living with conspecifics produces a variety of survival pressures that have a direct impact on reproductive success. High-ranking individuals have priority of access to available resources, particularly reproductive opportunities. Maximizing reproductive success, therefore, is intimately connected to maximizing one's rank, which brings us to the obvious question: Which factors determine dominance rank?

Dominance Hierarchies and Intelligent
Reasoning Functions

Common wisdom has it that dominance is merely a matter of brawn—biggest wins all. But in point of fact, this is not the case in many species. Among primates, and most notably chimpanzees, *dominance rank does not correlate with size.* Instead, attaining and maintaining a high-ranking position depends on a collection of *cognitive* traits.

First and foremost, one must be capable of *violation detection;* otherwise, one cannot maintain priority of access to resources or control the behavior of subordinates. One must have the cognitive wherewithal to recognize when a subordinate is violating a social norm. For example, high-ranking individuals often punish violations of social norms as benign as grooming or sharing food with forbidden individuals (de Waal 1992, pp. 246–249). And for good reason: in order to secure and maintain a high-ranking position, individuals must *form and maintain alliances through reciprocal obligations* (Chapais 1988, 1992; Datta 1983a, 1983b; de Waal 1989, 1992; Goodall 1986; Harcourt 1988; Harcourt and de Waal 1992; Harcourt and Stewart 1987; Riss and Goodall 1977; Seyfarth and Cheney 1984; Smuts 1985; Uehara et al. 1994). During contests of rank, individuals typically call for help, and *non-kin allies are most likely to supply that help if the individual in question has groomed them, shared food with them, or assisted them in agonistic encounters in the past* (Chapais 1992; Cheney and Seyfarth 1990, pp. 67–69; Prud'Homme and Chapais 1993; Seyfarth 1976; Seyfarth and Cheney 1984). These are reciprocal relationships in that the rate of intervention by individual A on behalf of B is proportional to the rate of intervention of B on behalf of A (de Waal 1989, 1992). Furthermore, there is a preference for forming alliances with high-ranking individuals (Chapais 1992; Prud'Homme and Chapais 1993).

All of this would be impossible if one did not have at least an implicit capacity to recognize individuals, to monitor one's dyadic relationships, and to update one's knowledge of them as they shift. But there are even more "hidden" cognitive traits at work here. The most important of these are recognizing (1) what is permitted and what is forbidden given one's rank, (2) what is obligated given one's history with particular individuals, and (3) violations of social norms (i.e., cheating). Without a cognitive function that allows one to quickly learn what is *forbidden* and what is *permitted* given one's rank, subordinates risk incurring the wrath of their higher ranking conspecifics, a situation that can (and does) result in ostracism and even death. Without a cognitive function that allows one to grasp the structure of an *obligation,* fruitful alliances cannot be formed and maintained. Without a *violation detection* function, high-ranking individuals cannot monopolize resources, nor can fruitful alliances be maintained. These, I argue, constitute basic and early emerging cognitive functions in social mammals, including humans.

Social Norms and Violation Detection in Human Primates

Psychological and philosophical treatments of human reasoning distinguish between deontic (or practical) reasoning and theoretical reasoning. Whenever one reasons about what one is *permitted, obligated,* or *forbidden* to do, one is reasoning deontically (Hilpinen 1971, 1981; Manktelow and Over 1991). This type of reasoning is distinct from discursive or theoretical reasoning, in which the reasoner is required to determine the epistemic status (truth) of a rule or other description of a state of affairs. When reasoning deontically, one is less concerned with what is true than choosing a correct or prudent course of action.

When reasoning about deontic rules (social norms), people spontaneously adopt a violation detection strategy; that is, *they look for cheaters* (Cheng and Holyoak 1985, 1989; Cosmides 1989; Cosmides and Tooby 1992; Cummins 1996a, 1996b, 1996c, 1996d, 1997a, 1997b, 1998a, 1998b; Manktelow and Over 1991, 1995). This extremely cogent and crucial reasoning strategy seems to be triggered almost exclusively by problems with deontic content, particularly permissions, obligations, prohibitions, promises, and warnings.

As a simple example, imagine someone tells you something odd about a mutual friend of yours, namely:

If Joan goes to the movies, she cleans her room first. (If <p>, then <q>.)

Information regarding Joan's recent activities is recorded on cards. One side of the card indicates whether or not she went to the movies, and the other side indicates whether or not she cleaned her room. You are shown four cards with the following information faceup:

Movies

No Movies

Cleaned Room

Didn't Clean Room

Which card(s) must be turned over to find out whether or not the statement is true? The typical answer on truth-testing problems like this is p and q ("Movies" and "Cleaned Room").

Now imagine that Joan is your teenage daughter and you expect her to obey the rule mentioned earlier. *Which card(s) must be turned over to find out whether or not Joan is obeying the rule?*

The typical answer on *deontic* problems like this is p and not-q ("Movies" and "Didn't Clean Room"). In other words, when reasoning about the *truth* of a conditional statement (hypothesis), people spontaneously seek to discover whether the antecedent (p) and the consequent (q) did in fact occur together. When reasoning about obedience to prescriptive rules *(social norms)*, they instead spontaneously look for possible cheating. But consider this: In the hypothesis-testing case, had the "Didn't Clean Room" card been turned over and "Movies" appeared on the other side, this would have provided incontrovertible proof that the statement was false. Yet it does not occur to us to look for potential violations of the statement in the hypothesis-testing case. The need only seems apparent in the deontic case.

The *deontic effect* does not just appear in the reasoning of adults. It has been observed in children as young as three years of age, making it one of the earliest emerging reasoning functions (Cummins 1996c). Children spontaneously adopt a violation detection strategy when attempting to determine whether or not a social rule is being followed but not when attempting to determine whether a conditional utterance is true or false. The magnitude of this effect is equivalent to the magnitude found in the adult literature. Furthermore, children also find it easier to recognize instances of cheating than instances that prove a rule false (Harris and Nuñez 1996).

Even more crucial to my argument is the observation that consideration of relative social rank strongly influences the likelihood that a cheater detection strategy will be evoked. Reasoners are far more likely to look for cheaters *when checking on individuals who are lower ranking than themselves* (65 percent) than when checking on individuals of equally high (20 percent), equally low (18 percent), or higher rank (20 percent) than themselves (Cummins 1997a). Social rank had no effect on the likelihood of adopting a violation detection strategy in a lie detection condition. (The percentage of "p and not-q" responses ranged from 15 to 18 across the rank manipulations in the lie detection task.) Similarly, L. Mealey, C. Daood, and M. Krage found that subjects were far better at remembering low-status cheaters than high-status cheaters or noncheaters of any rank (1996). Other studies have found that increases in blood pressure associated with anger or frustration in social situations can be eliminated if individuals are given an opportunity to aggress against the people who caused their distress (target), *but only if the target is of lower status than the retaliator*; if the target is of higher status, blood pressure remains at the frustration-induced elevated level (Hokanson 1961; Hokanson and Shetler 1961).

These results can be readily understood from the perspective offered here: Violation detection is a basic cognitive function that facilitates social regulation. It is a crucial function for ensuring that implicit (or explicit) social norms are honored and, more particularly, that higher ranking individuals can protect the status quo by regulating the behavior of those over whom they have power or authority.

The Selective Pressure for Thwarting
Social Norms through Guile

Conforming to social norms ensures social harmony. But in a social dominance hierarchy, social norms can take on a more insidious purpose—that of preserving high-ranking individuals' privileged access to resources. Low-ranking individuals must choose between conforming to the norms and resigning themselves to a much smaller (and perhaps entirely inadequate) share of resources, or *thwarting the norms by use of guile.* Violating norms in social dominance hierarchies means acquiring a larger share of resources than one is entitled to by virtue of one's rank, a situation that would immediately provoke cheater detection and punishment among those of higher rank—unless one were clever enough to avoid detection. Such a situation produces enormous pressure to develop—or evolve—a capacity for deception, and this is exactly what the ethology literature shows.

Nature is replete with instances of deception, much of it aimed at avoiding predation (as in the piping plover's broken wing display, which lures a would-be predator away from the nest) or *thwarting dominance in order to garner a larger share of resources.*

The following excerpt from Menzel 1974 illustrates the latter point quite dramatically. In this excerpt, Belle, a young female chimpanzee, is the only one shown the location of hidden food on successive trials. Although Belle is willing to share the food, Rock (to whom she is subordinate) repeatedly thwarted her by taking all of the food himself as soon as she uncovered it. Belle's subsequent actions were as follows:

> Belle, accordingly, stopped uncovering the food if Rock was close. She sat on it until Rock left. Rock, however, soon learned this, and when she sat in one place for more than a few seconds, he came over, shoved her aside, searched her sitting place, and got the food. Belle next stopped going all the way [to the food]. Rock, however, countered by steadily expanding the area of his search through the grass near where Belle had sat. Eventually, Belle sat farther and farther away, waiting until Rock looked in the opposite direction before she moved toward the food at all, and Rock in turn seemed to look away until Belle started to move somewhere. On some occasions Rock started to wander off, only to wheel around suddenly precisely as Belle was about to uncover some food . . . on a few trials, she actually started off a trial by leading the group in the opposite direction from the food, and then, while Rock was engaged in his search, she doubled back rapidly and got some food. (pp. 134–135)

It is clear that Belle is using whatever cognitive capacity she has at her disposal to elude detection by Rock and that Rock counters by using whatever cognitive capacity he has at his disposal to thwart her attempts to hide her illicit plans and actions.

But more important, *deception can be used more directly to enhance the reproductive success of subordinate individuals.* Recall that high-ranking individuals typically monopolize reproductive opportunities. Often only the alpha male mates with estrous females, and subordinates who are caught consorting (i.e., cheating) face severe punishment. This doesn't mean, however, that such matings don't occur. They do occur, but surreptitiously. For example, females will suppress their copulation cries when mating with subordinate males, thereby avoiding attracting the attention of dominant individuals, and both parties will attempt to move their clandestine trysts out of line of sight of dominant individuals (de Waal 1988; Kummer 1988). P. Gagneux, D. S. Woodruff, and C. Boesch (1997) report that over 50 percent of the offspring born to female chimpanzees in their study group were fathered by males from *other troops*. The females in question had surreptitiously disappeared around the times of their estrus and reappeared a few days later. During these times, they had apparently engaged in clandestine matings.

Deception is used not only to engage in clandestine matings but also to form illicit alliances that enable individuals to move up in rank. Recall that during contests of rank each contestant calls for support from allies and contestants are more likely to receive aid from non-kin if they have groomed or shared food with them (see Whiten and Byrne 1988 for numerous examples.) It is through these illicit exchanges of "goods" and services, therefore, that alliances are formed that allow low-ranking individuals to move up in rank.

Deception and the Evolution of Mental Representation

Deceptions are important to researchers interested in the evolution of mind not just because of their impact on reproductive success but also because they can be analyzed in terms of the complexity of the *mental representation* they require (Byrne 1995; Dennett 1988; Whiten and Byrne 1988).

Consider, for example, the hawk moth, which flicks open its hind wings in response to looming objects (Byrne 1995). The spots on its hind wings look strikingly similar to the eyes of a large hawk. The deception is strategic in that it is used only when something is looming at (threatening) the moth. But this sort of "deception" requires no capacity for mental representation.

In contrast, consider a cognitive system that is capable of intentional states such as

I *believe* (that the berries are ripe)

and

I *want* (the ripe berries).

Such a system is capable of first-order intentional mental states but cannot reflect on its own mental states or represent the mental states of others. Most higher order mammals (e.g., at the very least, those with a fully developed limbic system and a modicum of neocortex) surely are capable of such states. They behave purposively, display gustatory and other types of preferences, seek mates, defend territory, and so on. Lesioning the nervous system above the midbrain abolishes such purposive behavior, yielding an animal that behaves reflexively toward environmental stimulation. Without the basic motivations provided by the these higher neural structures, the animal essentially behaves "reflexively" to environmental stimuli, eating only when food is there rather than seeking it, climbing when placed on a climbable object rather than exploring the environment, and so forth.

The question becomes thornier when it comes to higher orders of intentionality that are reflected in hierarchically embedded mental representations such as

I *know* (that you *want* [my food cache])

I *want* (you to *believe* [that I *believe* (the food is in location A)])

and so on.

Notice that as the *capacity for hierarchical embeddings of mental representations increases, so does the capacity to represent the mental states of others and, concomitantly, so does one's capacity for deception.* An organism that is capable of forming second- or third-order embedded mental representations is also capable of engaging in stunning acts of deception—and of forming complex plans that involve deeply embedded goal structures. Dominating (or controlling) such an organism would constitute a daunting feat, as the interaction between Belle and Rock and the anecdote about Supinah amply illustrate.

Does this mean that other higher order mammals are capable of hierarchically embedded mental representation? This is a hotly debated topic in animal cognition (see, e.g., Bekoff 1998; Byrne 1995; Ristau 1998; and Whiten and Byrne 1988). As is apparent from AI work on robotics, the negotiating of the physical environment is not without its challenges. But if that environment is also imbued with agents who move of their own volition and are motivated by invisible internal states and whose behavior must be successfully forecast if one is to secure opportunities to leave progeny, these pressures enormously favor an adaptation for forming embedded mental representations. For this reason, many researchers have concluded that it was the exigencies of the social environment that forged the evolution of the mind (Byrne 1995; Byrne and Whiten 1988; Cheney and Seyfarth 1990; Cummins 1998a, 1998b, 1998c; Tomasello in press).

3. The Development of Mental State Attribution Skills in Childhood

When it comes to forming hierarchically embedded mental representations, humans clearly excel. It is apparent in our language, in our toolmaking, and in our capacity to represent the mental states of others. But more informative is the development of this capacity over the course of early childhood. In contrast to the early emergence of cheater detection, the capacity for mental state attribution exhibits a more gradual developmental pace, with separate subskills developing at different rates. For this reason, the development of *theory of mind reasoning*, as this type of reasoning is called, is a case where "ontogeny recapitulates phylogeny" is perhaps more than metaphor.

By age three, children can clearly identify acts of cheating, but identifying lies is another story. Typically, children in this age group fail to take into account a speaker's knowledge when evaluating utterances and simply label inaccurate statements as lies. For example, if puppet A watches an event, then lies about it to puppet B, who then innocently passes the inaccurate information on to puppet C, children in this age group will call both A and B liars (Strichartz and Burton 1990; Wimmer, Gruber, and Perner 1984). It is not until about the seventh or eighth year of life that consideration of what speakers believe or know reliably appears in their judgments. (See Bussey 1992 and Haugaard and Reppucci 1992 for reviews of this literature.)

Prior to about age four, children also perform inconsistently on tasks that require attributing false beliefs to others. In the standard false-belief task, children watch while a puppet hides a toy in location A and then leaves. A second puppet then appears, finds the toy, and hides it in location B. The child is then asked where the first puppet left the toy, where the toy is now, and where the first puppet thinks the toy is. Prior to about age four, children answer the first two questions correctly yet believe the first puppet thinks the toy is in the current location (location B). Their behavior is typically explained as a failure or inability to attribute false beliefs to others (see Gopnik and Wellman 1994 and Leslie 1994 for reviews of this literature.)

What deception and false-belief tasks have in common is that they require appreciating the knowledge/belief states of others. In the deception task, puppet A knew one thing but falsely reported another, but puppet B reported accurately what it knew. In the false-belief task, the first puppet can't know that the toy was moved because it didn't see the toy get moved. But with both types of tasks, young children seem to focus almost exclusively on accuracy or current reality. They seemingly fail to take into account what others saw, knew, or believe, particularly if that knowledge or belief may be contrary to fact. Clearly, there is something about creating and/or manipulating representations of the mental states of others that very young children find difficult. That something is probably the ability to construct hierarchically embedded mental representations, representations that allow one to distinguish between what one believes to be true and what others (perhaps falsely) believe to be true.

This pattern of results would suggest that forming hierarchically embedded representations of the mental states of others (a skill at which humans excel compared to other species) emerges later during ontogeny than does cheater detection (a skill we seem to have in common with other mammals). Consistent with this interpretation is the fact that it is not until about ages five to seven that children can reliably perform tasks that require understanding statements that express second-order intentionality such as "John wants his mother to think that . . ." (Perner and Wimmer 1985).

Was it the social environment that produced the types of pressure that favored the evolution of this capacity? The direct relationship between dominance, deception, and reproductive success strongly suggests that it was. So does the fact that theory of mind reasoning emerges earlier in laterborns than firstborns, suggesting that the capacity to mentally represent the mental states of others can serve the very useful purpose of thwarting dominance through guile (Jenkins and Astington 1996; Lewis et al. 1996; Perner, Ruffman, and Leekam 1994; Ruffman et al. 1998).

4. Summary

Like all social animals, humans live in social environments that exert extraordinary cognitive and socioemotional pressures. Extracting the social

norms that implicitly (or explicitly) regulate our behavior and allow continued group membership is crucially important, as is developing the capacity
to read the intentions, desires, and beliefs of others. I propose that our basic
cognitive architecture contains functions that enable fast-track learning of
the social norms crucial to our survival and facilitate detecting violations
of such norms and a latent capacity for forming hierarchically embedded
mental representations that is triggered through adequate interactions with
animate beings, particularly conspecifics. In short, our reasoning architecture is replete with domain-specificity, and the domains in which we as reasoners excel are also those that have a very deep evolutionary history.

REFERENCES

Altmann, J., S. C. Alberts, S. A. Haines, J. Dubach, P. Muruth, T. Coote, E. Geffen,
D. J. Cheesman, R. A. Mututua, S. N. Saiyalel, R. K. Wayne, R. C. Lacy, and
M. W. Bruford (1996). Behavior predicts genetic structure in a wild primate
group. *Proceedings of the National Academy of Sciences* 93:5795–5801.
Aruguete, M. (1994). Cognition, tradition, and the explanation of social behavior in non-human primates. Review of *Social Processes and Mental Abilities
in Non-Human Primates*, by F. D. Burton. *American Journal of Primatology*
33:71–74.
Bekoff, M. (1998). Playing with play: What can we learn about cognition, nego-
tiation, and evolution? In D. Dellarosa Cummins and C. A. Allen (eds.), *The
Evolution of Mind*, pp. 162–182. New York: Oxford University Press.
Bertram, B. C. R. (1976). Kin selection in lions and evolution. In P. P. G. Bateson
and R. A. Hinde (eds.), *Growing Points in Ethology*, pp. 281–302. Cambridge:
Cambridge University Press.
Boehm, C. (1992). Segmentary "warfare" and the management of conflict: Com-
parison of East African chimpanzees and patrilineal-patrilocal humans. In
A. H. Harcourt and F. B. M. de Waal (eds.), *Coalitions and Alliances in Humans
and Other Animals*, pp. 137–174. Oxford: Oxford University Press.
Bussey, K. (1992). Children's lying and truthfulness: Implications for children's
testimony. In S. J. Ceci, M. De Simone Leichtman, and M. Putnick (eds.), *Cog-
nitive and Social Factors in Early Deception*, pp. 89–110. Hillsdale, NJ: Erlbaum.
Bygott, J. D., B. C. R. Bertram, and J. P. Hanby (1979). Male lions in large coali-
tions gain reproductive advantage. *Nature* 282:839–841.
Byrne, R. (1995). *The Thinking Ape: Evolutionary Origins of Intelligence*. Oxford:
Oxford University Press.
Byrne, R., and A. E. Russon (1998). Learning by imitation: A hierarchical
approach. *Behavioral and Brain Sciences*: 21, 667–721.
Byrne, R., and A. Whiten (eds.) (1988). *Machiavellian Intelligence*. Oxford: Oxford
University Press.
Chapais, B. (1988). Rank maintenance in female Japanese macaques: Experi-
mental evidence for social dependency. *Behavior* 104:41–59.
Chapais, B. (1992). Role of alliances in the social inheritance of rank among
female primates. In A. Harcourt and F. B. M de Waal (eds.), *Coalitions and
Alliances in Humans and Other Animals*, pp. 29–60. Oxford: Oxford University
Press.
Cheney, D. L., and R. M. Seyfarth (1990). *How Monkeys See the World*. Chicago:
University of Chicago Press.

Cheng, P., and K. Holyoak (1985). Pragmatic reasoning schemas. *Cognitive Psychology* 17:391–416.

Cheng, P., and K. Holyoak (1989). On the natural selection of reasoning theories. *Cognition* 33:285–313.

Clutton-Brock, T. H. (1988). Reproductive success. In T. H. Clutton-Brock (ed.), *Reproductive Success*, pp. 472–485. Chicago: University of Chicago Press.

Clutton-Brock, T. H., and P. H. Harvey (1976). Evolutionary rules and primate societies. In P. P. G. Bateson and R. A. Hinde (eds.), *Growing Points in Ethology*, pp. 195–238. Cambridge: Cambridge University Press.

Cosmides, L. (1989). The logic of social exchange: Has natural selection shaped how humans reason? Studies with the Wason selection task. *Cognition* 31:187–276.

Cosmides, L., and J. Tooby (1992). Cognitive adaptations for social exchange. In J. Barkow, L. Cosmides, and J. Tooby (eds.), *The Adapted Mind: Evolutionary Psychology and the Generation of Culture*, pp. 163–228. New York: Oxford University Press.

Cummins, D. D. (1996a). Dominance hierarchies and the evolution of human reasoning. *Minds and Machines* 6:463–480.

Cummins, D. D. (1996b). Evidence for the innateness of deontic reasoning. *Mind and Language* 11:160–190.

Cummins, D. D. (1996c). Evidence of deontic reasoning in 3- and 4-year-olds. *Memory and Cognition* 24:823–829.

Cummins, D. D. (1996d). Human reasoning from an evolutionary perspective. *Proceedings of 18th Annual Meeting of the Cognitive Science Society* 18:50–51.

Cummins, D. D. (1997a). Cheater detection is modified by social rank. Paper presented at the meetings of the Human Behavior and Evolution Society, University of Arizona, Tucson, June 1997.

Cummins, D. D. (1997b). Rationality: Biological, psychological, and normative theories. *Cahiers de psychologie cognitive* (Current psychology of cognition) 16:78–86.

Cummins, D. D. (1998a). Can humans form hierarchically embedded mental representations? Commentary on R. W. Byrne and A. E. Russon, Learning by imitation: A hierarchical approach. *Behavioral and Brain Sciences* 21:687.

Cummins, D. D. (1998b). Social norms and other minds: The evolutionary roots of higher cognition. In D. D. Cummins and C. A. Allen (eds.), *The Evolution of Mind*, pp. 30–50. New York: Oxford University Press.

Datta, S. B. (1983a). Relative power and the acquisition of rank. In R. A. Hinde (ed.), *Primate Social Relationships*, pp. 93–102. Oxford: Blackwell.

Datta, S. B. (1983b). Relative power and the maintenance of rank. In R. A. Hinde (ed.), *Primate Social Relationships*, pp. 103–111. Oxford: Blackwell.

Dennett, D. (1984). *Elbow Room*. Cambridge: Bradford/MIT Press.

Dennett, D. (1988). The intentional stance in theory and practice. In R. W. Byrne and A. Whiten (eds.), *Machiavellian Intelligence*, pp. 180–202. Oxford: Oxford University Press.

de Waal, F. B. M. (1982). *Chimpanzee Politics*. Baltimore: Johns Hopkins University Press.

de Waal, F. B. M. (1988). Chimpanzee politics. In R. W. Byrne and A. Whiten (eds.), *Machiavellian Intelligence*, pp. 122–131. Oxford: Oxford University Press.

de Waal, F. B. M. (1989). Food sharing and reciprocal obligations among chimpanzees. *Journal of Human Evolution* 18:433–459.

de Waal, F. B. M. (1992). Coalitions as part of reciprocal relations in the Arnhem chimpanzee colony. In A. H. Harcourt and F. B. M. de Waal (eds.), *Coalitions and Alliances in Humans and Other Animals*, pp. 233–258. Oxford: Oxford University Press.

Dewsbury, D. A. (1982). Dominance rank, copulatory behavior and differential reproduction. *Quarterly Review of Biology* 57:135–159.

Ellis, L. (1995). Dominance and reproductive success among nonhuman animals: A cross-species Comparison. *Ethology and Sociobiology* 16:257–333.

Fedigan, L. (1983). Dominance and reproductive success in primates. *Yearbook of Physical Anthropology* 26:91–129.

Gagneux, P., D. S. Woodruff, and C. Boesch (1997). Furtive mating in female chimpanzees. *Nature* 387:358–369.

Goodall, J. (1986). *The Chimpanzees of Gombe*. Cambridge: Belknap Press.

Gopnik, A., and H. M. Wellman (1994). The theory theory. In L. A. Hirschfeld and S. A. Gelman (eds.), *Mapping the Mind: Domain Specificity in Cognition and Culture*, pp. 157–181. Cambridge: Cambridge University Press.

Hall, K. R. L. (1964). Aggression in monkey and ape societies. In J. Carthy and F. Ebling (eds.), *The Natural History of Aggression*, pp. 51–64. London: Academic Press.

Harcourt, A. H. (1988). Alliances in contests and social intelligence. In R. W. Byrne and A. Whiten (eds.), *Machiavellian Intelligence*, pp. 131–152. Oxford: Oxford University Press.

Harcourt, A. H., and K. J. Stewart (1987). The influence of help in contests on dominance rank in primates: Hints from gorillas. *Animal Behaviour* 35: 182–190.

Harcourt, A. H., and F. B. M. de Waal (eds.) (1992). *Coalitions and Alliances in Humans and Other Animals*. Oxford: Oxford University Press.

Harris, P., and M. Nuñez (1996). Understanding of permission rules by preschool children. *Child Development* 67:1572–1591.

Haugaard, J., and N. D. Reppucci (1992). Children and the truth. In S. J. Ceci, M. De Simone Leichtman, and M. Putnick (eds.), *Cognitive and Social Factors in Early Deception*, pp. 29–46. Hillsdale, NJ: Erlbaum.

Hausfater, G. (1975). Dominance and reproduction in baboons (*Papio cynocephalus*): A quantitative analysis. *Contributions in Primatology* 7:1–150.

Hilpinen, R. (1971). *Deontic Logic: Introductory and Systematic Readings*. Boston: Reidel/Kluwer.

Hokanson, J. E. (1961). The effect of frustration and anxiety on overt aggression. *Journal of Abnormal and Social Psychology* 62:346–351.

Hokanson, J. E., and S. Shetler (1961). The effect of overt aggression on physiological arousal. *Journal of Abnormal and Social Psychology* 63:446–448.

Jenkins, J., and J. W. Astington (1996). Cognitive factors and family structure associated with theory of mind development in young children. *Developmental Psychology* 32:70–78.

Kummer, H. (1988). Tripartite relations in hamadryas baboons. In Richard Byrne and Andrew Whiten (eds.), *Machiavellian Intelligence*, pp. 113–121. Oxford: Oxford University Press.

Leslie, A. (1994). ToMM, ToBY, and agency: Core architecture and domain specificity. In L. A. Hirschfeld and S. A. Gelman (eds.), *Mapping the Mind: Domain Specificity in Cognition and Culture*, pp. 119–148. Cambridge: Cambridge University Press.

Lewis, C., N. Freeman, C. Kyriakidou, K. Maridaki-Kassotaki, and D. Berridge (1996). Social influences on false belief access: Specific contagion or general apprenticeship? *Child Development* 67:2930–2947.

Manktelow, K. I., and D. Over (1991). Social roles and utilities in reasoning with deontic conditionals. *Cognition* 39:85–105.

Manktelow, K. I., and D. Over (1995). Deontic reasoning. In S. E. Newstead and J. St. B. Evans (eds.), *Perspectives on Thinking and Reasoning*, pp. 91–114. Englewood Cliffs, NJ: Erlbaum.

McCann, T. S. (1981). Aggression and sexual activity of male southern elephant seals (*Mirounga leonina*). *Journal of Zoology* 19:295–310.

Mealey, L., C. Daood, and M. Krage (1996). Enhanced memory for faces of cheaters. *Ethology and Sociobiology* 17:119–128.

Menzel, E. W. (1974). A group of chimpanzees in a 1-acre field: Leadership and communication. In A. M. Schrier and F. Stollnitz (eds.), *Behavior of Nonhuman Primates*, pp. 83–153. New York: Academic Press.

Nishida, T. (1983). Alpha status and agonistic alliance in wild chimpanzees (*Pan troglodytes schweinfurthii*). *Primates* 24:318–336.

Perner, J., T. Ruffman, and S. R. Leekam (1994). Theory of mind is contagious: You catch it from your sibs. *Child Development* 65:1228–1238.

Perner, J., and H. Wimmer (1985). John thinks that Mary thinks that . . . : Attribution of second-order beliefs by 5–10-year-old children. *Journal of Experimental Child Psychology* 38:437–471.

Prud'homme, J., and B. Chapais (1993). Aggressive interventions and matrilineal dominance relations in semifree-ranging Barbary macaques. *Primates* 34:271–283.

Riss, D. C., and J. Goodall (1977). The recent rise to the alpha-rank in a population of free-living chimpanzees. *Folia Primatologica* 27:134–151.

Ristau, C. A. (1998). Cognitive ethology: The minds of children and animals. In D. D. Cummins and C. Allen (eds.), *The Evolution of Mind*, pp. 127–161. New York: Oxford University Press.

Robinson, J. G. (1982). Intrasexual competition and mate choice in primates. *American Journal of Primatology* 1 (Supplement): 131–144.

Ruffman, T., J. Perner, M. Naito, L. Parkin, and W. C. Clements (1998). Older (but not younger) siblings facilitate false belief understanding. *Developmental Psychology* 34:161–174.

Seyfarth, R. M. (1976). Social relationships among adult female monkeys. *Animal Behavior* 24:917–938.

Seyfarth, R. M., and D. L. Cheney (1984). Grooming, alliances, and reciprocal altruism in vervet monkeys. *Nature* 308:541–543.

Silk, J. B. (1987). Social behavior in evolutionary perspective. In B. B. Smuts, D. L. Cheney, R. M. Seyfarth, R. W. Wrangham, and T. T. Struhsaker (eds.), *Primate Societies*, pp. 318–329. Chicago: University of Chicago Press.

Smuts, B. (1985). *Sex and Friendship in Baboons*. Hawthorne, NY: Aldine Press.

Strichartz, A. F., and R. Burton (1990). Lies and the truth: A study of the development of the concept. *Child Development* 61:211–220.

Tomasello, M. (in press). Uniquely primate, uniquely human. *Developmental Science*.

Tutin, C. E. G. (1979). Mating patterns and reproductive strategies in a community of wild chimpanzees (*Pan troglodytes schweinfurtü*). *Behavioral Ecology and Sociobiology* 6:29–38.

Uehara, S., M. Hiraiwa-Hasegawa, K. Hosaka, and M. Hamai (1994). The fate of defeated alpha male chimpanzees in relation to their social networks. *Primates* 35:49–55.

Watts, C. R., and A. W. Stokes (1971). The social order of turkeys. *Scientific American* 224:112–118.

Whiten, A., and R. W. Byrne (1988). The manipulation of attention in primate tactical deception. In R. W. Byrne, and A. Whiten (eds.), *Machiavellian Intelligence*, pp. 211–224. Oxford: Oxford University Press.

Wimmer, H., S. Gruber, and J. Perner (1984). Young children's conception of lying: Lexical realism–moral subjectivism. *Journal of Experimental Child Psychology* 37:1–30.

Wooldridge, D. (1963). *The Machinery of the Brain.* New York: McGraw-Hill.

8

How Good Are Fast and Frugal Heuristics?

GERD GIGERENZER,

JEAN CZERLINSKI, &

LAURA MARTIGNON

1. Introduction

Rationality and optimality are the guiding concepts of the Bayesian approach to cognition, but they are not the only reasonable guiding concepts. Two concepts from the other end of the spectrum, simplicity and frugality, have also inspired models of cognition. These fast and frugal models are justified by their psychological plausibility and adaptedness to natural environments. For example, the real world provides only scarce information, the real world forces us to rush when gathering and processing information, and the real world does not cut itself up into variables whose errors are conveniently independently normally distributed, as many optimal models assume.

However, recent optimal models already address these constraints. There are many methods for dealing with missing information. Optimal models can also be extended to take into account the cost of acquiring information. Finally, variables with unusual distributions can be transformed into nearly normal distributions, and outliers can be excluded. So what's the big deal?

This chapter previously appeared in James Shanteau, Barbara Mellers, and David Schum (eds.), *Decision Science and Technology: Reflections on the Contributions of Ward Edwards* (Boston: Kluwer Academic Press, 1999), pp. 81–103, and is reprinted by permission.

Optimal models seem to have met the challenge of adapting to natural environments. And if people do not already use these models, then they would want to learn how to use them since they are, after all, optimal.

Thus, it would seem that there is no need to turn to fast and frugal heuristics, which appear doomed to be both simplistic and inaccurate. Besides, there is an even stronger reason to shun simplicity and frugality as the basis for human cognition. They deny some of the most striking self-images *Homo sapiens* has constructed of itself: from *l'homme éclairé* of the Enlightenment to *Homo economicus* of modern business schools (Gigerenzer et al. 1989).

These are the typical intuitive arguments in the debate between optimality and rationality on the one hand and simplicity and frugality on the other. But before you pass judgment on where you stand, move beyond these mere intuitions to consider the real substance of the two approaches and the actual relationship between them. This chapter provides some food for your thoughts on these issues in the form of a review of our recent findings on fast and frugal heuristics (Gigerenzer, Todd, and the ABC group 1999). How great is the advantage in terms of speed and simplicity? How large is the loss of accuracy? How robust are fast and frugal heuristics under a variety of conditions—and under which conditions should we avoid using them? We answer these questions by comparing fast and frugal heuristics with benchmark models from the optimality and rationality tradition. Our intention is not to rule out one set of guiding concepts or the other, forcing us to choose rationality and optimality *or* simplicity and frugality. Rather, we wish to explore how far we can get with simple heuristics that may be more realistic models of how humans make inferences under constraints of limited time and knowledge.

But first we have to understand the guiding concepts. The fundamental distinction in approaches to reasonableness is between unbounded rationality and bounded rationality (e.g., Simon 1982, 1992). Unbounded rationality suggests building models that perform as well as possible with little or no regard for how time-consuming or informationally greedy these models may be. This approach includes Bayesian models and expected utility maximization models (e.g., Edwards 1954, 1961). In contrast, bounded rationality suggests designing models specifically to reflect the peculiar properties and limits of the mind and the environment. The decision maker is bounded in time, knowledge, and computational power. In addition, each environment has a variety of irregular informational structures, such as departures from normality.

There are, however, two approaches that compete for the title of bounded rationality: constrained maximization and satisficing (Figure 8.1). *Constrained maximization* means maximization under deliberation cost constraints. This demands even more knowledge and computation than unbounded rationality, because the decision maker has to compute the optimal trade-off between accuracy and various costs, such as information search costs and opportunity costs. The paradoxical result is that "limited" minds are assumed to have the knowledge and computational ability of mathematically sophisticated econometricians and their statistical software

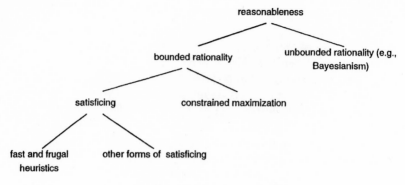

FIGURE 8.1. Visions of reasonableness

packages (e.g., Sargent 1993). The "father" of bounded rationality, Herbert Simon, has vehemently rejected this approach. In personal conversation, he once remarked in a mixture of anger and humor that he had thought of suing authors who misuse his concept of bounded rationality to construct ever more complicated models of human decision making.

Simon's view of bounded rationality is that of satisficing, which he con- trasts to constrained maximization. In the satisficing interpretation, the two sides of bounded rationality, limited minds and structured environments, are not merely two additional complications to the optimality story. Rather, they form a happy and beneficial marriage: subtle environmental structures that were neglected by standard rational models are potentially exploitable by simple heuristics (E. Brunswik in particular has emphasized the inter- relationship of cognition and environment, e.g., Brunswik 1964). Satisficing asserts that our minds have evolved all sorts of nimble tricks to perform well in the quirky structures of the real world.

The types of models developed by the satisficing view are thus fairly simple, in stark contrast to those of the constrained maximization view. For instance, one of the best-known examples of Simon's satisficing is to start with an aspiration level and then choose the first object encountered that satisfies this level (e.g., buy the first acceptable house). Still, satisficing can employ rather computationally expensive procedures (e.g., Simon 1956). We use the term *fast and frugal heuristics* for a subset of satisficing strategies that work with a minimum of knowledge, time, and computations. We call these heuristics "fast" because they process information in a relatively simple way, and we call them "frugal" because they use little information. The next section presents several examples of such heuristics.

2. Satisficing by Fast and Frugal Heuristics

There are infinitely many kinds of tasks that heuristics can be designed to perform. This chapter focuses on the task of predicting or inferring which of two objects scores higher on a criterion. Which soccer team will win? Which of two cities has a higher homelessness rate? Which applicant will do a better

TABLE 8.1. Cues for predicting homelessness in U.S. cities

	Los Angeles	Chicago	New York	New Orleans
Homeless per million	10,526	6,618	5,024	2,671
Rent control (1 is yes)	1	0	1	0
Vacancy rate (1 is below median)	1	1	1	0
Temperature (1 is above median)	1	0	1	1
Unemployment (1 is above median)	1	1	1	1
Poverty (1 is above median)	1	1	1	1
Public housing (1 is below median)	1	1	0	0

Note: Cues are ordered by validity, with rent control having the highest validity (.90). See text for further explanation.

Source: Tucker 1987.

job? To make such predictions, the heuristics use uncertain cues that indicate, with some probability, higher values on the criterion.

Consider, for example, the task of inferring which of two cities has a higher homelessness rate, using the data on fifty U.S. cities from an article by W. Tucker (1987). An excerpt from this data that includes the values for Los Angeles, Chicago, New York, and New Orleans on six cues and the criterion is shown in Table 8.1. One cue (rent control) is binary, and the other five have been dichotomized at the median. Unitary cue values (1) indicate higher values on the criterion, and zero cue values (0) indicate lower values. For example, since cities with rent control more often have a higher homelessness rate than cities without rent control, cities that have rent control are marked with a cue value of 1 for this cue. (In contrast, if cities without rent control more often had the higher homelessness rate, then having rent control would be marked by a 0.)

Of course, people generally do not have such tables of information handy; they have to search for information, in their memories or in libraries. But how could one construct a heuristic that cheaply (rather than optimally) limits search and computations? Two examples of such heuristics are Minimalist and Take The Best, which are drawn from a family of fast and frugal heuristics (Gigerenzer and Goldstein 1996; Gigerenzer, Hoffrage, and Kleinbolting 1991; Gigerenzer, Todd, and the ABC group 1999).

Minimalist

The minimal knowledge needed for cue-based inference is in which direction a cue "points." For instance, the heuristic needs to know whether warmer or cooler weather indicates a city with a higher rate of homelessness. In the fifty U.S. cities, warmer weather is indeed associated more often with higher homelessness rates than with lower rates, so a cue value of 1 is assigned to cities with warmer weather. Minimalist has only this minimal knowledge. Nothing is known about which cues have higher validity than others. The ignorant strategy of Minimalist is to look up cues in random order, choosing the city that has a cue value of 1 when the other city does not. Minimalist can be expressed in the following steps:

> Step 1. Random search: Randomly select a cue and look up the cue values of the two objects.

> Step 2. Stopping rule: If one object has a cue value of one (1) and the other does not, then stop search. Otherwise go back to Step 1 and search for another cue. If no further cue is found, guess.

> Step 3. Decision rule: Predict that the object with the cue value of one (1) has the higher value in the criterion.

For instance, when inferring whether Chicago or New Orleans has a higher homelessness rate, the unemployment cue might be the first cue randomly selected, and the cue values are found to be 1 and 1 (Table 8.1). Search is continued, the public housing cue is randomly selected, and the cue values are 1 and 0. Search is stopped and the inference is made that Chicago has a higher homelessness rate, as it indeed does.

So far, the only thing a person needs to know is which direction a cue points, that is, whether it indicates a higher or a lower value on the criterion. But there exist environments for which humans know not just the sign of cues but also roughly how predictive they are. If people can order cues according to their validities—whether or not this subjective order corresponds to the ecological order—then search can follow this order of cues. One of the heuristics that differs from the Minimalist in only this respect is called Take The Best; its motto is "Take the best; ignore the rest."

Take The Best

This heuristic is exactly like the Minimalist except that the cue with the highest validity, rather than a random cue, is tried first. If this cue does not discriminate, the next-best cue is tried, and so forth. Thus, Take The Best differs from Minimalist only in Step 1:

> Step 1. Ordered search: Select the cue with the highest validity and look up the cue values of the two objects.

The *validity* v_i of cue i is the number of right (correct) inferences, R_i, divided by the number of right and wrong inferences, $R_i + W_i$, based on cue i alone, independent of the other cues. We count which inferences are right and wrong across all possible inferences in a reference class of objects. That is,

$$v_i = \frac{\text{right inferences}}{\text{right inferences} + \text{wrong inferences}} = \frac{R_i}{R_i + W_i}$$

For example, since Los Angeles has a cue value of 1 for rent control while Chicago has a cue value of 0, the rent control cue suggests that Los Angeles has a higher homelessness rate; since Los Angeles does have a higher homelessness rate, this counts as a right inference. Between Chicago and New York, the rent control cue makes a wrong inference. And between Chicago and New Orleans, it does not discriminate—and cannot make an inference —because both cities have 0 cue values for rent control. If we count the number of right and wrong inferences for all possible pairings of the fifty U.S. cities, we find that 90 percent of the inferences based on rent control are right; thus, the cue validity of rent control is .90. Note that we only count as inferences the cases that are discriminated, that is, in which one object has a positive cue value and the other does not. Thus, the sum of all right and wrong inferences in the denominator is equal to the number of pairs of cities on which the cue discriminates. In the simulations that follow we compute the validity from the actual, ecological cue values. But when Take The Best is used as a model of human inference, the validities are computed only from the cue values the person actually knows (or believes).

For instance, when inferring whether Chicago or New Orleans has a higher homelessness rate, Take The Best looks up first the cue values of the two cities for rent control, since it is the cue with the highest validity (.90). Unfortunately, this cue does not discriminate—both cities have cue values of 0 (Table 8.1). So Take The Best looks up the second-best cue, the vacancy rate cue (validity .73). This cue does discriminate, so search is stopped. Take The Best infers that Chicago, the city with the unitary cue value in contrast to New Orleans's 0, has the higher homelessness rate.

Take The Best and Minimalist are constructed from several building blocks of fast and frugal heuristics (Gigerenzer and Goldstein 1996). These building blocks help us both in understanding the heuristics and in generating new heuristics.

The first building block is *step-by-step procedures*, that is, a cognitive strategy that searches for some information and checks whether this is sufficient to make a decision; if not, it searches for more information, checks whether this is sufficient, and so on (e.g., Miller, Galanter, and Pribram 1960).

The second building block is *simple stopping rules*, which specify computationally simple conditions for halting the gathering of more cue information. There are a number of heuristics that use stopping rules, especially those that already use "attribute-based" rather than "alternative-based" information gathering (to use the terminology of Payne, Bettman, and Johnson 1988). In the constrained maximization paradigm, for example, information search is halted when the marginal cost of another piece of information outweighs the marginal gain in accuracy expected. But calculating these marginals is a difficult game. In contrast, we propose stopping rules with uncomplicated criteria. Take The Best and Minimalist stop gathering further cue information if one object has a unitary (1) value for a cue and the other does not (i.e., has a zero, 0, or unknown value for that cue).

This simple stopping rule is in harmony with our third building block, *one-reason decision making*. Once search is stopped, a variety of computations could be performed on the information collected thus far. For example, multiple regression integrates all the cue values in a linear sum, and Bayesian models usually condition their probabilities on the values of several cues. But since Minimalist and Take The Best stop after the first piece of information that discriminates between the two objects, they base their decision only on this recent information, the last cue considered. Conflicts and trade-offs between cues never surface. The purpose behind such one-reason decision making is to avoid conflicts and avoid integrating information. Thus, the process that underlies decisions is noncompensatory. Note that one-reason decision making could be employed with less simple stopping rules, such as gathering a larger number of cues (e.g., in a situation where one has to justify one's decision); the decision, however, is based on only one cue.

To summarize, Minimalist and Take The Best employ the following building blocks:

- Step-by-step procedures
- Simple stopping rules
- One-reason decision making

In the following sections we will see how these building blocks exploit certain structures of environments. We will not deal here with how they exploit a lack of knowledge (see Gigerenzer and Goldstein 1996).

Some of these building blocks appear in other heuristics, which are related to Take The Best. Lexicographic strategies (e.g., Keeney and Raiffa 1976; Payne, Bettman, and Johnson 1993) are very close to Take The Best but not Minimalist. The term *lexicographic* signifies that cues are looked up in a fixed order and the first discriminating cue makes the decision, as in the alphabetic ordering used to decide which of two words comes first in a dictionary. A more distantly related strategy is Elimination By Aspects (Tversky 1972), which is also an attribute-based information processor and also has a stopping rule. Elimination By Aspects (EBA) differs from Take The Best in several respects; for instance, EBA chooses cues not according to the order of their validities but by another probabilistic criterion, and it deals with preference rather than inference. Another related strategy is Classification And Regression Trees (CART), which deals with classification and estimation rather than two alternative prediction tasks. The key difference is that in CARTs heavy computation and optimizing are used to determine the trees and the stopping rules.

In this section we have defined two fast and frugal heuristics. These heuristics violate two maxims of rational reasoning: they do not search for all available information, and they do not integrate information. Thus, Minimalist and Take The Best are fast and frugal, but at what price? How much more accurate are benchmark models that use and integrate all information when predicting unknown aspects of real environments?

This question was posed by Gigerenzer and D. G. Goldstein (1996), who studied the price of frugality in inferring city populations. The surprising result was that Take The Best made as many accurate inferences as linear models, including multiple regression, which uses both more computational power and more information. Minimalist generated only slightly less accurate inferences. In section 3 we test whether these results generalize to other real-world environments and to situations in which the training set and the test set are different. For simplicity, we will only study the performance of the heuristics under complete knowledge of cue values, whereas Gigerenzer and Goldstein (1996) varied the degree of limited knowledge. In section 4, we analyze the structure of information in real-world environments that fast and frugal heuristics can exploit, that is, their ecological rationality. Finally, in section 5, we take up W. Edwards's challenge to compare the performance of fast and frugal heuristics with more powerful strategies than multiple regression, in particular with Bayesian models.

3. Fast and Frugal at What Price?

Some psychologists propose multiple linear regression as a description of human judgment; others argue that it is too complex a model for humans to instinctively perform. Nevertheless, both camps often regard it as an approximation of the optimal strategy people should use, Bayesian models aside. A more psychologically plausible version of a linear strategy employs unit weights (rather than beta weights), as suggested by R. Dawes (e.g., 1979). This heuristic adds up the number of unitary (1) cue values and subtracts the number of zero (0) cue values. Thus, it is fast (it does not involve much computation) but not frugal (it looks up all cues). For simplicity, we call this heuristic *Dawes's Rule*.[1]

In this section, we will compare the performance of fast and frugal heuristics against these standard linear models. We begin by describing a single task in detail: to predict which U.S. cities have higher homelessness rates. Thereafter, we present the full data—the average results of the contests in twenty empirical data sets. But performance isn't everything—we also want to know what price we must pay for our accuracy. For example, heuristic *A* might need twice as many cue values as heuristic *B* in order to make its inferences but might be only a few percentage points more accurate. We will determine these accuracy-effort trade-offs for our heuristics, using measures of computational simplicity and frugality of cue use.

Predicting Homelessness

The first contest deals with a problem prevalent in many cities, homelessness, and we challenge our heuristics to predict which cities have higher homelessness rates. As mentioned earlier, the data stem from an article by W. Tucker (1987) that explores the causes of homelessness. He presents data for six possible factors for homelessness in fifty U.S. cities. Some possible factors have an obvious relationship to homelessness because they affect the ability of citizens to pay for housing, such as the unemployment rate and the percentage of inhabitants below the poverty line. Other possible causes affect the ability to find housing, such as high vacancy rates. When many apartments are vacant, tenants have more rental options and landlords are forced to lower rents in order to get any tenants at all. Rent control is also believed to affect ability to find housing. It is usually instituted to make housing more affordable, but many economists believe landlords would rather have no rent than low rent. Thus, less housing is available for rent and more people must live on the streets when rent control is in effect. The percentage of public housing also affects the ability to find housing because more public housing means that more cheap housing options are available. Finally, one possible cause does not relate directly to the landlord–tenant relationship. Average temperature in a city can affect how tolerable it is to sleep outside, leading to a number of possible effects, all of which suggest that warmer cities will have higher homelessness rates; warmer cities might attract the homeless from cooler cities, landlords might feel less guilty about throwing people out in warmer cities, and tenants might fight less adamantly against being thrown out in more tolerable climates.

We will ask our heuristics to use these six (dichotomized) cues to predict homelessness rates in the fifty cities.[2] The heuristics will be required to choose the city with more homelessness for all $50 \times 49/2 = 1{,}225$ pairs of cities. Regression will use the matrix of cue values to derive optimal weightings of the cues (possible causes).[3] There will be two types of competitions. In the first competition, the test set is the same as the training set (from which a strategy learns the information it needs, such as the weights of the cues). In the second, more realistic competition, the test set is different from the training set (also known as cross-validation). The second competition can reveal how much a heuristic overfits the data. Only the first type of competition was studied in Gigerenzer and Goldstein 1996.

Performance: Test Set = Training Set

We begin with the case of learning the entire data set and trying to fit it as well as possible. Performance is measured by the percentage of the 1,225 inferences that are correct (which city has higher homelessness?). Sometimes the heuristics must guess, for example between New Orleans and Miami, which have the same characteristics on the six cues (both are 1 on temperature, both are 0 on rent control, both are 1 on poverty, etc.). When a heuristic guesses, it earns a score of .5 correct, on the grounds that half the time the heuristic will be correct in its guess.

How well do the heuristics predict homelessness? Table 8.2 shows the results for the situation when the test set coincides with the training set. There are two surprises in these numbers. The first is that Take The Best, which uses only 2.4 cues on average, scores higher than Dawes's Rule, which uses all 6 of them. The second surprise is that Take The Best is almost as good as multiple regression, which not only looks up all the cues but also performs complicated calculations on them. So it seems that fast and frugal heuristics can be about as accurate as the more computationally expensive multiple regression! This confirms the findings of Gigerenzer and Goldstein (1996) in a task of predicting city populations.

TABLE 8.2. Trade-off between accuracy and cues looked up in predicting homelessness, for two kinds of competition

Strategy	Average number of cues looked up	% correct when test set same as training set	% correct when test set different from training set
Minimalist	2.1	61	56
Take The Best	2.4	69	63
Dawes's Rule	6	66	58
Multiple regression	6	70	61

Note: The average number of cues looked up was about the same for both kinds of competition (test set = training set and test set ≠ training set).

Although Take The Best's accuracy is very close to that of regression, its absolute value does not seem to be very high. What is the upper limit on performance? The upper limit is not 100 percent but 82 percent. This would be obtained by an individual who could memorize the whole table of cue values and, for each pair of cue profiles, memorize which one has the higher homelessness rate (but for the purpose of the test forgets the city names). If a pair of cue profiles appears more than once, this Profile Memorization Method goes for the profile that leads to the right answer more often.[4] The Profile Memorization Method results in 82 percent correct inferences for the homelessness data (see section 5).

Performance: Test Set ≠ Training Set

The prediction task we have considered thus far is limited to static situations, when we are merely trying to "fit" a phenomenon about which we already have all information. How well do the heuristics perform if the test set is different from the training set? This situation is a version of one-step learning and prediction. The data set is broken into two halves, with random assignment of cities to one or the other half. The heuristics are allowed to use one half to build their models (calculate regression weights, get cue orders, determine cue direction); then they must make predictions on the other half, using the parameters estimated on the first half, and their accuracy is scored. This process is repeated 1,000 times, with 1,000 random ways of breaking the data into two halves in order to average out any particularly helpful or hurtful ways of halving the data.

Training might not seem to affect Dawes's Rule and Minimalist, but in fact it does. Both strategies use the first half of the data set to estimate the direction of the cue (whether a higher or a lower cue value signals a higher criterion value). When the test set was different from the training set, the performance of Minimalist dropped from 61 percent correct to 56 percent and that of Dawes's Rule from 66 percent to 58 percent (Table 8.2). Take The Best requires learning more than merely the direction of the cues; one must also learn the order of the cue validities. With this slight additional

TABLE 8.3. Trade-off between accuracy and cues looked up, averaged across twenty data sets, for two kinds of competitions

Strategy	Average number of cues looked up	% correct when test set same as training set	% correct when test set different from training set
Minimalist	2.2	70	65
Take The Best	2.4	76	71
Dawes's Rule	7.4	73	70
Multiple regression	7.4	78	67

Note: The average number of cues looked up was about the same for both kinds of competition (test set = training set and test set ≠ training set).

knowledge, Take The Best scores 63 percent correct, down from 69 percent. Regression requires learning not only the direction of the cues but also their interrelationship in order to determine the best linear weighting scheme. Despite all this knowledge, regression's performance falls more than that of Take The Best. While regression scored 70 percent correct when it merely had to fit the data, it scores only 61 percent correct in the cross-validated case, falling to second place.

In summary, when heuristics built their models on half of the data and inferred on the other half, Take The Best was the most accurate strategy for predicting homelessness, followed closely by regression. This seems counter-intuitive, since Take The Best looks up only 2.4 of the 6 cues and (as we will soon see) is computationally simpler.

Note that we no longer determine the upper limit by the Profile Memorization Method. This method cannot be used if cue profiles that were not present in the first half are present in the second half.

Generalization

How well do these results generalize to making predictions about other environments? We now consider results across twenty data sets (explained in detail in Czerlinski, Gigerenzer, and Goldstein 1999). These data sets have real-world structure in them rather than artificial, multivariate normal structures. In order to make our conclusions as robust as possible, we also tried to choose as wide a range of empirical environments as possible. So they range from having 17 objects to 395 objects and from three cues (the minimum to distinguish between the heuristics) to nineteen cues. Their content ranges from social topics like high school dropout rates, to chemical ones such as the amount of oxidant produced from a reaction, to biological ones like the number of eggs found in individual fish.

Table 8.3 shows the performance of the heuristics averaged across the twenty data sets. When the task is merely fitting the given data (test set same as training set), multiple linear regression is the most accurate strategy, by two percentage points, followed by Take The Best. But when the task is to predict from a training set to a test set, Take The Best is most accurate. It out-performs multiple regression by four percentage points. Note that multiple regression has all the information Take The Best uses and more. Dawes's Rule lives up to its reputation for robustness in the literature (Dawes 1979) by taking second place and beating regression by three percentage points. Finally, Minimalist performs surprisingly well, only two percentage points behind regression. In short, Dawes's Rule is not the only robust yet simple model; Take The Best and Minimalist are also fairly accurate and robust under a broad variety of conditions. In fact, Take The Best is even slightly more accurate than Dawes's Rule, although it is more frugal. In section 4, we will explore how this is possible—how fast and frugal heuristics can also be accurate.

How Much Information Processing Is Performed?

We established empirically that Take The Best and Minimalist are frugal—on average, they stopped search and made a prediction after having looked up less than one-third of the cues. But are the heuristics also fast, that is, simple in their computations? Given that Take The Best performs so well, it must be doing some work, perhaps hidden in the training phase of the cross-validation, if not in the test phase. Thus, we now wish to be more precise about measuring how fast (computationally simple) our heuristics are, in both the training and test phase.

Let us begin by measuring the amount of learning required by the heuristics to build their models in order to perform their predictions later. We can use the suggestion of Newell and Simon (1972) and J. W. Payne, J. R. Bettman, and E. J. Johnson (1990) to count the number of Elementary Information Processing (EIP) units necessary for the training phase. These EIPs include addition, subtraction, multiplication, division, comparison of two numbers, reading a number, writing a number, and so on. For each such operation, we count one unit. These EIP units are easy to count, and Payne, Bettman, and Johnson (1990) present experimental evidence that they are a reasonable estimate of the cognitive effort involved in executing a particular choice strategy in a specific task environment. For our tasks, the number of EIPs required depends on N, the number of objects, and M, the number of cues in the data set. Table 8.4 specifies both the approximate number of EIPs used, for any values of N and M that a data set has and the number of EIPs for the specific case of predicting homelessness, with $N = 50$ and $M = 6$.

Fast and frugal heuristics require significantly less calculation in the training phase than multiple regression. This is the case even though in cal-culating the number of EIPs in regression we neglected the usual inevitabil-ity and computer overflow checks, so 20,000 EIPs is really a lower bound. In practical applications, fast and frugal heuristics might be as much as 1/100 simpler. Note that we differ from earlier theorists such as Dawes (1979) in including learning the direction of cues as a real problem; other theorists have assumed this is known already, making fast and frugal heuristics even simpler.

TABLE 8.4. Approximate number of Elementary Information Processing units (EIPs) needed for the training phase of each strategy

Strategy	Knowledge about cues obtained in training phase	Approximate number of EIPs used in training phase for any N, M	Number of EIPs used in training phase for homelessness ($N = 50, M = 6$)
Minimalist	Direction	$\approx 10NM$	3,398
Take The Best	Direction + order	$\approx 10NM$	3,448
Dawes's Rule	Direction	$\approx 10NM$	3,398
Multiple regression	Beta weights	$\approx 10NM^2$	20,020

Note: The task is predicting homelessness. N = number of objects; M = number of cues (for details see Czerlinski 1997).

Of course, learning a model of the data is only the first step. Implementing the heuristic has a cost, too. Table 8.5 specifies the number of EIPs in the test phase. Fast and frugal heuristics are always at least as efficient as the others because they look up fewer cues and perform fewer calculations on those cues. Since fast and frugal heuristics generally do not use all of the available cues, we also need to consider the "actual" number of cues looked up, M_a. For example, Take The Best uses on average only 2.4 cues for predicting homelessness.

Table 8.5 clearly shows that the cue-based predictions of Minimalist and Take The Best are highly efficient, about five times simpler than the simplest linear model, Dawes's Rule, and about ten times simpler than multiple regression. We now have a measure of how "fast" (computationally simple)

TABLE 8.5. Number of Elementary Information Processing units (EIPs) needed for the test phase of each strategy

Strategy	Process of inference	Formula for EIPs used in test phase for any N, M, M_a	Number of EIPs used in inferring homelessness ($N = 50, M = 6$)
Minimalist	Search through cues randomly until decision possible	$3M_a$	6.2 ($M_a = 2.1$)
Take The Best	Search through ordered cues until decision possible	$3M_a$	7.2 ($M_a = 2.4$)
Dawes's Rule	Count number of unitary and zero cue values; compare	$8M - 7$	41
Multiple regression	Linearly use beta weights to estimate criterion; compare	$16M - 7$	89

Note: The task is predicting homelessness. N = number of objects; M = number of cues; M_a = average number of cues used (for details see Czerlinski 1997).

the heuristics are, and we have shown that fast and frugal heuristics can be from five to ten times faster theoretically than regression (and practically even more). The calculation of EIPs does not have to assume serial processing; if the brain implements certain aspects of the calculation in parallel, then the total number of calculations would be the same, but they would be completed more quickly. For example, if we could compute the validity of all cues in parallel, we would effectively have $M = 1$, and this could be plugged into the formulae given earlier. However, even under such conditions, fast heuristics could not be slower than regression and could still be faster, just not as much faster as they are under the assumption of serial processing. And, of course, they would still be more frugal.

In summary, our fast and frugal heuristics learn with less information, perform fewer computations while learning, look up less information in the test phase, and perform fewer computations when predicting. Nevertheless, fast and frugal heuristics can be almost as accurate as multiple regression when fitting data. Even more counterintuitively, one of these fast and frugal heuristics, Take The Best, was on average more accurate than regression in the more realistic situation where the training set and test set were not the same (cross-validation). How is this possible?

4. Ecological Rationality: Why and When Are Fast and Frugal Heuristics Good?

Note first that these data sets have been collected from "real-world" situations. What are the characteristics of information in real-world environments that make Take The Best a better predictor than other heuristics, and where will it fail? When we talk of properties of information, we mean the information about an environment known to a decision maker. We discuss three properties. The first of these properties is one that characterizes many real-world situations: the available information is *scarce*. Take The Best is smarter than its competitors when information is scarce.

Scarce Information

In order to illustrate the concept of scarce information, let us recall an important fact from information theory: a class of N objects contains $log N$ bits of information. This means that if we were to encode each object in the class by means of binary cue profiles of the same length, this length should be at least $log N$ if each object is to have a unique profile. The example in Table 8.6 illustrates this relation for $N = 8$ objects. The eight objects are perfectly predictable by the three ($log 8 = 3$) binary cues. If there were only two cues, perfect predictability could simply not be achieved.

Theorem
If the number of cues is less than $log N$, the Profile Memorization Method will never achieve 100 percent correct inferences. Thus, no other strategy will, either.

TABLE 8.6. Illustration of the fact that eight objects can be perfectly predicted by $log8 = 3$ binary cues

Objects	First cue	Second cue	Third cue
A	1	1	1
B	1	1	0
C	1	0	1
D	1	0	0
E	0	1	1
F	0	1	0
G	0	0	1
H	0	0	0

This theorem motivates the following definition:

> A set of M cues provides *scarce* information for a reference class of N objects if $M \leq log N$.

We can now formulate a theorem that relates the performance of Take The Best to that of Dawes's Rule:

> In the case of scarce information, Take The Best is on average more accurate than Dawes's Rule.

The proof is in Martignon, Hoffrage, and Kriegeskorte 1997. The phrase "on average" means across all possible environments, that is, all combinations of binary entries for $N \times M$ matrices. The intuition that underlies the theorem is the following: in scarce environments, Dawes's Rule can take little advantage of its strongest property, namely, compensation. If in a scarce environment cues are *redundant*, that is, if a subset of these cues does not add new information, things will be even worse for Dawes's Rule. Take The Best suffers less from redundancy because decisions are taken at a very early stage.

Abundant Information

Adding cues to a scarce environment will do little for Take The Best if the best cues in the original environment are already highly valid, but it may compensate for various mistakes Dawes's Rule would have made based on the first cues. In fact, by adding and adding cues we can make Dawes's Rule achieve perfection. This is true even if all cues are favorable (i.e., their validity is >.5) but uncertain (i.e., their validity is <1).

Theorem
If an environment consists of all possible uncertain but favorable cues, Dawes's Rule will discriminate among all objects and make only correct inferences.

The proof is given in Martignon, Hoffrage, and Kriegeskorte (1997). Note that we are using the term *cue* to denote a binary valued function on the reference class. Therefore, the number of different cues on a finite reference class is finite. The theorem can be generalized to linear models that use cue validities as weights rather than unit weights. As a consequence, Take The Best will be outperformed on average by linear models in abundant environments.

Noncompensatory Information

Environments may be compensatory or noncompensatory. Among the twenty environments studied in section 3, we found four in which the weights for the linear models were noncompensatory (i.e., each weight is larger than the sum of all other weights to come, such as $1/2, 1/4, 1/8, \ldots$). The following theorem states an important property of noncompensatory models and is easily proved (Martignon et al. 1997):

> Take The Best is equivalent—in performance—to a weighted linear model whose weights form a noncompensatory set.

If multiple regression happens to have a noncompensatory set of weights (where the order of this set corresponds to the order of cue validities), then its accuracy is equivalent to that of Take The Best.

Why Is Take The Best So Robust?

The answer is simple: Take The Best uses few cues (only 2.4 cues on average in the data sets presented here). Thus, its performance depends on very few parameters. The top cues usually have high validity. In general, highly valid cues will remain highly valid across different subsets of the same class of objects. Even the order of their cue validities tends to be fairly stable. The stability of highly valid cues is a main factor for the robustness of Take The Best, in cross-validation as well as in other forms of incremental learning.

Strategies that use all cues must estimate a number of parameters larger than or equal to the number of cues. Some, like multiple regression, use a huge number of parameters. Thus, they suffer from overfitting, in particular with small data sets.

To conclude: Scarceness and redundancy of information are characteristics of information gathered by humans. Humans are not always good at finding large numbers of cues for making predictions. The magic number 7 ± 2 seems to represent the basic information capacity human minds work with in a short time interval. Further, humans are not always good at detecting redundancies between cues and quantitatively estimating the degree of these redundancies. Fast and frugal Take The Best is a heuristic that works well with scarce information and does not even try to estimate redundancies and cue intercorrelations. In this way, it compensates for the limits in human information processing. If the structure of the information available to an organism is scarce or noncompensatory, then Take The Best will be not only fast and frugal but also fairly accurate, even relative to more computationally expensive strategies.

5. How Does Take The Best Compare with Good Bayesian Models?

It happened that Edwards was a reviewer of one of our group's first papers on fast and frugal heuristics (Goldstein and Gigerenzer 1996). Ward sent us a personal copy of his review, as he always does. No surprise, his first point was "specify how a truly optimal Bayesian model would operate." But Ward did not tell us which Bayesian model of the task (to predict the populations of cities) he would consider truly optimal.

In this section, we present a possible Bayesian approach to the type of task discussed in the previous sections. We do not see Bayesian models and fast and frugal heuristics as incompatible or even opposed. On the contrary, considering the computational complexity Bayesian models require and the fact (as we will see) that fast and frugal heuristics do not fall too far behind in accuracy, one can be a satisficer when one has limited time and knowledge and a Bayesian when one is in no hurry and has a computer at hand. A Bayesian can decide when it is safe and profitable to be a satisficer.

Bayesian Networks

If training set and test set coincide, Bayesians know what they will do: they will use the Profile Memorization Method. If training set and test set are different, Bayesians have to construct a good model. Regression is not necessarily the first model that would come to a Bayesian's mind. Given this kind of task, Bayesians may tend to choose from the flexible family of Bayesian networks. Another possibility is a Bayesian CART, and a third is a mixture of these two.

The task is to infer which of two objects A or B scores higher on a criterion, based on the values of a set of binary cues (results explained in detail in Martignon and Laskey 1999). Assume, furthermore, that the decision maker has nine cues at his or her disposal and has full knowledge of the values these cues take on A and B. To work out a concrete example, let A and B have the cue profiles (100101010) and (011000011) respectively. Bayesians ask themselves: What is the probability that an object with cue profile (100101010) scores higher than an object with cue profile (011000011) on the established criterion? In symbols:

$$\text{Prob}(A > B \,|\, A \,@\, (100101010), B \,@\, (011000011)) = ? \quad (*)$$

Here the symbol @ is used to signify "has the cue profile." As a concrete example, let us discuss the task investigated in Gigerenzer and Goldstein 1996, where pairs of German cities were compared as to which had a larger population. There were nine cues: "Is the city the national capital?" (NC); "Is the city a state capital?" (SC); "Does the city have a soccer team in the major national league?" (SO); "Was the city once an exposition site?" (EX); "Is the city on the intercity train line?" (IT); "Is the abbreviation of the city on the license plate only one letter long?" (LP); "Is the city home to a university?"

(UN); "Is the city in the industrial belt?" (IB); and "Is the city in former West Germany?" (WG).

A network for our type of task considers pairs of objects (A, B) and the possible states of the cues, which are the four pairs of binary values $(0, 0)$, $(0, 1)$, $(1, 0)$, $(1, 1)$ on pairs of objects. A very simple Bayesian network would neglect all interdependencies between cues. This is known as Idiot Bayes. It computes (*) from the product of the different probabilities of success of all cues. Forced to a deterministic answer, Idiot Bayes will predict that A scores higher than B on the criterion if the probability of "A larger than B" computed in terms of this product is larger than the probability of "B larger than A." Due to its simplicity, Idiot Bayes is sometimes used as a crude estimate of probability distributions. This is not the procedure Bayesians will use if they want accuracy.

The other extreme in the family of Bayesian networks is the fully connected network, where each pair of nodes is connected both ways. Computing (*) in terms of this network when training and test set coincide amounts to using the Profile Memorization Method. Both these extremes, namely, Idiot Bayes and the fully connected network, are far from being optimal when training set and test set differ. A more accurate Bayesian network has to take into account the conditional dependencies between cues, as some dependencies are more relevant than others. Some may be so weak that it is convenient to neglect them, in order to avoid overfitting. Bayesians need a Bayesian strategy to decide which are the relevant links that should remain and to prune all the irrelevant ones. They need a strategy to search through the possible networks and evaluate each network in terms of its performance. Bayesian techniques for performing this type of search in a smart, efficient way have been developed in both statistics and AI. These methods are effcient in learning both structure and parameters. N. Friedman and L. Goldszmit (1996), for instance, have devised software[5] for searching over networks and finding a good fit for a given set of data in a classification task. Since our task is basically a classification task (we are determining whether a pair of objects is rightly ordered or not), we are able to make use of Friedman and Goldszmit's network. But even a smart Bayesian network is often too complex to be computed. The following theorem offers a way to reduce the huge number of computations that would be, at first glance, necessary for computing (*) based on a Bayesian network. In a Bayesian network the nodes with arrows that point to a fixed node are called the *parents* of that node. The node itself is called a *child* of its parents. What follows is a fundamental rule for operating with Bayesian networks:

Theorem
The conditional probability of a node j being in a certain state given knowledge on the state of all other nodes in the network is proportional to the product of the conditional probability of the node given its parents times the conditional probability of each of its children given its parents. In symbols:

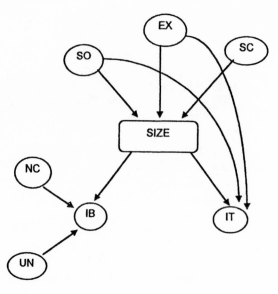

FIGURE 8.2. A Bayesian network for predicting population size (which of two German cities *A* or *B* is larger). The cues are SO = soccer team; EX = exposition site; SC = state capital; IB = industrial belt; NC = national capital; UN = university; IT = intercity train.

Prob(node *j* | other nodes)

= *K* × Prob(node *j* | parents of *j*) × Π Prob(child *k* of *j* | parents of *k*).

Here *K* is a normalizing constant. The set that consists of a node, its parents, its children, and the other parents of its children is called the *Markov Blanket* of that node. What the theorem states is that the Markov Blanket of a node determines the state of the node regardless of the state of all other nodes not in the Blanket.

The theorem just stated, based essentially on Bayes's rule, represents an enormous computational reduction in the calculation of probability distributions. It is precisely due to this type of reduction of computational complexity that Bayesian networks have become a popular tool both in statistics and in AI in the last decade.

Figure 8.2 shows the Bayesian network obtained with Friedman's search method, for the task of comparing German cities according to their population, as in Gigerenzer and Goldstein 1996. In that paper, the reference class of the eighty-three German cities with more than 100,000 inhabitants was analyzed. The Bayesian network reveals that two of the nine cues, LP and WG, are irrelevant when the other seven cues are known. Figure 8.2 illustrates the Markov Blanket of the node size, which represents the hypothesis "city *A* has more inhabitants than city *B*" and obviously can be in two states (the other state is "city *B* has more inhabitants than city *A*"). According to the theorem specified earlier,

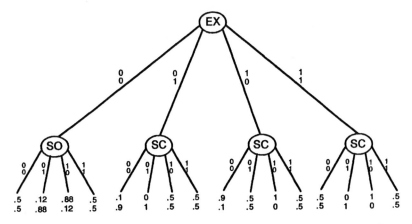

FIGURE 8.3. CART (Classification And Regression Tree) for quick computation of Prob (size | SO, EX, SC). For instance, if neither of the two cities A and B is an exposition site (symbolized by the two os in the left branch), then the only relevant cue is SO, that is, whether a city has a soccer team in the major league (SC is irrelevant). If A has a soccer team, but B does not (1 and 0), then Prob(A > B | SO, EX, SC) = .88, and Prob(A > B | SO, EX, SC) = .12 "A > B" stands for "A has larger population than B."

$$\text{Prob(size | UN, NC, IB, SO, EX, SC, IT)} = K \times \text{Prob(size | SO, EX, SC)} \times$$
$$\text{Prob(IB | size, UN, NC)} \times \text{Prob(IT | size)}$$

where K is a constant. In order to determine each of the probabilities on the right-hand side of the equation the program produces simple decision trees (actually CARTs), as illustrated in Figure 8.3 for Prob(size | SO, EX, SC). The program searches among all possible trees for the one that fits the data best, pruning all irrelevant branches. That is, this approach combines a Bayesian network with a CART step at the end. CART models were popularized in the statistical community by the seminal book by L. Breiman, J. H. Friedman, R. A. Olshen, and C. J. Stone (1984).

This method, a mixture of a Bayesian network and CART, is much more computationally intensive than multiple regression, not to speak of Take The Best. In fact, if we were to compute its ElPs as we did in the previous section, we would clearly reach a function of M and N that contains an exponential term in M.

How much more accurate is such a computationally complex Bayesian network than the simple Take The Best? Table 8.7 shows the performance of the Bayesian network and the Profile Memorization Method (the upper limit) when training and test set coincide. Performance was tested in four environments: Which of two German cities has the higher population? Which of two U.S. cities has a higher homelessness rate? Which of two individual female Arctic char fish produces more eggs? Which of two professors at a midwestern college has a higher salary?

For predicting city populations, the Bayesian network gets two percentage points more correct answers than Take The Best. The upper limit of

TABLE 8.7. Percentage of correct inferences when test set = training set

	Take The Best	Multiple regression	Bayesian network	Profile Memorization Method
City population	74	74	76	80
Homelessness	69	70	77	82
Fish fertility	73	75	75	75
Professors' salaries	80	83	84	87

correct predictions can be computed by the Profile Memorization Method as 80 percent, which is four percentage points above the performance of the Bayesian network. When the test set is different from the training set (Table 8.8), then multiple regression takes a slightly larger loss than Take The Best and the Bayesian network. Recall that the upper limit cannot be calculated by the Profile Memorization Method when the test set is different from the training set.

When predicting homelessness, the Bayesian network performs eight percentage points better than Take The Best (Table 8.7). This difference is reduced to two percentage points when the test set is different from the training set (Table 8.8). Here Take The Best is the most robust heuristic under cross-validation.

The fish fertility data set is of particular interest, because it contains a large set of objects (395 individual fish). The cues for the criterion (numbers of eggs found in a given fish) were weight of fish, age of fish, and average weight of her eggs. Here, as one would expect for a reasonably large data set, all results are quite stable when one cross-validates.

The next problem is to predict which of two professors at a midwestern college has a higher salary. The cues are gender, his or her current rank, the number of years in current rank, the highest degree earned, and the number of years since highest degree earned. When the test set is the same as the training set, Take The Best makes four percentage points less accurate inferences than the Bayesian network. However, when the test set is different from the training set, then Take The Best almost matches the Bayesian network.

TABLE 8.8. Percentage of correct inferences when test set is different from training set (cross-validation)

	Take The Best	Multiple regression	Bayesian network
City population	72	71	74
Homelessness	63	62	65
Fish fertility	73	75	75
Professors' salaries	80	80	81

Across these four environments, the following generalizations emerge:

1. When the test set is the same as the training set, the Bayesian network is considerably more accurate than Take The Best. On average, it was only three points behind the Profile Memorization Method, which attains maximal accuracy. However, when the test set is different from the training set, the accuracy of Take The Best is, on average, only one to two percentage points less than that of the Bayesian network. This result is noteworthy given the simplicity and frugality of Take The Best compared with the computational complexity of the Bayesian network.

2. Take The Best is more robust—measured in loss of accuracy from Table 8.7 to Table 8.8—than both multiple regression and the Bayesian network.

What is extraordinary about fast and frugal Take The Best is that it does not fall too far behind the complex Bayesian network. And it can easily compete in twenty different environments (section 3) with Dawes's Rule and multiple regression.

6. Conclusions

L. J. Savage wrote that the only decision we have to make in our lives is how to live our lives (1954, p. 83). But "how to live our lives" means basically "how to make decisions." Are we going to adopt Bayesian decision making or use some simple heuristics, like the satisficing ones presented in this chapter? This might not be an exclusive "or": fast and frugal heuristics can have their place in everyday affairs where time is limited and knowledge is scarce, and Bayesian tools can be the choice for someone who is in no hurry and has a computer in his or her bag (von Winterfeldt and Edwards 1986). A Bayesian who tries to maximize under deliberation constraints must choose a strategy under a combination of criteria, such as computational cost, frugality, accuracy, and perhaps even transparency. Thus, it may happen that this Bayesian may choose Take The Best or another fast and frugal heuristic over expensive but less robust Bayesian networks in some situations. Bayesian reasoning itself may tell us when to satisfice.

The major results summarized in this chapter are the following. First, across twenty real-world environments, the fast and frugal Take The Best outperformed multiple regression in situations with learning (test set ≠ training set), while even the simpler Minimalist came within two percentage points of it. Second, we specified which characteristics of information in real-world environments enable Take The Best to match or outperform linear models. Third, we showed that sophisticated Bayesian networks were only slightly more accurate than Take The Best.

The results reported in this chapter were obtained with real-world data but must be evaluated with respect to the conditions used, which include the following: First, we studied inferences only under complete knowledge, unlike Gigerenzer and Goldstein (1996), who studied the performance of heuristics under limited knowledge. Limited knowledge (e.g., knowing only a fraction of all cue values) is a realistic condition that applies to many situations in which predictions must be made. In the simulations reported by Gigerenzer and Goldstein, the major result was that the more limited the knowledge, the smaller the discrepancy between Minimalist and other heuristics becomes. Thus, Minimalist, whose respectable scores were nevertheless always the lowest, really flourishes when there is only limited knowledge. Gigerenzer and Goldstein (1996) also develop circumstances under which the counterintuitive less-is-more effect is possible, when knowing less information can lead to better performance than knowing more information.

Other conditions of the studies reported here include the use of binary and dichotomized data, which can be a disadvantage to multiple regression and Bayesian networks. Finally, we have used only correct data and not studied predictions under the realistic assumption that some of the information is wrong.

Some of the results obtained are reminiscent of the phenomenon of flat maxima. If many sets of weights, even unit weights, can perform about as well as the optimal set of weights in a linear model, this is called a flat maximum. The work by Dawes and others (e.g., Dawes and Corrigan 1974) made this phenomenon known to decision researchers, but it is actually much older (see John, Edwards, and von Winterfeldt n.d.). The performance of fast and frugal heuristics in some of the environments indicates that a flat maximum can extend beyond the issue of weights: inferences based solely on the best cue can be as accurate as those based on any weighted linear combination of all cues. The results in section 4, in particular the theorem on noncompensatory information, explain conditions under which we can predict flat maxima.

The success of fast and frugal heuristics emphasizes the importance of studying the structure of the information in the environment. Such a program is a Brunswikian program, but it is one that dispenses with multiple regression as *the* tool for describing both the processes of the mind and the structure of the environment. Fast and frugal heuristics can be ecologically rational in the sense that they exploit specific and possibly recurrent characteristics of the environment's structure. Models of reasonable judgment should look outside of the mind, to its environment. And models of reasonableness do not have to forsake accuracy for simplicity. The mind can have it both ways.

NOTES

We know Ward Edwards as a poet of limericks, as the ghostwriter who jazzes up the boring titles of our talks at the annual Bayesian meetings, as the rare reviewer who sends his reviews directly to the authors, and as the man who envisions the twenty-first century as "the century of Bayes." In research Ward has found a calling. Rather than promoting himself, he has chosen to promote the truth. For instance, he was strong enough to set the popular cognitive illusions program in motion and then jump off his own bandwagon, knowing that staying on it would have boosted his career. Ward is always willing to criticize his own thinking and reconsider his past views. The only possible exception is his dedicated Bayesianism. A great physicist once said of Max Planck, "You can certainly be of a different opinion from Planck's, but you can only doubt his upright, honorable character if you have none yourself." This statement could just as well have been made about Ward Edwards.

1. R. Dawes and B. Corrigan (1974) write: "The whole trick is to decide what variables to look at and then to know how to add" (p. 104). The problem of what variables to look at is, however, not defined: it is the job of the expert to determine both the cues and their directional relationship with the criterion (Dawes 1979). In our simulations we will use the full set of cues and simply calculate the actual direction of the cues (rather than asking an expert).

2. In contrast to Gigerenzer and Goldstein (1996), we always provide full information for the algorithms (no unknown cue values).

3. Note that if the optimal weight is negative, then regression says the cue points in the opposite direction from that indicated by the 1s and 0s. This can happen because the 1s and 0s are calculated for each cue independently while regression operates on all cues simultaneously, taking their interrelationship into account.

4. The Profile Memorization Method is essentially a Bayesian method. If there are several pairs of objects with the same one pair of cue profiles, the Profile Memorization Method looks at all such pairs and determines the frequency with which a city with the first cue profile has more homeless than a city with the second cue profile. This proportion is the probability that the first city scores higher on this criterion. If forced to give a deterministic answer and if the penalty for incorrectly guessing city 1 is the same as the penalty for incorrectly guessing city 2, the method dictates picking the object that has the highest probability of a high value on the criterion (e.g., a higher homelessness rate). Thus, in this situation the Bayesian becomes a frequentist who makes optimal use of every bit of information.

5. The software for this procedure has been kindly put to the disposition of Kathy Laskey and Laura Martignon by Neal Friedman.

REFERENCES

Breiman, L., J. H. Friedman, R. A. Olshen, and C. J. Stone (1984). *Classification and Regression Trees*. New York: Chapman and Hall.

Brunswik, E. (1964). Scope and aspects of the cognitive problem. In University of Colorado (Boulder Campus) Department of Psychology (ed.), *Contemporary Approaches to Cognition*, pp. 5–31. Cambridge: Harvard University Press.

Czerlinski, J. (1997). Algorithm calculation costs measured by ElPs. Unpublished manuscript, Max Planck Institute for Psychological Research, Munich.

Czerlinski, J., G. Gigerenzer, and D. Goldstein (1999). How good are simple heuristics? In G. Gigerenzer, P. Todd, and the ABC group, *Simple Heuristics That Make Us Smart*, pp. 97–118. New York: Oxford University Press.

Dawes, R. (1979). The robust beauty of improper linear models in decision making. *American Psychologist* 34:571–582.

Dawes, R., and B. Corrigan (1974). Linear models in decision making. *Psychological Bulletin* 81:95–106.

Edwards, W. (1954). The theory of decision making. *Psychological Bulletin* 51:380–417.

Edwards, W. (1961). Behavioral decision theory. *Annual Review of Psychology* 12:473–498.

Friedman, N., and L. Goldszmit (1996). A software for learning Bayesian networks. (Not released for public use.)

Gigerenzer, G., and D. G. Goldstein (1996). Reasoning the fast and frugal way: Models of bounded rationality. *Psychological Review* 103:650–669.

Gigerenzer, G., U. Hoffrage, and H. Kleinbölting (1991). Probabilistic mental models: A Brunswikian theory of confidence. *Psychological Review* 98:506–528.

Gigerenzer, G., Z. Swijtink, T. Porter, L. Daston, J. Beatty, and L. Krüger (1989). *The Empire of Chance: How Probability Changed Science and Everyday Life.* Cambridge: Cambridge University Press.

Gigerenzer, G., P. Todd, and the ABC group (1999). *Simple Heuristics That Make Us Smart.* New York: Oxford University Press.

Goldstein, D. G., and G. Gigerenzer (1996). Satisficing inference and the perks of ignorance. In G. W. Cottrell (ed.), *Proceedings of the Eighteenth Annual Conference of the Cognitive Science Society,* pp. 1347–1141. Mahwah, NJ: Erlbaum.

John, R. S., W. Edwards, and D. von Winterfeldt (n.d.). *Equal Weights, Flat Maxima, and Trivial Decisions.* Research Report 80-2. Social Science Research Institute, University of Southern California.

Keeney, R. L., and H. Raiffa (1976). *Decisions with Multiple Objectives: Preferences and Value Trade-offs.* Cambridge: Cambridge University Press.

Martignon, L., U. Hoffrage, and N. Kriegeskorte (1997). Lexicographic comparison under uncertainty: A satisficing cognitive algorithm. Unpublished manuscript.

Martignon, L., and K. Laskey (1999). Bayesian benchmarks for fast and frugal heuristics. In G. Gigerenzer, P. Todd, and the ABC group, *Simple Heuristics That Make Us Smart,* pp. 169–188. New York: Oxford University Press.

Miller, G. A., E. Galanter, and K. H. Pribram (1960). *Plans and the Structure of Behavior.* New York: Holt.

Payne, J. W., J. R. Bettman, and E. J. Johnson (1988). Adaptive strategy selection in decision making. *Journal of Experimental Psychology: Learning, Memory, and Cognition* 14:534–552.

Payne, J. W., J. R. Bettman, and E. J. Johnson (1990). The adaptive decision maker: Effort and accuracy in choice. In R. M. Hogarth (ed.), *Insights in Decision Making: A Tribute to Hillel J. Einhorn,* pp. 129–153. Chicago: University of Chicago Press.

Payne, J. W., J. R. Bettman, and E. J. Johnson (1993). *The Adaptive Decision Maker.* New York: Cambridge University Press.

Sargent, T. J. (1993). *Bounded Rationality in Macroeconomics.* Oxford: Clarendon Press.

Savage, L. J. (1954). *The Foundations of Statistics.* New York: Wiley.

Simon, H. A. (1956). Dynamic programming under uncertainty with a quadratic criterion function. *Econometrica* 24:19–33.

Simon, H. A. (1982). *Models of Bounded Rationality.* 2 vols. Cambridge: MIT Press.

Simon, H. A. (1992). *Economics, Bounded Rationality, and the Cognitive Revolution.* Aldershot Hants, England: Elgar.

Tucker, W. (1987). Where do the homeless come from? *National Review*, September 25, pp. 34–44.

Tversky, A. (1972). Elimination by aspects: A theory of choice. *Psychological Review* 79:281–299.

von Winterfeldt, D., and W. Edwards (1986). *Decision Analysis and Behavioral Research.* Cambridge: Cambridge University Press.

9

Commonsense Reasoning, Logic, and Human Rationality

MIKE OAKSFORD & NICK CHATER

1. Introduction

In cognitive psychology it is widely assumed that our understanding of human deductive reasoning will generalize to provide an understanding of everyday, commonsense reasoning and of human thought in general (Johnson-Laird 1983; Johnson-Laird and Byrne 1991; Rips 1994). This assumption presupposes that, in everyday life, much of human reasoning is deductive. Contrary to this view, we argue that almost no commonsense inferences are deductive. Moreover, we view this fact as diagnostic of the mismatch between the normative principles of logic and actual reasoning behavior on "deductive" reasoning tasks (e.g., Evans 1982, 1989; Evans, Newstead, and Byrne 1993; Johnson-Laird 1983; Johnson-Laird and Byrne 1991; Rips 1994; Wason and Johnson-Laird 1972). This mismatch has been taken to argue that humans may be irrational (Stein 1996; Stich 1985, 1990). In contrast, we argue that behavior on these tasks reflects rational, commonsense reasoning strategies that are appropriate to reasoning about our uncertain world. We thereby throw into question the significance of current psychological theories of deductive inference for understanding commonsense reasoning. We suggest that performance on many existing laboratory reasoning tasks can be better understood in nondeductive, commonsense terms.

Our argument is as follows: The most important issue for the cognitive science of reasoning is whether deduction provides a *computational*-level theory (Marr 1982) of a substantial amount of everyday, commonsense thought. Three sources of evidence appear to have the potential to settle the question decisively. These are the analysis of corpora of commonsense inferences; direct tests of performance on "deductive" reasoning tasks; and a priori considerations from computer science. We show that despite their superficial plausibility, none of these sources of evidence decides the question at issue. However, a more sophisticated interpretation of these sources of evidence can provide answers. First, the analysis of corpora circularly presupposes a standard logical analysis of individual arguments. It is more appropriate to investigate directly the kinds of reasoning that underpin organized systems of knowledge in which particular natural-language arguments (such as would be found in a corpus) are embedded. This is the subject matter of epistemology and the philosophy of science. Second, the study of reasoning tasks circularly presupposes that people interpret the tasks as deductive reasoning problems. It is more appropriate to contrast deductive and nondeductive characterizations of *both* interpretation and reasoning and see which provides the best account of the empirical data. This is the domain of the psychology of reasoning. Third, a priori considerations from computer science (suggesting that all computations are, in a sense, deductive) are too abstract to bear on issues relevant to the cognitive science of reasoning. It is more appropriate to consider whether computational systems based on deductive reasoning, in the sense employed in cognitive science, can provide the basis for systems that can reason about the everyday, commonsense world. This project has been extensively considered in AI. We argue that these lines of argument, from three different fields of inquiry—epistemology, AI, and psychology of reasoning—converge on the conclusion that deduction plays no significant role in commonsense reasoning about the everyday world.

This chapter is organized as follows: We begin by outlining what deduction is, in abstract terms, and then consider various ways in which it can be related to human reasoning, using the framework of D. Marr's (1982) levels of explanation. We argue that the fundamental issue for the cognitive science of reasoning is whether deductive logic provides a computational-level theory of human reasoning. We then consider how this question can be addressed. We first consider and reject the three superficially plausible methods of resolving the question of the prevalence of deduction introduced earlier. We then develop three more sophisticated lines of argument, from epistemology, AI, and the psychology of reasoning. We show that each argument supports our conclusion that deduction has no significant role in commonsense reasoning. Finally, we consider the implications of rejecting deduction for the cognitive science of human reasoning.

2. What Is Deduction?

Classically, in a valid deductive argument, the conclusion must be true if the premises are true. That is, deductive inferences are certain. Such inferences guarantee that the conclusion is true, if the premises are true, independent of any other information. Therefore, if a conclusion follows deductively from a set of premises, then it must also follow deductively from that set of premises conjoined with any set of additional premises (see Oaksford and Chater 1998, chapter 1). That is, nothing can overturn a deductive inference. Suppose, for example, that the commutativity of addition (that is, $x + y = y + x$, for all x and y) can be deduced from some axiomatic formulation of arithmetic. It therefore follows that commutativity holds, *whatever* further axioms are added. This property is known as monotonicity, and it is a crucial property of axiomatic systems in mathematics. Moreover, many logicians regard this property as the defining feature of a logical system (Curry 1956).

Other modes of reasoning, which are not deductively valid, are "nonmonotonic"—adding premises can lead to conclusions being withdrawn. An important example is induction, in which general laws or regularities are inferred from particular observations. At any time it is possible that a new observation may conflict with the regularity and undermine it. For example, a new observation of a nonblack raven logically undermines the inductive inference that *all ravens are black* based on the observation of numerous black ravens. Thus, adding a new premise (a new observation) can remove the conclusion, and hence induction is nonmonotonic. Another example is abduction, which typically involves inferring causes from their effects. For example, in a detective mystery a particular set of clues might, for example, suggest that the butler is the murderer. But a new and decisive clue (e.g., the chauffeur's bloodstained shirt) might overturn this conclusion. Thus, abduction is also nonmonotonic and hence not deductive.

3. Deduction and Reasoning?

The claim that human reasoning involves deduction can be understood in a number of different ways. We can understand these different interpretations in terms of two of Marr's (1982) three levels of computational explanation.

Marr's highest level of analysis is the *computational* level, where "the performance of the device is characterized as a mapping from one kind of information to another, the abstract properties of this mapping are defined precisely, and its appropriateness and adequacy for the task at hand are demonstrated" (1982, p. 24). Marr uses the example of a cash register. The theory of arithmetic provides the computational-level analysis of this device, and its appropriateness is demonstrated by showing that our intuitive constraints on the operation of a cash register map directly onto this mathematical theory (1982, p. 22). In the case of human reasoning, psychologists have typically assumed that deductive logic plays the role that arithmetic plays for the cash register; that is, logic characterizes the inferences people draw. Whether or not this is true is clearly an empirical question, just as it is an empirical question whether or not a particular piece of machinery functions as a cash register.

Marr's *algorithmic* level describes how to compute the function specified at the computational level. This level also involves specifying the representations that the algorithm manipulates in computing the function. Thus, in the case of the cash register, using Arabic numerals as the representations involves using the standard rules "about adding the least significant digits first and 'carrying' the sum if it exceeds 9" (1982, p. 22) as an algorithm. Although the choice of algorithm is constrained by the choice of representation, it is not uniquely constrained—there may be several ways of computing a certain function that use the same representation. It could be the case that deduction provides a crucial component at the algorithmic level. In computer science, this idea is embodied in theorem provers, which are computational systems for proving logical theorems. Theorem provers can be used to reason about the everyday world, given axioms that embody everyday knowledge. They have also been used to construct general programming languages, such as PROLOG (Clocksin and Mellish 1984).

Hypotheses about deductive reasoning at the computational and algorithmic levels have been prevalent within the psychology of deductive reasoning. Many theorists argue for deduction at both levels. For example, B. Inhelder and J. Piaget (1958, p. 305) go as far as to say that human "reasoning is nothing more than the propositional calculus itself." For Piaget, attainment of the formal operational stage in cognitive development is, by definition, revealed in the ability to show logical reasoning behavior. Thus, logic is viewed as an appropriate computational-level description of mature human behavior. But, moreover, the quotation earlier reveals that the mechanism that achieves this performance is itself logic. This view is still widely advocated in current psychology of reasoning, by advocates of "mental logic" (Braine 1978; Braine and O'Brien 1991; Henle 1962; Lea et al. 1990; O'Brien, Braine, and Yang 1994; Pollitzer and Braine 1991; Rips 1983, 1994; for a collection on these issues, see Macnamara and Reyes 1994). For example, Rips (1994, p. viii) argues for what he calls the Deduction System Hypothesis: that logical "principles . . . are central to cognition because they underlie many other cognitive abilities . . . [and] that the mental life of every human embodies certain deduction principles."

Although the claims that logic has a role at the computational and algorithmic levels are often held together, they are clearly independent. It is possible that while logic characterizes the behavior of a device at the computational level, the algorithms that produce the behavior are not themselves logical. This viewpoint is explicitly advocated in the psychology of reasoning by J. Macnamara, who also places deductive logic at the center of human cognition but articulates this thesis more guardedly: "A logic that is true to intuition in a certain area constitutes a competence theory [in Chomsky's (1965) sense] for the corresponding area for cognitive psychology" (Macnamara 1986, p. 22). As Marr (1982) notes, "competence theory" is simply another way of talking about a computational-level account. Mental model theory (Johnson-Laird 1983; Johnson-Laird and Byrne 1991) explicitly takes the view that logic is part of the computational-level theory of reasoning.[1] But mental model theory is typically viewed as not involving logical inference at the algorithmic level. Instead mental model theory assumes that deductive reasoning involves the construction and manipulation of mental models.[2]

The converse position is also possible. The algorithms that underlie thought might follow deductive logic, but the behavior that results from those algorithms might be best characterized in nondeductive terms. For example, a theorem prover could implement list-handling operations or arithmetic. Therefore, the computational-level characterization of what the program is doing will involve descriptions of list manipulation or arithmetical calculation, rather than logical proof. Within the psychology of reasoning, this viewpoint has not been explicitly advocated, as far as we know.[3] However, it is reasonable to interpret influential theorists in the foundations of cognitive science, such as J. A. Fodor, as advocating this position. Thus, Fodor and Z. W. Pylyshyn (1988, pp. 29–30) argue that "it would not be unreasonable to describe Classical Cognitive Science as an extended attempt to apply the methods of proof theory to the modeling of thought," and they proceed to defend this position strongly. Because proof theory is the mechanism by which deductive inferences are made, this amounts to the claim that cognition is deductive at the algorithmic level. But Fodor (1983) also argues extensively that almost all aspects of thought are "nondemonstrative," that is, nondeductive, in character (and we shall outline some of these arguments later). Therefore, Fodor seems to reject deduction as a computational-level theory of reasoning but embraces logic as an algorithmic theory.

In this chapter, we shall focus primarily on whether deductive logic provides an appropriate *computational*-level description of human reasoning, rather than dealing with the algorithmic level. As we have seen, the assumption that deduction does provide a computational-level description for much human inference is shared by many contemporary researchers on reasoning, including advocates of mental logics and mental models. Of course, no theorist would propose that deductive logic could provide a computational-level theory of all aspects of human reasoning, such as reasoning under uncertainty (Tversky and Kahneman 1974), decision making (Baron 1994; Tversky and Kahneman 1986), and abductive (Gluck and Bower 1988), and inductive (Gorman and Gorman 1984; Wason 1960) reasoning. Instead, deductive logic is assumed to provide a computational-level account of an important class of human reasoning. Moreover, deductive logic is assumed to play at least a partial role in almost every other aspect of cognition (Johnson-Laird and Byrne 1991; Macnamara and Reyes 1994; Rips 1994). For example, P. N. Johnson-Laird and R. M. J. Byrne (1991, pp. 2–3) argue for the centrality of deduction

> because of its intrinsic importance: it plays a crucial role in many tasks. You need to make deductions in order to formulate plans and to evaluate actions; to determine the consequences of assumptions and hypotheses; to interpret and formulate instructions, rules and general principles; to pursue arguments and negotiations; to weigh evidence and to assess data; to decide between competing theories; and to solve problems.

Thus, the idea that a deductive competence theory is central to human cognition both has a long pedigree and is widely held by many leading figures in the psychology of reasoning.

In this chapter, we argue against this tradition in the psychology of reasoning. We claim that almost no commonsense human reasoning can be characterized deductively or has any significant deductive component. Although many theorists have argued that deduction is at the core of cognition, we argue that it is at the periphery. From this point of view, we shall argue that the "errors and biases" observed in "deductive" tasks in psychological experiments should be understood not as failed deductive reasoning but as successful nondeductive reasoning. Consequently, these "biases" do not provide evidence for human irrationality; rather, they reveal the nature of people's commonsense reasoning strategies. Other theorists have argued for a similar position (e.g., Cheng and Holyoak 1985; Cosmides 1989; Fischhoff and Beyth-Marom 1983; Gigerenzer and Hug 1992; Holland et al. 1986; Holyoak and Spellman 1993; Klayman and Ha 1987). But these theorists have focused on whether particular tasks are deductive, rather than on whether deduction provides a satisfactory computational-level description of real, commonsense reasoning.[4] It is this wider question that is the central concern of this chapter.

4. Deduction and Common Sense: False Trails

There are three methods of investigating the question of how much commonsense reasoning is deductive at the computational level, which initially appear to provide decisive answers. First, the collection and analysis of corpora of commonsense arguments promises to reveal the statistical prevalence of deductive reasoning directly. Second, presenting people with deductive reasoning tasks should directly tap any underlying deductive competence. Third, a priori considerations from computer science appear to decide the question, before any empirical investigation is carried out: specifically, any computational process whatever can be viewed as deductive. In this section, we show that none of these considerations can decide the question. In the next section, we show that when these sources of evidence are viewed from a more sophisticated perspective the question can be genuinely addressed. The three sources of evidence provide three criteria of adequacy on theories of reasoning, from epistemology, AI, and the psychology of reasoning, none of which can be met by a cognitive science of reasoning using deduction as its computational-level theory.

Looking at Commonsense Argument

This strategy involves collecting and analyzing corpora of commonsense natural-language arguments and deciding what fraction of them are deductively valid. If deduction is prevalent in commonsense argument, it is also likely to be prevalent in reasoning, on the reasonable assumption that what people say is closely related to what they think.

The problem is that whether or not a natural-language argument is deductive cannot be straightforwardly ascertained by purely logical analysis. Consider, for example, the argument:

Birds fly.
Tweety is a bird.
Therefore, Tweety flies.

One way of assessing the validity of this argument is to translate it into a logical formalism, such as the predicate calculus, as follows:

$$\forall x(bird(x) \rightarrow flies(x))$$
$$\underline{bird(Tweety)}$$
$$flies(Tweety)$$

According to the logical properties of the predicate calculus, this is a deductively valid argument: in logical terms, there is no model in which the premises are true, but the conclusion is false.

But this only means that the original argument is deductively valid if the *translation* from natural language into the logical language is accepted as capturing the "logical form" of natural-language statements (Haack 1978). In practice, this step is frequently highly controversial. For example, even the logical terms ¬, ∧, and ∨ are notoriously distant relatives of their natural-language counterparts *not, and* and *or* (e.g., Hodges 1977; Horn 1989; Lemmon 1965). The relation between quantifiers ∀ and ∃ and universal and existential quantification in natural language is even more complex (Barwise and Cooper 1981). This is particularly true when, as in our example sentence "Birds fly," the quantification is not explicit. Should this sentence be treated as meaning that *all* birds fly? Or is a better interpretation that *most* birds fly, that *normal* birds fly (McCarthy 1980), or perhaps that it is reasonable to assume that a bird flies unless there is reason to believe the contrary (Reiter 1980, 1985)? On any of these latter interpretations, the conclusion of the preceding inference does not follow deductively—Tweety may be one of the exceptional nonflying birds. Therefore, whether or not a natural-language argument is deductive depends on how the premises and conclusions are translated into logic—and this translation is a highly controversial matter.

Moreover, both philosophers (e.g., Davidson 1984; Quine 1960) and psychologists (Smedslund 1970) have pointed out that there is a circularity in the relationship between studying reasoning and studying the meaning of what people say. That is, which translation of a natural-language statement is correct depends on how people *reason* with that statement.[5] For example, is the statement rejected as soon as a counterexample is found? Will a person wager an arbitrarily large sum of money against the possibility that the premises are true but the conclusion false? The logical form of a statement is intended to capture the patterns of reasoning in which it figures, and hence the nature of reasoning with the statement constrains the choice of translation. But, of course, discovering how people reason with a statement is a question in the psychology of reasoning. So psychologists cannot look to a purely logical analysis of natural-language arguments as a neutral way of assessing how much deduction people do, because the appropriateness of any particular logical analysis itself depends on how people reason.

The fact that logical analysis of natural-language arguments itself depends on psychological considerations rules out the obvious methodological strategy of collecting and analyzing a corpus of commonsense arguments.

Using Deductive Reasoning Tasks

Instead of collecting a corpus, a more appropriate strategy might be to experimentally test people's ability to solve deductive reasoning problems. However, the problem that logical analysis is not psychologically neutral also applies to the interpretation of materials in psychological experiments (Smedslund 1970). In setting up putative "deductive reasoning problems," psychologists have typically assumed a particular logical analysis of the natural-language statements that people are asked to reason over. This analysis is typically accepted uncritically from logical texts, and the psychological presuppositions involved in adopting a particular analysis are not examined. But if the logical analysis chosen turns out to be psychologically inappropriate (for example, a quantifier is interpreted as meaning "all" when it should be interpreted as "almost all"), then serious consequences may follow. First, the psychologist may not be studying deductive reasoning at all. Second, the logical misanalysis will lead the psychologist to assume that people are making reasoning errors (in terms of the wrong logical analysis), while they may be reasoning correctly (in terms of the psychologically appropriate analysis). Third, the psychologist will postulate biases and other reasoning limitations to explain the apparent reasoning errors and will be unable to discover any rational pattern in people's performance. In our discussion of the psychology of reasoning later, we argue that these problems lie at the heart of current theories of the psychology of deductive reasoning. We argue that most "deductive" reasoning tasks are not deductive at all and that human data can be rationally explained as involving uncertain, commonsense reasoning, rather than deduction.

At the heart of this issue is the question "what is the appropriate computational-level description of human behavior on 'deductive' reasoning tasks?" Although logic may have inspired a particular task, it is an empirical question whether people interpret the task deductively. We illustrate this point by an analogy with discovering the function of an unknown device. Suppose it has a keypad on it, a digital readout, and a coin slot. You therefore form the reasonable hypothesis that it is a public pay calculator; that is, its function is to perform arithmetic calculations for you when you put a coin in the slot. To test this reasonable hypothesis you may enter a coin and punch in some numbers in the following sequence: "2," "*," "4," "=." Your hypothesis leads you to predict that the digital readout some short time later will be "8." Three possibilities arise: (1) Suppose that the readout is indeed "8," which seems to confirm your hypothesis. It would not take many more such successful tests before you were reasonably confident that this device was indeed a pay calculator. (2) Suppose, however, that you adopt the same hypothesis, but now, after placing your coin in the slot and pressing the appropriate keys in the preceding test, the digital readout was "10." This would seem to suggest that the device was not a calculator after all. However, you continue to test the device in the same way—perhaps you think quite reasonably that even machines can make occasional mistakes— and still find no consistent arithmetic relation between the inputs and the outputs. At this point you should become reasonably convinced that the device is not a calculator. (3) You then notice that the number that comes up at each trial in fact corresponds to the value of the coin you insert into the device. You therefore come to the conclusion that the device is actually a pay phone.

We suggest that contemporary psychology of reasoning theory is in situation (2) earlier. Researchers have assumed that the tasks they present people are deductive but then fail to elicit logical performance. However, rather than abandon the view that people interpret these tasks logically, researchers have inferred that people have error-full deductive mechanisms. We will argue that reasoning researchers should instead search for more appropriate computational-level theories—specifically, they should explore computational-level theories of nonmonotonic, uncertain reasoning, rather than computational-level theories based on deduction.

In sum, the strategy of presenting people directly with deductive reasoning problems confronts the same problem of interpretation as studying corpora—you can never tell which arguments in the corpus, or which experimental tasks, are indeed deductive. Moreover, illogical performance on a task need not bear on whether people are rational, because they may interpret the task in such a way that some other normative theory applies by whose standards their reasoning is perfectly sound.

An Answer from Computer Science?

Perhaps all these empirical considerations are wholly unnecessary. Cognitive science is built on the assumption that cognition is computation. And there are deep results in computer science that suggest that all computations can be viewed as deductive, that is, logical, inferences.

All computational devices are equivalent to Turing machines (assuming the Church-Turing thesis). It is simple to write logical axioms that perfectly model the behavior of any Turing machine (Boolos and Jeffrey 1980). Thus, logic (assuming the appropriate axioms) provides a computational-level theory of the behavior of the device. In this sense, logic can provide a computational-level account of any computational process, including any postulated in cognitive science. Furthermore, the steps that underlie the Turing machine's behavior each correspond to a step in a logical derivation.

Therefore, logic also provides an algorithmic-level account of the Turing machine's behavior.

Similarly, programming languages are typically given two kinds of semantics, according to which they can be understood as performing logical inferences. Operational semantics maps the programming language onto machine operations. Denotational semantics typically maps the programming language onto some abstract mathematical structure, according to which, for example, algorithmic correctness can be proved (Girard 1989; Scott and Strachey 1971). According to both approaches, logic can provide a computational- and an algorithmic-level theory for any programming language.

It would therefore appear that the question of how much deduction there is in human cognition is decided the moment we adopt the assumption that cognition is computation. Any behavior that we can explain in computational terms must automatically have a logical interpretation both at the algorithmic and at the computational level. Consequently, it appears that *all* cognitive processes are ipso facto deductive.

However, there is clearly something seriously wrong with this line of argument. If it is accepted, then any cognitive task is necessarily a logical task. This would mean that arithmetic, reading, probabilistic reasoning, motor control, perceptual processing, syntactic analysis, and so on are all examples of logical reasoning. Furthermore, this means that all mundane computations, such as doing spreadsheets, word processing, solving differential equations, and doing actuarial calculations, have deductive logic as their computational-level theory. But this is close to a reductio ad absurdum of this line of reasoning. The point of computational-level theory is that it describes both the purpose of the computation and the objects and relations it is *about*. Thus, a computational-level theory of a cash register must involve numbers and numerical operations; a computational-level theory of syntactic analysis must deal with words, phrases, and sentences of natural languages; and so on. However, the objects utilized in providing the overarching logical analyses outlined earlier involve states and possible state transitions of a Turing machine or mathematical objects in abstract function spaces. A logical description in terms of these objects provides a computational-level description of a sort, but at such an abstract level of specification that it says nothing about the *point* of the computation. At this level of description, it is not possible to discriminate a computational process that carries out actuarial calculations from one that does word processing or produces natural-language utterances. The whole point of Marr's (1982) computational-level analysis is to make exactly these distinctions, to which these highly abstract analyses are insensitive.

In the case of human reasoning, it is crucial that a computational-level theory view human reasoning as about the objects and relations in the everyday world. The claim that an inference from "Birds fly" and "Tweety is a bird" to "Tweety flies" is (or is not) deductive only makes sense where we interpret these statements as referring to birds, flying, and Tweety, not to either states of a computational device or to objects in an abstract function space.

Therefore, the apparently decisive a priori arguments from computer science turn out to be entirely beside the point in determining whether or not human inference should be understood deductively. The results from computer science only apply to a level of analysis so abstract as to be of no practical value in constructing computational- or algorithmic-level theories of human reasoning.

Summary

The three possible ways of answering our question concerning the relationship between commonsense and deductive reasoning turned out, on closer inspection, to be inadequate. The first and second cases, analyzing corpora of inferences or directly testing people with "deductive" reasoning tasks, both founder on the same problem. This is that the interpretations of arguments and of tasks both circularly involve assumptions about how people reason. Moreover, a priori concerns from computer science are too abstract to differentiate deductive from nondeductive reasoning in any sense interesting to cognitive theory.

Each of these sources of evidence can, however, when viewed from a more sophisticated perspective, bear on the prevalence of human deductive reasoning at Marr's computational level of description. First, we have argued that analyzing natural-language corpora of inferences piecemeal would be futile, because of the problem of interpretation. This issue is directly addressed in philosophy, by classical epistemology and its contemporary counterpart, the philosophy of science. These philosophical projects attempt to characterize the inference patterns that underpin whole bodies of beliefs (such as scientific theories), in which specific arguments and inferences are embedded. Second, we have argued that simply testing people on "deductive" reasoning tasks confronts the same problem—that how participants interpret the task is unclear. But empirical psychology can answer this question, by providing theories of how tasks are interpreted *and* how to characterize people's reasoning given these interpretations, that is, by providing a computational-level explanation. Competing explanations at this level (e.g., involving or not involving deduction) can then be compared with the data to see which provides the best characterization of human reasoning behavior. Third, we have argued that a priori considerations from computer science are too abstract to be useful. But computer science can inform the question of how much deduction there is in commonsense reasoning via the practical attempt to build intelligent reasoning systems using logical methods (where logic is employed at the level relevant to psychology). This is not merely an abstract possibility but has been a popular research strategy in much of AI (Charniak and McDermott 1985). Therefore, the success or failure of this strategy can inform the viability of a deductive characterization of human thought. We now consider each of these more sophisticated approaches and argue that each reveals that little or no commonsense human reasoning is deductive.

5. Common Sense and Deduction: Lines of Evidence

If real human reasoning is based on deduction, then three criteria of adequacy can be adduced, which correspond to three more sophisticated research strategies mentioned earlier. First, unless we are to give up the claim that human reasoning has any rational justification, then a deductive account of how people *should* reason about the world must be viable. That is, deduction must be central to our theories of epistemology, which define the very standards of rationality against which we measure actual human reasoning performance. Second, any psychological theory must be computationally viable. Therefore, if deduction is the foundation of human thought, then it must be possible to design and successfully implement AI systems that reason about the real world using deduction. Third, a good psychological theory must, of course, be consistent with the data. Psychological theories of reasoning based on deduction should provide better fits to the data than accounts that reject deduction.

We argue that the claim that human reasoning is based on deduction at the computational level fails on all three counts: it represents an epistemologically outmoded tradition; it has not proved viable in AI; and, moreover, nondeductive accounts of human reasoning provide better fits to the empirical data.

Epistemological Adequacy

In this section our argument is in three parts. First, we argue that the view that deduction is the foundation for reasoning about the world reflects an outmoded epistemological tradition. Second, we consider what aspects of reasoning might be deductive and conclude that the obvious candidates turn out to be nondeductive in character. Third, we briefly consider and reject a possible defense of the centrality of deduction in psychology, which seeks to exploit the fact that epistemology considers how we *should* reason, whereas cognitive science is concerned with how people actually *do* reason.

DEDUCTION: A FOUNDATION FOR THOUGHT? Euclid provided the first systematic exploration of deductive reasoning (Coolidge 1940). Beginning with definitions and apparently self-evident axioms, he showed how purely deductive argument could establish a large class of geometrical truths. The Euclidean method has proved to be enormously productive not just in geometry but throughout mathematics.

But mathematical reasoning does not seem, superficially, to have much in common with commonsense thought. In particular, mathematics appears to be about establishing certainties that concern abstract objects (see Putnam and Benacerraf 1983 for discussion). In contrast, commonsense thought appears to be about making the best sense possible of an ill-defined, concrete external world, in which certainty is rarely, if ever, encountered

(Barwise and Perry 1983). Can deduction extend beyond the mathematical realm and provide a route to knowledge that concerns the external world? This question is crucial for the psychology of reasoning, for it concerns the scope that human reasoning might have. It is also a central question in the history of epistemology (Russell 1946).

Euclid's astonishing successes in geometry and the absence of any comparably impressive achievements that use other reasoning methods suggested that deductive reasoning could also provide a foundation for knowledge of the external world. From Plato to Kant, an influential line of philosophers has attempted to establish nonmathematical knowledge using deductive argument. Attempts to model scientific inquiry on Euclid's deductive model had a profound influence on Greek and medieval science (Russell 1946). Spinoza even went as far as using the Euclidean method in his *Ethics*, with definitions, axioms, and "proofs." It would not be unreasonable to suggest, then, that psychologists of reasoning have simply taken over a preoccupation with deduction that has been evident more widely in Western thought since Plato.

However, more recently, the view that science derives knowledge of the world by deduction from self-evident foundations has fallen into disrepute (Lakatos 1977a, 1977b; Popper 1959). Contrary to the Euclidean picture, science appears to proceed by plausible conjecture on the basis of observation, not by deductively certain inference. For example, Bacon explicitly advocated alternative inferential methods for what he called inductive reasoning (James 1975). In the twentieth century, it has become increasingly accepted that people derive knowledge of the world by different means from knowledge of mathematics (see, for example, Russell 1919). The nondeductive origin of scientific knowledge is a common thread that links diverse views in modern philosophy of science (e.g., Glymour 1980; Howson and Urbach 1993; Kuhn 1962; Lakatos 1970; Putnam 1974; Thagard 1988; Toulmin 1961; Van Frassen 1980). In epistemology more generally there is agreement that knowledge of the world does not have a deductive basis (see, e.g., Goldman 1986; Lehrer 1990; Pollock 1986; and Thagard 1988).

The deductive picture has, however, remained influential as an apparently unattainable standard against which philosophers may assess other knowledge-gathering methods. In particular, skepticism concerning knowledge of the world, from Descartes onward, has its roots in the distance between the certainty that deduction can assure and the lack of certainty that nondeductive empirical methods of inquiry provide (Burnyeat 1983). That no one has met the skeptical challenge to provide a certain grounding for knowledge reinforces our thesis that science does not obtain knowledge by deductive means.

So it seems that we have two paradigms of thought: mathematical knowledge, where deductive inference appears to be of primary importance; and empirical, scientific knowledge, in which deductive inference plays at most a secondary role. Both within epistemology and in psychology, there is agreement that we should view human thought as generally analogous to scientific, rather than mathematical, inquiry (Fodor 1983). For example, many philosophers advocate the view that common sense and science are parts of the same general project of understanding the world, differing only by degree of systematicity and rigor (e.g., Goodman 1951; Quine 1960, 1990). Developmental psychologists frequently view the child as a "naive scientist" (Carey 1988; Karmiloff-Smith 1988); accounts of causal reasoning in adults also use the naive-scientist metaphor (Jaspars, Fincham, and Hewstone 1983; Kelley 1967). Further, psychologists view learning from experience in any domain as involving inductive inference (Holland et al. 1986), and so on.

As mentioned earlier, Fodor (1983) argues strongly for the nondeductive character of thought. He notes that the perceptual system attempts to infer the causes in the external world of the inputs to the sensory receptors and that such reasoning is an instance of inference to the best explanation (Harman 1965). This pattern of inference, like induction, is uncontroversially nonmonotonic. From a distance, the perceptual system may misclassify sensory input as being generated by a horse. However, on moving closer it may be apparent that it is actually a cow. The addition of new information overturns the original conclusion—additional information that indicates another explanation is better overturns what was previously the best explanation. Thus, perception involves nonmonotonic and hence nondeductive reasoning. Moreover, Fodor argues that what he calls "central" cognitive processes, of belief revision and commonsense thought, face a problem analogous to scientific inference. For reasons similar to those we have outlined earlier, Fodor believes that scientific inference is nonmonotonic and that it is not deductively formalizable. He therefore concludes that central cognitive processes will likewise be nondeductive in character.

To sum up so far: There is a long tradition in epistemology, initially inspired by Euclidean geometry, that attempts to provide deductive foundations for nonmathematical knowledge. According to this model, it seems quite reasonable to postulate that deduction is the foundation of human thought. However, the rise of science has involved plausible but uncertain inferences that do not fit this deductive pattern. Furthermore, human cognition is related to empirical, nondeductive inquiry, rather than deductive, mathematical inquiry. So the view that deduction provides the foundation for human thought may be unworkable, a vestige of an outmoded epistemological tradition.

DEDUCTIVE ASPECTS OF THOUGHT? The conclusion that deduction is not the foundation for thought does not, of course, imply that no thought is deductive. From the point of view of the psychology of reasoning, the study of deduction may still be of wide significance to psychology, if some substantial and important aspects of human reasoning are deductive. Indeed, many psychologists of reasoning appear, at least in some passages, to advocate this relatively modest position. Johnson-Laird and Byrne (1991), who advocate a central role for deduction, nonetheless concede that much human reasoning is not deductive in character. For example, they point out that even Sherlock Holmes, whose "powers of deduction" are legendary, does not really solve problems deductively at all. Johnson-Laird and Byrne note that Holmes's inferences are plausible conjectures, which although ubiquitous in everyday life are not the consequences of deductively valid arguments.

Pursuing the analogy with science, it is interesting that although philosophers of science have generally abandoned the view that scientific inference might be deductive, some continue to advocate the view that certain aspects of science involve deductive inference. Roughly, the view is that although forming theories does not involve deductive inference, deduction is crucially involved in prediction, explanation, and theory testing. Most notably the hypothetico-deductive account of prediction and hypothesis testing (Popper 1959) and the deductive nomological view of scientific explanation and prediction (Hempel 1965) advocate this view. If this view is right, we can conjecture that deduction plays an analogous role in human thought as in science. Thus, perhaps deduction does have an important, if not exclusive, role in human cognition.[6]

However, deductive views of science provide little support for the deductively inclined psychologist of reasoning. Contrary to the views of C. Hempel and K. R. Popper, recent philosophy of science has suggested that prediction, explanation, and hypothesis testing in science are not really deductive in character. Taking prediction as an example, according to the deductive view a prediction is a deductive consequence of a theory or a hypothesis together with some initial conditions. So, according to Hempel's view, we have the following picture:

(1)   Theory $(T) \wedge$ Initial Conditions $(I) |= $ Prediction (P)

where the theory and initial conditions form the antecedent of an entailment and the prediction the consequent. For example, Newton's laws (T) together with information (I) about the state of the solar system at time, t_0, deductively imply particular trajectories (P) for the planets at subsequent times $t > t_0$. However, as critics have pointed out (Duhem 1954; Lakatos 1970, 1977a, 1977b; Putnam 1974; Quine 1953), this conclusion only follows *all other things being equal*. Real physical systems are not causally sealed off from external forces; they are open systems. Consequently there are limitless possible intervening forces and factors, that is, "auxiliary hypotheses" (Putnam 1974), that could intervene to make the prediction fail—unexpected frictional, electromagnetic, or as yet undiscovered forces, changes in physical constants in different parts of space/time, and so on.

The nondeductive character of scientific prediction becomes clear when the prediction does not fit with observation. If the prediction followed deductively from the theory, then the theory would automatically be falsified. However, in practice, the theory may be fine, because auxiliary hypotheses such as those noted earlier may be the cause of the mismatch between prediction and observation. H. Putnam (1974) notes, for example, that Newton's laws are entirely compatible with square orbits, given appropriate additional forces.

One possible defense for the deductive view is to argue that the predictions follow deductively from the conjunction of the theory under test and the auxiliary hypotheses. This suggestion involves modifying the antecedent of the entailment in (1) as follows:

(2) $T \wedge I \wedge AH_1 \wedge AH_2 \wedge \ldots \wedge AH_n \models$ Prediction (P)

If the prediction turns out to be false, then the scientist may reject one of these auxiliary hypotheses, not the theory under test, thus bringing prediction and observation back into line. However, this requires a complete enumeration of all the auxiliary hypotheses, which appears to be impossible, even in principle (Putnam 1974; Quine 1953). Science is concerned with causally open systems where there are indefinitely many unexpected external factors. It is impossible to exhaustively enumerate these other possible factors, and hence scientific prediction cannot be made to fit into the deductive mold.

We have considered prediction in science at length because precisely analogous considerations arise in attempting to model commonsense reasoning in deductive terms (e.g., Schiffer 1987), as we shall see in the discussion of default rules in AI later.

We have so far argued that deduction is not appropriate for formalizing predictive and explanatory reasoning: that is, the derivation of empirical predictions about the world does not proceed by deductive inference. The final position we consider is that deductive reasoning leads not to empirical predictions but to conceptual or analytic truths. For example, perhaps it follows deductively from what it is to be a bachelor that bachelors must be male. Kant's program for establishing the properties of space, causality, and the like pursued this line: the idea was that these properties are not really properties of the external world but conceptual necessities of human thought (Scruton 1982). Perhaps this kind of inference is deductive.

Modern epistemology suggests that it is not, because the distinction between conceptual and empirical claims cannot be maintained. For example, W. V. O. Quine (1953) has forcefully argued that there is no noncircular way to characterize the distinction between analytic, conceptual truths and synthetic, empirical truths. According to contemporary epistemology, all statements are revisable in the light of experience—none are purely conceptual truths derived by deductive argument alone (although see Katz 1990 for an opposing point of view). Furthermore, the development of mathematics and physics since Kant has shown that "conceptual necessity" is unexpectedly flexible. For example, Kant took the Euclidean character of space to be conceptually necessary, but modern science has shown that space is in fact non-Euclidean (Putnam 1975). Hence, what appears to be conceptual knowledge, which might potentially be the result of deduction, may be empirical and thus not derived by deduction.[7] In sum, epistemological considerations suggest that deduction is not central to human thought in either making empirical predictions or establishing conceptual truths.

From the first part of the epistemological argument, we concluded that deduction cannot be the primary means of acquiring knowledge of the world. In the second part, we have searched for a substantial residual role for deductive reasoning and failed to find one. From an epistemological point of view, one might suspect that deduction plays only a small role in human reasoning.

We have shown that deduction does not provide an adequate epistemology. If deduction is never or rarely *justified*, then it seems unlikely to provide a useful design principle for intelligent systems, whether human or artificial. This suggestion is reinforced by the next two arguments, which concern AI and the empirical data.

A POSSIBLE DEFENSE?   Epistemology and the philosophy of science are concerned with how people *should* reason, rather than how they *do* reason: it is *normative* rather than descriptive. This appears to leave open the possibility that the epistemological arguments described earlier may be accepted, but that they imply only that people *should not* use deduction in everyday life. This seems not to preclude the possibility that people actually *do* reason deductively about the everyday world.

But this defense fails for a number of reasons. First, notice that epistemological considerations show that interesting conclusions never (or almost never) follow deductively from known premises about the real world. This means that if people do reason deductively, then the conclusions that they will be able to draw will be entirely uninteresting: they will not support induction of general rules, allow predictions about or explanations of the everyday world, or even reveal conceptual "analytic" truths. The arguments from contemporary epistemology earlier show that reasoning deductively about the world would not yield conclusions of any interest, despite a long philosophical tradition to the contrary. Therefore, it would seem bizarre, to say the least, to suppose that deduction is central to human thought, even though the results of deduction would never be useful.

Second, it is clear that people *do* predict, explain, and find regularities in the scientific and everyday worlds and use this knowledge as a basis for decisions and action. These abilities are of fundamental cognitive significance. So even if one were, in desperation, to maintain that much reasoning is perversely based on deduction (and reaches no useful conclusions about the everyday world), it would still be necessary to grant that reasoning that does lead to substantial and interesting conclusions about the everyday world is not based on deduction. But given that these concessions must be granted, deductive reasoning is clearly marginal, rather than central, to cognition, which is the conclusion for which we are arguing.

Third, the attempt to drive a wedge between how people *should* reason and how they *do* reason is beside the point in this context, because the epistemological arguments that we discussed earlier are themselves derived from the actual practice of scientific reasoning. The tendency to make inductive leaps with no deductive justification, the Quine-Duhem thesis, the failure to automatically reject hypotheses when their predictions are disconfirmed, and so on are not merely abstract methodological recommendations. They are manifest in the history of science (e.g., Kuhn 1962). Indeed, in philosophy of science and contemporary epistemology more generally the constraints between accounts of how people *should* and *do* reason are so tight that many philosophers have argued that they cannot be separated (Kornblith 1994; Quine 1969; Thagard 1988).

A final defense might be that people do derive interesting conclusions about the world (e.g., prediction, explanation, and the like), that they use deduction to do this, and that epistemology simply shows that these deductions are not valid. But admitting that people's actual deductions are invalid amounts to giving up deduction as a *computational-level explanation* of human reasoning. This is because, by assumption, people's actual deductions are not valid, and hence their reasoning behavior cannot be characterized by deductive logic. Moreover, the degree to which human reasoning about the world is successful is left entirely mysterious on the view that human reasoning is merely bungled deductive logic.

We have seen that the view that deduction characterizes people's reasoning about the world at the computational level is epistemologically unviable. Reasoning about the everyday world *should not be* and *is not* deductively valid. This conclusion is reinforced by considerations from our two other sources of evidence: AI and the psychology of reasoning.

Artificial Intelligence

A cognitive scientific approach to reasoning assumes that reasoning is a kind of computation. Any adequate cognitive theory must therefore be computationally viable. But, we shall argue, this minimal condition is violated by theories of reasoning that use deduction as their computational-level theory. The fundamental reason should already be clear from our discussion of epistemology: that real-world inferences are not deductively valid and must be outside the scope of any theory based on deduction. But AI provides an ideal testing ground for the hypothesis that reasoning is deductive, because it has adopted the practical project of attempting to formalize (fragments of) human knowledge and build computational systems that reason using this knowledge (e.g., Charniak and McDermott 1985). As we now see, research in AI reinforces the conclusion from epistemology that deductive inference has little or no role in reasoning about the everyday world.

First, let us briefly consider inductive reasoning and inference to the best explanation, as they are studied in AI. According to Hempel's (1965) deductive-nomological view of explanation and Popper's (1959) hypothetico-deductive approach to prediction and theory testing, deduction might be expected to play an important role in computational systems that perform such reasoning. Similarly, according to Rips (1994) and Johnson-Laird and Byrne (1991), who argue that deduction plays an important role in almost all cognitive processes, it might be expected that deduction would have an important role to play. But in fact, as might be expected in the light of the epistemological arguments outlined earlier, AI has found no useful role for deduction in inductive and abductive reasoning. Induction, which is studied in the AI and engineering literatures on machine learning (e.g., Michalski, Carbonell, and Mitchell 1983), pattern recognition (e.g., Duda and Hart

1973), and neural networks (e.g., Hertz, Krogh, and Palmer 1991), has no place for deduction. Inference to the best explanation, which we mentioned in the previous section, is known as abduction in AI. AI systems for abductive inference are generally nondeductive in character (Josephson and Josephson 1994). Furthermore, making predictions, where deduction at least seems prima facie to be appropriate, is no more deductive in the domain of commonsense reasoning than we found it to be in science.

Consider, for example, the prediction that if you drop an egg it will break, based on knowledge about eggs, the floor surface, the height from which you drop the egg, and so on. This inference is uncertain: you may catch the egg before it lands, you may have hardened the shell by artificial means, and so on. As an alternative, reconsider our inference that Tweety flies, from the general proposition that birds fly and the knowledge that Tweety is a bird. This inference, too, is uncertain, since Tweety may be a penguin, have an injury, be newborn, have clipped wings, and so on. Different areas of cognitive science, from cognitive psychology and philosophy to AI, give many different labels to this phenomenon. Commonsense inference is "context-sensitive" (Barsalou 1987), "holds only relative to background conditions" (Barwise and Perry 1983), is "defeasible" (Minsky 1977), "admits exceptions" (Holland et al. 1986), "lacks generality" (Goodman 1983), and has categories that are "intention-relative" (Winograd and Flores 1986). Borrowing a term from AI, we shall call inferences that use rules that allow exceptions *default* inferences.

How can deductive logic, the calculus of certainty, be used to model the uncertainty of default inference? An initial suggestion is to deny that prediction really is uncertain; instead, the conclusion follows deductively from the premises and fails only when one or more of the premises do not apply. According to this view, prediction only appears to be uncertain because some of the premises are left unstated. In the case cited earlier, for example, additional premises such that the egg falls unimpeded, no one has artificially tampered with the shell, and so on are required to deduce the conclusion that the egg will break. If those premises are true, so the story goes, the conclusion follows with certainty.

We saw that this approach does not appear to be successful in the context of scientific reasoning, where we noted that because systems under study are open there will always be indefinitely many unexpected factors that can defeat our predictions. Open systems are also the concern of commonsense reasoning about the everyday world, and so here, too, similar problems arise. In formalizing commonsense reasoning, as in formalizing science, it is not possible to restore certainty by including all these possible additional factors as extra premises in the argument. Even if we rule out the possibility that the dropped egg has an artificially hardened shell or that you catch the egg before it lands, there remain possibilities, such as that room is in free fall or is flooded, that the egg is caught by a net, and so on, that defeat the conclusion that the egg will break. Whatever additional premises we add, there are always further additional factors, not ruled out by those premises, that will overturn the conclusion.[8]

It seems that the majority of inferences about the real world, whether commonsense or scientific, are uncertain rather than deductive. In particular, we have seen that prediction in both science and common sense is nondeductive. Recent research in AI, in contrast to the psychology of reasoning, has abandoned the attempt to model commonsense reasoning purely deductively and has recognized the need for a calculus of default reasoning that goes beyond deduction (Ginsberg 1987).

There are three broad approaches to dealing with uncertainty in AI, none of which maintains that commonsense inference is deductively valid:

1. *The logicist approach.* This approach attempts to develop non-monotonic logics (or related methods) where future premises can overturn conclusions; that is, they sacrifice deductive validity (McCarthy 1980; McDermott 1982; McDermott and Doyle 1980; Reiter 1980, 1985). Within logic, there have been other attempts to extend logical methods so that they handle the uncertain, nondeductive character of inference that concerns the real world, situation theory (Barwise and Perry 1983) being a notable example. We may view these approaches as broadening the notion of deduction, rather than abandoning it. We should not underestimate the magnitude of the change, however. From an epistemological point of view, giving up certainty is, of course, of fundamental significance; from a formal and computational point of view, nonmonotonic reasoning has different properties from standard monotonic reasoning, partly because these systems must continually reevaluate past conclusions in the light of new information, to see if they still follow (Brachman and Levesque 1985; Ginsberg 1987; Harman 1986; Oaksford and Chater 1991). As noted earlier, in this chapter we restrict deduction to monotonic reasoning, as this is the sense used in the psychology of reasoning; according to this usage, these nonmonotonic reasoning schemes are not deductive. Indeed, psychologists of reasoning have generally rejected the use of nonmonotonic logics (Johnson-Laird 1986; Johnson-Laird and Byrne 1991; Rips 1994). Indeed, Johnson-Laird and Byrne (1991) and A. Garnham (1993) suggest that the psychology of reasoning does not need to appeal to nonmonotonic logics to understand how people carry out nonmonotonic reasoning (although see Chater 1993; Chater and Oaksford 1993; Oaksford 1993; and Oaksford and Chater 1991 for critiques of such approaches).

2. *The probabilistic approach.* This approach to uncertainty in human reasoning uses the mathematical theory of uncertainty, probability theory, or related formalisms (Dempster 1967; Pearl 1988; Shafer 1976). This approach reconstructs commonsense inferences as establishing that a conclusion is probable, rather than deductively certain, given a set of premises. In cases in which conditional probabilities are close to 1, then the probabilistic style of reasoning becomes increasingly close to logical inference. Pearl (1988)

exploits this fact in developing a nonmonotonic logic that he justifies as a limiting case of probabilistic inference. This approach has the advantage of dealing with defeasibility naturally without many of the problems inherent in the nonmonotonic logic approach (Oaksford and Chater 1998). Moreover, it provides a set of normative principles against which to assess human rationality. Later on we will show that this approach permits us to reinterpret some important results in the psychology of reasoning that had previously been thought to impugn human rationality. We show that these results conform to the normative principles of probability theory (Oaksford and Chater 1994a).

3. *The proceduralist approach.* This approach involves devising procedures that solve particular inference problems, but without attempting to ground such procedures in any formal theory of inference (McDermott 1987). A fortiori, this approach rejects the reconstruction of commonsense inference as *deductive* inference.

We have seen that none of these three approaches to uncertainty rely on deductively valid inference. Thus, we might expect that cognitive psychologists concerned with computational models of the mind would similarly have rejected deductive inference as the central mechanism for human thinking. Indeed, it appears that cognitive psychology has implicitly recognized this point, although the implications of this fact do not appear to have touched the psychology of reasoning.

Outside the psychology of reasoning, cognitive psychology has used AI models to provide theoretical proposals about how to organize world knowledge to support commonsense reasoning. We now discuss three approaches that have been influential in psychology: semantic networks, schemas, and production systems. All of these approaches contain mechanisms for dealing with default inference. We shall consider how these theories relate to the three-way classification of AI approaches to default reasoning, arguing that they are all examples of the proceduralist approach.

Semantic networks (e.g., Collins and Loftus 1975; Collins and Quillian 1969) use a hierarchical organization of knowledge and associate properties of objects with nodes in the hierarchy. Suppose that the BIRD node is associated with the property of FLYING, but that the PENGUIN node is associated with the property of NOT_FLYING. On encountering Tweety, a specific penguin, the system can infer both that Tweety cannot fly (because Tweety is a penguin) and that Tweety can fly (because Tweety is a bird). To resolve the conflict the system assumes that information lower in the hierarchy (i.e., more specific information) takes precedence. Thus, the system infers that Tweety does not fly. This method involves a particular approach to a certain kind of default rule—rules that apply to most of the objects in a class but not to some subclasses of that class (rather than default rules that intervening external factors may override, such as those we discussed in the section on epistemology). However, as it stands, the approach is very unconstrained. For example, the label NOT_FLYING may apply to all varieties of bird, although

FLYING may still attach to the class BIRD, and other bizarre possibilities (see Woods 1975 for related discussion).

Schema theories and production systems use essentially similar mechanisms for dealing with default inference. In schema or frame theories (e.g., Minsky 1977; Schank and Abelson 1977), incoming information fills "slots" in rules that are organized into domain-specific compartments or "schemas." Slots have associated default values, which further information can override. For example, Tweety may fill the BIRD slot in a rule such as IF **hears**(*BIRD, bang*), THEN **flees**(*BIRD*) (i.e., if a bird hears a bang it flees). The slot for BIRD will carry the default assumption that birds fly and hence that Tweety can fly. This may lead, for example, to the inference that Tweety will flee by flying away on hearing the bang. But if you know Tweety is a penguin, then this will override the default using much the same mechanism as in the semantic network, and you may infer that Tweety will waddle rather than fly away. Production systems (e.g., Anderson 1983; Newell 1990) encode knowledge in conditional rules much as in the preceding example. Default inferences arise out of conflicts between different conditional rules, for example, between the rule that IF **bird**(x), THEN **flies**(x) and IF **penguin**(x), THEN NOT(**flies**[x]). On encountering Tweety, to which both rules apply, the system resolves the conflict by choosing the most specific rule, as with semantic networks. Production systems also embody a variety of other procedures, in addition to specificity, for resolving conflicting defaults, including use of production *strength*, goodness of match with the antecedent of the conditional, and so on (Anderson 1983).

Semantic networks, schemas, and productions are all procedural approaches in the sense discussed earlier, specifically in regard to their approach to default reasoning. They handle defaults by simple procedural strategies, such as preferring rules whose antecedents are at a lower level in a default hierarchy. Although the nondefault aspects of some of these systems can be formalized using standard monotonic logic (for example, regarding semantic networks see Woods 1975; for schemas see Hayes 1979), the default inferences are simply treated as procedures without any logical justification. For this reason, none of these systems simply implement logical inference. Hence, since almost all knowledge is defeasible, as we have already discussed, the majority of inferences drawn will be nondeductive in character.

It seems that from the perspective of constructing practical AI systems, as well as from the point of view of epistemology, thought about the world (rather than about mathematics) does not appear to be deductive in character. Thus, AI, as well as epistemology, strongly suggests that psychological theories should not place deductive reasoning at the center of human thought. We now turn to a more direct source of evidence for this view from experimental studies in the psychology of reasoning.

The Argument from Psychology

It is symptomatic of the focus on deduction in the psychology of reasoning that the defeasible, nondeductive character of commonsense inference has not been a major focus of research. In other areas of psychology, though, discussion of such inferences is ubiquitous. We have already noted the popular views that cognitive development is akin to scientific theory change, that commonsense inference is equivalent to the problem of confirmation in science, that perception is inference to the best explanation, and that learning from experience, in whatever domain, involves induction. We have also observed that theories of the organization of knowledge and commonsense inference borrowed by psychologists from AI, including semantic networks, schemas, and production systems, were specifically developed to deal with nondeductive default inference. It is easy to add more examples of aspects of psychology where default inference is central: in text comprehension, the wealth of "bridging" and "elaborative" inferences (e.g., Clark 1977; Garrod and Sanford 1977; Kintsch and van Dijk 1978; O'Brien et al. 1988) required to understand a text do not follow deductively from what is said; similarly, pragmatic inferences about speakers' intentions do not follow deductively from what is said but are a special case of inference to the best explanation (e.g., Levinson 1983; Sperber and Wilson 1986). In memory, elaborative inferences, which importantly affect memory performance, are not deductive inferences from what people must recall—rather, they go beyond and elaborate what people hear (e.g., Craik and Lockhart 1972; Craik and Tulving 1975). Research on decision making and probabilistic reasoning has directly focused on nondeductive forms of inference (e.g., Kahneman, Slovic, and Tversky 1982). Moreover, within the psychology of reasoning itself there has been interest in inductive reasoning tasks (e.g., Klahr and Dunbar 1988; Mynatt, Doherty, and Tweeny 1977; Oaksford and Chater 1994b; Wason 1960).

Mainstream psychology of reasoning has, however, concentrated on what are regarded as deductive reasoning tasks. Our discussions of epistemology and AI suggest that deductive reasoning is rather rare in everyday life; we submit that it is also rather rarer in the laboratory than many reasoning theorists have suspected. At a superficial level, this is because subjects do not appear to perform many deductively valid inferences in laboratory tasks and draw many inferences that are not deductively valid (e.g., Evans, Newstead, and Byrne 1993). In the psychology of reasoning, however, this mismatch between human performance and deductive expectations has not discouraged researchers from proposing theories of reasoning that postulate a core deductive component and explaining away the experimental data as performance errors. We argue that there is a deeper reason that reasoning researchers rarely observe deduction in laboratory reasoning tasks. This is because many tasks that experimenters assume tap deductive reasoning are not really deductive tasks at all. Moreover, experimental data on these tasks are better modeled as uncertain, nondeductive reasoning, rather than as error-full deductive reasoning. We consider two examples that have been of central importance in the psychology of reasoning: P. C. Wason's selection task and conditional inference tasks.

WASON'S SELECTION TASK Wason's selection task (1966, 1968) is perhaps the most intensively studied task in the psychology of reasoning. Subjects must assess whether some evidence is relevant to the truth or falsity of a conditional rule of the form *if p then q*, where by convention *p* stands for the antecedent clause of the conditional and *q* for the consequent clause. In the standard abstract version of the task, the rule concerns cards, which have a number on one side and a letter on the other. The rule is *if there is a vowel on one side (p), then there is an even number on the other side (q)*. Four cards are placed before the subject, so that just one side is visible; the visible faces show an "A" (*p* card), a "K" (*not-p* card), a "2" (*q* card), and a "7" (*not-q* card). Subjects then select those cards they must turn over to determine whether the rule is true or false. Typical results were: *p* and *q* cards, 46 percent; *p* card only, 33 percent; *p, q,* and *not-q* cards, 7 percent; and *p* and *not-q* cards, 4 percent (Johnson-Laird and Wason 1970).

The task subjects confront is analogous to a central problem of experimental science: the problem of which experiment to perform. The scientist has a hypothesis (or a set of hypotheses) that he or she must assess (for the subject, the hypothesis is the conditional rule) and must choose which experiment (card) will be likely to provide data (i.e., what is on the reverse of the card) that bears on the truth of the hypothesis.

In the light of the epistemological arguments we have already considered, it may seem unlikely that this kind of scientific reasoning will be deductive in character. Nonetheless, the psychology of reasoning has viewed the selection task as paradigmatically deductive (e.g., Evans 1982; Evans, Newstead, and Byrne 1993), although a number of authors have argued for a non-deductive conception of the task (Fischhoff and Beyth-Marom 1983; Kirby 1994; Klayman and Ha 1987; Rips 1990).[9]

The assumption that the selection task is deductive in character arises from the fact that psychologists of reasoning have tacitly accepted Popper's hypothetico-deductive philosophy of science. Popper (1959) assumes that evidence can falsify but not confirm scientific theories. Falsification occurs when predictions that follow deductively from the theory do not accord with observation. This leads to a recommendation for the choice of experiments: to only conduct experiments that have the potential to falsify the hypothesis under test.

Applying the falsificationist account to the selection task, the recommendation is that subjects should only turn cards that are potentially logically incompatible with the conditional rule. When viewed in these terms, the selection task has a deductive component, in that the participant must deduce which cards would be logically incompatible with the conditional rule. According to the rendition of the conditional as material implication (which is standard in the propositional and predicate calculi; see Haack 1978), the only observation that is incompatible with the conditional rule *if p then q* is a card with *p* on one side and *not-q* on the other. Hence, subjects should select only cards that could potentially falsify the rule. That is, they should turn the *p* card, since it might have a *not-q* on the back, and the *not-q* card, since it might have a *p* on the back.

This pattern of selections is rarely observed in the experimental results outlined earlier.[10] Subjects typically select cards that could *confirm* the rule, that is, the *p* and *q* cards. However, according to falsification the choice of the *q* card is irrational and is an example of so-called confirmation bias (Evans and Lynch 1973; Wason and Johnson-Laird 1972). The rejection of confirmation as a rational strategy follows directly from the falsificationist perspective.

We have argued that the usual standard of "correctness" in the selection task follows from Popper's hypothetico-deductive view of science. Rejecting the falsificationist picture would eliminate the role of logic and hence deduction in the selection task. In the preceding section on epistemology, we have already seen that the hypothetico-deductive view faces considerable difficulties as a theory of scientific reasoning. This suggests that psychologists should explore alternative views of scientific inference that may provide different normative accounts of experiment choice and hence might lead to a different "correct" answer in the selection task. Perhaps the dictates of an alternative theory might more closely model human performance and hence be consistent with the possibility of human rationality.

We (Oaksford and Chater 1994a) adopt this approach, adapting the Bayesian approach to philosophy of science (Earman 1992; Horwich 1982; Howson and Urbach 1989), rather than the hypothetico-deductive view, to provide a rational analysis (Anderson 1990, 1991) of the selection task. We view the selection task in probabilistic terms, as a problem of Bayesian optimal data selection (Good 1966; Lindley 1956; MacKay 1992). Suppose that you are interested in the hypothesis that eating tripe makes people feel sick. Should known tripe eaters or tripe avoiders be asked whether they feel sick? Should people known to be or not to be sick be asked whether they have eaten tripe? This case is analogous to the selection task. Logically, you can write the hypothesis as a conditional sentence: if you eat tripe (*p*), then you feel sick (*q*). The groups of people that you may investigate then correspond to the various visible card options, *p*, *not-p*, *q*, and *not-q*. In practice, who is available will influence decisions about which people you question. The selection task abstracts away from this factor by presenting one example of each potential source of data. In terms of our everyday example, it is like coming across four people, one known tripe eater, one known not to have eaten tripe, one known to feel sick, and one known not to feel sick. The task is to decide who to question about how they feel or what they have eaten.

We (Oaksford and Chater 1994a) suggest that hypothesis testers should choose experiments (select cards) to provide the greatest possible "expected information gain" in deciding between two hypotheses: (1) that the task rule, if *p* then *q*, is true, that is, *p*s are invariably associated with *q*s, and (2) that the occurrences, of *p*s and *q*s are independent. For each hypothesis, we (1994a) define a probability model that derives from the prior probability of each hypothesis (which for most purposes we assume to be equally likely, i.e., both = .5) and the probabilities of p and of q in the task rule. We define information gain as the difference between the uncertainty *before* receiving some data and the uncertainty *after* receiving that data where we measure uncertainty using Shannon-Wiener information. Thus, we define the information gain of data D as:

$$\text{Information before receiving } D: I(H_i) = -\sum_{i=1}^{n} P(H_i)\log_2 P(H_i)$$

$$\text{Information after receiving } D: I(H_i \mid D) = -\sum_{i=1}^{n} P(H_i \mid D)\log_2 P(H_i \mid D)$$

$$\text{Information gain: } I_g = I(H_i) - I(H_i \mid D)$$

We calculate the $P(H_i \mid D)$ terms using Bayes's theorem. Thus, information gain is the difference between the information contained in the *prior* probability of a hypothesis (H_i) and the information contained in the *posterior* probability of that hypothesis given some data D.[11]

When choosing which experiment to conduct (that is, which card to turn), the subjects do not know what that data will be (that is, what will be on the back of the card). So they cannot calculate actual information gain. However, subjects can compute *expected* information gain. Expected information gain is calculated with respect to all possible data outcomes, for example, for the p card: q and *not-q*, and both hypotheses.

We (1994a) calculated the expected information gain of each card assuming that the properties described in p and q are rare. J. Klayman and Y. Ha (1987) make a similar assumption in accounting for related data on Wason's (1960) 2-4-6 task. The order in expected information gain is:

$$E(Ig[p]) > E(Ig[q]) > E(Ig[not\text{-}q]) > E(Ig[not\text{-}p])$$

This corresponds to the observed frequency of card selections in Wason's task: $p > q > not\text{-}p > not\text{-}p$ and thus explains the predominance of p and q card selections as a rational inductive strategy. We (1994a) also show how our model generalizes to all the main patterns of results in the selection task (for discussions of this account see Almor and Sloman 1996; Evans and Over 1996; and Laming 1996 and for a response see Oaksford and Chater 1996). Specifically, it accounts for the nonindependence of card selections (Pollard 1985), the negations paradigm (e.g., Evans and Lynch 1973), the therapy experiments (e.g., Wason 1969), the reduced array selection task (Johnson-Laird and Wason 1970), work on so-called fictional outcomes (Kirby 1994), and deontic versions of the selection task (e.g., Cheng and Holyoak 1985), including perspective and rule-type manipulations (e.g., Cosmides 1989; Gigerenzer and Hug 1992), the manipulation of probabilities and utilities in deontic tasks (Kirby 1994), and effects of relevance (Oaksford and Chater 1995a; Sperber, Cara, and Girotto 1995).

We noted earlier that the philosophy of science that underlies the "deductive" conception of the selection task now has few adherents. The consensus is that scientific theories do not deductively imply predictions and hence that the general problem of choosing which experiment to perform (or, analogously, which card to turn in the selection task) cannot be reconstructed deductively. Further, our (Oaksford and Chater 1994a) probabilistic and hence nonmonotonic account provides a better model of human performance on the selection task. According to this model, people do not use deduction when solving the selection task—rather, they use a nonmonotonic inferential strategy. Crucially, this model preserves human rationality: the optimal data selection model shows that under certain minimal assumptions (the rarity assumption: real-world properties only apply to small subsets of all the objects in the world) people's behavior on the selection task conforms to the principles of a normative theory.

CONDITIONAL INFERENCE TASKS   The selection task is perhaps the most celebrated "deductive" reasoning task. However, the conditional inference task is perhaps the task that seems most unequivocally to engage deductive reasoning processes. For example, Rips (1994) uses example (3) as the paradigm example of deductive inference in introducing his mental logic theory of reasoning. Therefore, if human reasoning is not deductive even in this task, then it seems unlikely that other areas of human reasoning will be well explained in deductive terms. For this reason, the conditional reasoning task is a particularly crucial test case for theories of reasoning that employ deductive logic as a computational-level theory.

In the standard conditional inference task, subjects see a conditional rule, *if p then q*, and an additional premise (*p, q, not-p*, or *not-q*) and are asked whether a given conclusion (again, *p, q, not-p*, or *not-q*) follows. Consider the simplest form of the task, where the premises are *p* and *if p then q* and subjects decide whether *q* follows. This appears to be an example of the paradigmatic deductive inference of *modus ponens*. Rips's (1994) central example of deductive inference appears to have this form:

(3)   If Calvin deposits 50 cents, he'll get a Coke.
       Calvin deposits 50 cents.
       Therefore, Calvin will get a Coke.

As we have argued earlier, interpreting this natural-language argument involves applying a standard logical analysis, which presupposes that it should be viewed in deductive terms. But in the light of our discussion of epistemology and AI, this inference seems to be a typical example of default inference and not an instance of the deductive reasoning at all, despite Rips. Calvin won't get the Coke if the machine is broken, if the Cokes have run out, if the power is turned off, and so on. That is, additional premises can overturn the conclusion, which monotonic deductive inference does not allow. Thus, although the task is *intended* as a test of deductive reasoning, the subject may be more likely to *interpret* the reasoning materials so that it involves nonmonotonic, nondeductive reasoning.

The question for the psychology of reasoning, then, is which account of how people interpret and reason with the materials in the task provides the best fit with reasoning performance. It turns out that the experimental data support the claim that people treat such inferences as defeasible rather than deductive. Work on conditional inference indicates that subjects interpret conditional sentences as default rules (Holyoak and Spellman 1993) even in laboratory tasks (Oaksford, Chater, and Stenning 1990). Byrne (1989) and Cummins, T. Lubart, O. Alksnis, and R. Rist (1991) have shown that background information derived from stored world knowledge can affect inferential performance (see also Markovits 1984, 1985). Specifically, they showed that *additional antecedents* influence the inferences conditional statements allow. For example:

(4)   If you turn the key the car starts.

(5)   *Additional Antecedent*: You are out of gas.

Example (4) could be used to predict that the car will start if you turn the key. This is an inference by *modus ponens*. However, including information about an additional antecedent, example (5), *defeats* this inference (Byrne 1989). Moreover, confidence reduces in this inference for rules that possess many alternative antecedents even when this information is only implicit (Cummins et al. 1991). Additional antecedents also affect inferences by *modus tollens*. If the car does not start, you can infer that you didn't turn the key, unless you are out of gas. Explicitly providing information about alternative antecedents undermines the use of *modus tollens* (Byrne 1989) and reduces confidence in rules that possess many alternative antecedents even when this information is only implicit (Cummins et al. 1991). This result was very striking and unexpected within the context of the psychology of reasoning. However, from the point of view of epistemology and AI it is just what we would expect. Human inferences about Coke machines, like those about the rest of the external world, are defeasible.

In sum, the experimental data seem to show that people treat conditionals in laboratory reasoning tasks as default rules. So it seems that even the commonsense inferences that some reasoning researchers regard as paradigmatic examples of deduction, like example (3), are not examples of deductive inference at all. If defeasibility infects even such paradigmatic cases of deductive reasoning, then it threatens to leave the advocate of deductive reasoning with no commonsense reasoning at all to explain.

How can theories in the psychology of reasoning that place deduction at center stage in human cognition attempt to account for the ubiquity of defeasibility? A popular view is that defeasibility is illusory. The idea is that encountering a fresh premise defeats one of the existing premises and it is this that now allows the rejection of the conclusion.

For example, G. Politzer and M. D. S. Braine (1991)[12] and D. P. O'Brien (1993) argue that the observed effects on reasoning of additional premises do not show that the major premise is defeasible (thereby invoking some nonmonotonic inference regime) but simply show that it is false, according to the standard, nondefeasible, interpretation of the conditional. However, if this is how people interpret conditionals, then the only conditionals that people should believe are true will be those that never admit of counterexamples. Because any commonsense conditional, including example (4), admits exceptions, then all such conditionals will be false. Clearly, people do not reject such conditionals out of hand but freely assert them, argue about whether they are true, and use them to guide their behavior. This makes perfect sense if people interpret conditionals as default rules; it makes no sense at all if they interpret these conditionals logically.

A related line of argument is that people assume that the conditional premise is true until additional premises force them to question it. Before encountering such premises, they reason by *modus ponens* but retract this inference when additional information casts doubt on this premise (e.g., Garnham 1993; Johnson-Laird and Byrne 1991; Politzer and Braine 1991; Stevenson and Over 1995; see Chater 1993; Chater and Oaksford 1993; and Oaksford 1993 for discussion). The idea is that subjects start off assuming the truth of the conditional *if you turn the key the car starts*. If told that *you turn the key*, they infer by *modus ponens* that *the car starts*. However, on encountering the additional premise that *you are out of gas*, subjects question the conditional—this is because general knowledge tells them that the conditional does not apply to cars that are out of gas.

The proposal is that people treat conditional rules as rigid, rather than defeasible, and that people use them deductively. General knowledge acts as a "shield" for cases of apparent defeasible reasoning; general knowledge specifies that the rule does not apply in certain contexts (e.g., when the car is out of gas). The superficial plausibility of this story evaporates once we consider *when* general knowledge operates in the process of inference (see Chater and Oaksford 1993 and Oaksford and Chater 1991, 1995b, for detailed discussion of these issues). Suppose that it operates post hoc; that is, *after* you are presented with a particular problem: you apply *modus ponens* as usual; your general knowledge then determines whether to accept the conclusion; if not, you reject the conclusion, shielding the conditional inference from counterexample by deciding that it was not applicable in that instance. This story is viable only by virtue of being completely vacuous. The inferential processes are exactly those that would occur if the conditional were a default rule, except that every time you find a counterexample you put it aside by assuming that the inference did not apply. In a similar vein, one might maintain that all birds fly and cope with any apparent counterexamples by insisting post hoc that these are not birds. Such a strategy is clearly absurd: it only holds the counterexamples at bay by removing any empirical content from the generalization—it would be held true whatever the state of the world.

Suppose, however, that people adopt a strategy that prespecifies general knowledge of the conditions under which the rule applies. This means that the rule that the subject believes to be true is not that *if you turn the key, the car starts* but that *if you turn the key and there is gas in the car, the car starts*. This rule clearly does not apply to the case where there is no gas in the car. However, in the light of our discussion of epistemology and AI, it should be clear that prespecifying the conditions under which a default rule is true is an endless and impossible task. However many additional conditions you add, further uneliminated counterexamples are always available.[13]

What of apparent demonstrations of logically competent performance on reasoning tasks? (Braine 1978; Braine and O'Brien 1991; Henle 1962; Lea et al. 1990; O'Brien, Braine, and Yang 1994; Pollitzer and Braine 1991; Rips 1983, 1994). If subjects show correct logical inference on some tasks, then surely we cannot dismiss logic as having a role in human thought? All such demonstrations, however, involve particular inference rules, such as *modus ponens* or *and*-elimination (Braine, Reiser, and Rumain 1984). Such demonstrations bear on the question of whether people are logical but are in themselves far from conclusive. The point of providing a logic is to specify a whole system of inference determined by the logical terms of a language. Logicality can only be determined by conformity to all the patterns of inference licensed by a logic. Isolated conformity to one or another rule does not mean that behavior is logical, because other explanations are equally as plausible and usually more parsimonious than attributing people with the inferential power of deductive logic. For example, isolated logical performance is explicable by procedural accounts that do not attempt to provide any rational basis for cognition. Consequently, in the face of the widespread illogicality observed in reasoning tasks, that behavior conforms to one or two logical rules provides little evidence that people are logical.

Supporters of mental logic get around people's apparent illogicality by arguing that people do not possess various rules or that some inferences are more complex than others. Such attempts to square logic with people's behavior on laboratory tasks cannot, however, resolve the central problem that scientific and commonsense inference is invariably nonlogical. Hence, theories based on logic and derived to explain behavior in laboratory tasks cannot generalize to real inference in the everyday world (Oaksford and Chater 1993, 1995b). Further, as we have argued, even in the laboratory it is clear that conditionals are regarded not as rigid logical rules but as default rules (Cummins et al. 1991; Holyoak and Spellman 1993). Ultimately, however, within the psychology of reasoning, the issue will only be decided by which theories provide the best fits to the empirical data. In this respect nonlogical, probabilistic accounts seem to do better than logical accounts. For example, as we indicated earlier, our account of the selection task (Oaksford and Chater 1994a) provides good fits to most of the existing data.

In short, psychologists of reasoning must conclude, along with philosophers and workers in AI, that human conditional reasoning (outside mathematical domains) is defeasible and not deductive.

Deduction at the Algorithmic Level?

We have argued that deduction cannot provide a computational-level theory of commonsense inference, as has been widely assumed (e.g., Johnson-Laird and Byrne 1991; Macnamara 1986; Rips 1994). But this leaves open the possibility that deduction may be important at the algorithmic, but not the computational, level. We now argue that this position, too, is not viable.

First, note that the principal reason that psychologists (Inhelder and Piaget 1958; Rips 1994) have postulated deduction at the algorithmic level is because it explains how people can reason deductively. But if people cannot reason deductively, then there is no need to postulate a deductive machinery (e.g., a mental logic) to explain reasoning performance.

Second, it remains conceivable in principle that logical procedures at the algorithmic level are used to implement nonlogical reasoning, in the same way as a computer program to perform arithmetic, manipulate lists, or carry out probabilistic calculations might be written in the logic programming language PROLOG. But it seems unlikely that the cognitive system uses algorithms based on logic, if only because it is so computationally expensive to convert procedures into steps of logical inference. Indeed, in practice, programs written in PROLOG run slowly, and moreover, practical programming requires extensive use of nonlogical tricks to reduce the complexity of the program (such as PROLOG's "cut," Clocksin and Mellish 1984). More generally, the "purer" the logical programming style used (i.e., the more nonlogical tricks are avoided), the more rapidly computational complexity grows. Indeed, results from computational complexity theory show that computational systems based solely on logic must be computationally intractable, even when the logical language is just the propositional calculus (Garey and Johnson 1979; for implications for the psychology of reasoning, see Oaksford and Chater 1991, 1993, 1995b and Chater and Oaksford 1993). Moreover, these computational complexity results apply to serial and parallel computational systems and hence must apply to the cognitive system (see Oaksford and Chater 1991).

In sum, then, it seems unlikely that deduction has a significant role in reasoning at either the computational or the algorithmic level.

6. Conclusions

We began by considering the view that deductive reasoning is central to human cognition. However, we have found that the scope of deductive reasoning is remarkably small: it includes neither scientific reasoning, commonsense reasoning, nor important paradigmatic laboratory "deductive" reasoning tasks. It is nondeductive, uncertain reasoning that appears to be cognitively ubiquitous. What does this imply for the psychology of reasoning?

The mental logic account of human reasoning (Braine 1978; Rips 1983, 1994), which advocates deduction at both computational and algorithmic levels of explanation, is directly under threat from this line of argument, for it seems that the deductive inferences for which the mental logic purports to account are actually extremely rare. According to the arguments we have presented, the vast majority of the examples of reasoning that mental logicians reconstruct deductively are not, in fact, deductive inferences at all.

Equally under threat is the mental model view of human inference (Johnson-Laird 1983; Johnson-Laird and Byrne 1991), for which deduction is part of the computational level of explanation. At a general level, this is because the apparatus of mental model theory simply provides a specific way of drawing deductive, logical inferences: ". . . the [mental] model theory is in no way incompatible with logic: it merely gives up the formal approach (rules of inference) for a semantic approach (search for counter-examples)" (Johnson-Laird and Byrne 1991, p. 212). Since the mental model view relies on the search for counterexamples, it cannot extend beyond monotonic deductive inference. In nonmonotonic inference, it is, by definition, possible for the premises to be true but the conclusions false: that is, counterexamples will always be possible. Any approach based on search for counterexamples will reject all nonmonotonic inferences as invalid (Chater and Oaksford 1993).

If human reasoning is not deductive, how can it be modeled? Epistemology may provide valuable qualitative constraints on patterns of uncertain human reasoning, which have been subject to particularly intensive study in the philosophy of science. Furthermore, each of the three approaches to uncertain reasoning in AI provides possible psychological mechanisms. The logicist wants to somehow extend logical methods to handle uncertain reasoning, the probabilistic account uses probability theory and related formalisms as a starting point, and the procedural approach abandons the search for a rational underpinning for thought and proposes heuristics for particular types of uncertain reasoning.

To what extent are these approaches being taken up within the psychology of reasoning? As we have noted, theorists who argue for mental logics have been surprisingly unwilling to propose nonmonotonic logics as psychological mechanisms but have attempted to maintain that nonmonotonic logics are (at least in a large range of cases) unnecessary (Johnson-Laird 1986; Johnson-Laird and Byrne 1991; Rips 1994). The proceduralist approach has also been relatively little investigated, although J. St. B. T. Evans (1982, 1983, 1984, 1989) can be viewed as taking up this approach, in that he focuses on processing-based explanations of reasoning data. Nonetheless, Evans is not a full-blown proceduralist. He views his procedures only as *supplements* to accounts of deductive competence, to explain systematic errors and biases in people's deductive reasoning (1991). J. H. Holland, K. J. Holyoak, R. E. Nisbett, and P. R. Thagard (1986) provide a more thoroughgoing proceduralist account of default reasoning, which, however, they have not directly applied to reasoning research. They view knowledge as organized into hierarchies of default rules in a production system. Although such systems seem directly applicable to commonsense human reasoning, no detailed modeling of experimental reasoning data has so far been carried out. A number of researchers have taken up the probabilistic approach (Cheng and Novick 1992; Fischhoff and Beyth-Marom 1983; Gigerenzer and Hug 1992; Kirby 1994; Klayman and Ha 1987; Manktelow and Over 1991), including our work on the selection task described earlier (Oaksford and Chater 1994a). We view this approach as the most promising because it successfully explains some of the most problematic data on human reasoning as conforming to the principles of a normative theory; that is, it preserves the rationality of people's reasoning and thus explains why cognition is successful. Nonetheless, only further research within each of these three approaches will provide an answer to the question of which is the most appropriate framework for studying human reasoning.

NOTES

1. They argue that logic must be supplemented with additional principles that constrain which logical inferences people actually draw (Johnson-Laird and Byrne 1991).

2. There is ambiguity over whether the algorithmic level postulated by mental models is really a kind of logical proof theory, based on semantic principles (like truth tables or semantic tableaux). For example, this viewpoint seems implicit in Johnson-Laird and Byrne (1991, p. 212): "The [mental] model theory is in no way incompatible with logic: it merely gives up the formal (rules of inference) for a semantic approach (search for counterexamples)."

3. However, advocates of mental logic, for example, do explicitly argue that deductive reasoning has an important role in many nondeductive reasoning tasks, such as induction and decision making (e.g., Rips 1994).

4. Although J. H. Holland, K. J. Holyoak, R. E. Nisbett, and P. R. Thagard's (1986) assumption that knowledge is organized as hierarchies of default rules does implicitly involve a general rejection of the idea that much of cognition is deductive in character.

5. This view is explicitly taken in formal semantics, where the goal of logical analysis is typically to capture the inferences that people draw from a statement (e.g., Cresswell 1985; Kamp and Reyle 1993; Montague 1974). The set of these entailments is closely related to or even identical with its meaning.

6. Of course, many scientific theories make only probabilistic predictions, and these predictions are not readily modeled in deductive terms. It is worth noting that many predictions of commonsense thinking often appear to have this character: I predict that if I am late to the bus stop, I will miss the bus; but this prediction is only probabilistic, since the bus is late, say, 5 percent of the time. Although probabilistic cases were of considerable concern to Popper (1959) and also to Hempel (1965), who dubbed them "inductive-statistical" inference, we leave this complication aside here.

7. Indeed, even the deductive character of mathematics is under threat from this point of view (Lakatos 1976).

8. The open character of the everyday world is often dealt with by fiat in AI— by simply making a "closed-world" assumption (Clark 1978) that the current contents of the system's database include all relevant factors. Even within the closed world, however, researchers must assume that inference is nonmonotonic, and hence nondeductive, which is all we are concerned with in this chapter. As it happens, the open character of the commonsense world means that many inferences that follow from the closed-world assumption are clearly invalid from outside the perspective of that closed world.

9. J. St. B. T. Evans and D. Over (1996) suggest that the selection task is a "decision making task," rather than a deductive reasoning task—a decision must be made concerning which cards to choose. But it appears that, at this level of abstraction, almost any psychological task involves "decision making," in the trivial sense that the subject must decide how to respond. It is therefore not clear whether Evans and Over's viewpoint amounts to accepting that reasoning in the task involves uncertain inductive inference, as we argue.

10. As few as 4 percent of subjects make this response, and hence, according to the deductive view, the bulk of the experimental data must be explained in terms of performance error.

11. In response to Evans and Over's (1996) observation that information gains may sometimes be negative and that this is intuitively unattractive, we (Oaksford and Chater 1996) develop an alternative motivation for their account, based on expected Kullback-Liebler distance. This revised account is mathematically identical to the current account but is somewhat more complex to derive, so we have retained our original account here. We also note here that the equations here have the opposite sign to those used in Oaksford and Chater (1994a): that is, information gains are all positive rather than negative.

12. See Oaksford and Chater 1995b for a formal demonstration of the fallacy in Politzer and Braine's (1991) argument.

13. Such shielding of rules would seem to preclude any role for counterexamples to refute rules, and hence inferences like reductio ad absurdum would no longer be possible. We don't believe this to be a problem because inferences like reductio can apply but now become more a matter of degree. The situation is analogous to I. Lakatos's (1970) account of the "protective belt" that surrounds a theory, protecting it from simple falsification by counterexample. Although the theory will survive many counterexamples by invoking auxiliary assumptions in its protective belt, there is a point at which this is no longer viable and at which counterexamples penetrate to falsify the theory.

REFERENCES

Almor, A., and S. A. Sloman (1996). Is deontic reasoning special? *Psychological Review* 103:374–380.

Anderson, J. R. (1983). *The Architecture of Cognition*. Cambridge: Harvard University Press.

Anderson, J. R. (1990). *The Adaptive Character of Thought*. Hillsdale, NJ: Erlbaum.

Anderson, J. R. (1991). Is human cognition adaptive? *Behavioral and Brain Sciences* 14:471–517.

Baron, J. (1994). *Thinking and Deciding*. Cambridge: Cambridge University Press.

Barsalou, L. W. (1987). The instability of graded structures: Implications for the nature of concepts. In U. Neisser (ed.), *Concepts and Conceptual Development*, pp. 101–140. Cambridge: Cambridge University Press.

Barwise, J., and R. Cooper (1981). Generalized quantifiers and natural languages. *Linguistics and Philosophy* 4:159–219.

Barwise, J., and J. Perry (1983). *Situation and Attitudes*. Cambridge: MIT Press.

Boolos, G. S., and R. C. Jeffrey (1980). *Computability and Logic*. Cambridge: Cambridge University Press.

Brachman, R. J., and H. Levesque (eds.) (1985). *Readings in Knowledge Representation*. Los Altos, CA: Morgan Kaufmann.

Braine, M. D. S. (1978). On the relation between the natural logic of reasoning and standard logic. *Psychological Review* 85:1–21.

Braine, M. D. S., and D. P. O'Brien (1991). A theory of *if*: Lexical entry, reasoning program and pragmatic principles. *Psychological Review* 98:182–203.

Braine, M. D. S., B. J. Reiser, and B. Rumain (1984). Some empirical justification for a theory of natural propositional logic. In G. Bower (ed.), *The Psychology of Learning and Motivation: Advances in Research and Theory*, vol. 18, pp. 313–370. New York: Academic Press.

Burnyeat, M. (1983). *The Skeptical Tradition*. Berkeley: University of California Press.

Byrne, R. M. J. (1989). Suppressing valid inferences with conditionals. *Cognition* 31:1–21.

Carey, S. (1988). Conceptual differences between children and adults. *Mind and Language* 3:167–181.

Charniak, E., and D. McDermott (1985). *An Introduction to Artificial Intelligence*. Reading, MA: Addison-Wesley.

Chater, N. (1993). Mental models and non-monotonic reasoning. *Behavioral and Brain Sciences* 16:340–341.

Chater, N., and M. Oaksford (1993). Logicism, mental models and everyday reasoning. *Mind and Language* 8:72–89.

Cheng, P. W., and K. J. Holyoak (1985). Pragmatic reasoning schemas. *Cognitive Psychology* 17:391–416.

Cheng, P. W., and L. R. Novick (1992). Covariation in natural causal induction. *Psychological Review* 99:365–382.

Chomsky, N. (1965). *Aspects of the Theory of Syntax*. Cambridge: MIT Press.

Clark, H. H. (1977). Bridging. In P. N. Johnson-Laird and P. C. Wason (eds.), *Thinking: Readings in Cognitive Science*, pp. 411–420. Cambridge: Cambridge University Press.

Clark, K. L. (1978). Negation as failure. In H. Gallaire and J. Minker (eds.), *Logic and Data Bases*, pp. 293–322. New York: Plenum Press.

Clocksin, W. F., and C. S. Mellish (1984). *Programming in PROLOG*. Berlin: Springer-Verlag.

Collins, A. M., and E. F. Loftus (1975). A spreading activation theory of semantic processing. *Psychological Review* 82:407–428.

Collins, A. M., and M. R. Quillian (1969). Retrieval from semantic memory. *Journal of Verbal Learning and Verbal Behavior* 8:240–247.

Coolidge, J. L. (1940). *A History of Geometrical Methods*. Oxford: Clarendon Press.

Cosmides, L. (1989). The logic of social exchange: Has natural selection shaped how humans reason? Studies with the Wason selection task. *Cognition* 31: 187–276.

Craik, F. I. M., and R. S. Lockhart (1972). Levels of processing: A framework for memory research. *Journal of Verbal Learning and Verbal Behavior* 11:671–684.

Craik, F. I. M., and E. Tulving (1975). Depth of processing and the retention of words in episodic memory. *Journal of Experimental Psychology: General* 104:268–294.

Cresswell, M. J. (1985). *Structured Meanings*. Cambridge: MIT Press.

Cummins, D. D., T. Lubart, O. Alksnis, and R. Rist (1991). Conditional reasoning and causation. *Memory and Cognition* 19:274–282.

Curry, H. B. (1956). *An Introduction to Mathematical Logic*. Amsterdam: Van Nostrand.

Davidson, D. (1984). *Inquiries into Truth and Interpretation*. Oxford: Clarendon Press.

Dempster, A. P. (1967). Upper and lower probabilities induced by a multivalued mapping. *Annals of Mathematical Statistics* 38:325–339.

Duda, R. O., and P. E. Hart (1973). *Pattern Classification and Scene Analysis*. New York: Wiley.

Duhem, P. ([1914] 1954). *The Aim and Structure of Physical Theory*. Princeton: Princeton University Press.

Earman, J. (1992). *Bayes or Bust?* Cambridge: MIT Press.

Evans, J. St. B. T. (1982). *The Psychology of Deductive Reasoning*. London: Routledge and Kegan Paul.

Evans, J. St. B. T. (1983). Linguistic determinants of bias in conditional reasoning. *Quarterly Journal of Experimental Psychology* 35A:635–644.

Evans, J. St. B. T. (1984). Heuristic and analytic processes in reasoning. *British Journal of Psychology* 75:451–468.

Evans, J. St. B. T. (1989). *Bias in Human Reasoning: Causes and Consequences*. Hillsdale, NJ: Erlbaum.

Evans, J. St. B. T. (1991). Theories of human reasoning: The fragmented state of the art. *Theory and Psychology* 1:83–106.

Evans, J. St. B. T., and J. S. Lynch (1973). Matching bias in the selection task. *British Journal of Psychology* 64:391–397.

Evans, J. St. B. T., S. E. Newstead, and R. M. J. Byrne (1993). *Human Reasoning: The Psychology of Deduction*. Hillsdale, NJ: Erlbaum.

Evans, J. St. B. T., and D. Over (1996). Rationality in the selection task: Epistemic utility vs. uncertainty reduction. *Psychological Review* 103:356–363.

Fischhoff, B., and R. Beyth-Marom (1983). Hypothesis evaluation from a Bayesian perspective. *Psychological Review* 90:239–260.

Fodor, J. A. (1983). *Modularity of Mind: An Essay on Faculty Psychology*. Cambridge: MIT Press.

Fodor, J. A., and Z. W. Pylyshyn (1988). Connectionism and cognitive architecture: A critical analysis. *Cognition* 28:3–71.

Garey, M., and M. Johnson (1979). *Computers and Tractability*. San Francisco: W. H. Freeman.

Garnham, A. (1993). Is logicist cognitive science possible? *Mind and Language* 8:49–71.

Garrod, S., and A. J. Sanford (1977). Interpreting anaphoric relations: The integration of semantic information while reading. *Journal of Verbal Learning and Verbal Behavior* 16:77–90.

Gigerenzer, G., and K. Hug (1992). Domain-specific reasoning: Social contracts, cheating and perspective change. *Cognition* 43:127–171.

Ginsberg, M. L. (ed.), (1987). *Readings in Nonmonotonic Reasoning*. Los Altos, CA: Morgan Kaufmann.

Girard, J.-Y. (1989). *Proofs and Types*. Cambridge: Cambridge University Press.

Gluck, M. A., and G. H. Bower (1988). Evaluating an adaptive network model of human learning. *Memory and Language* 27:166–195.

Glymour, C. (1980). *Theory and Evidence*. Princeton: Princeton University Press.

Goldman, A. I. (1986). *Epistemology and Cognition*. Cambridge: Harvard University Press.

Good, I. J. (1966). A derivation of the probabilistic explication of information. *Journal of the Royal Statistical Society, Series B*, 28:578–581.

Goodman, N. (1951). *The Structure of Appearance*. Cambridge: Harvard University Press.

Goodman, N. ([1954] 1983). *Fact, Fiction, and Forecast*, 4th edition. Cambridge: Harvard University Press.

Gorman, M. E., and M. E. Gorman (1984). A comparison of disconfirmatory, confirmatory and control strategies on Wason's 2-4-6 task. *Quarterly Journal of Experimental Psychology* 36A:629–648.

Haack, S. (1978). *Philosophy of Logics*. Cambridge: Cambridge University Press.

Harman, G. (1965). The inference to the best explanation. *Philosophical Review* 74:88–95.

Harman, G. (1986). *Change in View: Principles of Reasoning.* Cambridge: MIT Press Bradford.

Hayes, P. (1979). The logic of frames. In D. Metzing (ed.), *Frame Conceptions in Text Understanding,* pp. 46–61. Berlin: Walter de Gruyter.

Hempel, C. (1965). *Aspects of Scientific Explanation and Other Essays in the Philosophy of Science.* New York: Free Press.

Henle, M. (1962). The relation between logic and thinking. *Psychological Review* 69:366–378.

Hertz, J., A. Krogh, and R. G. Palmer (1991). *Introduction to the Theory of Neural Computation.* Menlo Park, CA: Addison-Wesley.

Hodges, W. (1977). *Logic.* Harmondsworth, UK: Penguin.

Holland, J. H., K. J. Holyoak, R. E. Nisbett, and P. R. Thagard (1986). *Induction: Processes of Inference, Learning and Discovery.* Cambridge: MIT Press.

Holyoak, K. J., and B. A. Spellman (1993). Thinking. *Annual Review of Psychology* 44:265–315.

Horn, L. R. (1989). *A Natural History of Negation.* Chicago: University of Chicago Press.

Horwich, P. (1982). *Probability and Evidence.* Cambridge: Cambridge University Press.

Howson, C., and P. Urbach (1989). *Scientific Reasoning: The Bayesian Approach.* La Salle, IL: Open Court.

Inhelder, B., and J. Piaget (1958). *The Growth of Logical Reasoning.* New York: Basic Books.

James, S. (1975). *Francis Bacon and the Style of Science.* Chicago: University of Chicago Press.

Jaspars, J. M. F., M. R. C. Hewstone, and F. D. Fincham (1983). Attribution theory and research: The state of the art. In J. M. F. Jaspars, F. D. Fincham, and M. R. C. Hewstone (eds.), *Attribution Theory: Essays and Experiments,* pp. 3–36. Orlando, FL: Academic Press.

Johnson-Laird, P. N. (1983). *Mental Models.* Cambridge: Cambridge University Press.

Johnson-Laird, P. N. (1986). Reasoning without logic. In T. Myers, K. Brown, and B. McGonigle (eds.), *Reasoning and Discourse Processes,* pp. 13–50. London: Academic Press.

Johnson-Laird, P. N., and R. M. J. Byrne (1991). *Deduction.* Hillsdale, NJ: Erlbaum.

Johnson-Laird, P. N., and P. C. Wason (1970). Insight into a logical relation. *Quarterly Journal of Experimental Psychology* 22:49–61.

Josephson, J. R., and S. G. Josephson (1994). *Abductive Inference: Computation, Philosophy, Technology.* Cambridge: Cambridge University Press.

Kahneman, D., P. Slovic, and A. Tversky (eds.) (1982). *Judgment under Uncertainty: Heuristics and Biases.* Cambridge: Cambridge University Press.

Kamp, H., and U. Reyle (1993). *From Discourse to Logic: Introduction to Model Theoretic Semantics for Natural Language, Formal Logic and Discourse Representation Theory.* Kluwer: Dordrecht.

Karmiloff-Smith, A. (1988). The child is a theoretician, not an inductivist. *Mind and Language* 3:183–196.

Katz, J. J. (1990). *The Metaphysics of Meaning.* Cambridge: MIT Press.

Kelley, H. H. (1967). Attribution theory in social psychology. In D. Levine (ed.), *Nebraska Symposium on Motivation,* vol. 15, pp. 192–238. Lincoln: University of Nebraska Press.

Kintsch, W., and T. A. Van Dijk (1978). Toward a model of text comprehension and production. *Psychological Review* 85:363–394.

Kirby, K. N. (1994). Probabilities and utilities of fictional outcomes in Wason's four-card selection task. *Cognition* 51:1–28.

Klahr, D., and K. Dunbar (1988). Dual space search during scientific reasoning. *Cognitive Science* 12:1–48.

Klayman, J., and Y. Ha (1987). Confirmation, disconfirmation and information in hypothesis testing. *Psychological Review* 94:211–228.

Kornblith, H. (ed.) (1994). *Naturalizing Epistemology.* Cambridge: MIT Press.

Kuhn, T. S. (1962). *The Structure of Scientific Revolutions.* Chicago: University of Chicago Press.

Lakatos, I. (1970). Falsification and the methodology of scientific research programmes. In I. Lakatos and A. Musgrave (eds.), *Criticism and the Growth of Knowledge,* pp. 91–196. Cambridge: Cambridge University Press.

Lakatos, I. (1976). *Proofs and Refutations: The Logic of Mathematical Discovery.* Cambridge: Cambridge University Press.

Lakatos, I. (1977a). *Philosophical Papers,* vol. 1: *The Methodology of Scientific Research Programmes.* Cambridge: Cambridge University Press.

Lakatos, I. (1977b). *Philosophical Papers,* vol. 2: *Mathematics, Science and Epistemology.* Cambridge: Cambridge University Press.

Laming, D. (1996). On the analysis of irrational data selection: A critique of Oaksford and Chater (1994). *Psychological Review* 103:364–373.

Lea, R. B., D. P. O'Brien, S. M. Fisch, I. A. Noveck, and M. D. S. Braine (1990). Predicting propositional logic inferences in text comprehension. *Journal of Memory and Language* 29:361–387.

Lehrer, K. (1990). *Theory of Knowledge.* Boulder: Westview.

Lemmon, E. J. (1965). *Beginning Logic.* London: Nelson.

Levinson, S. (1983). *Pragmatics.* Cambridge: Cambridge University Press.

Lindley, D. V. (1956). On a measure of the information provided by an experiment. *Annals of Mathematical Statistics* 27:986–1005.

MacKay, D. J. C. (1992). Information-based objective functions for active data selection. *Neural Computation* 4:590–604.

Macnamara, J. (1986). *A Border Dispute: The Place of Logic in Psychology.* Cambridge: MIT Press.

Macnamara, J., and G. E. Reyes (eds.) (1994). *The Logical Foundations of Cognition.* Oxford: Oxford University Press.

Manktelow, K. I., and D. E. Over (1991). Social roles and utilities in reasoning with deontic conditionals. *Cognition* 39:85–105.

Markovits, H. (1984). Awareness of the "possible" as a mediator of formal thinking in conditional reasoning problems. *British Journal of Psychology* 75:367–376.

Markovits, H. (1985). Incorrect conditional reasoning among adults: Competence or performance. *British Journal of Psychology* 76:241–247.

Marr, D. (1982). *Vision.* San Francisco: W. H. Freeman.

McCarthy, J. M. (1980). Circumscription: A form of nonmonotonic reasoning. *Artificial Intelligence* 13:27–39.

McDermott, D. (1982). Non-monotonic logic II: Non-monotonic modal theories. *Journal of the Association for Computing Machinery* 29(1): 33–57.

McDermott, D. (1987). A critique of pure reason. *Computational Intelligence* 3:151–160.

McDermott, D., and J. Doyle (1980). Non-monotonic logic I. *Artificial Intelligence* 13:41–72.

Michalski, R., J. G. Carbonell, and T. Mitchell (1983). *Machine Learning: An Artificial Intelligence Approach*. Palo Alto, CA: Tioga.

Minsky, M. (1977). Frame system theory. In P. N. Johnson-Laird and P. C. Wason (eds.), *Thinking: Readings in Cognitive Science*, pp. 355–376. Cambridge: Cambridge University Press.

Montague, R. (1974). *Formal Philosophy: Selected Papers of Richard Montague*. R. H. Thomason (ed.). New Haven: Yale University Press.

Mynatt, C. R., M. E. Doherty, and R. D. Tweney (1977). Confirmation bias in a simulated research environment: An experimental study of scientific inference. *Quarterly Journal of Experimental Psychology* 29:85–95.

Newell, A. (1990). *Unified Theories of Cognition*. Cambridge: Harvard University Press.

Oaksford, M. (1993). Mental models and the tractability of everyday reasoning. *Behavioral and Brain Sciences* 16:360–361.

Oaksford, M., and N. Chater (1991). Against logicist cognitive science. *Mind and Language* 6:1–38.

Oaksford, M., and N. Chater (1993). Reasoning theories and bounded rationality. In K. I. Manktelow and D. E. Over (eds.), *Rationality*, pp. 31–60. London: Routledge.

Oaksford, M., and N. Chater (1994a). A rational analysis of the selection task as optimal data selection. *Psychological Review* 101:608–631.

Oaksford, M., and N. Chater (1994b). Another look at eliminative and enumerative behaviour in a conceptual task. *European Journal of Cognitive Psychology* 6:149–169.

Oaksford, M., and N. Chater (1995a). Information gain explains relevance which explains the selection task. *Cognition* 57:97–108.

Oaksford, M., and N. Chater (1995b). Theories of reasoning and the computational explanation of everyday inference. *Thinking and Reasoning* 1:121–152.

Oaksford, M., and N. Chater (1996). Rational explanation of the selection task. *Psychological Review* 103:381–391.

Oaksford, M., and N. Chater (1998). *Rationality in an Uncertain World: Essays on the Cognitive Science of Human Reasoning*. Hove, East Sussex: Psychology Press.

Oaksford, M., N. Chater, and K. Stenning (1990). Connectionism, classical cognitive science and experimental psychology. *AI and Society* 4:73–90.

O'Brien, D. P. (1993). Mental logic and human irrationality. In K. I. Manktelow and D. E. Over (eds.), *Rationality*, pp. 110–135. London: Routledge.

O'Brien, D. P., M. D. S. Braine, and Y. Yang (1994). Propositional reasoning by mental models? Simple to refute in principle and in practice. *Psychological Review* 101:711–724.

O'Brien, E. J., D. M. Shank, J. L. Myers, and K. Rayner (1988). Elaborative inference during reading: Do they occur on line? *Journal of Experimental Psychology: Learning, Memory and Cognition* 14:410–420.

Pearl, J. (1988). *Probabilistic Reasoning in Intelligent Systems*. San Mateo, CA: Morgan Kaufmann.

Politzer, G., and M. D. S. Braine (1991). Responses to inconsistent premises cannot count as suppression of valid inferences. *Cognition* 38:103–108.

Pollard, P. (1985). Non-independence of selections on the Wason selection task. *Bulletin of the Psychonomic Society* 23:317–320.

Pollock, J. L. (1986). *Contemporary Theories of Knowledge*. Totowa: Rowman Littlefield.

Popper, K. R. ([1935] 1959). *The Logic of Scientific Discovery*. London: Hutchinson.

Putnam, H. (1974). The "corroboration" of theories. In P. A. Schilpp (ed.), *The Philosophy of Karl Popper*, vol. 1, pp. 221–240. La Salle, IL: Open Court.

Putnam, H. ([1962] 1975). The analytic and the synthetic. In H. Putnam (ed.), *Philosophical Papers*, vol. 2: *Mind, Language and Reality*, pp. 33–69. Cambridge: Cambridge University Press.

Putnam, H., and P. Benacerraf (eds.) (1983). *Philosophy of Mathematics: Selected Readings*, 2nd ed. Cambridge: Cambridge University Press.

Quine, W. V. O. (1953). Two dogmas of empiricism. In *From a Logical Point of View*, pp. 20–46. Cambridge: Harvard University Press.

Quine, W. V. O. (1960). *Word and Object*. Cambridge: MIT Press.

Quine, W. V. O. (1969). Epistemology naturalized. In *Ontological Relativity and Other Essays*, pp. 69–90. New York: Columbia University Press.

Quine, W. V. O. (1990). *Pursuit of Truth*. Cambridge: MIT Press.

Reiter, R. (1980). A logic for default reasoning. *Artificial Intelligence* 13:81–132.

Reiter, R. ([1978] 1985). One reasoning by default. In R. J. Brachman and H. Levesque (eds.), *Readings in Knowledge Representation*, pp. 401–410. Los Altos, CA: Morgan Kaufmann.

Rips, L. J. (1983). Cognitive processes in propositional reasoning. *Psychological Review* 90:38–71.

Rips, L. J. (1990). Reasoning. *Annual Review of Psychology* 41:321–353.

Rips, L. J. (1994). *The Psychology of Proof: Deductive Reasoning in Human Thinking*. Cambridge: MIT Press.

Russell, B. (1919). *Introduction to Mathematical Philosophy*. New York: Macmillan.

Russell, B. (1946). *History of Western Philosophy*. London: Macmillan.

Schank, R. C., and R. P. Abelson (1977). *Scripts, Plans, Goals, and Understanding*. Hillsdale, NJ: Erlbaum.

Schiffer, S. (1987). *Remnants of Meaning*. Cambridge: MIT Press.

Scott, D., and C. Strachey (1971). *Toward a Mathematical Semantics for Computer Languages*. Oxford: Oxford University Press.

Scruton, R. (1982). *Kant*. Oxford: Oxford University Press.

Shafer, G. (1976). *A Mathematical Theory of Evidence*. Princeton: Princeton University Press.

Smedslund, J. (1970). On the circular relation between logic and understanding. *Scandinavian Journal of Psychology* 11:217–219.

Sperber, D., F. Cara, and V. Girotto (1995). Relevance explains the selection task. *Cognition* 57:31–95.

Sperber, D., and D. Wilson (1986). *Relevance: Communication and Cognition*. Oxford: Basil Blackwell.

Stein, E. (1996). *Without Good Reason: The Rationality Debate in Philosophy and Cognitive Science*. Oxford: Oxford University Press.

Stevenson, R. J., and D. E. Over (1995). Deduction from uncertain premises. *Quarterly Journal of Experimental Psychology* 48:613–643.

Stich, S. (1985). Could man be an irrational animal? *Synthese* 64:115–135.

Stich, S. (1990). *The Fragmentation of Reason*. Cambridge: MIT Press.

Thagard, P. (1988). *Computational Philosophy of Science*. Cambridge: MIT Press Bradford.

Toulmin, S. (1961). *Foresight and Understanding*. London: Hutchinson.

Tversky, A., and D. Kahneman (1974). Judgment under Uncertainty: Heuristics and biases. *Science* 125:1124–1131.

Tversky, A., and D. Kahneman (1986). Rational choice and the framing of decisions. *Journal of Business* 59:251–278.

Van Fraassen, B. (1980). *The Scientific Image*. Oxford: Oxford University Press.

Wason, P. C. (1960). On the failure to eliminate hypotheses in a conceptual task. *Quarterly Journal of Experimental Psychology* 12:129–140.

Wason, P. C. (1966). Reasoning. In B. Foss (ed.), *New Horizons in Psychology*, pp. 135–151. Harmondsworth, Middlesex: Penguin.

Wason, P. C. (1968). Reasoning about a rule. *Quarterly Journal of Experimental Psychology* 20:273–281.

Wason, P. C. (1969). Regression in reasoning. *British Journal of Psychology* 60:471–480.

Wason, P. C., and P. N. Johnson-Laird (1972). *The Psychology of Reasoning: Structure and Content*. Cambridge: Harvard University Press.

Winograd, T., and F. Flores (1986). *Understanding Computers and Cognition*. Reading, MA: Addison-Wesley.

Woods, W. A. (1975). What's in a link: Foundations for semantic networks. In D. G. Bobrow and A. M. Collins (eds.), *Representation and Understanding: Studies in Cognitive Science*, pp. 35–82. New York: Academic Press.

10

Reasoning Imperialism

LANCE J. RIPS

1. Introduction

As everybody knows by now, scientists are the last great imperialists. All your colleagues have their eyes on your lab space. Go away for a couple days and you can expect to find gangs of grad students from other labs "borrowing" your workstations. To make things worse, this sort of territorial ambition extends into the theoretical domain as well. Once a theorist has come up with a model of hippopotamus anatomy, you can be sure it won't be long before he or she is asserting that the theory applies perfectly generally to anything from tomatoes to toasters, and soon you've got a Theory of Everything.

It also won't come as a surprise that cognitive psychologists who study reasoning are not immune to this version of manifest destiny. I am a sorry example of this tendency, since I've argued that deductive reasoning might play a central role in cognitive architecture (Rips 1994). I'm happy to say that I won't be defending this theory here. I'm mentioning it because I'm about to criticize a similar expansionist tendency in others, and it seems only fair to acknowledge the same drive.

The difficulty that I *do* want to discuss concerns people's ability to recognize certain arguments as deductively correct and other arguments as inductively strong. Argument (1), for example, is the sort that seems deductively correct and gives experimental subjects no trouble at all when they're quizzed about it.

(1)   Broccoli contains vitamin Y and cauliflower contains vitamin Y.
          Therefore, broccoli contains vitamin Y.

In the relevant experiments, the subjects read arguments like this, and they're asked to decide whether the conclusion is necessarily true whenever the premise is true. This being one of the simplest examples, nearly all subjects say that the conclusion follows (100 percent of the undergraduates in an experiment by M. D. S. Braine, B. J. Reiser, and B. Rumain [1984]; 91 percent of adolescents in experiments by D. N. Osherson [1975]). Argument (2), however, is the sort of example that has been used in experiments on inductive strength (e.g., Osherson, et al. 1990; Rips 1975; Sloman 1993):

(2)   Broccoli contains vitamin Y.
          Therefore, cauliflower contains vitamin Y.

No one would suppose that the conclusion is necessarily true when the premise is, but subjects do say that the premise makes the conclusion more plausible. They also find (2) more convincing than a similar argument in which, for example, *french fries* is substituted for *cauliflower*.

But here's where the imperialist temptation arises. If you've got a theory that explains how people recognize (1) as deductively correct, then maybe you can weaken the theory's criteria to get an explanation of why they think that (2) isn't so bad. In the other direction, if you've got a theory that explains how people determine the convincingness of arguments like (2), then maybe you can use the theory to handle (1) as a special case of maximum convincingness.[1]

If you have these sorts of ambitions over all reasoning, then there are two possible strategies that you can adopt. One is to take the distinction between judgments of deductive correctness and judgments of inductive strength as psychologically real and then claim that your theory is powerful enough to account for both processes. According to this view, people can reliably distinguish deductive correctness from inductive strength; they have some mental procedure that tells them when an argument is deductively correct and when it is (merely) strong. The theory, however, is powerful enough to explain both types of decision. Flip one switch, and you've got a validity detector; flip another switch, and you've got a strength detector. That's the basic idea, and I'll label it the *two-mode* strategy in what follows. The other strategy for conquering the reasoning domain is to deny that the distinction applies at a psychological level, so only one type of theory is needed to explain the data. You could claim, for example, that people don't have a grasp of deductive correctness apart from inductive strength, so your theory of inductive strength is all that's required to deal with human reasoning. I'll call this alternative the *one-mode* strategy.

My guess is that neither of these strategies works. What I'd like to argue is that first, current proposals along the lines of the two-mode strategy seriously underestimate the difficulties of extending theories of deductive correctness in the direction of inductive strength (or underestimate the difficulties of extending theories of inductive strength to handle deductive correctness). Maybe someone will come along with a cognitive theory that's powerful enough to handle both with the flip of a switch, but current candidates don't do this. Second, the one-mode strategy of denying that people can distinguish deductive correctness and inductive strength doesn't square with the data. It's certainly possible that people sometimes confuse deductive correctness and inductive strength: sometimes they may make judgments of inductive strength when they're officially supposed to be making judgments of deductive correctness. But this is a confusion of two *different* operations, like adding two numbers when you were supposed to be multiplying them. The data that bear on this issue are relatively new, coming from a pair of recent imaging studies; but if they hold up, there are some concrete reasons to reject one-mode theories. In short, if these arguments are correct, imperialist approaches aren't going to be successful, and for the moment, at any rate, we should all go back to our own labs and stop these raids on neighboring territory.

Two terminological points before pushing on, though, one that concerns one- versus two-mode strategies and the other that concerns deductive correctness versus inductive strength. As I've just drawn it, the one-mode/two-mode split has to do with whether people can *reliably* distinguish inductive strength from deductive correctness, and because of the emphasis on reliability, the boundary between the strategies is vague. People can easily discriminate arguments like (1) and (2) in these terms, but we can obviously up the ante, for example, by concocting invalid arguments with very high inductive strength. How good does a person's discrimination have to be in order to count as "reliable" for these purposes? I hope to make the distinction between one-mode and two-mode strategies a bit crisper in sections 2 and 3. Some residual vagueness is inevitable but shouldn't beg any questions against the theories that I consider here.

Along similar lines, there are boundary conditions on one-mode and two-mode strategies that tend to reduce the potential difference between them. From one direction, the "modes" of two-mode theories obviously can't be so dissimilar that they supply entirely different explanations for strength and validity judgments. If the modes of a theory have few commonalities, then it's not a unified theory of reasoning, and it would concede the issue to the anti-imperialist forces. From the opposite direction, one-mode theories would be trivially false if they predicted that people make exactly the same evaluative responses to clear-cut arguments such as (1) and (2). To have room to maneuver, one-mode theories have to be able to hold arguments to different standards when evaluating them for deductive correctness than when evaluating them for inductive strength. The trouble is that the greater the difference between the types of standards, the more the one-mode theory looks like a two-mode approach. As a result, we may sometimes have difficulty deciding whether to classify a theory as having one or two modes. But as in the case of vagueness associated with reliability, vagueness about the degree of difference between one- and two-mode mechanics isn't going to cause mayhem. As long as the considerations about an individual theory are correct, it won't much matter on which side of the expository fence it sits.

The distinction between deductive correctness and inductive strength is a little more delicate, since certain ways of characterizing the difference will become an issue in section 3. Unlike the one-mode/two-mode difference, the difference between deductive correctness and inductive strength is not vague (so I'll be arguing), but we do have a choice in the approach we should take in thinking about it. In order to have some neutral ground for the debate, let's say, for the time being, that a deductively correct argument is one in which the conclusion is necessarily true whenever the premises are true. Unlike deductive correctness, inductive strength is a matter of degree. But we can say that the degree of inductive strength depends on the extent to which the conclusion is plausible whenever the premises are true. These construals of deductive correctness and inductive strength have the advantage that they are close to the standard way in which investigators instruct subjects about their task in experiments on reasoning, so the results from the experiments will bear on the current issues. Of course, the paraphrase of deductive correctness depends on how we interpret *necessarily* in this context (and similarly for *strength* and *plausibility*), and so it can't by itself serve as a satisfactory analysis of this concept. But at least the paraphrases can buy us some time until we are able to get a clearer view of the opposing positions. To go along with this neutral stance, I'll continue to use the term *deductive correctness* instead of *validity* or *derivability*, since the latter terms may presuppose special ways of thinking about correctness.

2. Can We Get Deductive Correctness from Strength?

I'd like to start by examining the two-mode strategy. So until further notice I'm going to assume that ordinary folk can discriminate deductive correctness from mere inductive strength, with a view toward finding out whether there are any psychological theories around that can handle both sorts of judgment. In principle, one might start with a theory of inductive strength and try to extend it to deductive correctness, or one could work in the opposite direction. I don't, in fact, know anyone who claims that his or her theory of inductive strength can explain deductive correctness; it's the opposite direction that's apparently more tempting, as we'll see in a minute. Still, it's worth considering why psychological theories of inductive strength aren't extendable.

As a test case, let's consider one hypothetical attempt to get a theory of strength to capture deductive correctness. Suppose your theory says that people evaluate the strength of arguments by calculating the conditional probability of the conclusion given the premises. So Argument (2), for example, would be strong to the extent that the probability is high of cauliflower having vitamin Y given that broccoli has it. In order to get a two-mode theory that can also handle deductive correctness, you might assume that if the conditional probability turns out to be 1, the argument is *perfectly* strong or deductively correct. Thus, in induction mode the theory tests arguments for high conditional probability, whereas in deduction mode the theory tests them for a conditional probability of 1. In line with this theory, the usual axioms of probability theory confer a conditional probability of 1 on arguments that are deductively correct in classical logic (provided the premises are not contradictory).[2] But what about the reverse direction? Does having a conditional probability of I guarantee deductive correctness?

Here's an easy probability quiz that may help clarify this issue. For each of the arguments in (3), calculate the conditional probability of the conclusion given the premise:

(3a)   Calvin rolls a die where the six faces of the die have an equal probability of ending faceup.
        Therefore, Calvin rolls a 1, 2, or 3.

(3b)   Calvin rolls a die where the six faces of the die have an equal probability of ending faceup.
        Therefore, Calvin rolls a 1, 2, 3, 4, or 5.

(3c)   Calvin rolls a die where the six faces of the die have an equal probability of ending faceup.
        Therefore, Calvin rolls a 1, 2, 3, 4, 5, or 6.

If you answered 1/2, 5/6, and 1, you get an A+. But notice that even though the conclusion of (3c) given its premise is 1, this argument is obviously invalid. There are possible states in which rolling a die magically makes new spots materialize on the faces or makes them disappear, so the conclusion needn't be true when the premise is. Were we wrong about the conditional probability being 1 in (3c), then? I think the answer has to be "no," on pain of never being able to assert a conditional probability of 1 in simple sampling or randomizing experiments. The trouble is that in standard probability theory, the conditional probability depends on how things are in the single sample space of the problem (e.g., Feller 1950). But how things are in a single sample space isn't enough to guarantee deductive correctness. We need to look at other possible states of affairs to check that the argument is deductively correct.

As another example, consider situations in which there are an infinite number of possible outcomes, as in (4):

(4a)   A real number between 3 and 4 is randomly sampled.
        Therefore, the sampled number is π.

(4b)   A real number between 3 and 4 is randomly sampled.
        Therefore, the sampled number is not π.

The conditional probability of choosing π is presumably 0, so the complementary conditional probability that the chosen number is not π is 1. However, (4b) is not a deductively correct argument, since the premise is true and the conclusion false in case π really is the number selected.[3]

In fact, it *is* possible to get deductive correctness out of probability theory. H. H. Field (1977) outlines one way to do this. However, this method requires generalizing over sample spaces, that is, considering all possible assignments of probabilities to the atomic events in the model. It seems safe to say that no psychological theories for inductive reasoning have anything like the power to perform this kind of generalization.

One reason that it's safe to assume this is that most existing models for induction are based on a much weaker relation than standard probability. For example, Osherson et al. (1990) propose that people assess the strength of (2) by computing the similarity of broccoli to cauliflower, computing the similarity of broccoli to other items in the lowest-level natural category in which both broccoli and cauliflower are members (vegetables, presumably), and then combining these two similarities. (Rips 1975 presents a model in the same style.) S. A. Sloman (1993) proposed a connectionist version in which properties of the premise category are associated with the predicate. In (2), for example, properties of broccoli like being green, edible, and so on, are connected to a representation for vitamin Y. The conclusion category "cauliflower" is also decomposed into properties, such as being white, edible, and so forth. Some of the cauliflower properties will overlap the broccoli properties. The greater the overlap, the larger the activation that cauliflower gives to vitamin Y and the higher the judged strength of the argument, according to this story.

None of these authors is under the illusion that these very simple models will work for all inductively strong arguments (for qualifications, see the original papers, as well as Coley, Medin, and Atran 1997; Heit and Rubinstein 1994; and Sloman 1994). The point is that if they don't work for all inductively strong arguments, they're very unlikely to be able to identify deductively correct ones. As an example, Argument (5a) is deductively correct and Argument (5b) isn't, but these models predict that the premise and the conclusion are more similar in (5b) than in (5a) (Sloman and Rips 1998). The deductively incorrect argument ends up stronger than the deductively correct one.

(5a)   Broccoli has vitamin Y and cauliflower has vitamin Y and turnips have vitamin Y and parsnips have vitamin Y.
        Therefore, broccoli has vitamin Y.

(5b)   Broccoli has vitamin Y and cauliflower has vitamin Y and turnips have vitamin Y and parsnips have vitamin Y.
        Therefore, broccoli has vitamin Y and cauliflower has vitamin Y and turnips have vitamin Y and parsnips have vitamin Y and carrots have vitamin Y.

There may be psychologists who believe that evaluating inductive strength is all that's needed to account for subjects' performance in experiments that ask for evaluation of deductive correctness, but that's because these psychologists think subjects don't have a grasp of deductive correctness at all. Remember we're assuming, for the time being, that this isn't so—that subjects can tell us that (5a) is deductively correct and that (5b) is strong but not deductively correct.

3. Can We Get Strength from Deductive Correctness?

The idea that you can get a theory of deductive correctness from a theory of inductive strength hasn't been especially popular, but raids in the other direction have proved tempting. One attempt, for example, has sometimes been associated with the hypothetico-deductive method in the philosophy of science. The idea was roughly that if you can deduce a testable conclusion from a set of premises drawn from your theory (together with premises that state background conditions), then a positive outcome for the test inductively confirms the theory. In our terms, if we have a deductively correct argument from a premise to a conclusion, then the reverse argument from the conclusion to the premise is inductively strong: "The logical process by which we seem to pass directly from examined to unexamined cases consists in an inverse application of deductive inference, so that all reasoning may be said to be either directly or inversely deductive" (Jevons 1892, p. 152).

A cognitive example might go like this: Consider the relation between working memory span (i.e., the maximum number of letters, digits, or other items that you can repeat back immediately after hearing them) and item recognition time (the amount of time it takes to say that a particular item, say the letter Q, is a member of a short list of items—e.g., W, E, Q, G—that you've seen a few seconds before). Let m be the memory span for a given type of item (e.g., letters) and t be the item recognition rate (total recognition time divided by the number of items on the memorized list). Suppose you hypothesize on the basis of preliminary data that recognition rate is inversely related to memory span: the more items that will fit in working memory, the less time it takes to check any one of them. In particular, suppose the preliminary data suggests that $t = 250/m$, where t is measured in milliseconds (Cavanagh 1972). Then if you find that the memory span of some new type of item (e.g., people's first names) is ten items, you can *deduce* from your hypothesis and the new data point that t ought to be twenty-five milliseconds/item for recognition of the same item type. Should it turn out in a further experiment that this prediction is correct, then the *inductive* argument from the data to the hypothesis is strong. We can represent the relevant deductively correct argument as (6a) and the derived inductively strong argument as (6b):

(6a) $t = 250/m$ (hypothesis) and $m = 10$ (initial condition).
        Therefore, $t = 25$ (predicted datum).

(6b) $t = 25$ (observed datum).
        Therefore, $t = 250/m$ (hypothesis) and $m = 10$ (initial condition).

These days, philosophers of science tend to reject this approach (although they usually don't deny that deduction plays some role in deriving new predictions). One reason for this is that there are apparent counterexamples in which reversing a deductively correct argument produces an argument that has little or no inductive strength. For example, Argument (7a) is deductively correct, but the reverse (7b) seems nearly worthless:

(7a)   Shepard's theory of second-order isomorphism is true and broccoli has vitamin Y.
         Therefore, broccoli has vitamin Y.

(7b)   Broccoli has vitamin Y.
         Therefore, Shepard's theory of second-order isomorphism is true and broccoli has vitamin Y.

Osherson, E. E. Smith, and E. Shafir (1986) discuss a number of these attempts to pull the rabbit of inductive strength from the hat of deductive correctness and ably demonstrate their deficiencies. There is no reason to go over the same ground here, so let me concentrate on a more recent proposal that might get around some of the earlier problems.

A Model-Based Theory of Inductive Strength

This new approach comes from P. N. Johnson-Laird (1994), and it consists of two main pieces: one piece is a theoretical proposal formulated in terms of possible worlds, and the other is a psychological proposal formulated in terms of his own brand of mental models. The theoretical proposal starts by defining the strength of an inductive inference in terms of possible worlds, as follows (p. 197):

> a set of premises, including implicit premises provided by general and-contextual knowledge, lend *strength* to a conclusion according to two principles:
>
> 1. The conclusion is true in at least one of the possible states of affairs in which the premises are true; that is, the conclusion is at least consistent with the premises. If there is no such state of affairs, then the conclusion is inconsistent with the premises: the inference has no strength whatever. . . .
>
> 2. Possible states of affairs in which the premises are true but the conclusion false (i.e., counterexamples) weaken the argument. If there are no counterexamples, then the argument is maximally strong—the conclusion follows validly from the premises. If there are counterexamples, then the strength of the argument equals the proportion of states of affairs consistent with the premises in which the conclusion is also true.

In other words, the inductive strength of an argument is the ratio of the number of possible worlds in which the premises and conclusion are all true to the number of possible worlds in which the premises are true. Johnson-Laird also explicitly identifies this ratio with the conditional probability of the conclusion given the premises ("the strength of an inference is accordingly equivalent to the probability of the conclusion given the premises"

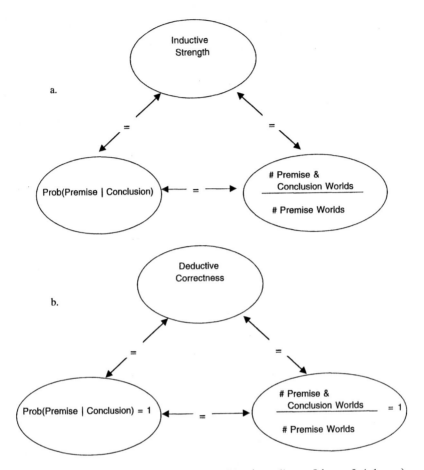

FIGURE 10.1a. The hypothetical relationships (according to Johnson-Laird 1994) among the inductive strength of an argument, the conditional probability of its conclusion given its premises, and the ratio of possible worlds in which both premises and conclusion are true to possible worlds in which the premises are true.

FIGURE 10.1b. The hypothetical relationships (according to Johnson-Laird 1994) among the deductive correctness of an argument, unit conditional probability of its conclusion given its premises, and unit ratio of possible worlds in which both premises and conclusion are true to possible worlds in which the premises are true.

[1994, p. 197]). So we have the equivalences that you see in Figure 10.1a for the general case. In the special case in which this ratio of possible worlds is 1, the conditional probability of the conclusion given the premises will also be 1, and the argument is deductively correct, as shown in Figure 10.1b.

Johnson-Laird notes, however, that as a psychological proposal this one has "the obvious disadvantage . . . that it is completely impractical. No one can consider all the infinitely many states of affairs consistent with a set of premises" (pp. 198–199). So how do people evaluate the strength of an argument? Johnson-Laird's answer is that people substitute mental models for possible worlds (p. 201):

> The *strength* of an inference depends, as we have seen, on the relative proportion of two sorts of possible states of affairs consistent with the premises: those in which the conclusion is true and those in which it is false. Reasoners can estimate these proportions by constructing models of the premises and attending to the proportions with which the two sorts of models come to mind, and perhaps to the relative ease of constructing them.

The estimates in question don't have the elegant properties of statistical estimators. According to Johnson-Laird, they can be "rudimentary, biased and governed by heuristics" (p. 202), so there is no guarantee that they will reflect the theoretical strength of an argument, as defined earlier.

To evaluate this proposal, let's postpone discussing mental models for a moment and start with Johnson-Laird's initial idea that the strength of an argument is equal to the ratio of premise-and-conclusion possible worlds to premise possible worlds. In order to get a deductively correct argument when this ratio is 1, as Johnson-Laird stipulates in the second part of his definition, we need to understand the possible states of affairs or possible worlds in question to be all logically possible states of affairs. Restricting the set of worlds to a smaller subset would mean that arguments that do not follow logically will mistakenly count as deductively correct. But including all logically possible states means that for arguments about probabilistic matters, such as those in (3), the preceding ratio will differ from standard calculations of the conditional probability of the conclusion given the premise. There are many possible worlds in which the premise of (3c) will be true and the conclusion false—worlds like those envisaged earlier, in which rolling a die supernaturally changes the spots on its faces. So Johnson-Laird's ratio of possible worlds will be less than 1 in this situation. As we would normally calculate it, however, the probability of the conclusion of (3c) given the premise is exactly 1. Something has gone wrong.[4] Extreme conditional probability can't be identified with deductive correctness.

In retrospect, this shouldn't have been surprising. Calculation of probabilities in arguments like (3) leaves in place ordinary causal laws, including laws that govern the behavior of devices like dice and urns (see Pollock 1990 for the relation between probability and physically possible worlds). But the assessment of deductive correctness doesn't observe these constraints.

Is there any way to restore the picture in Figure 10.1 in which deductive correctness is the same as extreme conditional probability? Perhaps the most natural way to do this within the confines of Johnson-Laird's approach is to assume that when we evaluate an argument's inductive strength we add to the explicit premises new ones that specify the relevant causal factors. (Remember that Johnson-Laird evaluates the strength of an argument through use of not just the premises that explicitly appear in the argument but also "implicit premises provided by general and contextual knowledge" [p. 197].) In other words, in assessing the inductive strength of an argument, as opposed to its deductive correctness, we consider the argument as an enthymeme, supply the necessary causal or contextual premises, and then determine strength using the ratio-of-possible-worlds method.

But even granting that all relevant causal principles can be formulated as a list of premises, this maneuver just acknowledges that inductive strength and deductive correctness are relative to a different set of worlds. This is the set of worlds consistent with the explicit premises in the case of deductive correctness but consistent with the explicit-premises-plus-causal-laws in the case of inductive strength. Although we might be able to think of both validity testing and strength testing as comparing possible worlds, these two kinds of assessment would require distinct theories of what's logically possible and what's causally possible. If this seems like a unified theory of deductive correctness and inductive strength, it's only because we're abstracting over what makes them interestingly and substantively different.

Moreover, even if we add causally relevant implicit premises in order to make an argument like (3c) come out right, we're still left with the problem posed by Argument (4b). It's clear that adding causal laws to (4b)'s explicit premise (i.e., a real number between 3 and 4 is randomly sampled) won't eliminate the (physical) possibility that the chosen number is π. So supplementing the premise with causal laws doesn't turn it into a valid argument.

Let's summarize what's wrong with the picture in Figure 10.1. First, although deductive correctness implies a conditional probability of 1, the converse doesn't hold in general. Second, because we have to take into account an infinite number of worlds (to deal with Argument [4b], for example), the ratio of premise-and-conclusion worlds to premise worlds is sometimes undefined (see note 4). Even if we patch up the computation so that the comparison of worlds coincides with conditional probability, then the comparison of worlds won't imply deductive correctness.

Inductive Strength and Mental Models

But what about the second half of Johnson-Laird's proposal? Even if we jettison the theoretical idea that deductive correctness and inductive strength fall on the same continuum, might it not still be true that when people actually attempt to evaluate arguments they do so in such a way that deductive correctness is the end point of inductive strength? Maybe people believe that an argument is strong if most of their mental models of the premises are mental models of the conclusion and believe it is deductively correct if all of their mental models of the premises are mental models of the conclusion. Johnson-Laird and F. Savary (1996, p. 72) have emphasized that mental models are supposed to account for how "intelligent, but mathematically ignorant, individuals—such as Aristotle!—reason about probabilities. . . . It remains to be seen how far the theory can be extended to cope with numerical probabilities." So perhaps the fact that numerical values of conditional probabilities don't line up with ratios of logically possible models isn't

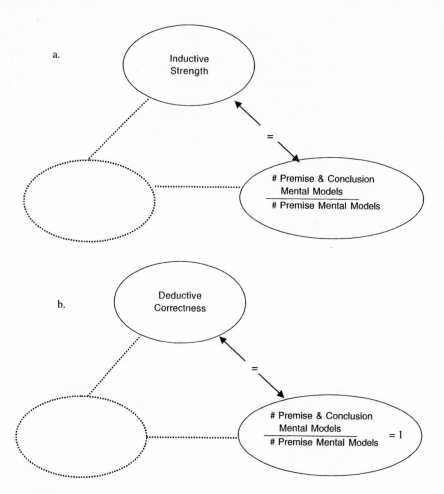

FIGURE 10.2a. The hypothetical relationship (according to Johnson-Laird 1994) between inductive strength and the ratio of number of mental models in which both the premises and conclusion are true to the number of mental models in which the premises are true.

FIGURE 10.2b. The hypothetical relationship (according to Johnson-Laird 1994) between deductive correctness and the unit ratio of number of mental models in which both the premises and conclusion are true to the number of mental models in which the premises are true.

an issue; perhaps for "mathematically ignorant individuals" impressions of strength do line up with ratios of mental models. Let's consider the simpler set of equivalences in Figure 10.2, then, where we have eliminated numerical conditional probabilities and have substituted mental models for possible worlds.[5]

It turns out, however, that the same difficulties we've just considered militate against assessing inductive strength using the same mental models that one would use to assess deductive correctness. To see why, consider Argument (3c) again (*Calvin rolls a die with equi-probable faces; therefore, Calvin rolls a 1-6*). As we saw earlier, it's easy to imagine lots of sci-fi counterexamples in which the premise is true and the conclusion false (e.g., Calvin's rolling the die allows new spots to materialize, so Calvin rolls a 7 or an 8 or . . .). The problem is that the cumulative effect of these counterexamples (an indefinitely large number of them) on the strength of Argument (3c) is nil. This isn't because it's hard to bring these examples to mind; I just told you about them, so little effort on your part is needed. It's also impossible to dismiss these counterexamples on the grounds that they're implausible. Plausibility is itself a function of inductive strength, so even though the counterexamples are indeed implausible, overlooking them for this reason begs the question at issue. Moreover, the same counterexamples do suffice to show that (3c) is not deductively correct, and this means that eliminating such counterexamples for purposes of evaluating inductive strength concedes that strength and deductive correctness don't draw on the same set of models or situations.

What seems to be going on is that counterexamples like these are simply irrelevant to the strength of (3c), since the strength of (3c) depends only on situations in which the usual causal laws apply. Assessments of strength, like assessments of conditional probability in our earlier examples, fix these causal relations or, at least, fix as many of them as are consistent with the premises of the argument. But there are no such constraints on the evaluation of deductive correctness, and so deductive correctness and inductive strength must be relative to different models. As in the earlier discussion, it is possible that (3c) is an enthymeme, with the missing premises supplying the relevant causal information. However, there is no evidence that people treat arguments like these as incomplete (see Sellars 1953 for arguments against the enthymeme approach). And, in any case, there is nothing at all in the mental model theory that explains how we determine these missing causal principles; the theory supplies no explicit theory of causality that we can draw on for these purposes.

Even in the case of simple arguments like (2), it is completely up for grabs how many mental models there are in which both broccoli and cauliflower have vitamin Y relative to the number in which broccoli has vitamin Y. People might reason that because broccoli and cauliflower share many of their biological properties, it's quite likely that there are lots of models in which cauliflower has vitamin Y if broccoli does. But it's apparent that what's doing the work in such an estimate is people's knowledge of biological properties and not the number of models. We might as well say more simply that people reason that because broccoli and cauliflower share relevant biological properties, it's likely that cauliflower has vitamin Y if broccoli does and drop talk of mental models altogether. About knowledge of biological properties mental model theory has nothing to add.

I think what's right about mental models in this context is the underlying intuition that we sometimes recall and count the number of individual events we have experienced in determining the overall frequency or probability of an event class (see Tourangeau, Rips, and Rasinski 2000, chapter 5, for a review of frequency and probability estimation). In estimating the probability that new computer programs have bugs, for example, you might count the number of new programs you can remember that have bugs and the number of new programs you can remember and calculate the quotient. We could also use the quotient as an estimate of the strength of an argument from *X is a new program* to *X has bugs*. But the idea that we sometimes use remembered events to estimate frequencies doesn't provide much support for mental models, and for two reasons. First, all that's required to determine these frequencies is representations of individual events; there is no special need for mental models per se. Representation of events could take the form of natural-language sentences, sentences in mentalese, or instantiated schemes, among other possibilities. Mental models are specialized representations that, by definition, have parts that are isomorphic to the parts of their referents: "Mental models have a structure that corresponds to the structure of what they represent. They are accordingly akin to architect's models of buildings, to molecular biologists' models of complex molecules, and to physicists' diagrams of particle interactions" (Johnson-Laird, Girotto, and Legrenzi 1998, p. 2). In order to count remembered events, however, any means of representing distinct events is sufficient, and diagrammatic representations like these have no special advantages.

Second, once we're out of the domain of our immediate experience, counting remembered events isn't sufficient to determine probability or strength. In order to estimate the strength of (2), we can't call to mind remembered incidents in which broccoli has vitamin Y and count the number of such events in which cauliflower also has vitamin Y. We might try *imagining* events to do the computations, using mental models or some other means. But we've just seen that this tactic requires some independent way to determine which imagined events are relevant for these purposes. If we try to spell out "relevant" as "plausible," "probable," or the like, we've only pirouetted around the issue.[6]

4. Can People Distinguish Strength and Deductive Correctness?

So far we've been examining the two-mode strategy of using the same psychological theory to explain both deductive correctness and inductive strength. If these ruminations are correct, then we've found that there are no existing theories that are able to account for both these types of evaluation. On one hand, current theories of inductive strength are too weak to provide an adequate explanation of judgments of deductive correctness, and on the other hand, current theories of deduction don't specialize in the right way to give an explanation of strength. These are complaints about existing theories, and, as such, they don't demonstrate that general-purpose theories are impossible. Still, there seems to be something systematic about these failures. In order to handle strength, theories have to build in causal constraints (and perhaps other constraints) that govern the behavior of the entities that the arguments describe. These causal factors, however, are irrelevant to deductive correctness. It might be possible to produce a theory that worked by imposing causal restrictions when it evaluates strength, lifting these restrictions when it evaluates deductive correctness, but determining exactly what these causal factors amount to psychologically is, to say the least, a nontrivial task. Current theories aren't able to formulate these causal constraints in anything like a general way. That's why current theories for inductive strength are so feeble and why they aren't general-purpose reasoning engines.

There is another way, however, that theories could aspire to the role of general-purpose reasoners. It might turn out that people are only capable of performing one type of argument evaluation, in which case it becomes much easier for a single theory to explain all the facts. We've been assuming that people distinguish inductive strength from deductive correctness, so a general-purpose theory has to explain both. But, of course, if they are only able to assess strength or only able to assess deductive correctness, then perhaps one of the current theories is all we need. This is the one-mode strategy that I mentioned at the beginning, and I think that many psychologists implicitly hold a position somewhere in this vicinity. Their pattern of thinking goes something like this:

We clearly need to do some form of inductive or probabilistic reasoning in order to accomplish mundane tasks like walking across the street without being run down by a truck. Our early ancestors must have had to do similar sorts of reasoning in order to keep from being eaten by large, hungry animals or in order to maintain social order in the clan, so our ability to do some form of inductive reasoning may even be innate. Evaluating deductive correctness, however, is an enormously specialized cognitive skill. Unless we've been brainwashed in a logic course, we never really get the hang of it. As evidence, even when bright undergraduates have to decide explicitly whether a conclusion follows logically from a set of premises, they make all sorts of errors, including relying on the plausibility of the conclusion.[7] So it's fair to think that most people can't evaluate arguments for deductive correctness; they just make do with inductive assessments. Many cognitive psychologists who specialize in reasoning—for example, those who believe in pragmatic reasoning schemes (Cheng and Holyoak 1985) and those who believe in reasoning by social contracts (Cosmides 1989)—hold a view related to this one, but they wisely tend to hedge their bets. They agree that deductive correctness isn't terribly important for everyday reasoning and thinking, but they sometimes allow that people can evaluate arguments for deductive correctness, provided that the arguments are extremely simple and transparent and provided that there is no simpler method of evaluation on hand.

Why pull back from the view that inductive reasoning is all we need? One reason might be that people appreciate the deductive correctness of certain schematic arguments in which the only possible clue to correctness is the pattern of logical connectives they contain. For example, people go along with *and*-elimination arguments, such as (1), even when the component propositions are about arbitrary arrangements of letters and numbers (Braine, Reiser, and Rumain 1984; Osherson 1975). It might be possible to disrupt people's success with such arguments by embedding them in a context that imposes its own pragmatic implications. However, the fact that people appreciate these arguments in minimal formats is difficult to explain except by crediting them with an understanding of conjunction and its entailments. And grasping conjunction's entailments just *is* having a rudimentary notion of deductive correctness.

Although I think the foregoing reason is decisive, further support for a qualitative difference between evaluations of inductive strength and of deductive correctness comes from two recent neuroimaging studies—one by V. Goel, B. Gold, S. Kapur, and S. Houle (1997) and the other by Osherson, D. Perani, S. Cappa, T. Schnur, F. Grassi, and F. Fazio (1998). Both experiments used PET imaging of subjects who, in one condition, judged the deductive correctness of arguments and, in a second condition, judged the plausibility of arguments. (In Osherson et al., the arguments were identical in the relevant portion of the tasks.) Although the two studies differ in their conclusions about exactly which brain regions are implicated in the deduction task, both agree that induction and deduction recruit different brain areas. The Osherson study (1998, p. 374) asserts on the basis of this evidence that "brain structures responsible for deductive and probabilistic reasoning appear to be substantially distinct," and the Goel study (1997, p. 1309) concludes similarly that "the classical distinction between deduction and induction has a neurophysiological basis contrary to the predictions made by the unitary cognitive models of reasoning."

At this early stage in the research, of course, there are potential interpretive problems in assessing these conclusions. First, it's difficult to eliminate competing explanations. In the Goel (1997) study, subjects evaluated distinct sets of arguments for deductive correctness and for strength, so it's conceivable that the outcome is due to factors associated with the individual items. The Osherson study (1998) used the same (deductively incorrect) arguments on critical trials, but these items varied in their inductive strength; thus, subjects should have given the arguments a negative evaluation in the deduction condition but either a positive or a negative evaluation in the induction condition. Perhaps the difference in type of evaluation contributed to the imaging results. It's also true that the categorical syllogisms that served as stimuli in the Osherson study (and as some of the items in Goel et al. 1997) may have promoted special strategies that subjects had learned in school (e.g., use of Euler circles), and such strategies may also have influenced the results, as Osherson et al. note. It would be of interest to look at arguments of less familiar types to see whether the dissociation persists.

Second, a pessimistic view of the imaging evidence might be that it tells us no more than what we already knew. We know that people will say that an argument like (2)—broccoli has vitamin Y; therefore, cauliflower has vitamin Y—is strong but not deductively correct, so they can distinguish deductively correct arguments from strong ones in easy cases. There must be some cognitive and physiological mechanisms to support this distinction, and for this reason it's obvious that we will find some difference or other in brain functioning when people evaluate inductive strength versus deductive correctness. But perhaps this doesn't show that there's any interesting way in which assessments of strength and deductive correctness are distinct. Maybe it only shows that the imaging is sensitive to the difference between medium values of inductive strength (e.g., in the case of [2]) and very high values of inductive strength (e.g., in the case of [1]), in which case the one-mode view still has a chance.

These interpretative difficulties are inevitable at this stage of the research, and they provide no reason to dismiss it out of hand. We need to wait until more details are filled in. If, as these investigators claim, the inductive and deductive tasks give rise to big differences in brain activation and these different areas of activation are themselves associated with disparate functions, then we shouldn't be too ready to explain away the evidence as due to some simple change, such as a shift in response or shift in threshold.

5. Conclusion

Looking back on the failed attempts in this area, you can easily see what motivates psychologists to try to construct general theories of reasoning that will explain both judgments of deductive correctness and judgments of inductive strength. Besides the obvious attraction of having a theory that will explain everything, there's a feeling that deductive correctness and inductive strength just can't be unbridgeably different. Arguments seem to vary continuously in how much plausibility the premises lend the conclusion. Why not think of the end point of this continuum as deductive correctness, so that both types of argument evaluation refer to the same attribute and differ only in their cutoff point? In addition, standard probability axioms are such that logical tautologies turn out to have a probability of 1, which lends support to the same identification.

I've been arguing that, for all its attractions, this sort of convergence isn't available. Although all deductively correct arguments could be said to be maximally strong, arguments with maximal strength aren't necessarily deductively correct. We evaluate some arguments as maximally strong when they conform to causal constraints (Jackson and Pargetter 1980), entrenchment constraints (Goodman 1955), constraints on allowable variability (e.g., Nisbett et al. 1983; Rips 1989), and perhaps others that are part of our understanding of how things operate and how we explain things. This sort of knowledge has to be built into a theory of inductive strength, but because it's irrelevant to theories of deductive correctness, we need separate theoretical specifications.

Why do we have this kind of double standard in evaluating arguments? I think the obvious answer is that we have different reasons for evaluating arguments and we hold them to different standards depending on these reasons. Sometimes what we want to know is how the argument fares in establishing its conclusion in view of our knowledge of how the world works.

At other times, we're interested in a more abstract examination. We want to know how well the argument does in establishing its conclusion according to properties of statements that preserve significant chunks of logical or mathematical structure and that abstract over other elements of the statement. Our need to evaluate arguments in different ways isn't astonishing, since we evaluate almost everything of importance according to multiple criteria.

I'm all for building bridges between different areas of psychology, but there's no use pretending that you've got a unified theory if you haven't. Psychologists who study reasoning should take seriously the idea that evaluating the plausibility or the strength of an argument responds to different pressures than evaluating deductive correctness. Unless they can account for both the differences and the similarities in a substantive way, they haven't unified anything—they've just plastered over the cracks.

NOTES

NSF grant SBR-9514491 supported this research. Thanks to Gilbert Harman and Reid Hastie for expert comments on an earlier version of this chapter and to James Booth and Edward Smith for discussion of the imaging studies mentioned in section 4.

1. I'm making the standard assumption that an argument is a set of statements, one of which is the conclusion and the remaining statements (possibly null) the premises. Thus, an argument is not itself a psychological entity, and the deductive correctness or inductive strength of an argument is not a psychological property. Nevertheless, people can evaluate the deductive correctness or strength of an argument, and the processes they use to do so are, of course, psychological processes. It's a matter of debate whether the process that evaluates deductive correctness is distinct from the one that evaluates strength, and some of the data I mention in section 4 are relevant to this issue.

2. How come? Suppose that an argument is deductively correct. Then any state of affairs in which all the premises are true is a state of affairs in which the conclusion is true. In other words, if P is the set of states in which all the premises are true and C is the set of states in which the conclusion is true, then $P \subset C$. Hence, $P \cap C = P$. According to the definition of conditional probability, $\text{Prob}(C \mid P) = \text{Prob}(P \cap C) / \text{Prob}(P)$, and substituting the preceding equality, we get $\text{Prob}(C \mid P) = \text{Prob}(P) / \text{Prob}(P) = 1$. If the premises are contradictory, $\text{Prob}(P) = 0$, and the preceding quotient is undefined.

3. Gilbert Harman suggested this example (personal communication 1998). For similar reasons, the one-way relationship between deductive correctness and conditional probability of 1 also holds in R. Carnap's (1962) system. Although the conditional probability of a deductively correct argument is 1, arguments with conditional probabilities of 1 are not necessarily deductively correct. See Carnap (1962, pp. 322–323).

4. The deficiency here isn't just restricted to arguments that involve conditional probabilities of 0 and 1, but it affects all probability values. For example, the conditional probability of the conclusion of (3b) given the premise is 5/6 on standard reckoning. But first, there are an infinite number of possible worlds in which the premise is true and an infinite number in which both premise

and conclusion are true; hence, the ratio of possible worlds is undefined. Second, even if we can get around the first problem by taking limits (or by some other means), we're still faced with the problem that there are logically possible worlds in which new spots appear when a die is thrown, so the probability could converge to something less than 5/6. The difficulty is that the set of possible worlds that we have to take into account in evaluating deductive correctness is broader than what's involved in calculating conditional probabilities, so logically possible worlds don't provide a guide to the relevant conditional probability.

5. Another reason for cutting conditional probability out of the picture in Figure 10.2 is that conditional probability sometimes doesn't track people's impressions of strength, as A. Tversky and D. Kahneman (1980) have demonstrated.

6. It is also worth noticing that people don't always estimate frequency or probability by counting events (Tourangeau, Rips, and Rasinski 2000). This is the moral of many of Kahneman and Tversky's classic demonstrations. For example, in Tversky and Kahneman's (1983) conjunction fallacy, subjects judge that Linda, a college student with a deep sense of social justice and an activist background, is more likely to become a feminist bank teller than a bank teller. But in any mental model in which Linda is a feminist bank teller, she's also a bank teller. Hence, mental models can't account for these heuristic judgments, as Johnson-Laird, A. Legrenzi, V. Girotto, M. S. Legrenzi, and J.-P. Caverni (in press) have recently acknowledged. For further deficiencies of the mental-model approach, see, e.g., Bonatti 1994a, 1994b; O'Brien, Braine, and Yang 1994; and Rips 1986, 1994.

7. For a review of plausibility effects, see Evans, Newstead, and Byrne 1993, chapter 8.

REFERENCES

Bonatti, L. (1994a). Propositional reasoning by model? *Psychological Review* 101:725–733.

Bonatti, L. (1994b). Why should we abandon the mental logic hypothesis? *Cognition* 50:17–39.

Braine, M. D. S., B. J. Reiser, and B. Rumain (1984). Some empirical justification for a theory of natural propositional reasoning. In G. H. Bower (ed.), *Psychology of Learning and Motivation*, vol. 18, pp. 313–371. New York: Academic Press.

Carnap, R. ([1950] 1962). *Logical Foundations of Probability*, 2nd edition. Chicago: University of Chicago Press.

Cavanagh, J. P. (1972). Relation between immediate memory span and the memory search rate. *Psychological Review* 79:525–530.

Cheng, P. W., and K. J. Holyoak (1985). Pragmatic reasoning schemes. *Cognitive Psychology* 17:391–416.

Coley, J. D., D. L. Medin, and S. Atran (1997). Does rank have its privilege? Inductive inference within folkbiological taxonomies. *Cognition* 64:73–112.

Cosmides, L. (1989). The logic of social exchange: Has natural selection shaped how humans reason? Studies with the Wason selection task. *Cognition* 31:187–276.

Evans, J. St. B. T., S. E. Newstead, and R. M. J. Byrne (1993). *Human Reasoning.* Hillsdale, NJ: Erlbaum.

Feller, W. (1950). *An Introduction to Probability Theory and Its Applications*, vol. 1. New York: Wiley.

Field, H. H. (1977). Logic, meaning, and conceptual role. *Journal of Philosophy* 74:379–409.

Goel, V., B. Gold, S. Kapur, and S. Houle (1997). The seats of reason? An imaging study of deductive and inductive reasoning. *NeuroReport* 8:1305–1310.

Goodman, N. (1955). *Fact, Fiction, and Forecast*. Cambridge: Harvard University Press.

Heit, E., and J. Rubinstein (1994). Similarity and property effects in inductive reasoning. *Journal of Experimental Psychology: Learning, Memory, and Cognition* 20:411–422.

Jackson, F., and R. Pargetter (1980). Confirmation and the nomological. *Canadian Journal of Philosophy* 10:415–428.

Jevons, W. S. (1892). *The Principles of Science*. London: Macmillan.

Johnson-Laird, P. N. (1994). Mental models and probabilistic thinking. *Cognition* 50:189–209.

Johnson-Laird, P. N., V. Girotto, and P. Legrenzi (1998). Mental models: A gentle guide for outsiders. Unpublished manuscript, Princeton University.

Johnson-Laird, P. N., P. Legrenzi, V. Girotto, M. S. Legrenzi, and J.-P. Caverni (in press). Naive probability: A mental model theory of extensional reasoning. *Psychological Review*.

Johnson-Laird, P. N., and F. Savary (1996). Illusory inferences about probabilities. *Acta Psychologica* 93:69–90.

Nisbett, R. E., D. H. Krantz, D. Jepson, and Z. Kunda (1983). The use of statistical heuristics in everyday inductive reasoning. *Psychological Review* 90:339–363.

O'Brien, D. P., M. D. S. Braine, and Y. Yang (1994). Propositional reasoning by mental models? Simple to refute in principle and in practice. *Psychological Review* 101:711–724.

Osherson, D. N. (1975). *Logical Abilities in Children*, vol. 3. Hillsdale, NJ: Erlbaum.

Osherson, D., D. Perani, S. Cappa, T. Schnur, F. Grassi, and F. Fazio (1998). Distinct brain loci in deductive versus probabilistic reasoning. *Neuropsychologia* 36:369–376.

Osherson, D. N., E. E. Smith, and E. Shafir (1986). Some origins of belief. *Cognition* 24:197–224.

Osherson, D. N., E. E. Smith, O. Wilkie, A. Lopez, and E. Shafir (1990). Category-based induction. *Psychological Review* 97:185–200.

Pollock, J. L. (1990). *Nomic Probability and the Foundations of Induction*. Oxford: Oxford University Press.

Rips, L. J. (1975). Inductive judgments about natural categories. *Journal of Verbal Learning and Verbal Behavior* 14:665–681.

Rips, L. J. (1986). Mental muddles. In M. Brand and R. M. Harnish (eds.), *The Representation of Knowledge and Belief*, pp. 258–286. Tucson: University of Arizona Press.

Rips, L. J. (1989). Similarity, typicality, and categorization. In S. Vosniadou and A. Ortony (eds.), *Similarity and Analogical Reasoning*, pp. 21–59. Cambridge: Cambridge University Press.

Rips, L. J. (1994). *The Psychology of Proof: Deductive Reasoning in Human Thinking*. Cambridge: MIT Press.

Sellars, W. (1953). Inference and meaning. *Mind* 62:313–338.

Sloman, S. A. (1993). Feature-based induction. *Cognitive Psychology* 25:231–280.

Sloman, S. A. (1994). When explanations compete: The role of explanatory coherence on judgments of likelihood. *Cognition* 52:1–21.

Sloman, S. A., and L. J. Rips (1998). Similarity as an explanatory construct. *Cognition* 65:87–101.

Tourangeau, R., L. J. Rips, and K. Rasinski (2000). *Psychology of Survey Responses.* Cambridge: Cambridge University Press.

Tversky, A., and D. Kahneman (1980). Causal schemes in judgments under uncertainty. In M. Fishbein (ed.), *Progress in Social Psychology*, pp. 49–72. Hillsdale, NJ: Erlbaum.

Tversky, A., and D. Kahneman (1983). Extensional versus intuitive reasoning: The conjunction fallacy in probability judgments. *Psychological Review* 90: 293–315.

11

Ending the Rationality Wars

How to Make Disputes about Human
Rationality Disappear

RICHARD SAMUELS, STEPHEN STICH,
& MICHAEL BISHOP

Blessed are the peacemakers; for they shall be called the
children of God.

Matthew 5:9

1. Introduction

During the last twenty-five years, researchers who studied human reasoning and judgment in what has become known as the heuristics and
biases tradition have produced an impressive body of experimental work
that many have seen as having "bleak implications" for the rationality of
ordinary people (Nisbett and Borgida 1975). According to one proponent
of this view, when we reason about probability we fall victim to "inevitable
illusions" (Piattelli-Palmarini 1994). Other proponents maintain that the
human mind is prone to "systematic deviations from rationality" (Bazerman
and Neale 1986) and is "not built to work by the rules of probability" (Gould
1992). It has even been suggested that human beings are "a species that
is uniformly probability-blind" (Piattelli-Palmarini 1994). This provocative
and pessimistic interpretation of the experimental findings has been challenged from many different directions over the years. One of the most recent
and energetic of these challenges has come from the newly emerging field

of evolutionary psychology, where it has been argued that it's singularly implausible to claim that our species would have evolved with no "instinct for probability" and, hence, be "blind to chance" (Pinker 1997, p. 351). Though evolutionary psychologists concede that it is possible to design experiments that "trick our probability calculators," they go on to claim that "when people are given information in a format that meshes with the way they naturally think about probability" (Pinker 1997, pp. 347, 351) the inevitable illusions turn out to be, to use Gerd Gigerenzer's memorable term, "evitable" (Gigerenzer 1998). Indeed, in many cases evolutionary psychologists claim that the illusions simply "disappear" (Gigerenzer 1991a).

On the face of it, the dispute between evolutionary psychology and the heuristics and biases tradition would appear to be a deep disagreement over the extent of human rationality—a conflict between two sharply divergent assessments of human reasoning. This impression is strengthened by the heated exchanges that pepper the academic literature and reinforced by steamy reports of the debate that have appeared in the popular press (Bower 1996). It is our contention, however, that the alleged conflict between evolutionary psychologists and advocates of the heuristics and biases program has been greatly exaggerated. The claims made on either side of the dispute can, we maintain, be plausibly divided into *core claims* and mere *rhetorical flourishes*.[1] And once one puts the rhetoric to one side almost all of the apparent disagreement dissolves. When one focuses on the core claims that are central to the heuristics and biases tradition and best supported by the experimental results, it turns out that these claims are not *challenged* by the evolutionary psychologists. On the contrary, some of the most intriguing avenues of research pursued by evolutionary psychologists in recent years simply make no sense unless they are interpreted as *endorsing* these central theses of the heuristics and biases tradition. Moreover, the agreement runs in the opposite direction as well. When we put aside the rhetoric of evolutionary psychologists and attend instead to their central claims about reasoning and cognitive architecture, it becomes clear that advocates of the heuristics and biases tradition have no reason at all to object to any of these claims and, in some cases, clearly should and do endorse them. Thus, we maintain that much of the dispute between evolutionary psychologists and those in the heuristics and biases tradition is itself an illusion. The fireworks generated by each side focusing on the rhetorical excesses of the other have distracted attention from what we claim is, in fact, an emerging *consensus* about the scope and limits of human rationality and about the cognitive architecture that supports it.

Our central goal in this chapter is to refocus the discussion away from the rhetoric of the debate between evolutionary psychology and the heuristics and biases tradition and toward this emerging consensus on fundamental points. To work toward this goal we will proceed as follows: In section 2, we will briefly outline the two research programs and explain what we take to be the core claims and the rhetorical excesses on both sides. Then, in section 3, we will argue that it is implausible to maintain that either research program rejects the core claims of the other. Once this is accomplished we think the illusion that evolutionary psychology and the heuristics and biases tradition have a deep disagreement about how rational human beings are should disappear. This is not to say, however, that there are *no* genuine disagreements between these two research programs. In the fourth section of this chapter, we briefly outline and discuss what we take to be some genuine disagreements between evolutionary psychology and the heuristics and biases tradition.

2. The Apparent Conflict

This section has two major parts. In the first half, we will begin by offering a few illustrations of the sorts of striking experimental findings that have been produced in the heuristics and biases tradition. Next, we will illustrate the sorts of explanations that those in the heuristics and biases tradition have offered for those findings. Finally, we will outline what we take to be the core claims of the heuristics and biases program and contrast them with some of the more rhetorically flamboyant claims that have been made. In the second half of this section, we start with an overview of the basic claims of evolutionary psychology and proceed on to a quick sketch of some of the experimental findings about probabilistic reasoning that evolutionary psychologists have presented. We'll then explain what we take to be the core claims of the evolutionary psychological approach to reasoning and assemble another short catalog of rhetorically flamboyant claims—this time claims about the implications of the evolutionary psychologists' results. Against this backdrop we'll go on, in the following section, to argue that despite all the colorful rhetoric, evolutionary psychologists and proponents of the heuristics and biases program don't really disagree at all about the extent to which human beings are rational or about any other claim that is central to either program.

The Heuristics and Biases Tradition: Experiments, Explanations, Core Claims, and Rhetoric

On the familiar Bayesian account, the probability of a hypothesis on a given body of evidence depends, in part, on the prior probability of the hypothesis. However, in a series of elegant experiments, D. Kahneman and A. Tversky (1973) showed that subjects often seriously undervalue the importance of prior probabilities. One of these experiments presented half of the subjects with the following "cover story":

> A panel of psychologists has interviewed and administered personality tests to 30 engineers and 70 lawyers, all successful in their respective fields. On the basis of this information, thumbnail descriptions of the 30 engineers and 70 lawyers have been written. You will find on your forms five descriptions, chosen at random from the 100 available descriptions. For each description, please indicate your probability that the person described is an engineer, on a scale from 0 to 100.

The other half of the subjects were presented with the same text, except the "base rates" were reversed. They were told that the personality tests had been administered to seventy engineers and thirty lawyers. Some of the descriptions that were provided were designed to be compatible with the subjects' stereotypes of engineers, though not with their stereotypes of lawyers. Others were designed to fit the lawyer stereotype but not the engineer stereotype. And one was intended to be quite neutral, giving subjects no information at all that would be of use in making their decision. Here are two examples, the first intended to sound like an engineer, the second intended to sound neutral:

> Jack is a forty-five-year-old man. He is married and has four children. He is generally conservative, careful, and ambitious. He shows no interest in political and social issues and spends most of his free time on his many hobbies, which include home carpentry, sailing, and mathematical puzzles.
>
> Dick is a thirty-year-old man. He is married with no children. A man of high ability and high motivation, he promises to be quite successful in his field. He is well liked by his colleagues.

As expected, subjects in both groups thought that the probability that Jack was an engineer was quite high. Moreover, in what seems to be a clear violation of Bayesian principles, the difference in cover stories between the two groups of subjects had almost no effect at all. The neglect of base-rate information was even more striking in the case of Dick. That description was constructed to be totally uninformative with regard to Dick's profession. Thus, the only useful information that subjects had was the base-rate information provided in the cover story. But that information was entirely ignored. The median probability estimate in both groups of subjects was 50 percent.

How might we explain these results and the results of many similar experiments that have been reported in the psychological literature? The basic explanatory strategy that proponents of the heuristics and biases program have pursued is to posit the existence of reasoning heuristics: rules of thumb that we employ when reasoning. In the specific case of the preceding experiments, the hypothesis that Kahneman and Tversky offer is that in making probabilistic judgments people often rely on what they call *the representativeness heuristic*:

> Given specific evidence (e.g., a personality sketch), the outcomes under consideration (e.g., occupations or levels of achievement) can be ordered by the degree to which they are representative of that evidence. The thesis of this paper is that people predict by representativeness, that is, they select or order outcomes by the degree to which the outcomes represent the essential features of the evidence. In many situations, representative outcomes are indeed more likely than others. However, this is not always the case, because there are factors (e.g., prior probabilities of outcomes and the reliability of evidence) which affect the likelihood of outcomes but not their representativeness. Because these factors are ignored, intuitive predictions violate statistical rules of prediction in systematic and fundamental ways. (1973, p. 48)

Though many of the reasoning problems explored in the heuristics and biases literature have no great practical importance, there are some notable exceptions. In a well-known and very disquieting study, W. Casscells, A. Schoenberger, and T. Grayboys (1978) presented the following problem to a group of faculty, staff, and fourth-year students at Harvard Medical School:

> If a test to detect a disease whose prevalence is 1/1,000 has a false positive rate of 5%, what is the chance that a person found to have a positive result actually has the disease, assuming that you know nothing about the person's symptoms or signs? ____%

Under the most plausible interpretation of the problem, the correct Bayesian answer is 2 percent. But only 18 percent of the Harvard audience gave an answer close to 2 percent. Forty-five percent of this distinguished group completely ignored the base-rate information and said that the answer was 95 percent.

What do these results and the many similar results in the heuristics and biases literature tell us about the quality of ordinary people's probabilistic reasoning and about the mental mechanisms that underlie that reasoning? Though we will return to the issue in section 3, let us grant for the time being that some of the answers that subjects provide are mistaken—that they deviate from appropriate norms of rationality. Then, since studies like those we've mentioned are both numerous and readily replicable, the following holds:

(1)   people's intuitive judgments on a large number of problems that involve probability or uncertainty regularly deviate from appropriate norms of rationality.

This is clearly a core claim of the heuristics and biases program. As Kahneman and Tversky have said, "Although errors of judgment are but a method by which some cognitive processes are studied, the method has become a significant part of the message" (1982, p. 124). In addition, however, it is clear that proponents of the heuristics and biases program also endorse as a core claim a thesis about how to explain these deviations from appropriate norms of rationality, namely:

(2)   Many of the instances in which our probabilistic judgments deviate from appropriate norms of rationality are to be explained by the fact that, in making these judgments, people rely on heuristics like representativeness "which sometimes yield reasonable judgments and sometimes lead to severe and systematic errors." (Kahneman and Tversky 1973, p. 48)

Moreover, if we adopt the (standard) assumption that a cognitive mechanism or program is normatively appropriate or "correct" only to the extent that it yields normatively appropriate judgments, then, given (1) and (2), it is eminently plausible to conclude, along with P. Slovic, B. Fischhoff, and S. Lichtenstein, that "people lack the correct programs for many important judgmental tasks" (1976, p. 174).

Slovic, Fischhoff, and Lichtenstein are not content, however, to stop with this relatively modest conclusion. Instead, they go on to make the much more sweeping claim that "[we] have not had the opportunity to evolve an intellect capable of dealing conceptually with uncertainty" (p. 174), thus suggesting not merely that we lack the correct programs for many tasks but also that, in dealing with uncertainty, we lack the correct programs for *all* judgmental tasks. In other words, they appear to be suggesting the following:

(3)   The *only* cognitive tools that are available to untutored people when dealing with problems that involve probability or uncertainty are normatively problematic heuristics such as representativeness.

This expansive theme echoes passages like the following, in which Kahneman and Tversky, the founders of the heuristics and biases program, seem to endorse the view that people use representativeness and other normatively defective heuristics not just in some or many cases but in *all* cases—including those cases in which they get the right answer:

In making predictions and judgments under uncertainty, people do not appear to follow the calculus of chance or the statistical theory of prediction. Instead, they rely on a limited number of heuristics which sometimes yield reasonable judgments and sometimes lead to severe and systematic errors. (1973, p. 48)

In light of passages like this, it is perhaps unsurprising that both friends and foes of the heuristics and biases tradition suppose that it is committed to the claim that, as Gerd Gigerenzer has put it, "the untutored mind is running on shoddy software, that is, on programs that work *only* with a handful of heuristics" (1991b, p. 235). In another paper Gigerenzer suggests that the heuristics and biases tradition views people "as 'cognitive misers' relying on a few general heuristics due to their limited information-processing abilities" (1991a, p. 109). After describing one of Kahneman and Tversky's best-known experiments, S. Gould asks: "Why do we consistently make this simple logical error?" His answer is: "Tversky and Kahneman argue, correctly I think, that our minds are not built (for whatever reason) to work by the rules of probability" (1992, p. 469).[2]

If proponents of the heuristics and biases program would really have us believe (3), then the picture of human reasoning that they paint is bleak indeed! But should we accept this claim as anything more than mere rhetorical flourish? For several rather different reasons, we maintain that the answer is no. First, although we shall not defend this claim in detail here, it is simply not plausible to maintain that (3) is supported by the currently available experimental evidence. At *most*, what could be plausibly claimed is that we have reason to think that, in *many* instances, human beings use normatively defective heuristics. The further claim that these normatively problematic heuristics are the *only* cognitive tools that untutored folk have available is vastly stronger than anything the available evidence will support. Second, when they are being careful about what they say, leading advocates of the heuristics and biases program make it clear that they do not endorse (3). Thus, for example, Kahneman and Tversky state very clearly that the use of normatively problematic heuristics "does not preclude the use of other procedures" and insist that the currently available data do not support (3) but only the "more moderate hypothesis that intuitive predictions and probability judgments are highly sensitive to representativeness" (Tversky and Kahneman 1983, p. 88). This, of course, is entirely compatible with the suggestion that in many circumstances we use methods other than normatively problematic heuristics. Finally, as will become apparent in the remainder of this chapter, the heuristics and biases account of human reasoning does not presuppose a commitment to (3). It is not a central element in the heuristics and biases research program.

Evolutionary Psychology: Theory, Data, Core Claims, and Rhetoric

Though the interdisciplinary field of evolutionary psychology is too new to have developed any precise and widely agreed upon body of doctrine, there are three basic theses that are clearly central. The first is that the mind contains a large number of special-purpose systems—often called modules or mental organs. These modules are invariably conceived of as a type of computational mechanism: namely, computational devices that are specialized or domain-specific. Many evolutionary psychologists also urge that modules are both innate and present in all normal members of the species. While this characterization of modules raises lots of interesting issues—issues about which we have had a fair amount to say elsewhere (Samuels forthcoming; Samuels, Stich, and Tremoulet forthcoming)—in this chapter we propose to put them to one side. The second central thesis of evolutionary psychology is that, contrary to what has been argued by Fodor (1983) and others, the modular structure of the mind is not restricted to input systems (those responsible for perception and language processing) and output systems (those responsible for producing actions). According to evolutionary psychologists, modules also subserve many so-called central capacities, such as reasoning and belief fixation.[3] The third thesis is that mental modules are *adaptations*—they were, as J. Tooby and L. Cosmides have put it, "invented by natural selection during the species' evolutionary history to produce adaptive ends in the species' natural environment" (1995, p. xiii). Here is a passage in which Tooby and Cosmides offer a particularly colorful statement of these central tenets of evolutionary psychology:

> Our cognitive architecture resembles a confederation of hundreds or thousands of functionally dedicated computers (often called modules) designed to solve adaptive problems endemic to our hunter-gatherer ancestors. Each of these devices has its own agenda and imposes its own exotic organization on different fragments of the world. There are specialized systems for grammar induction, for face recognition, for dead reckoning, for construing objects and for recognizing emotions from the face. There are mechanisms to detect animacy, eye direction, and cheating. There is a

"theory of mind" module . . . a variety of social inference modules . . . and a multitude of other elegant machines. (1995, p. xiv)

If much of central cognition is indeed subserved by cognitive modules that were designed to deal with the adaptive problems posed by the environment in which our primate forebears lived, then we should expect that the modules responsible for reasoning would do their best job when information is provided in a format similar to the format in which information was available in the ancestral environment. And, as Gigerenzer has argued, though there was a great deal of useful probabilistic information available in that environment, this information would have been represented "as frequencies of events, sequentially encoded as experienced—for example, *3 out of* 20 as opposed to 15 percent or p = 0.15" (1994, p. 142). Cosmides and Tooby make much the same point as follows:

> Our hominid ancestors were immersed in a rich flow of observable frequencies that could be used to improve decision-making, given procedures that could take advantage of them. So if we have adaptations for inductive reasoning, they should take frequency information as input. (1996, pp. 15–16)

On the basis of such evolutionary considerations, Gigerenzer, Cosmides, and Tooby have proposed and defended a psychological hypothesis that they refer to as the *Frequentist Hypothesis*: ". . . some of our inductive reasoning mechanisms do embody aspects of a calculus of probability, but they are designed to take frequency information as input and produce frequencies as output" (Cosmides and Tooby 1996, p. 3).

This speculation led Cosmides and Tooby to pursue an intriguing series of experiments in which the Harvard Medical School problem used by Casscells, Schoenberger, and Grayboys was systematically transformed into a problem in which both the input and the response required were formulated in terms of frequencies. Here is one example from their study in which frequency information is made particularly salient:

> 1 out of every 1,000 Americans has disease X. A test has been developed to detect when a person has disease X. Every time the test is given to a person who has the disease, the test comes out positive. But sometimes the test also comes out positive when it is given to a person who is completely healthy. Specifically, out of every 1,000 people who are perfectly healthy, 50 of them test positive for the disease.
> Imagine that we have assembled a random sample of 1,000 Americans. They were selected by lottery. Those who conducted the lottery had no information about the health status of any of these people.
> Given the information above: on average, how many people who test positive for the disease will *actually* have the disease? ____out of ____.

In sharp contrast to the original Casscells experiment, in which only 18 percent of subjects gave the correct Bayesian response, this problem elicited the correct Bayesian answer from 76 percent of Cosmides and Tooby's subjects. Nor is this an isolated case in which "frequentist versions" of probabilistic reasoning problems elicit high levels of performance. On the contrary, it seems that in many instances, when problems are framed in terms of frequencies rather than probabilities, subjects tend to reason in a normatively appropriate manner (Gigerenzer 1991a, 1996; Kahneman and Tversky 1996; Tversky and Kahneman 1983). Though it remains contentious how precisely to explain this fact, the phenomenon itself is now generally accepted by evolutionary psychologists and proponents of heuristics and biases alike.

It is still a matter of some controversy what precisely results of this sort show about the nature and extent of human rationality. What is clear, however, is that evolutionary psychologists take them to suggest the truth of two claims. First, they clearly think the data suggest the following:

(4)   There are many reasoning problems that involve probability or uncertainty on which people's intuitive judgments *do not* deviate from appropriate norms of rationality.

Specifically, for many problems involving frequencies we reason in a normatively appropriate fashion (Cosmides and Tooby 1996; Gigerenzer 1991a, 1996). Moreover, evolutionary psychologists clearly think that the results cited earlier also provide some support for the following thesis:

(5)   Many of the instances in which our probabilistic judgments accord with appropriate norms of rationality are to be explained by the fact that, in making these judgments, we rely on mental modules that were designed by natural selection to do a good job at nondemonstrative reasoning when provided with the sort of input that was common in the environment of evolutionary adaptation (EEA).

So, for example, as we have already seen, evolutionary psychologists maintain that the mind contains one or more frequentist modules that have been designed by natural selection and tend to produce normatively appropriate judgments when provided with the appropriate input. We take it that (4) and (5) are core claims of the evolutionary psychological research on probabilistic reasoning.

Like their heuristics and biases counterparts, however, evolutionary psychologists have also on occasion issued exuberant proclamations that go well beyond the core claims of the research program and cannot plausibly be viewed as anything other than rhetorical excess. In particular, evolutionary psychologists sometimes appear to maintain the following:

(6)   Our probabilistic reasoning is subserved by "elegant machines" designed by natural selection and any concerns about systematic irrationality are unfounded.

This view is suggested in numerous passages in the evolutionary psychology literature. Moreover, these rhetorical flourishes tend to suggest, in our view incorrectly, that evolutionary psychology poses a direct challenge to the heuristics and biases tradition. Thus, for example, the paper in which

Cosmides and Tooby reported their data on the Harvard Medical School problem appeared with the title "Are Humans Good Intuitive Statisticians after All? Rethinking Some Conclusions from the Literature on Judgment under Uncertainty." Five years earlier, while Cosmides and Tooby's research was still in progress, Gigerenzer reported some of their early findings in a paper with the provocative title "How to Make Cognitive Illusions Disappear: Beyond 'Heuristics and Biases.'" The clear suggestion, in both of these titles, is that the findings they report pose a head-on challenge to the pessimism of the heuristics and biases tradition and to its core claim that human beings are prone to systematic deviations from appropriate norms of rationality. Nor were these suggestions restricted to titles. In paper after paper, Gigerenzer has said things like "we need not necessarily worry about human rationality" (1998b, p. 280); "more optimism is in order" (1991b, p. 245); and "Keep distinct meanings of probability straight, and much can be done—cognitive illusions disappear" (1991b, p. 245), and he has maintained that his view "supports intuition as basically rational" (1991b, p. 242). Since comments like these are widespread in the literature, it is hardly surprising that many observers have concluded that the view of the mind and of human rationality proposed by evolutionary psychologists is fundamentally at odds with the view offered by proponents of the heuristics and biases program.

3. Making the Dispute Disappear

So far we've outlined in broad strokes the dispute between evolutionary psychology and the heuristics and biases tradition. If we are to believe the rhetoric, then it would appear that these two research programs are locked in a deep disagreement over the nature and extent of human rationality. However, in this section we propose to argue that the air of apparent conflict between evolutionary psychology and the heuristics and biases program is, in large part, an illusion engendered by a failure to distinguish the core claims of the two research programs from the rhetorical embellishments to which advocates on both sides occasionally succumb. We'll argue that once one puts the rhetoric aside and tries to formulate the dispute in more precise terms, it becomes clear that there is much less disagreement here than meets the eye. To defend this surprising contention, we need to start by drawing some distinctions. In particular, we need to distinguish between (1) a variety of proposals about *what* precisely is being assessed (what the *objects of epistemic evaluation* are) in the psychological literature on rationality and (2) a range of proposals about the *standards* (the normative yardsticks) against which epistemic evaluations should be made. With these distinctions in hand, we will then argue that on any plausible understanding of the dispute over the extent of human rationality between evolutionary psychology and the heuristics and biases tradition there is, in fact, no genuine disagreement. Though the rhetoric would suggest otherwise, evolutionary psychologists and their heuristics and biases counterparts are in substantial *agreement* over the extent to which human beings are rational.

TABLE 11.1. Eight different kinds of epistemic evaluation

	Judgments	Mechanisms
"Standard picture"		
Accuracy in the actual domain		
Accuracy in the proper domain		
Optimal given relevant constraints		

The Objects and Standards of Epistemic Evaluation

In order to make an epistemic evaluation, one must adopt—perhaps explicitly but more often than not implicitly—positions on the following two issues: First of all, one needs to make assumptions about *what* exactly is being assessed—what the *objects* of epistemic evaluation are. In the dispute between evolutionary psychologists and advocates of the heuristics and biases tradition, there are at least two kinds of entity that might plausibly be construed as the objects of evaluation. One option is that the researchers are aiming to assess the *judgments* that subjects make—for example, the answer "95 percent" in response to the Harvard Medical School problem. If this is what is being evaluated, then it might be that the disagreement between evolutionary psychology and the heuristics and biases tradition concerns the extent to which human *judgments* about probability are normatively problematic. A second option is that psychologists who study human reason are aiming to assess the *cognitive mechanisms* that produce these judgments. In that case, the disagreement might concern the extent to which these *mechanisms* are normatively problematic.

Second, in addition to making assumptions about *what* is being assessed, the task of epistemic evaluation also requires that one adopt, if only implicitly, some *normative standard*—some yardstick—against which the evaluation is to be made. As we see it, there have been four main kinds of normative standard that have been invoked in the debate between evolutionary psychology and the heuristics and biases tradition:

1. What E. Stein (1996) calls the "standard picture"
2. Two accuracy-based normative standards:
   (a) Accuracy in the actual domain of a cognitive mechanism
   (b) Accuracy in the proper domain of a cognitive mechanism
3. An optimality-based normative standard

We will soon elaborate on these epistemic standards in some detail. For the moment, however, we wish merely to point out that when we combine them with the two objects of epistemic evaluation mentioned earlier, we can generate a 2 × 4 array of options (see Table 11.1); there are eight different kinds of epistemic evaluation that need to be kept distinct. In the remainder of this section we will argue that for each of these options there is no genuine disagreement between evolutionary psychologists and psychologists in the heuristics and biases tradition.

The Standard Picture

When evaluating human reasoning, both evolutionary psychologists and proponents of the heuristics and biases program typically presuppose what Stein has called the standard picture of rationality:

> According to this picture, to be rational is to reason in accordance with principles of reasoning that are based on rules of logic, probability theory and so forth. If the standard picture of reasoning is right, principles of reasoning that are based on such rules are normative principles of reasoning, namely they are the principles we ought to reason in accordance with. (1996, p. 4)

Thus, the standard picture maintains that the appropriate criteria against which to evaluate human reasoning are the rules derived from formal theories such as classical logic, probability theory, and decision theory.[4] So, for example, one might derive something like the following principle of reasoning from the conjunction rule of probability theory:

> Conjunction Principle
> One ought not assign a lower degree of probability to the occurrence of event A than one does to the occurrence of A and some (distinct) event B. (Stein 1996, p. 6)

Given principles of this kind, one can evaluate the specific judgments issued by human subjects and the mechanisms that produce them. To the extent that a person's judgments accord with the principles of the standard picture these judgments are rational, and to the extent that they violate such principles the judgments fail to be rational. Similarly, to the extent that a reasoning mechanism produces judgments that accord with the principles of the standard picture the mechanism is rational, and to the extent that it fails to do so it is not rational. As M. Piattelli-Palmarini puts the point:

> The universal principles of logic, arithmetic, and probability calculus . . . tell us what we *should* . . . think, not what we in fact think. . . . If our intuition does in fact lead us to results incompatible with logic, we conclude that our intuition is at fault. (1994, p. 158)

THE STANDARD PICTURE AND THE EVALUATION OF JUDGMENTS Proponents of the heuristics and biases program often appear to be in the business of evaluating the intuitive *judgments* that subjects make against the yardstick of the standard picture. As we noted earlier, Kahneman and Tversky say that "although errors of judgment are but a method by which some cognitive processes are studied, the method has become a significant part of the message" (1982, p. 124). And the method-turned-message appears to be that many of our probabilistic judgments *systematically* deviate from the norms of rationality prescribed by the standard picture, specifically from those norms derived from probability theory (Kahneman and Tversky 1972, p. 431; Piatelli-Pallmarini 1994, p. 140). A recurrent theme in the heuristics and biases literature is that many of our intuitive judgments about probabilities deviate from the canons of probability theory in such a way that the deviations can be reliably reproduced under a wide range of circumstances that are related in their possession of certain key characteristics— for example, the manner in which information is presented to people or the content of the information about which people are asked to reason.

At first sight, this would appear to be a claim that evolutionary psychologists reject. Thus, Gigerenzer asserts that "most so-called errors or cognitive illusions are, contrary to the assertions of the literature, in fact *not* violations of probability theory" (1991a, p. 86). But on closer scrutiny, it is hard to see how evolutionary psychologists *could* reject the claim that many of our intuitive judgments systematically deviate from norms derived from probability theory. This is because some of the central features of their research program commit them to saying that human judgments *do* systematically deviate from these norms. In order to make this point we will focus on two features of the evolutionary psychological research program: (1) the empirical thesis that formulating probabilistic problems in terms of frequencies improves performance and (2) the ameliorative project of improving statistical reasoning by teaching subjects to reformulate probabilistic problems in terms of frequencies.

As we saw in section 2, evolutionary psychologists maintain that when problems are explicitly formulated in terms of frequencies performance improves dramatically. Consider, for example, the experiments on base-rate neglect. We have already discussed the Casscells study's Harvard Medical School problem and noted that it appears to show that, under certain circumstances, human beings systematically ignore information about base rates when performing diagnostic tasks (Cascells, Schoenberger, and Grayboys 1978). For our current purposes, the crucial point to notice about the Casscells et al. experiment is that the problem was formulated in a *nonfrequentist* format. Subjects were asked about the probability of single events—the probability that a *specific* person has a disease—and were provided with probabilistic information in percentile and decimal formats. The results were disconcerting: 82 percent of subjects failed to provide the appropriate Bayesian answer to the problem. By contrast, we have already seen that, when presented with variants of the Harvard Medical School problem in which frequencies rather than percentages and single event probabilities were emphasized, subjects performed far better than they did in the original Cascells experiment. Although a number of different factors affect performance, according to Cosmides and Tooby, two predominate: "Asking for the answer as a frequency produces the largest effect, followed closely by presenting the problem information as frequencies" (1996, p. 58).

One central conclusion that evolutionary psychologists have wanted to draw from these experiments is that human probabilistic judgment *improves* when problems are reformulated in terms of frequencies.[5] So, for example, Cosmides and Tooby claim that "good statistical reasoning reappears, when problems are posed in frequentist terms" (1996, p. 62). This, however, poses a serious problem for the view that evolutionary psychologists reject the heuristics and biases thesis that human beings perform poorly in many judgmental tasks that involve probabilities. After all, it's hard to make sense of the claim that probabilistic judgment *improves* or that good statistical reasoning *reappears* in frequentist tasks unless performance on nonfrequency problems was *poor*, or at any rate less good, in the first place. Moreover, it is clear that the metric that evolutionary psychologists are employing in order to evaluate whether or not probabilistic judgment improves is precisely the same as the one adopted by proponents of the heuristics and biases program: namely, the standard axioms and theorems of probability theory. It is precisely *because* judgments on many frequentist tasks accord with Bayes's theorem (and judgments on nonfrequentist tasks do not) that Cosmides and Tooby claim that good statistical reasoning reappears when problems are posed in terms of frequencies. The interpretation that evolutionary psychologists impose on their own experimental data—namely, that performance improves in frequentist tasks—*commits* them to accepting the heuristics and biases thesis that many of our probabilistic judgments deviate from appropriate norms of probabilistic reasoning.

A similar point applies to another central feature of evolutionary psychological research on human reasoning—the ameliorative project of trying to improve human probabilistic inference. In addition to providing empirical hypotheses about the cognitive mechanisms responsible for inductive reasoning, evolutionary psychologists have also been concerned with trying to improve the quality of probabilistic inference. This practical project has been vigorously pursued by Gigerenzer and his colleagues. And in a series of papers with titles such as "How to Improve Bayesian Reasoning without Instruction: Frequency Formats" and "How to Improve Diagnostic Inferences in Physicians" they have shown how probabilistic judgment can be improved by teaching subjects to convert problems into a frequentist format (Gigerenzer and Hoffrage 1995; Hoffrage, Gigerenzer, and Ebert in press). So, for example, Gigerenzer and his colleagues suggest that if physicians convert diagnostic problems into a frequentist format, then they are more likely to be accurate in their diagnoses.

This sort of ameliorative project, once again, poses a serious problem for the contention that evolutionary psychologists reject the heuristics and biases thesis that human beings perform poorly in many judgmental tasks that involve probabilities. For it is extremely hard to see how we can make sense of the idea that performance can be *improved* by converting problems into a frequency format *unless subjects were previously doing something wrong.* If there was nothing wrong, for example, with the answers that physicians provided to diagnostic problems that were formulated in nonfrequentist terms, then diagnosis *couldn't* be improved by formulating the problem in a

TABLE 11.2.   Kinds of epistemic dispute narrowed to seven options

	Judgments	Mechanisms
"Standard picture"	*no dispute*	
Accuracy in the actual domain		
Accuracy in the proper domain		
Optimal given relevant constraints		

frequentist format.[6] This is, we think, an entirely uncontroversial conceptual point. According to conventional wisdom, "If it ain't broken, don't fix it." Our point is rather more basic: if it ain't broken, you *can't* fix it.

It is hard, then, to sustain the view that evolutionary psychologists reject the claim that many of our probabilistic judgments deviate from the norms of probability theory. What about a disagreement in the other direction? Do proponents of the heuristics and biases tradition deny the evolutionary psychologists' claim that many of our intuitive judgments about probability *accord* with the principles of probability theory? This is a suggestion that is hard to take seriously in the light of overwhelming textual evidence to the contrary. Kahneman, Tversky, and other advocates of the heuristics and biases program note repeatedly that normatively problematic heuristics like "representativeness" often get the *right* answer. Moreover, Kahneman and Tversky maintain (correctly) that they were responsible for discovering that formulating many judgmental problems in terms of frequencies leads to a dramatic improvement in performance (1996). And, as we'll see later on, they have also attempted to explain this phenomenon by providing an analysis of how the "extensional cues" provided by frequentist formulations of probabilistic problems facilitate reasoning. It is, therefore, singularly implausible to maintain that proponents of heuristics and biases deny that there are many probabilistic problems in which subjects' judgments accord with the probability calculus. We conclude that if there is a dispute between evolutionary psychologists and proponents of heuristics and biases, it is not located in the first box in Table 11.1. So it is time to replace Table 11.1 with Table 11.2.

THE STANDARD PICTURE AND THE EVALUATION OF MECHANISMS   If there is no substantive disagreement between evolutionary psychologists and proponents of the heuristics and biases tradition over whether or not our probabilistic *judgments* accord with the principles of the standard picture, then perhaps a disagreement exists over whether or not the cognitive *mechanisms* that subserve probabilistic reasoning accord with these principles? Certainly much of what has been said by participants in the debate suggests such a disagreement. Thus, for example, Cosmides and

Tooby explicitly represent their project as a challenge to what they see as "the conclusion most common in the literature on judgment under uncertainty —that our inductive reasoning mechanisms do not embody a calculus of probability" (1996, p. 1). But when one considers the issue more carefully it becomes difficult to sustain the view that there is any genuine disagreement here—or so we shall argue.

In order to defend this claim, we'll start by arguing that the positive accounts of probabilistic reasoning that evolutionary psychologists and proponents of heuristics and biases have developed are not incompatible. Indeed, rather than being incompatible, the views that have emerged from these two research programs about the nature of probabilistic reasoning mechanisms are to a surprising degree complementary. For while the heuristics and biases program has been primarily concerned with finding cases where subjects do a bad job in their probabilistic reasoning and proposing mechanisms to explain these shortcomings, evolutionary psychologists have been more concerned with positing mechanisms in order to explain those instances in which our probabilistic reasoning is normatively unproblematic. In short, the two research programs have simply focused on different phenomena.

Evolutionary psychologists have endorsed a range of claims about the mechanisms that subserve probabilistic inference in human beings. One often-repeated claim is that the human mind contains a "multitude of elegant machines" for inductive reasoning: "many different ones, each appropriate to a different kind of decision-making problem" (Cosmides and Tooby 1996, p. 63). Moreover, evolutionary psychologists contend that at least some of these mechanisms—specifically, frequentist mechanisms— are normatively appropriate relative to precisely the same standard that the heuristics and biases program endorses, namely, their input-output patterns match what would be required by the Bayesian theory of probability. Thus, Cosmides and Tooby suggest that "people do have reliably developing mechanisms that allow them to apply the calculus of probability" (1996, p. 18).

It is important to stress, however, that these frequentist mechanisms are supposed to be *format-restricted*; they are only able to process information that is presented in the appropriate format. More specifically, frequentist mechanisms "are designed to accept probabilistic information when it is in the form of a frequency, and to produce a frequency as their output" (Cosmides and Tooby 1996, p. 18). When probabilistic problems are presented in a nonfrequentist format, however, evolutionary psychologists contend that our judgments will deviate from those prescribed by the calculus of probability because the frequentist mechanisms will be unable to process the information.[7] In short: according to evolutionary psychology, whether or not our probabilistic reasoning mechanisms produce judgments that accord with the probability calculus depends crucially on the format in which the information is presented.

The previous two paragraphs provide a brief description of the main *positive* theses that evolutionary psychologists endorse about probabilistic inference in humans. But it is important to stress that this cannot be the entire story. Nor, for that matter, do evolutionary psychologists suggest that it is. Indeed, they *insist* that we may well need to posit a wide range of other inductive mechanisms, each of which operates according to different principles, in order to explain human reasoning (Cosmides and Tooby 1996, p. 63). One class of phenomena that is clearly in need of explanation is that of those instances in which subjects respond to probabilistic problems in ways that deviate from the norms of the probability calculus. These responses are not random but systematic in character. And presumably a complete account of human probabilistic reasoning needs to explain the inferential patterns that occur when we deviate from the probability calculus as well as those that occur when we get things right. Though evolutionary psychologists clearly accept this point and are prepared to posit additional mechanisms in order to explain the results, they have, as yet, provided no detailed theory that accounts for these results.[8] Nevertheless, they require an explanation. And presumably the explanation will need to invoke mechanisms in addition to the frequentist mechanisms discussed earlier. Moreover, these additional mechanisms will not map inputs onto the same outputs that the probability calculus would and, hence, *they will be normatively problematic by the lights of the standard picture.*

Is there any reason to think that proponents of the heuristics and biases program would or should disagree with any of this? As far as we can see, the answer is no. First of all, it is important to see that, according to the preceding picture of our reasoning architecture, the total system will yield lots of mistakes, though it will also yield lots of correct answers. And this is entirely consistent with the heuristics and biases account. Moreover, proponents of the heuristics and biases program will clearly not want to reject the claim that we possess cognitive mechanisms that *fail* to produce the input-output mappings that are sanctioned by the probability calculus. That there are such mechanisms is a central claim of the heuristics and biases approach to human probabilistic reasoning. Indeed, it would appear that the positive views that evolutionary psychologists endorse about the nature of our reasoning architecture are consistent with the claim that the systems responsible for producing non-Bayesian judgments employ the sorts of heuristics that Kahneman, Tversky, and their followers have invoked in order to explain deviations from the probability calculus. So, for example, it may be the case that some of the normatively problematic mechanisms that evolutionary psychologists must posit to explain normatively problematic judgments implement the representativeness and availability heuristics.

At this point it might be suggested that proponents of the heuristics and biases program reject the existence of mechanisms that operate according to principles of the probability calculus. This could be because either (1) they reject the existence of more than one reasoning mechanism or (2) while they accept the existence of more than one reasoning mechanism, they deny that any of them operate according to the principles of probability. Let's consider these options in turn.

Evolutionary psychologists sometimes appear to suggest that proponents of the heuristics and biases program are wedded to the assumptions that there are no domain-specific or modular mechanisms for reasoning and that all reasoning is subserved by general-purpose processes and mechanisms. So, for example, Cosmides and Tooby appear to attribute to the heuristics and biases program "a certain old-fashioned image of the mind: that it has the architecture of an early model, limited-resource general-purpose computer" (1996, p. 13). There is plenty of textual evidence, however, that proponents of the heuristics and biases program do not endorse such a picture of the mind. So, for example, in a passage that anticipates a central theme in the work of evolutionary psychologists, Kahneman and Tversky compare the processes involved in the solving of probabilistic problems "with the operation of a flexible computer program that incorporates a variety of potentially useful subroutines" (1983, p. 88).[9] Elsewhere, they are even more explicit on the matter and claim that "the actual reasoning process is schema-bound or content-bound so that different operations or inferential rules are available in different contexts" and that "consequently, human reasoning cannot be adequately described in terms of content-independent formal rules" (Tversky and Kahneman 1983, p. 499). Piattelli-Palmarini is still more explicit in his endorsement of a domain-specific conception of human reasoning and goes so far as to suggest (rightly or wrongly) that judgmental errors are "a demonstration of what modern cognitive science calls the 'modularity' of the mind" (1994, p. 32). In other words, Piattelli-Palmarini appears to be endorsing the claim that we possess modules for reasoning.

So proponents of the heuristics and biases program do not appear to be adverse to the idea that human reasoning is subserved by a variety of domain-specific cognitive mechanisms. Do they, perhaps, deny that any of these mechanisms operate according to the principles of the probability calculus? If they did maintain this position, then there would be a genuine disagreement between evolutionary psychologists and proponents of the heuristics and biases program. But there is, in fact, no reason to suppose that they do hold such a view. First of all, nowhere in the heuristics and biases literature have we been able to find a single passage in which it is *explicitly* denied that we possess some cognitive mechanisms that operate according to the principles of the probability calculus. What we do find, however, are passages that may be interpreted as *suggesting* that there are no such mechanisms. So, for example, as we noted earlier, Kahneman and Tversky (1973) claim that

in making predictions and judgments under uncertainty, people do not appear to follow the calculus of chance or the statistical theory of prediction. Instead, they rely on a limited number of heuristics which sometimes yield reasonable judgments and sometimes lead to severe and systematic errors. (p. 48)

This and other similar passages in the heuristics and biases literature might be thought to have the conversational implicature that we *only* use normatively problematic heuristics in our probabilistic reasoning and hence possess no reasoning mechanisms that operate according to the principles of the probability calculus.

We maintain, however, that there are extremely good reasons to treat such claims as instances of rhetorical excess. First, as we pointed out in section 2, the claim that we possess *no* normatively unproblematic mechanisms for probabilistic reasoning is clearly not supported by the available empirical evidence. Such a claim is vastly stronger than anything the available evidence will support. And this provides us with some reason to treat it as a rhetorical flourish rather than a core claim of the heuristics and biases research program.

Second, all the quotations from the heuristics and biases literature we have found that suggest humans possess no normatively appropriate reasoning mechanisms manifest a tendency that Kahneman and Tversky have themselves lamented—the tendency to overstate one's position by "omitting relevant quantifiers" (1996, p. 589). Kahneman and Tversky raise this point in response to Gigerenzer's claim that cognitive illusions disappear when problems are formulated in terms of frequencies. They suggest that "because Gigerenzer must be aware of the evidence that judgments of frequency . . . are subject to systematic error, a charitable interpretation of his position is that he has overstated his case by omitting relevant quantifiers" (1996, p. 589). We maintain that much the same may be said of the position that Kahneman, Tversky, and their followers sometimes appear to endorse regarding the normative status of our reasoning mechanisms. Consider, for example, the preceding quotation from Kahneman and Tversky 1973. The natural reading of this passage is that Kahneman and Tversky are claiming that humans *always* "rely on a limited number of heuristics" (1973, p. 48). But notice that the relevant quantifier is omitted. It is left unspecified whether they are claiming that we *always* use normatively problematic heuristics rather than (for example) claiming that we *typically* or *often* use such heuristics. And because they must know that the truth of the natural reading is vastly underdetermined by the data, it is surely charitable to interpret this as an instance of rhetorical excess—an overstatement of their position that results from omitting relevant quantifiers. Moreover, this point generalizes: in *all* the passages from the heuristics and biases literature that we have found which suggest that humans possess no normatively appropriate reasoning mechanisms, *relevant quantifiers are systematically omitted*. We suggest, therefore, that because proponents of the heuristics and biases program are presumably aware that the available evidence fails to support the claim that humans possess *no* normatively unproblematic reasoning mechanisms, the charitable interpretation of these quotations is that they overstate the position by omitting relevant quantifiers.

A final point that further supports the conclusion of the previous paragraph is that in their more reflective moments—when quantifiers are not omitted—advocates of the heuristics and biases tradition make it clear that they are not maintaining that we *always* use normatively problematic heuristics and mechanisms in our intuitive reasoning. Instead, they explicitly claim

TABLE 11.3. Kinds of epistemic dispute narrowed to
six options

	Judgments	Mechanisms
"Standard picture"	*no dispute*	*no dispute*
Accuracy in the actual domain		
Accuracy in the proper domain		
Optimal given relevant constraints		

only that we *sometimes* or *often* use such heuristics and mechanisms. So, for example, when they are being careful, Kahneman and Tversky claim only that "intuitive predictions and judgments are *often* mediated by a small number of distinct mental operations . . . [or] . . . judgmental heuristics" (1996, p. 582). But this position is entirely compatible with the evolutionary psychological view that we also possess some normatively unproblematic reasoning mechanisms. In short: when proponents of the heuristics and biases tradition express their views carefully and fill in the appropriate quantifiers, they end up maintaining a position about the normative status of our reasoning mechanisms that does not conflict with the claims of evolutionary psychologists. It is time, then, to replace Table 11.2 with Table 11.3.

Accuracy-Based Assessments

Though the standard picture is the normative yardstick most commonly invoked in the dispute between evolutionary psychology and the heuristics and biases program, it is not the only one. Another kind of normative standard is suggested by Gigerenzer's discussion of Take The Best and other members of a class of satisfying algorithms that he calls fast and frugal procedures (Gigerenzer and Goldstein 1996; Gigerenzer, Hoffrage, and Kleinbölting 1991). According to Gigerenzer, a central consideration when evaluating reasoning is its *accuracy* (Gigerenzer and Goldstein 1996, p. 665). And because fast and frugal algorithms get the correct answer at least as often as other computationally more expensive, "rational"[10] methods (such as standard statistical linear models) Gigerenzer clearly thinks that they are normatively unproblematic. Indeed, he thinks that the fact that these simple algorithms are accurate constitutes a refutation of the claim that only "rational" algorithms can be accurate and goes some way toward overcoming the "opposition between the rational and the psychological and . . . reunit[ing] the two" (Gigerenzer and Goldstein 1996, p. 666).

Although the notion of accuracy applies to both judgments and cognitive mechanisms, Gigerenzer and other evolutionary psychologists are concerned primarily with the accuracy of mechanisms (Cosmides and Tooby

1996; Gigerenzer and Goldstein 1996). Moreover, it is also clear that once we address the issue of whether or not evolutionary psychologists and proponents of the heuristics and biases tradition disagree about the accuracy of our cognitive mechanisms, the same considerations apply *mutatis mutandis* to the putative disagreement over judgments. For this reason we will focus primarily on whether or not there is any genuine disagreement between evolutionary psychology and the heuristics and biases program over the accuracy of our cognitive mechanisms.

When applied to cognitive mechanisms, Gigerenzer's accuracy-based criterion for epistemic evaluation bears an intimate relationship to the reliabilist tradition in epistemology according to which (very roughly) a cognitive mechanism is rational just in case it tends to produce true beliefs and avoid producing false ones (Goldman 1986; Nozick 1993).[11] One frequently observed consequence of reliabilist and accuracy-based approaches to the evaluation of cognitive mechanisms is that assessments must be relativized to some environment or domain of information (Goldman 1986; Nozick 1993; Stich 1990). A visual system, for example, is not reliable or unreliable *simpliciter* but only reliable or accurate relative to a (set of) environment(s) or a domain of information.[12] Moreover, there is an indefinitely wide range of environments or domains to which evaluations might be relativized. For current purposes, however, let's focus on two that have been suggested by D. Sperber to be particularly relevant to understanding the evolutionary psychological approach to reasoning—what he calls the *actual domain* and the *proper domain* for a cognitive mechanism (1994). The actual domain for a given reasoning module is "all the information in the organism's environment that may (once processed by perceptual modules, and possibly by other conceptual modules) satisfy the module's input conditions" (pp. 51–52). By "input conditions" Sperber means those conditions that must be satisfied in order for the module to be able to process a given item of information. So, for example, if a module requires that a problem be stated in a particular format, then any information not stated in that format fails to satisfy the module's input conditions. By contrast, the proper domain for a cognitive mechanism is all the information that it is the mechanism's "biological function to process" (p. 52). The proper domain is the information that the mechanism was designed to process by natural selection. In recent years, many philosophers of biology have come to regard the notion of a biological function as a particularly slippery one.[13] For current purposes we can rely on the following very rough characterization: the biological functions of a system are the activities or effects of the system in virtue of which the system has remained a stable feature of an enduring species.

Do evolutionary psychologists and proponents of the heuristics and biases tradition disagree about the accuracy of reasoning mechanisms in their *proper* domains? Clearly not. For while evolutionary psychologists have maintained that cognitive mechanisms will tend to perform accurately in their proper domains—on the kinds of information that they are designed to process—the heuristics and biases tradition has been entirely silent on the issue. Determining the accuracy of cognitive mechanisms *in the proper domain* is simply not the line of work that proponents of heuristics and biases are engaged in. So there could be no disagreement here.

It is similarly implausible to maintain that evolutionary psychologists and advocates of the heuristics and biases tradition disagree over the accuracy of our reasoning mechanisms in the *actual* domain. Clearly, evolutionary psychologists think that *some* of our reasoning mechanisms are accurate in the actual domain. But it is equally clear that they do not claim that *all* of these mechanisms are. They certainly cite no evidence that could support the claim that *all* of our reasoning mechanisms are accurate in the actual domain. And, what is more important, such a claim would be patently incompatible with their ameliorative project. If all our reasoning mechanisms are accurate in the actual domain, then there is little room for systematically *improving* human reasoning. So it must be the case that what evolutionary psychologists want to claim is that *some but not all* of our reasoning mechanisms are accurate in the actual domain.

Do proponents of the heuristics and biases tradition reject this claim? As far as we can see, the answer is no. They clearly think that *some* of our cognitive mechanisms are inaccurate in the actual domain. This, after all, is a central message of their research program. But they have been largely silent on the issue of whether or not we possess other reasoning mechanisms that are accurate in the actual domain. And this is simply because, as we mentioned earlier on, proponents of the heuristics and biases tradition have primarily focused on explaining instances of incorrect judgment rather than explaining instances of successful inference. Nonetheless, as we saw earlier, theorists working within the heuristics and biases tradition are not adverse to the idea that we have reasoning mechanisms other than the ones that employ normatively problematic heuristics and, to the extent that they say anything about these other mechanisms, they seem amenable to the idea that they may be accurate. So, for example, Kahneman and Tversky seem entirely comfortable with the idea that mechanisms that employ correct rules of probabilistic inference can produce highly accurate judgments in contexts where the problem is transparent and "extensional" cues are effective (Tversky and Kahneman 1983).

The situation is similar when we turn to the issue of whether or not evolutionary psychologists and advocates of the heuristics and biases approach disagree over the accuracy of our *judgments*. Evolutionary psychologists think that we tend to be accurate in the *proper* domain, whereas proponents of the heuristics and biases program are simply silent on the issue. And both parties appear to think that *many but not all* of our judgments are accurate in the *actual* domain. There are, of course, lots of issues of detail where the two research programs disagree. So, for example, Gigerenzer has challenged some of the interpretations that advocates of the heuristics and biases program have imposed on specific experiments. We will consider some of these cases in section 4. But we maintain that these disagreements are *merely* matters of detail and ought not to distract from the genuine consensus between evolutionary psychology and the heuristics and biases program. Both programs clearly accept that many of our judgments in the actual

TABLE 11.4. Kinds of epistemic dispute narrowed to two options

	Judgments	Mechanisms
"Standard picture"	*no dispute*	*no dispute*
Accuracy in the actual domain	*no dispute*	*no dispute*
Accuracy in the proper domain	*no dispute*	*no dispute*
Optimal given relevant constraints		

domain are inaccurate and that we are subject to systematic errors. This is a central claim of the heuristics and biases program, and evolutionary psychology is similarly committed to this view by virtue of endorsing the ameliorative project. Moreover, neither program insists that *all* of our judgments are inaccurate. Both, for example, think that our judgments about frequency can be highly accurate. Again, there is no disagreement. So we can now replace Table 11.3 with Table 11.4.

Constrained-Optimality Assessments

A final normative standard that has been invoked by participants in the debate between evolutionary psychology and the heuristics and biases tradition is one that applies only to the evaluation of cognitive mechanisms and not to the judgments that these mechanisms produce. The standard in question maintains that a reasoning mechanism is normatively unproblematic to the extent that it is *optimal given the constraints to which it is subject.* This proposal is alluded to by Gigerenzer when he suggests that some reasoning mechanisms may be optimal in the way that Herman von Helmholtz and Richard Gregory propose that visual processing mechanisms are optimal: they are *the best systems available for acquiring an accurate picture of the world given the constraints under which they must operate.* One crucial point to stress is that the best system (given the constraints under which it operates) need not be a system that never makes mistakes. As Gigerenzer points out, such "systems can be fooled and may break down when stable, long-term properties of the environment to which they are adapted change" (1997, p. 10). So, for example, Gregory maintains that visual "illusions will be a necessary part of all efficiently designed visual machines"—even the *best-designed* visual systems (Gregory, quoted in Gigerenzer 1991a, p. 228). Similarly, Gigerenzer suggests that, given the constraints under which real cognitive systems must operate, "cognitive illusions" or "biases" will be a necessary part of an efficiently designed reasoning mechanism. Thus, the Helmholtzian view "allows both for optimal cognitive functioning and for systematic illusions" (Gigerenzer 1991a, p. 240).

Is there any disagreement between evolutionary psychologists and proponents of the heuristics and biases program on the issue of whether or not we possess mechanisms that are optimally well designed (given the appropriate constraints) for probabilistic reasoning? Once again, we maintain, the answer is no. While evolutionary psychologists have suggested that we possess mechanisms that are optimal in the relevant sense, proponents of the heuristics and biases program need not and do not deny this claim. To see why, it is important to note that when evolutionary psychologists suggest that we possess reasoning mechanisms that are optimal given the constraints, they typically appear to have in mind the claim that we possess cognitive mechanisms that are optimally well designed for processing information in their *proper domains* (and under conditions similar to those our evolutionary ancestors would have encountered) and not the claim that we possess mechanisms that are optimally well designed for processing information in their *actual domains*. Thus, for example, Cosmides and Tooby suggest that

> our minds come equipped with very sophisticated intuitive competences that are well-engineered solutions to the problems humans normally encountered in natural environments . . . and that ecologically valid input (e.g., frequency formats) may be necessary to activate these competences. (1996, p. 9)

But if the notion of optimality invoked by evolutionary psychologists is indexed to the proper domain, then, as we have already seen, proponents of the heuristics and biases program do not disagree. The heuristics and biases program simply is not concerned with the performance of cognitive mechanisms in their proper domains.

Suppose, however, that, contrary to appearances, evolutionary psychologists do wish to maintain that we possess reasoning mechanisms that are optimal relative to the actual domain. Even so, they clearly could not maintain that *all* of our reasoning mechanisms are optimal since, once again, such a view would render their ameliorative project impossible. If all our reasoning mechanisms were the best that they could be, then we *couldn't* make them better. Here the (dis)analogy between visual systems and reasoning systems is illuminating. It is plausible to claim that when functioning normally our visual systems are optimal in the sense that they simply cannot be improved. By contrast, we *can* improve our reasoning—hence the ameliorative project. So the most that evolutionary psychologists could be claiming is that some or perhaps many of our cognitive mechanisms are optimal relative to the actual domain. But this is not a claim that proponents of the heuristics and biases tradition either do or should reject. To the best of our knowledge, proponents of the heuristics and biases program have never denied that we possess some reasoning mechanisms that are optimal in this sense. What they do deny is that *all* of the cognitive mechanisms that subserve reasoning are optimal in the sense that they always produce judgments that are correct and/or accord with the principles of the probability calculus. This, however, is a very different notion of optimality—a notion of

TABLE 11.5. Kinds of epistemic dispute narrowed to one option

	Judgments	Mechanisms
"Standard picture"	*no dispute*	*no dispute*
Accuracy in the actual domain	*no dispute*	*no dispute*
Accuracy in the proper domain	*no dispute*	*no dispute*
Optimal given relevant constraints		*no dispute*

optimality that does not take into consideration the constraints under which our reasoning systems must operate. There is no reason to suppose that the heuristics and biases program is committed to denying that we possess cognitive mechanisms that are optimal in the actual domain *given the constraints under which they operate*. For as we have already seen, the claim that a reasoning system is optimal (given the appropriate constraints) is perfectly consistent with the view that it is subject to lots of biases and cognitive illusions. Thus, proponents of the heuristics and biases program need not and do not deny that some or even many of our cognitive mechanisms may be optimal in the Helmholtzian sense that Gigerenzer and other evolutionary psychologists have in mind. And if this correct, then we can replace Table 11.4 with Table 11.5.

4. Some Real Disagreements

The main burden of this chapter has been to dispel the illusion that there is any substantive disagreement between evolutionary psychologists and advocates of the heuristics and biases tradition concerning the extent of human rationality. We do not intend to suggest, however, that there is nothing left for evolutionary psychologists and proponents of the heuristics and biases program to disagree about. Clearly there is. Indeed, there are a number of different disputes that remain. One of these disputes focuses on the issue of how we ought to apply probability theory to specific problems in the heuristics and biases literature—for example, the lawyer/engineer problem and the Harvard Medical School problem—and whether or not probability theory provides a uniquely correct answer to these problems. Though authors in the heuristics and biases tradition often appear to assume that there is only one normatively correct answer to these problems, Gigerenzer has argued that there are typically a number of equally reasonable ways of applying probability theory to the problems and that these different analyses result in distinct but equally correct answers (1991a, 1994).

Another very real dispute concerns the adequacy of the explanations proposed by proponents of the heuristics and biases tradition—explanations that invoke heuristics, such as availability and representativeness, in order to explain cognitive phenomena. Evolutionary psychologists have maintained that these "heuristics are too vague to count as explanations" and that psychologists who work in the heuristics and biases tradition have failed to "specify precise and falsifiable process models, to clarify the antecedent conditions that elicit various heuristics, and to work out the relationship between heuristics." (Gigerenzer 1996, p. 593). Proponents of the heuristics and biases tradition have responded by arguing that evolutionary psychologists have "missed the point" (Kahneman and Tversky 1996). They maintain that representativeness and other heuristics "can be assessed experimentally" and that testing the hypothesis that probability judgments are mediated by these heuristics "does not require a theoretical model" (Kahneman and Tversky 1996).

On our view, both of these disputes raise deep and interesting questions, which we plan to address elsewhere. In this section we propose to focus on a third very real dispute between evolutionary psychologists and proponents of the heuristics and biases tradition, one that has often been center stage in the literature. This is the disagreement over what interpretation of probability theory to adopt.

There has been a long-standing disagreement between proponents of the heuristics and biases program and evolutionary psychologists over what we should recognize as the correct interpretation of probability theory. In contrast with psychologists in the heuristics and biases tradition, Gigerenzer has urged that probability theory ought to be given a frequentist interpretation according to which probabilities are construed as relative frequencies of events in one class to events in another. As Gigerenzer points out, according to "this frequentist view, one cannot speak of a probability unless a reference class is defined" (1993, pp. 292–293). So, for example, "the relative frequency of an event such as death is only defined with respect to a reference class such as 'all male pub-owners fifty-years old living in Bavaria' " (Gigerenzer 1993, p. 292). One consequence of this that Gigerenzer is particularly keen to stress is that according to frequentism, it makes no sense to assign probabilities to single events. Claims about the probability of a single event are literally meaningless: "For a frequentist . . . the term "probability," when it refers to a single event, has no meaning at all for us" (1991a, p. 88). Moreover, Gigerenzer maintains that because of this "a strict frequentist" would argue that "the laws of probability are about frequencies and not about single events" and, hence, that "no judgment about single events can violate probability theory" (1993, pp. 292–293).

In stark contrast with Gigerenzer's frequentism, Kahneman, Tversky, and their followers insist that probability theory can be meaningfully applied to single events and hence that judgments about single events (e.g., Jack being a engineer or, in another well-known problem, Linda being a bank teller)[14] can violate probability theory. This disagreement emerges very clearly in Kahneman and Tversky's 1996 work, where they argue that Gigerenzer's treatment of judgment under uncertainty "appears far too restrictive" because it "does not apply to events that are unique for the individual and, therefore, excludes some of the most important evidential and decision problems in people's lives" (p. 589). Instead of adopting frequentism, Kahneman and Tversky suggest that some "subjectivist" or "Bayesian" account of probability may be preferable.

This disagreement over the interpretation of probability raises complex and important questions in the foundations of statistics and decision theory about the scope and limits of our formal treatment of probability. Moreover, the dispute between frequentists and subjectivists has been a central debate in the foundations of probability for much of the twentieth century (Mises 1957; Savage 1972). Needless to say, a satisfactory treatment of these issues is beyond the scope of this chapter. But we would like to comment briefly on what we take to be the central role that issues about the interpretation of probability theory play in the dispute between evolutionary psychologists and proponents of the heuristics and biases program. In particular, we will argue that Gigerenzer's use of frequentist considerations in this debate is deeply problematic.

Questions about the interpretation of probability entered the debate between evolutionary psychology and the heuristics and biases tradition primarily because it was realized by some theorists—most notably Gigerenzer—that these questions bear on the issue of whether or not human reasoning violates appropriate norms of rationality. As we have already seen, Gigerenzer argues that if frequentism is true, then statements about the probability of single events are meaningless and, hence, that judgments about single events *cannot* violate probability theory (1993, pp. 292–293). Gigerenzer clearly thinks that this conclusion can be put to work in order to dismantle part of the evidential base for the claim that human judgments and reasoning mechanisms violate appropriate norms. For as we have seen, participants in the debate between evolutionary psychology and the heuristics and biases tradition typically view probability theory as the source of appropriate normative constraints on probabilistic reasoning. And if frequentism is true, then no probabilistic judgments about single events will be normatively problematic (by this standard), since they will not violate probability theory. In which case, Gigerenzer gets to exclude all experimental results that involve judgments about single events as evidence for the existence of normatively problematic, probabilistic judgments and reasoning mechanisms.

On the face of it, Gigerenzer's strategy is quite persuasive. Nevertheless, we think that it is subject to serious objections. Frequentism itself is a hotly contested view, but even if we grant, for argument's sake, that frequentism is correct, there are still serious grounds for concern. First, as we observed in note 6, there is a serious tension between the claim that subjects don't make errors in reasoning about single events and the ameliorative project that evolutionary psychologists are engaged in. The current point is not that frequentism is false but merely that evolutionary psychologists cannot comfortably maintain both (1) that we don't violate appropriate norms of rationality when reasoning about the probabilities of single events and (2) that reasoning improves when single-event problems are converted into a frequentist format.

A second and perhaps more serious problem with Gigerenzer's use of frequentist considerations is that it is very plausible to maintain that *even if* statements about the probabilities of single events really are meaningless and hence do not violate the probability calculus, subjects are still guilty of making *some sort of error* when they deal with problems about single events. For if, as Gigerenzer would have us believe, judgments about the probabilities of single events are meaningless, then surely the correct answer to a (putative) problem about the probability of a single event is not some numerical value or rank ordering but rather: "Huh?" or, "That's utter nonsense!" or, "What on earth are you talking about?" Consider an analogous case, in which you are asked to answer a question like "Is Linda taller than?" or "How much taller than is Linda?" Obviously these questions are nonsense because they are incomplete. In order to answer them you must be told what the other relatum of the "taller than" relation is supposed to be. Unless this is done, answering yes or no or providing a numerical value would surely be normatively inappropriate. Now according to the frequentist, the question "What is the probability that Linda is a bank teller?" is nonsense for much the same reason that "Is Linda taller than?" is. So when subjects answer the single-event probability question by providing a *number* they are doing something that is clearly normatively inappropriate. The normatively appropriate answer is "Huh?," not, "Less than ten percent."

It might be suggested that the answers that subjects provide in experiments that involve single-event probabilities are an artifact of the demand characteristics of the experimental context. Subjects (one might claim) know, if only implicitly, that single-event probabilities are meaningless. But because they are presented with forced choice problems that require a probabilistic judgment, they end up giving silly answers. So one might think that the take-home message is: "Don't blame the subject for giving a silly answer. Blame the experimenter for putting the subject in a silly situation in the first place!" But this proposal is implausible for two reasons. First, as a matter of fact, ordinary people use judgments about single-event probabilities in all sorts of circumstances outside of the psychologist's laboratory. So it is implausible to think that *they* view single-event probabilities as meaningless. But second, even if subjects really did think that single-event probabilities were meaningless, presumably we should expect them to provide more or less random answers and not the sorts of systematic responses that are observed in the psychological literature. Again, consider the comparison with the question "Is Linda taller than?" It would be a truly stunning result if everyone who was pressured to respond said yes.

5. Conclusion

The main aim of this chapter has been to dispel an illusion: the illusion that evolutionary psychology and the heuristics and biases tradition are deeply divided in their assessments of human reasoning. We started by outlining the two research programs and disentangling their core claims from the rhetorical flourishes that have obscured an emerging consensus between the two programs about the scope and limits of human rationality and about the cognitive architecture that supports it. We then showed that, contrary to appearances, there is no substantial disagreement between evolutionary psychologists and advocates of the heuristics and biases program over the extent of human rationality. On a number of different readings of what the dispute is supposed to be, *neither research program denies the core claims of the other* and, in many cases, it is clear that they should and do endorse each other's core claims. Finally, we briefly focused on some of the points of disagreement that remain once the illusory dispute has disappeared. Though there are some important issues that divide evolutionary psychologists and advocates of the heuristics and biases program, there is also a surprising degree of consensus. Moreover, and this has been our central theme, they do not really have any deep disagreement over the extent of human rationality.

NOTES

An earlier version of this chapter was discussed at a workshop on the evolution of mind at the Hang Seng Centre for Cognitive Studies at the University of Sheffield. We are grateful for the many helpful comments and criticisms that were offered on that occasion. Special thanks are due to George Botterill, Richard Byrne, Peter Carruthers, Gerd Gigerenzer, Brian Loar, Adam Morton, and Michael Segal.

1. We classify a claim as a *core claim* in one of the two research traditions if (1) it is central to the research program, (2) it is not completely implausible to suppose that the claim is supported by the empirical evidence offered by advocates of the program, and (3) advocates of the program are prepared to endorse it in their more careful moments. *Rhetorical flourishes*, by contrast, are claims that (1) are not central to the research program, (2) are not supported by the evidence offered, and (3) are typically not endorsed by advocates of the program in question when they are being careful and reflective.

2. While Kahneman and Tversky's rhetoric, and Gould's, suggests that untutored people have nothing but normatively defective heuristics or "shoddy software" with which to tackle problems dealing with probability, M. Piattelli-Palmarini goes on to make the even more flamboyant claim that the shoddy software is more likely to get the wrong answer than the right one.

> We are . . . blind not only to the extremes of probability but also to intermediate probabilities—from which one might well adduce that we are blind about probabilities.

> I would like to suggest a simple, general, probabilistic law: Any probabilistic intuition by anyone not specifically tutored in probability calculus has a greater than 50 percent chance of being wrong. (1994, pp. 131–132)

This is not, however, a claim that any other proponents of heuristics and biases have been prepared to endorse even in their least careful statements. Nor is there any reason to think that they should, since it is utterly implausible to maintain that this thesis is supported by the available data. We will, therefore, treat Piattelli-Palmarini's "probabilistic law" as a particularly extreme instance of rhetorical excess and ignore it in the remainder of this chapter.

3. The conjunction of the first two central theses of evolutionary psychology constitutes what might be called the *Massive Modularity Hypothesis*. For more

on this hypothesis, see Samuels (forthcoming) and Samuels, Stich, and Tremoulet (forthcoming).

4. Precisely what it is for a principle of reasoning to be *derived from* the rules of logic, probability theory, and decision theory is far from clear. For as A. Goldman and Harman have both pointed out, rules of rational inference cannot literally be derived from logic and probability theory (Goldman 1986, p. 82; Harman 1986, chapter 2). Nor is it clear which of the rules of logic, probability theory, and decision theory our judgments and reasoning mechanisms must accord with in order to count as rational. Moreover, there are serious disagreements about which *versions* of logic, decision theory, and probability theory the correct principles of rationality ought to be derived from (see, for example, Gigerenzer 1991a). Nonetheless, the essential idea is that we use the rules from these formal theories as a guide in constructing normative principles that can then be employed in order to measure the extent to which human reasoning and judgment is rational.

5. Indeed, evolutionary psychologists take the fact that performance improves in frequentist tasks to *support* the frequentist hypothesis.

6. This also poses a serious problem for Gigerenzer's claim that problems about single-event probabilities are meaningless and that, as a result, subjects' responses to such problems are not violations of the probability calculus. If problems about single events are really meaningless, then subjects' answers to such problems *couldn't* be wrong by the lights of the probability calculus. In which case, it is extremely hard to see how performance on reasoning tasks could *improve* when problems are reformulated in terms of frequencies as opposed to single events. Indeed, if, as evolutionary psychologists often appear to suggest, the frequentist problems given to experimental subjects are supposed to be *reformulations* of single-event problems, then it is hard to see how (accurate) reformulations of the original (meaningless) problems could be anything other than meaningless. In short: it is exceedingly hard to see how it could be the case that both (1) human reasoning improves when problems are reformulated in terms of frequencies and (2) nonfrequentist problems are meaningless.

7. An analogy might help to illuminate the proposal: Consider a standard electronic calculator that is designed to take as inputs mathematical problems that are presented in a standard base-10 notation. We might suppose that such a machine is a well-designed, specialized computational device that reliably solves problems that are presented in the appropriate format—i.e., base-10 Arabic notation. But suppose that we were to use the calculator to solve a problem stated in terms of Roman numerals. Since there simply are no buttons for "X" and "L" and "I" there would be no way for the calculator to deal with the problem (unless, of course, we first translate it into Arabic notation).

8. One might think that the notion of format restriction provides us with at least the outline for an explanation of why we perform poorly on probabilistic problems that are presented in nonfrequentist formats: viz., frequentist mechanisms will be unable to "handle" these problems because they are encoded in the wrong format. But the fact that the normatively unproblematic mechanisms are format-restricted only tells us that problems with the wrong format *won't* be assigned to (or be handled by) them. So they must be handled by some other component of the mind. But that's *all* the notion of format restriction tells us, and that hardly counts as an explanation of why we give the wrong answer. Nor, of course, does it explain why we make the specific sorts of systematic errors that have been documented in the psychological literature. So, for

example, it clearly does not explain why, for nonfrequentist problems, base rates tend to be neglected rather than overstressed or why human beings tend to exhibit overconfidence rather than, say, underconfidence. The point that needs to be stressed here is that it is implausible to think that these normatively problematic responses are the product of normatively unproblematic, format-restricted mechanisms (both because the responses are normatively problematic and because they are in the wrong format). So there must be further mechanisms that are normatively problematic. And that is just what the heuristics and biases tradition says.

9. Compare to Tooby and Cosmides' own suggestion that the human mind "can be likened to a computer program with millions of lines of code and hundreds or thousands of functionally specialized subroutines" (1992, p. 39).

10. Evolutionary psychologists often use the term *rational* in scare quotes. When they do so, it is clear that they intend to refer to judgments, mechanisms, or procedures that are construed as rational by the lights of the standard picture.

11. There are also interesting questions about the relationship between the accuracy-based criterion and the standard picture, but we do not have the space to discuss them here.

12. So, for example, the human visual system may well be accurate relative to the range of information that it processes in the environments in which we typically live. But as Gigerenzer (1998a) notes, our color vision is singularly *un*-reliable in parking lots illuminated by mercury vapor lamps. And in the "world" of the psychophysicist with its array of exotic visual stimuli, other components of the visual system can be very unreliable indeed.

13. See, for example, Godfrey-Smith 1994, Neander 1991, and Plantinga 1993.

14. This problem was first studied by Tversky and Kahneman (1982), who presented subjects with the following task:

> Linda is 31 years old, single, outspoken, and very bright. She majored in philosophy. As a student, she was deeply concerned with issues of discrimination and social justice, and also participated in anti-nuclear demonstrations.
>
> Please rank the following statements by their probability, using 1 for the most probable and 8 for the least probable.
>
> (a) Linda is a teacher in elementary school.
> (b) Linda works in a bookstore and takes Yoga classes.
> (c) Linda is active in the feminist movement.
> (d) Linda is a psychiatric social worker.
> (e) Linda is a member of the League of Women Voters.
> (f) Linda is a bank teller.
> (g) Linda is an insurance salesperson.
> (h) Linda is a bank teller and is active in the feminist movement.

In a group of naive subjects with no background in probability and statistics, 89 percent judged that statement (h) was more probable than statement (f). For current purposes, the key point to notice is that subjects are asked to make judgments about a single event—e.g., that Linda is a bank teller—rather than a relative frequency. For this reason, Gigerenzer has insisted, contrary to the claims in the heuristics and biases literature, that ranking (h) as more probable than (f) "is not a violation of probability theory . . . [since] . . . for a frequentist, this problem has nothing to do with probability theory" (1991a, pp. 91–92).

REFERENCES

Bazerman, M., and M. Neale (1986). Heuristics in negotiation. In H. Arkes and K Hammond (eds.), *Judgment and Decision Making: An Interdisciplinary Reader*, pp. 311–321. Cambridge: Cambridge University Press.

Bower, B. (1996). Rational mind design: research into the ecology of thought treads on contested terrain. *Science News* 150:24–25.

Casscells, W., A. Schoenberger, and T. Grayboys (1978). Interpretation by physicians of clinical laboratory results. *New England Journal of Medicine* 299:999–1000.

Cosmides, L., and J. Tooby, (1996). Are humans good intuitive statisticians after all? Rethinking some conclusions from the literature on judgment under uncertainty. *Cognition* 58: 1–73.

Fodor, J. A. (1983). *Modularity of Mind: an Essay on Faculty Psychology.* Cambridge: MIT Press.

Gigerenzer, G. (1991a). How to make cognitive illusions disappear: Beyond "heuristics and biases." *European Review of Social Psychology* 2:83–115.

Gigerenzer, G. (1991b). On cognitive illusions and rationality. *Poznan Studies in the Philosophy of the Sciences and the Humanities* 21:225–249.

Gigerenzer, G. (1993). The bounded rationality of probabilistic mental models. In K. Manktelow and D. Over (eds.), *Rationality: Psychological and Philosophical Perspectives*, pp. 284–313. London: Routledge.

Gigerenzer, G. (1994). Why the distinction between single-event probabilities and frequencies is important for psychology (and vice versa). In G. Wright and P. Ayton (eds.), *Subjective Probability*, pp. 129–161. New York: Wiley.

Gigerenzer, G. (1996). On narrow norms and vague heuristics: A reply to Kahneman and Tversky (1996). *Psychological Review* 103:592–596.

Gigerenzer, G. (1997). The modularity of social intelligence. In A. Whiten and R. Byrne (eds.), *Machiavellian Intelligence II.*, pp. 264–280. Cambridge: Cambridge University Press.

Gigerenzer, G. (1998). Ecological intelligence: An adaptation for frequencies. In D. Cummins and C. Allen (eds)., *The Evolution of Mind*, pp. 9–29. New York: Oxford University Press.

Gigerenzer, G., and D. G. Goldstein (1996). Reasoning the fast and frugal way: Models of bounded rationality. *Psychological Review* 103:650–669.

Gigerenzer, G., and U. Hoffrage (1995). How to improve Bayesian reasoning without instruction: Frequency formats. *Psychological Review* 102: 684–704.

Gigerenzer, G., U. Hoffrage, and H. Kleinbölting (1991). Probabilistic mental models: A Brunswikian theory of confidence. *Psychological Review* 98: 506–528.

Godfrey-Smith, P. (1994). A modern history theory of functions. *Nous* 28: 344–362.

Goldman, A. I. (1986). *Epistemology and Cognition.* Cambridge, MA: Harvard University Press.

Gould, S. (1992). *Bully for Brontosaurus: Further Reflections in Natural History.* London: Penguin.

Harman, G. H. (1986). *Change in View: Principles of Reasoning.* Cambridge: MIT Press Bradford.

Hoffrage, U., G. Gigerenzer, and A. Ebert (in press). How to improve diagnostic inferences in physicians.

Kahneman, D., and A. Tversky (1972). Subjective probability: A judgment of representativeness. *Cognitive Psychology* 3:340–354.

Kahneman, D., and A. Tversky (1973). On the psychology of prediction. *Psychological Review* 80:237–251. Reprinted in D. Kahneman, P. Slovic, and A. Tversky eds., *Judgment under Uncertainty: Heuristics and Biases*, pp. 48–68. Cambridge: Cambridge University Press, 1982.

Kahneman, D., and A. Tversky (1996). On the reality of cognitive illusions: A reply to Gigerenzer's critique. *Psychological Review* 103:582–591.

Kahneman, D., P. Slovic, and A. Tversky (eds.) (1982). *Judgment under Uncertainty: Heuristics and Biases*. Cambridge: Cambridge University Press.

Mises, R. von (1957). *Probability, Statistics and Truth*. London: Allen and Unwin.

Neander, K. (1991). The teleological notion of "function." *Australasian Journal of Philosophy* 59:454–468.

Nisbett, R., and E. Borgida (1975). Attribution and the social psychology of prediction. *Journal of Personality and Social Psychology* 32:932–943.

Nozick, R. (1993). *The Nature of Rationality*. Princeton: Princeton University Press.

Piattelli-Palmarini, M. (1994). *Inevitable Illusions: How Mistakes of Reason Rule Our Minds*. New York: John Wiley.

Pinker, S. (1997). *How the Mind Works*. New York: W. W. Norton.

Plantinga, A. (1993). *Warrant and Proper Function*. Oxford: Oxford University Press.

Samuels, R. (forthcoming). Evolutionary psychology and the massive modularity hypothesis. *British Journal for the Philosophy of Science*.

Samuels, R., S. Stich, and P. Tremoulet (forthcoming). Rethinking rationality: From bleak implications to Darwinian modules. In E. LePore and Z. Pylyshyn (eds.), *Rutgers University Invitation to Cognitive Science*. Oxford: Basil Blackwell.

Savage, L. J. (1972). *The Foundations of Statistics*. London: Wiley.

Slovic, P., B. Fischhoff, and S. Lichtenstein (1976). Cognitive processes and societal risk taking. In J. S. Carol and J. W. Payne (eds.), *Cognition and Social Behavior*, pp. 165–184. Hillsdale, NJ: Erlbaum.

Sperber, D. (1994). The modularity of thought and the epidemiology of representations. In L. A. Hirschfeld and S. Gelman A. (eds.), *Mapping the Mind: Domain Specificity in Cognition and Culture*, pp. 39–67. Cambridge: Cambridge University Press.

Stein, E. (1996). *Without Good Reason: The Rationality Debate in Philosophy and Cognitive Science*. Oxford: Clarendon Press.

Stich, S. (1990). *The Fragmentation of Reason*. Cambridge: MIT Press.

Tooby, J., and L. Cosmides (1992). The psychological foundations of culture. In J. Barkow, L. Cosmides and J. Tooby (eds.), *The Adapted Mind: Evolutionary Psychology and the Generation of Culture*, pp. 19–136. Oxford: Oxford University Press.

Tooby, J., and L. Cosmides (1995). Foreword. In S. Baron-Cohen, *Mindblindness: An Essay on Autism and Theory of Mind*, pp. xi–xviii. Cambridge: MIT Press.

Tversky, A., and D. Kahneman (1982). Judgments of and by representativeness. In D. Kahneman, P. Slovic, and A. Tversky (eds.), *Judgment under Uncertainty: Heuristics and Biases*, pp. 84-98. Cambridge: Cambridge University Press.

Tversky, A., and D. Kahneman (1983). Extensional versus intuitive reasoning: The conjunction fallacy in probability judgments. *Psychological Review* 90: 293–315.

Name Index

Abelson, R. P., 195
Agre, P. E., 39
Alberts, S. C., 135
Alksnis, O., 201, 203
Allen, J., 39, 76 n. 6
Almor, A., 199
Aloimonos, J., 39
Altmann, J., 135
Anderson, J. R., 17, 19, 95, 195, 198
Aruguete, M., 134
Ashton, A., 12
Ashton, R., 12
Astington, J. W., 142
Atran, S., 220
Audi, R., 121

Bacchus, F., 12, 41
Baron, J., 12, 18, 178
Barsalou, L. W., 192
Barwise, J., 186, 192–193
Bazerman, M., 236
Beatty, J., 149
Bekoff, M., 141
Benacerraf, P., 185
Bender, J. W., 104
Berridge, D., 142
Bertram, B. C. R., 135
Bettman, J. R., 153–154, 159
Beyth-Marom, R., 179, 197, 205
Blackburn, S., 94
Boddy, M., 44
Boehm, C., 134
Boesch, C., 139
Bolker, E., 79
Bonatti, L., 233 n. 6
BonJour, L., 104
Boolos, G. S., 182
Borgida, E., 236
Bower, B., 237
Bower, G. H., 178
Brachman, R. J., 42, 193
Braine, M. D. S., 177, 201–204, 216, 230, 233 n. 6

Breese, J. S., 44, 56 n. 3
Breiman, L., 167
Brooks, R. A., 39, 55
Brown, J., 123
Bruford, M. W., 135
Brunswick, E., 150
Burnyeat, M., 186
Burton, R., 141
Bussey, K., 142
Bygott, J. D., 135
Byrne, M. D., 110
Byrne, R., 133, 140–141
Byrne, R. M. J., 5, 16, 174, 177–178, 187, 191, 193, 196–197, 201–205, 206 nn. 1–2, 233 n. 7

Cappa, S., 230
Cara, F., 199
Carbonnell, J. G., 191
Card, S. K., 95
Carey, S., 187
Carnap, R., 41, 79, 89, 232 n. 3
Cassandra, A. R., 49
Casscells, W., 240, 243, 248
Cavanagh, J. P., 221
Caverni, J.-P., 233 n. 6
Chapais, B., 136
Chapman, D., 39
Charniak, E., 184, 191
Chater, N., 12, 17, 19, 176, 193–194, 196–205, 207 nn. 11–12
Cheesman, D. J., 135
Cheney, D. L., 135–136, 141
Cheng, P. W., 12, 17, 31 n. 3, 137, 179, 199, 205, 229
Cherniak, C., 47
Chomsky, N., 96, 100, 177
Clark, H. H., 196, 206 n. 8
Clements, W. C., 142
Clocksin, W. E., 177, 204
Clutton-Brock, T. H., 135
Cohen, L. J., 6, 15
Coley, J. D., 220

Collins, A., 12, 194
Coolidge, J. L., 185
Coote, T., 135
Corrigan, B., 170
Cosmides, L., 17, 137, 179, 199, 229,
    242–245, 248–253, 255, 259
Craik, F. I. M., 196
Cresswell, M. J., 206 n. 5
Cummins, D. D., 137, 141, 201, 203
Curry, H. B., 176
Czerlinksi, J., 158, 160

Daood, C., 138
Daston, L., 149
Datta, S. B., 135
Davidson, D., 104, 180
Davies, P., 123
Davis, R., 45
Dawes, R., 155, 159, 170
Dean, T., 39, 44, 49
Dempster, A. P., 193
Dennett, D., 47, 133, 140
de Waal, F. B. M., 135–136, 139
Dewsbury, D. A., 135
Doherty, M. E., 196
Doyle, J., 7, 16, 42, 193
Dreyfus, H., 55
Dubach, J., 135
Duda, R. O., 191
Duhem, P., 188
Dunbar, K., 196

Earman, J., 198
Ebert, A., 249
Edwards, W., 155, 169, 170
Einhorn, H. J., 12
Eliasmith, C., 110, 120
Elio, R., 6, 12–13
Ellis, L., 135
Ephrati, E., 43
Evans, J. St. B. T., 5, 12, 21, 174, 196–197,
    199, 205, 206 n. 9, 207 n. 11, 233
    n. 7

Fazio, F., 230
Fedigan, L., 135
Fehling, M. R., 44, 46
Feller, W., 219
Field, H. H., 220
Fikes, R. E., 76 n. 3
Fincham, F. D., 187
Fisch, S. M., 177, 203
Fischhoff, B., 179, 197, 205, 240–241
Flores, F., 192
Fodor, J. A., 22, 178, 186–187, 242
Forbes, J., 50
Freeman, N., 142
Frege, G., 5, 114
Friedman, J. H., 167
Friedman, N., 165

Gabbay, D., 12
Gagneux, P., 139
Galanter, E., 153
Gärdenfors, P., 12
Garey, M., 204
Garnham, A., 193, 202
Garrod, S., 196
Geddis, D. F., 45
Geffen, E., 135
Gentner, D., 93
George, C., 12
Gigerenzer, G., 6, 16, 149, 151, 153–156,
    158, 164, 166, 170, 179, 199, 205,
    237, 241, 243–245, 248–249,
    254–258, 260–263
Ginsberg, M. L., 14, 45, 193
Girard, J.-Y., 183
Girotto, V., 199, 228, 233 n. 6
Gluck, M. A., 178
Glymour, C., 186
Godfrey-Smith, P., 266 n. 13
Goel, V., 230
Gold, B., 230
Goldman, A. I., 186, 256, 265 n. 4
Goldstein, D. G., 151, 153–156, 158, 164,
    166, 170, 255–256
Goldszmitz, L., 165
Good, I. J., 43, 198
Goodall, J., 136
Goodman, N., 71, 187
Gopnick, A., 142
Gorman, M. E., 178
Gould, S., 236, 241
Grassi, F., 230
Grayboys, T., 240, 243, 248
Gregory, R., 258
Grove, A., 12, 41
Gruber, S., 141
Guha, R. V., 31 n. 5

Ha, Y., 179, 197, 199, 205
Haack, S., 104–111, 197
Haines, S. A., 135
Hall, K. R. L., 135
Halpern, J. Y., 12–13
Hamai, M., 136
Hanby, J. P., 135
Hanks, S., 71–72, 76 n. 11
Harcourt, A. H., 136
Harman, G., 32 n. 10, 47, 90, 98, 100,
    104, 187, 193, 232 n. 3, 265 n. 4
Harris, P., 138
Hart, P. E., 191
Harvey, P. H., 135
Haugaard, J., 142
Hausfater, G., 135
Hayes, P., 8, 69, 93, 195
Heit, E., 220
Helmholtz, H., 258
Hempel, C., 78, 188, 191, 206 n. 6
Henle, N., 177, 203

Hertz, J., 192
Hewstone, M. R. C., 187
Hilpinen, R., 137
Hiraiwa-Hasegawa, M., 136
Hodges, W., 180
Hoffrage, U., 151, 162–163, 249, 255
Hogarth, R. M., 12
Hogger, C., 12
Hokanson, J. E., 138
Holland, J. H., 13, 179, 187, 192, 205, 206
    n. 4
Hollis, M., 32 n. 10
Holyoak, K. J., 13, 17, 111, 137, 179, 187,
    192, 199, 201, 203, 205, 206 n. 4,
    229
Horn, L. R., 180
Horvitz, E. J., 19, 44, 46, 56 n. 4
Horwich, P., 198
Hosaka, K., 136
Houle, S., 230
Howard, R. A., 43
Howson, C., 79, 186, 198
Huang, T., 50
Hug, K., 179, 199, 205
Husserl, E., 5

Jackson, F., 231
James, S., 186
Jaspars, J. M. F., 187
Jeffrey, R. C., 79, 182
Jenkins, J., 142
Jennings, R., 86
Jepson, D. H., 231
Jevons, W. S., 221
John, R. S., 170
Johnson, E. J., 153–154, 159
Johnson, M., 204
Johnson-Laird, P. N., 12, 16, 98, 174,
    177–178, 187, 191, 193, 197–198,
    202–205, 206 nn. 1–2, 222–225, 228,
    233 n. 6
Josephson, R. J., 192
Josephson, S. G., 192

Kaelbling, L. P., 49
Kahneman, D., 5–6, 14, 178, 196, 233 nn.
    5–6, 238–242, 244, 247–248, 250,
    252–255, 257, 261
Kalman, R. E., 50
Kamp, H., 206 n. 5
Kanazawa, K., 49
Kapur, S., 230
Karmiloff-Smith, A., 187
Katz, J. J., 189
Kautz, H., 42
Kearns, M., 52
Keeney, R. L., 41, 154
Kelly, H. H., 187
Kintsch, W., 196
Kirby, K. N., 197, 199, 205
Kitcher, P., 115

Klahr, D., 196
Klayman, J., 179, 197, 199, 205
Kleinbölting, H., 151, 255
Koffka, K., 117
Koller, D., 12
Kornblith, H., 191
Kosslyn, S., 116
Krage, M., 138
Krantz, D. H., 231
Kriegeskorte, N., 162–163
Krogh, A., 192
Krüger, L., 149
Kuhn, T. S., 186, 190
Kumar, P. R., 42
Kummer, H., 139
Kunda, D. H., 231
Kunda, Z., 119
Kunsch, M., 5, 6
Kyburg, H. E., Jr., 12, 79, 84, 91 n. 2
Kyriakidou, C., 142

Lacey, R. C., 134
Laird, J. E., 16, 53
Lakatos, I., 186, 188, 206 n. 7, 207 n. 13
Laming, D., 199
Laskey, K., 164
Lauritzen, S. L., 50
Lea, R. B., 177, 203
Leekam, S. R., 142
Legrenzi, M. S., 233 n. 6
Legrenzi, P., 228, 233 n. 6
Lehrer, K., 104, 186
Lemmon, E. J., 180
Lenat, D., 31 n. 5
Leslie, A., 142
Levesque, H. J., 42, 193
Levi, I., 79
Levinson, S., 196
Lewis, C., 142
Lewis, D., 99
Lichtenstein, S., 240–241
Lifschitz, V., 72, 76 n. 6
Lindley, D. V., 198
Littman, M. L., 49
Lockhart, R. S., 196
Loftus, E. F., 194
Lopez, A., 12, 220
Loui, R. P., 90
Lubart, T., 201, 203
Lukes, S., 32 n. 10
Lynch, J. S., 197–199

MacKay, D. J., 198
Macnamara, J., 6, 177–178, 203
Makinson, D., 12
Manktelow, K. I., 12, 15, 17, 137, 205
Marcus-Newhall, A., 110
Maridaki-Kassotaki, K., 142
Markovits, H., 201
Marr, D., 175–177, 183–184
Martignon, L., 162–164

Matheson, J. E., 44
McAllester, D., 76 n. 1
McCann, T. S., 135
McCarthy, J., 6, 8, 11, 31 n. 2, 69, 180, 193
McClelland, J. L., 126 n. 4
McDermott, D., 71–72, 76 n. 11, 184, 191, 193–194
Mealey, L., 138
Medin, D. L., 117, 220
Megiddo, N., 46
Mele, A. R., 32 n. 10
Mellish, C. S., 177, 204
Menzel, E. W., 139
Michalski, R., 12, 191
Miller, G. A., 153
Millgram, E., 119
Minsky, M., 192, 195
Minton, S., 45
Mitchell, T., 191
Montague, R., 206 n. 5
Moran, T. P., 95
Morgenstern, L., 12
Muruth, P., 135
Mututua, R. A., 135
Myers, J. L., 196
Mynatt, C. R., 196

Naito, M., 142
Neale, M., 236
Neander, K., 266 n. 13
Newell, A., 16, 18, 41–42, 53, 95, 159, 195
Newstead, S. E., 5, 174, 196–197, 233 n. 7
Nilsson, N. J., 76 n. 1
Nisbett, R., 13, 93, 179, 187, 192, 205, 206 n. 4, 231, 236
Nishida, T., 135
Norvig, P., 39, 49
Noveck, I. A., 177, 203
Novick, L. R., 205
Nowak, G., 110
Nozick, R., 256
Nuñez, M., 138

Oaksford, M., 12, 17, 19, 193–194, 196, 198–205, 207 nn. 11–12
O'Brien, D. P., 177, 196, 201, 203, 233 n. 6
Olshen, R. A., 167
Osherson, D. N., 12, 14, 216, 220, 222, 230
Over, D. E., 12, 15, 17, 21, 137, 199, 202, 205, 206 n. 9, 207 n. 11

Palmer, R. G., 192
Papadimitriou, C. H., 47
Pargetter, R., 231
Parkin, L., 142
Parr, R., 50
Patil, R. S., 42
Payne, J. W., 153–154, 159
Pearl, J., 11, 193
Pelletier, F. J., 6, 13
Penberthy, J. S., 76 n. 1

Perani, D., 230
Perner, J., 141–142
Perry, J., 186, 192–193
Petty, R. E., 12
Piaget, J., 177, 203
Piattelli-Palmarini, M., 236, 247–248, 253
Pinker, S., 237
Plantinga, A., 266 n. 13
Pojman, L. P., 122
Politzer, G., 177, 201–203
Pollock, J. L., 7–8, 21–22, 60, 70–72, 76 n. 8, 81, 98, 186, 224
Polya, G., 115
Popper, K. R., 186, 188, 197, 206 n. 6
Porter, T., 149
Pribram, K. H., 153
Priester, J. R., 12
Prud'Homme, J., 136
Putnam, H., 185–186, 188–189
Pylyshyn, Z. W., 22, 178

Quillian, M. R., 194
Quine, W. V., 93, 95, 180, 187–189, 191

Raghavan, S. A., 6
Raiffa, H., 41, 154
Ranney, M., 94, 110
Rasinski, K., 228
Rawls, J., 116
Rayner, K., 196
Read, S., 110
Reiser, B. J., 203, 216, 230
Reiter, R., 11, 180, 193
Reppucci, N. D., 142
Rescher, N., 13
Reyes, G. E., 177–178
Reyle, U., 206 n. 5
Rips, L. J., 6, 98, 174, 177–178, 191, 193, 197, 200, 203, 205, 206 n. 3, 215–216, 220, 228, 231
Riss, D. C., 136
Rist, R., 201, 203
Ristau, C. A., 141
Robinson, J. A., 12
Robinson, J. G., 135
Rock, I., 116
Rosenblitt, D., 76 n. 1
Rosenbloom, P. S., 16, 53
Rosenschein, J. S., 43
Ross, B., 117
Rubinstein, J., 220
Ruffman, T., 142
Rumain, B., 203, 216, 230
Rumelhart, D. E., 126
Russell, B., 96, 113–115, 186
Russell, S., 39, 43–46, 48–52
Russon, A. E., 133
Ryle, G., 95

Saiyalel, S. N., 135
Salmon, W., 115

Samuels, R., 242
Sanford, A. J., 196
Sargent, T. G., 150
Savage, L. J., 169, 262
Savary, F., 225
Schank, P., 110
Schank, R. C., 195
Schapire, R., 52
Schiffer, S., 189
Schnur, T., 230
Schoenberger, A., 240, 243, 248
Schotch, P., 86
Scott, D., 183
Scruton, R., 189
Sellars, W., 95, 227
Sellie, L., 52
Seyfarth, R. M., 135–136, 141
Shafer, G., 193
Shafir, E., 12, 220, 222
Shank, D. M., 196
Shetler, S., 138
Shoham, Y., 72
Silk, J. B., 135
Silverman, B. G., 6
Simon, H. A., 15, 18, 39, 44, 149–150,
    159
Sloman, S. A., 21, 199, 216, 220
Slovic, P., 196, 240–241
Smedslund, J., 180
Smith, E. E., 12, 220, 222
Smuts, B., 136
Soames, S., 99
Sondik, E. J., 49
Sowa, J., 11
Spellman, B. A., 179, 201, 203
Sperber, D., 196, 199, 256
Stalker, D., 76 n. 9
Stanovich, K. E., 15, 18, 21–22
Stein, E., 15, 17, 174, 246–247
Stenning, K., 201
Stevens, A. L., 93
Stevenson, R. J., 12, 202
Stewart, K. J., 136
Stich, S., 17, 174, 242, 256
Stokes, A. W., 135
Stone, C. J., 167
Strachey, C., 183
Strawson, P. F., 96
Strichartz, A. F., 141
Subramanian, D., 46–48, 50–52
Swijtink, Z., 149

Tadepalli, P., 53
Teng, C. M., 84, 85, 88

Thagard, P. R., 12, 13, 105, 107, 110–111,
    116, 119–120, 123–124, 179,
    186–187, 191–192, 205, 206 n. 5
Todd, P., 149, 151
Tomasello, M., 141
Tooby, J., 17, 137, 242–245, 248–253, 255,
    259
Toulmin, S., 186
Tourangeau, R., 228
Tremoulet, P., 242
Tsitsiklis, J. N., 52
Tucker, W., 151, 155
Tulving, E., 196
Tutin, C. E. G., 135
Tversky, A., 5–6, 14, 154, 178, 196, 233
    nn. 5–6, 238–242, 244, 247–248,
    250, 253, 255, 257, 261–262
Tweeny, R. D., 196

Uehara, S., 136
Urbach, P., 79, 186, 198

van Dijk, T. A., 196
Van Fraassen, B., 186
Van Roy, B., 52
Varaiya, P., 42
Verbeurgt, K., 105
von Mises, R., 262
von Winterfeldt, D., 169, 170

Wason, P. C., 93, 174, 178, 196–197, 199
Watts, C. R., 135
Wayne, R. K., 135
Wefald, E. H., 43–45, 52
Wegener, D. T., 12
Weld, D., 76 n. 1
Wellman, H. M., 142
Wellman, M. P., 41, 52
Whiten, A., 140–141
Wigderson, A., 46
Wilkie, O., 12, 220
Wilson, D., 196
Wimmer, H., 141–142
Winograd, T., 192
Witten, E., 123
Wittgenstein, L., 102
Woodruff, D. S., 139
Woods, W. A., 195
Wooldridge, D., 133

Yang, Y., 177, 203, 233 n. 6
Yannakakis, M., 47

Zilberstein, S., 44–45, 48, 51–52

Subject Index

abduction, 192

acceptance of uncertain evidence, 80–81, 84–88

adaptation
  and human cognitive mechanisms, 17, 132–142, 150, 242–243, 248–253, 255, 259
  and rationality, 19
  See also evolutionary psychology

agent
  formal definition of, 39–40, 46
  knowledge-level characterization of, 18, 41
  rational, 18, 39–41
  See also Principle of Rationality

agent architecture
  and meta-level reasoning, 41–46
  rationality and properties of, 14, 16, 20–21, 51–54
  See also human cognitive architecture

analogical reasoning, 110–114

artificial intelligence, 6, 8–12, 191
  and formal approaches to uncertain reasoning, 10–12, 191–195
  goals of, 37–38, 55–56

Bayesian theory
  and Bayesian networks, 11, 42, 50–51, 164–169
  and heuristic methods for decision making, 164–169
  and laboratory reasoning tasks, 198–200, 238–240
  as a normative standard for uncertain reasoning, 6, 242–244, 248–249
  and uncertain information, 82–83, 90–91
  and uncertain reasoning, 78–80
  See also frequentism and probability theory; statistical inference

belief justification
  deductive correctness vs. inductive strength, 216–232

and epistemic cognition, 60, 66
  foundationalist and coherence theories, 106–110, 122–123
  and uncertain evidence, 80–81, 84–88

belief revision, 12
  and coherence, 98, 121, 124
  as goal directed, 97–98
  and planning example, 31 n. 6
  principles for, 98
  See also nonmonotonic reasoning

biases and heuristics
  as descriptive account of human reasoning, 5, 14, 178, 196, 236–264
  and human cognitive architecture, 240–241

bounded optimality, 19, 38, 46–48, 50–54, 258–260. *See also* bounded rationality

bounded rationality, 15, 149–150

brain imaging studies, 230–231

Church-Turing Thesis, 182
  and computational models of human reasoning, 182–184

closed world assumption, 206 n. 8

cognitive architectures. *See* human cognitive architecture

coherence
  and analogical reasoning, 110–113
  and belief justification, 110
  and belief revision, 98
  constraint satisfaction algorithm for, 105–106, 120–122, 125–126
  and deductive reasoning, 113–116
  and explanation, 106–109
  and foundationalism, 106–110, 121
  objections to, 120–124
  and perception, 116–118
  as a theory of knowledge, 106–110, 120–123

common sense
  dictionary definition of, 3

commonsense knowledge
    and making inductive arguments,
        224–229
    scope and examples of, 8–9, 141–142
commonsense reasoning
    as belief revision, 10–12
    and closed world assumption, 206 n. 8
    development in childhood, 141–142
    and dual-process reasoning theories,
        21–23, 215–217
    inductive quality of, 13–14, 215–218,
        229
    as nonmonotonic reasoning, 10–11, 192
    and planning, 66–68
    as practical cognition, 66, 174
    related to scientific reasoning, 186–192
    and role of deductive inference, 174ff
    scope and examples, 8–9
    and social norms, 137–143
    and strength of inductive arguments,
        78–81, 215–228
    See also heuristics for reasoning;
        inductive inference; nonmonotonic
        reasoning
competence/performance distinction, 6,
    177
computational methods for commonsense
    reasoning
    Bayesian networks, 42, 50–51, 164–169
    classification and regression trees
        (CARTs), 154, 167
    connectionist methods, 120–121,
        125–129
    constraint satisfaction, 105–106,
        120–122, 125–126
    dynamic probabilistic networks, 49
    fast and frugal heuristics, 150–154
    Markov models, 49–51
    multiple regression, 155ff
    nonmonotonic logics, 193
    production systems, 194
    schema theory, 193
    See also heuristics for reasoning
computer models
    CYC, 31 n. 5
    ECHO, 107–110
    OSCAR, 76
    SOAR, 16, 53
computing science theory
    and computational models of human
        reasoning, 182–194
conditional inference, 200–202
connectionist methods, 120–121, 125–129
constraint satisfaction, 105–106, 120–122,
    125–126
cue-based inference, 151–153

decision making
    and acceptance of evidence, 80–81,
        84–88
    and bounded optimality, 46–47
    as deliberative coherence, 119

statistical vs. heuristic algorithms for,
    151–154, 155ff, 163
    See also agent architecture; human
        cognitive architecture; environment
decision theory, 7
    and metareasoning, 43–46
deductive inference
    and brain imaging studies, 230–231
    as coherence computation, 113–116,
        123–124
    and correctness of deductive
        arguments, 215–221, 228–231
    and laboratory reasoning tasks, 181,
        200–203
    and Marr's trilevel theory, 175–179,
        183–184, 203–204
    and mathematical reasoning, 113–116
    and relevance to common sense
        reasoning, 7, 9, 174ff
    as subsumed by inductive reasoning
        models, 215–221
deductive logic
    extended for uncertain reasoning,
        11–12, 180, 192–193
    as human competence theory, 177–
        178
    and impact on philosophy of science,
        186–189
    and mathematical reasoning, 185–187
    as normative standard for reasoning, 7,
        94–95, 190–191
    and scientific reasoning, 185–186
default logic, 11, 180, 193
default properties, 194–196. See also
    nonmonotonic reasoning; temporal
    projection
defeasible inference. See nonmonotonic
    reasoning
deontic reasoning, 17, 136–138, 229
    examples in primates, 138
    and laboratory reasoning tasks,
        137–138, 199
    and natural selection, 134–140
dual-process theories for reasoning, 21–23,
    215–217
dynamic probabilistic networks, 49

economic theory and rationality, 7, 41–43
environment
    complexity of and rationality, 42, 56
    dynamic properties of and planning,
        66–70
    in formal definitions of rationality, 40,
        46
    information structure of and reasoning
        heuristics, 161–163, 169
    as providing frequency vs. probability
        information, 161–163, 242–244
    and rational agent design, 6–7, 40,
        49–50
    real-time properties of and bounded
        optimality, 47–50, 148–149

environment (*continued*)
    and situated cognition, 39
    See also agent; social environment
epistemology
    and models of reasoning, 186–191
    and psychologism, 6
    theories of, 106–110, 120–123
    and truth conditions, 98–101
evolutionary psychology, 17–19, 133ff,
    236–264
explanation
    and analogy, 111–112
    and coherence theory, 106–110
    and role in scientific reasoning, 188–191

fast and frugal heuristics, 148–171
foundationalism, 106–110, 121
frame problem, 6, 12, 31 n. 8, 68ff
frequentism and probability theory, 6,
    80–81, 90, 261–263
    and laboratory reasoning tasks,
    242–244
    See also environment; statistical
    reasoning

game theory and bounded optimality,
    46–47
Gestalt principles, 117

heuristics and biases. *See* biases and
    heuristics
heuristics for reasoning
    compared to Bayesian methods,
    164–168
    and information structure in
    environment, 161–163
    as response to intractable problems, 14,
    42–43, 159–161, 204
    See also biases and heuristics
human cognitive architecture, 14–17,
    19–21, 23, 258–260
    and assessing rationality of, 246ff
    and deviations from normative
    standards, 240–241
    and evolutionary psychology
    perspective, 242–244, 253, 256
    and evolved reasoning heuristics,
    133–143, 255
    and materialism, 132–133
    See also agent architecture;
    environment; evolutionary
    psychology

induction
    and centrality to common sense
    reasoning, 13–14, 191–193, 229
    as mechanism for optimizing and
    adapting performance, 51–53
    and meta-level rationality, 45
    and reinforcement learning, 50
inductive inference
    and brain imaging studies, 230–231

and strength of inductive arguments,
    78–81, 215–228
    as subsumed by deductive reasoning
    models, 221–227
    and temporal projection, 71
inference to the best explanation, 97, 187
inference vs. implication, 96–97
intelligence
    as bounded optimality, 46–48
    defined as types of rationality, 38
    role of environment in, 6–7
intentionality. *See* theory of mind
intractability and complexity
    and commonsense reasoning, 14
    metareasoning as a solution to, 44–46
    and rational behavior, 41–43
    See also bounded optimality; heuristics
    for reasoning

knowledge and truth conditions, 98–100
knowledge-level characterization of
    rationality, 41

logic
    and centrality to commonsense
    reasoning, 175–178
    in constructing arguments and in
    reasoning, 96–97, 215–231
    form vs. content, 98–100
    implication vs. inference, 94–97, 101
    inductive vs. deductive arguments,
    215–232
    and Marr's trilevel theory, 176–177
    and nonmonotonic logics, 11, 84–87,
    180, 193
    as normative standard for inference,
    4–7, 94–97
    for ordinary language, 93–102
    See also deductive logic; inductive
    inference
lottery paradox, 81, 123

machine architecture. *See* agent
    architecture
Marr's trilevel theory, 175–179, 183–184,
    203–204
materialism, 133–134
mathematical reasoning
    and coherence theory of knowledge,
    114–116
    and deductive inference, 114–116,
    185–187
means-end reasoning, 61–76
    in primate behavior, 133, 139
    See also planning
mental logic, 98, 200, 203–204
mental model theory of reasoning, 98, 177
    and plausible inference, 222–228
metaknowledge, 45
meta-level reasoning, 43–46
    and constrained maximization,
    149–150, 153

modus ponens
and laboratory reasoning tasks,
200–202

natural language
and interpretation of logical statements,
180–181, 200–202
and knowledge of truth conditions,
98–100
a logic of, 93–102
quantifiers in, 101–102
nonmonotonic logic, 11, 180, 193
as formalization of commonsense
reasoning, 10–12, 192–194
and probabilistic acceptance of
information, 84–88
nonmonotonic reasoning
and Bayesian approaches, 79–80, 90
defined, 31 n. 7, 176
and errors of measurement, 81ff
examples, 10–12, 192
and planning, 65ff
and scientific reasoning, 187–189
as statistical inference, 88
normative models and standards, 4–8, 13,
17, 23, 89, 181, 246–260
calculative rationality, 41–43, 55–56
and common sense, 21
and descriptive models, 190–191
as directives for cognitive theories, 7
and epistemology, 190–191
for outcomes vs. mechanisms, 246–260
logic as, 4–8, 94–95
and prescriptive models, 18
and procedural vs. substantive
rationality, 246–260
and psychologism, 5
See also deductive logic; probability
theory

paraconsistent logic, 86
perception, 116–118
perfect rationality, 38. See also rationality
philosophy of science
and Bayesian framework, 198
and deductive logic in scientific
reasoning, 186–189
and epistemology, 186–191
and inductive vs. deductive arguments,
221–222
and laboratory reasoning tasks,
197–198
planning
AI theories and formalizations of, 50,
61–76
as commonsense reasoning, 10
and demands of the real world, 67–69,
75–76
examples in primates, 133, 139
and the frame problem, 68ff
means-ends reasoning, 61–76
and nonmonotonic quality, 65ff

as practical cognition, 60
and theory of mind, 141
plausible inference. See nonmonotonic
inference
prescriptive models, 18, 19. See also
normative models and standards
Principle of Rationality, 18
probability theory
and dynamic networks, 49
as formalizing nonmonotonic
reasoning, 11, 78–90, 193–194
and frequentism, 242–244, 248–249,
261–262
and laboratory reasoning tasks,
238–240
as normative standard for human
reasoning, 7, 247–255
in psychological models of reasoning,
205, 223–228, 237
and validity of deductive correctness,
218–221, 224
and validity of inductive arguments,
219–220
See also Bayesian theory; normative
models and standards
psychologism, 5–6, 13, 89

quantifiers in language, 101–102

rational agents, 39
rational
dictionary definition of, 3
rational analysis, 19–20
applied to selection task, 198–200
rationality
adaptive, 19, 133–134
as bounded optimality, 15, 18, 46–48,
148–150, 258–260
calculative, 38, 41–42, 45, 49–50
and computationally intractable
problems, 14, 38, 41–43, 45, 49–50,
150
definitions of, 1, 3, 15, 38, 42, 47, 150
of individual acts vs. policies for acting,
47
intelligence, 37–38, 55–56
meta-level, 38, 43–46
normative standards of, 17, 21,
246–260
of outcomes vs. mechanisms, 39,
246–260
perfect, 38, 40–41
philosophical views on, 47
principle of, 18
procedural vs. substantive, 39, 246–
260
situated, 17–19, 39–40
See also agent architecture; human
cognitive architecture; normative
models and standards
real-time decision making
and bounded optimality, 47–48

real-time decision making (*continued*)
Markov models for, 49–50
and metareasoning, 44
reasoning. *See* commonsense reasoning;
deductive inference; inductive
inference; nonmonotonic
reasoning
reference class problem, 90
reflective equilibrium, 116
reinforcement learning, 50

satisficing, 149–150
heuristics for, 150ff
See also bounded optimality
scientific reasoning
as commonsense reasoning, 187–
189
explanation and coherence theory,
110–112, 122–124
inductive aspect of, 221
and laboratory reasoning tasks,
197–198
as probabilistic reasoning, 198
and role of deductive logic in, 113–114,
185–191
and statistical inference with uncertain
information, 81–84, 88
selection task
Bayesian interpretation, 198–200
defined, 197, 206 n. 9
deontic reasoning effect, 137–138
rationality of human performance on,
93, 198–200
and scientific reasoning, 197–200
situated cognition and rationality, 17–19,
39. *See also* agent; environment

social environment
as shaping human cognitive
architecture, 134–136, 140–141
and social norms, 135–136
statistical inference
and acceptance of uncertain
information, 81–82, 88
and evolutionary psychology, 243–244
human errors in, 238–240, 243–244
and lottery paradox, 81, 123
and multiple regression as normative
model, 154–155, 159, 163
as nonmonotonic reasoning 88–89
and strength of inductive arguments,
219–221
See also frequentism and probability
theory; biases and heuristics
syllogistic inference, 16, 98

temporal projection, 70ff
theory of mind
as commonsense knowledge, 8
development in childhood, 141–142
examples in primates, 139
as explanatory and analogical
reasoning, 112–113
as product of natural selection, 133,
140–141
Type II rationality, 43. *See also* meta-level
reasoning

unbounded rationality, 149. *See also*
rationality
utility
and bounded optimality, 46–47
and metareasoning, 43–44